LITERATURE FROM THE BIBLE

Selected by
JOSEPH FRANK
University of Rochester

LiTERATURE

from the

BIBle

LITTLE, BROWN AND COMPANY   *Boston · Toronto*

contents

ISAIAH

JOB

JONAH

PSALMS

THE SONG OF SOLOMON

ECCLESIASTES

THE NEW TESTAMENT

THE GOSPELS

THE ACTS OF THE APOSTLES

THE EPISTLES OF PAUL

REVELATION

LITERATURE FROM THE BIBLE

INTRODUCTION

THE WORD *Bible* comes from the Greek *biblia*, meaning little books, and the Bible is, literally, a collection of little books. The earliest parts of some of them go back beyond 1200 B.C., the latest date from the middle of the second century after Christ. Thus this collection spans fourteen centuries, a coverage broader than an anthology of English Literature beginning with "Beowulf" and ending with an author of the twentieth century. The Bible is also a selective sampling of Hebrew literature. As such it contains a wide range of writing: folk tales, legends, sagas, fables, riddles, songs, history, philosophy, short stories, biography—and this list is not complete. Therefore, the Bible, quite apart from its theological and cultural importance, can serve as a valid and exciting introduction to the study of literature. Furthermore, this book has been pervasive in its influence on Western writing; from the works of Caedmon in the seventh century to the contemporary novels of Faulkner and Golding it has been instrumental in shaping the content and style of much of our imaginative literature. To describe this influence would require volumes, but each introduction to the separate sections that follow concludes with a list of suggested readings that can, collectively, point up how the Bible has been a keystone in the arch of great books.

Understandably, the Bible is both the all-time best seller and by far the most translated book in the world. For English-speaking people the most significant translation is the King James or Authorized Version, completed in 1611. It is this edition which Milton and Bunyan knew, which the pilgrims brought with them to Massachusetts, which American pioneers carried westward. Consequently it is the edition that has most strongly influenced English and American thought and expression. For this reason, and because of its widely acknowledged aesthetic superiority, the King James Version is used here.

1

Paradoxically, this magnificent translation was the work of a committee. But this committee, appointed by King James I in 1604, operated under favorable conditions. First, political and economic disputes in seventeenth-century England were so interlocked with problems of theology that religion was not something remote; and the vocabulary of religion—of, explicitly, the Protestant Bible—was used in forum, market place, and parlor, not just in the pulpit. Second, this was a period in which the English language was at its most dynamic and flexible. The first decade of the seventeenth century saw, for instance, the creation of Shakespeare's great tragedies, in which words old and new were shaped into dazzling and lasting combinations. Third, the committee was not starting from scratch.

Under Henry VIII, when the English church broke away from Rome, one of the immediate and urgent needs was for a Bible printed in the native language. In the 1520's and '30's William Tyndale, working from the Greek text of Erasmus, Luther's German edition, and the traditional Latin Bible (the Vulgate), published on the Continent his translations of most of the Bible. Much of the diction and rhythm, as well as many of the familiar phrases of the King James Version, are taken from Tyndale, and it is to him that the English Bible is deeply indebted for the forceful and often colloquial nature of its sentence structure and vocabulary. In 1535 the first complete Bible printed in English appeared. Its "author," Miles Coverdale, relied heavily on Tyndale but removed some of his controversial translations and marginal comments. Coverdale also supplied certain phrases of his own that have become part of our linguistic heritage. Two other significant Bibles followed. The Geneva Bible, published in 1560, was for half a century the translation used in most English homes, and, next to Tyndale's, it was the book from which King James' committee borrowed most heavily. (In all probability this was the version Shakespeare read, and it was the edition favored by the early Puritans.) Then in 1568 came the Bishops' Bible, a large and costly volume that, as the official Bible of the Church of England, likewise contributed to its replacement.

To create this new Authorized Version, fifty churchmen, working in six groups, spent six years revising earlier English Bibles. Two members from each group then acted as a board of review, and from them the copy went through a final check at the hands of two bishops. Not only was the committee's work scholarly and collective, but the final result represented a compromise between various doctrinal views. Yet the King James Version was almost immediately recognized as a classic, and it may well represent the rare instance of a translation which is as good as the original.

That original was worthy of the best in translations. But, like all classics, it must be reinterpreted by each generation; otherwise it dies. The fact that the Bible is very much alive raises the question, however, of how and why the ancient writings of a small and in many ways primitive group should be relevant to our own massive, fast-changing world. One answer is that the Bible is the word of God. Another answer, not necessarily contradictory, is that this record of Hebrew history and aspirations and of the beginnings of Christianity was compiled by men who profoundly investigated and expressed what it meant—and what it means—to be a human being.

The matrix from which these men came was not fixed. At first they belonged to groups of nomads, feeding their flocks in a sparsely populated area somewhat analogous to the western plains of America before the white men arrived. Later, as agriculture superseded sheep-herding, tribal groups amalgamated to form small city states. For a brief interval after 1000 B.C. Palestine was a self-sufficient kingdom. Then, since it was at the crossroads of the ancient world, it became the battleground and prize of a series of competing empires: Assyrian, Babylonian, Persian, Alexandrian, Roman. Civil wars, sectarian conflicts, class struggles added to the turmoil. Meanwhile the impact of immigration and emigration, of new ideas, of rival cultures further insured that the authors of the Bible would not become isolated or stagnant.

But the collection of little books which they wrote is not discontinuous. The idea of God, whether a localized tribal deity or a universal and all-powerful force, is vividly present in every part of both Testaments. Furthermore, the concept of a chosen people, a group whom God has both blessed and burdened with special responsibilities, runs through the entire collection. Finally, the belief in righteousness—the welding together of religion and morality—links Abraham with St. Paul, Moses with Christ. (The recently discovered Dead Sea Scrolls, written in the first centuries before and after Christ, underline this continuity between the Old

and New Testaments.) In short, the authors of the Bible sprang
from a tumultuous and changing background, though the rate of
change was much slower than it is today. They shared common
fears and aspirations, though these fears and aspirations have been
modified by history. Later authors knew and reverenced what their
predecessors had set down, though they had no hesitation in altering
or reinterpreting earlier sections. Consequently, on reading the
Bible, one is struck by both its variety and its underlying homo-
geneity: it is many little books, but it is also one big book.

Because it is, in every sense, a big book, an edition of selections
from it can be functional. In the following pages I have tried to
convey the range and diversity of the Bible and, at the same time,
to avoid excessive fragmentation. Most of the literary forms are
included, the sweep of Hebrew history and the beginnings of Christianity are shown, and those passages which generations of readers
have found most beautiful and moving are well represented. Thus
the basis of selection is, obviously, historical and literary rather than
theological. I have adhered closely to the King James Version, except
for the elimination of the verse numbers and marginal comments and
most genealogies. I have also modernized the spelling, enclosed
speeches in quotation marks, occasionally reparagraphed, and made
a few changes in punctuation and capitalization for the sake of
clarity. Footnotes are minimal, and are usually employed only to
define rare and obsolete words. Each section is preceded by an introduction intended to set that book of the Bible in its historical con-
text, to explain major problems of authorship, to point out certain
distinctive stylistic and conceptual characteristics, and to suggest
some of the literary classics that might be pertinent to that portion
of the Bible.

In making these selections and writing these introductions I owe
much to many. In particular, Professor William Hamilton of the
Colgate Rochester Divinity School has been invaluable as a sounding board and guide. Two of my colleagues at the University of
Rochester, Professors David Hadas and Robert Hinman, have been
generous in sharing their learning with me. Books have also been
my rod and my staff, especially the learned works of the late Robert
Pfeiffer and the indispensable twelve-volume *Interpreter's Bible;*
and the brief list which follows gives those works I found helpful
in compiling this edition:

Anderson, Bernhard W., *Understanding the Old Testament*, Englewood Cliffs, 1957.

Ballou, Robert O., ed., *The Bible of the World*. New York, 1939.

Bates, Ernest Sutherland, *The Bible Designed to be Read as Living Literature*, New York, 1952.

Burrows, Millar, *More Light on the Dead Sea Scrolls*, New York, 1958.

Chamberlin, Roy B., and Herman Feldman, *The Dartmouth Bible*, Boston, 1950.

Chase, Mary Ellen, *The Bible and the Common Reader*, New York, 1945.

Clarke, W. K. Lowther, *Concise Bible Commentary*, New York, 1953.
The Interpreter's Bible, Nashville and New York, 1952-1957, 12 vols.

Kee, Howard C., and Franklin W. Young, *Understanding the New Testament*, Englewood Cliffs, 1957.

Pfeiffer, Robert H., *History of New Testament Times, With an Introduction to the Apocrypha*, New York, 1949.
——, *Introduction to the Old Testament*, New York, 1948.
——, with William G. Pollard, *The Hebrew Iliad*, New York, 1957.

Pritchard, James, B., ed., *Ancient Near Eastern Texts Relating to the Old Testament*, Princeton, 1950.

Scott, Ernest Findlay, *The Literature of the New Testament*. New York, 1932.

State University of Iowa, *A College Bible*, New York, 1938.

Wright, George Ernest, and Floyd Vivian Filson, *The Westminster Historical Atlas to the Bible*, Philadelphia, 1946.

Wright, William Aldis, ed., *The Authorized Version of the English Bible, 1611*, Cambridge, 1909, 5 vols.

dates	events	authors
2000–1700 B.C.	**THE AGE OF THE PATRIARCHS:** Contemporaneous with the rise of the ancient Babylonian Empire.	Hammurabi (ca. 1700)
1700–1500	**THE PEACEFUL PERIOD OF THE HEBREWS IN EGYPT:** During most of this time the Hyksos ruled Egypt. In the north Babylonia declined, and between 1600 and 1500 the Old Hittite Empire flourished.	
1500–1290	**THE PERIOD OF OPPRESSION BY THE EGYPTIANS:** This followed the expulsion of the Hyksos from Egypt. In Mesopotamia a New Hittite Empire arose (1375–1200). After 1354 it had to compete with the growing power of Assyria. Meanwhile, from about 1400 on, Hebrew tribes from the east were infiltrating Palestine.	
1290–1225	**THE EXODUS AND THE CONQUEST OF PALESTINE:** Contemporaneous with the continued dominance in the north of Assyria.	Song of Miriam
1225–1025	**THE PERIOD OF THE JUDGES:** Sporadic resistance to Philistine control of Palestine. In Mesopotamia the New Hittite Empire came to an end, and the strength of Assyria temporarily declined.	

Period	Description	Literature
1025–930	**THE UNITED HEBREW MONARCHY:** Saul as king 1025–1005; David, 1005–970; Solomon, 970–930. The First Temple was built around 960. The temporary stability of the monarchy was aided by the continued decline of Assyria and the relative impotence of Egypt.	J; the author of the Saul-David story (Ahimaaz?)
930–721	**THE SEPARATE KINGDOMS: JUDAH IN THE SOUTH, ISRAEL IN THE NORTH:** During this period Assyria revived, and in 732 defeated Syria. In that year Judah became a tributary of Assyria, which in 721 conquered Israel.	Elijah; Homer; Amos; Hosea; E; First Isaiah
721–587	**THE SURVIVING KINGDOM OF JUDAH:** Judah survived, but not as a fully independent state. After the period of Assyrian dominance, Egypt briefly held sway over Judah (608–605), followed by Babylonia, which late in the seventh century replaced Assyria as the colossus of the north. In 598 Nebuchadnezzar captured Jerusalem and deported hundreds of its leading Jews to Babylon; in 587 he destroyed the city and deported a second group.	Micah; D; Jeremiah; Ezekiel
587–538	**THE BABYLONIAN CAPTIVITY:** In 581 a third deportation occurred; but after the middle of the sixth century the Persian empire superseded the Babylonian. In 538 the Persian king Cyrus permitted the return of the exiled Jews to Palestine.	Job; Second Isaiah

538–333	**PALESTINE AS A PROVINCE OF PERSIA:** This period came to an end with the conquests of Alexander the Great. The Second Temple was dedicated in 516.	P; Third Isaiah; Malachi; Herodotus; Ruth; Jonah
333–142	**GREEK RULE OF PALESTINE:** After Alexander's death in 323 his empire was divided among four of his generals, one of whom established Ptolemaic rule over Egypt and Palestine. This dynasty was succeeded by that of the Seleucids in 198. (The Seleucids, another dynasty originally founded by Alexander, had been in control of Syria and Mesopotamia.) Then in 167, under the leadership of the Maccabees, the Hebrews revolted, and in 142 achieved temporary independence.	Most of the Psalms; Song of Songs; Ecclesiastes; Daniel
142–63	**THE JEWISH STATE UNDER THE MACCABEAN PRIEST-KINGS:** Until the coming of the Roman legions, and except for a brief period of Seleucid control (134–129), Palestine was relatively independent.	
63 B.C.–150 A.D.	**ROMAN RULE OF PALESTINE:** Pompey occupied Palestine in 63 B.C. and the area remained a province of Rome until the late fourth century A.D., when it became part of the Eastern Empire. Christ's dates are now usually given as 4 B.C. to 30 A.D. Beginning in 6 B.C. Palestine was ruled by Roman procurators (governors), and Pontius Pilate held that office from 26 to 36 A.D. The missionary journeys of Paul occurred between 48 or 49 and 61 A.D., when he was taken to Rome. In 66 A.D. the Jews rebelled against Roman rule, but within four years the revolt had been crushed, the temple destroyed, and many Jews deported.	Virgil; Paul; Mark; Matthew; Luke; John (the author of Revelation); John (the author of the Fourth Gospel); Peter

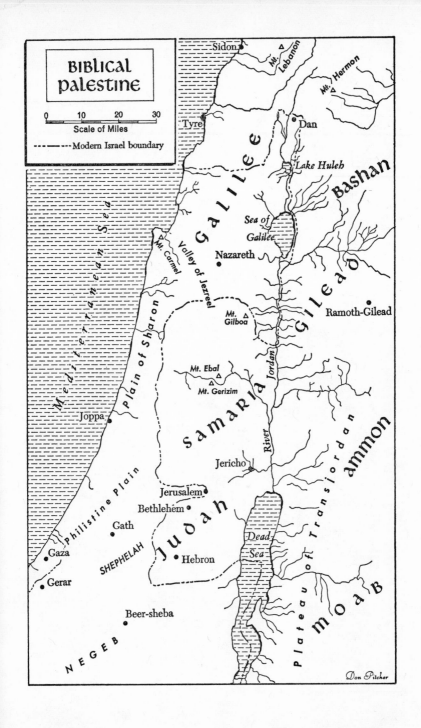

BIBLICAL
palestine

0   10   20   30
Scale of Miles
- - - - - Modern Israel boundary

Sidon

Mt. Lebanon

Mt. Hermon

Tyre

Dan

Lake Huleh

Bashan

G a l i l e e

Sea of
Galilee

Mt. Carmel

Nazareth

Valley of Jezreel

Mediterranean Sea

Ramoth-Gilead

Plain of Sharon

Mt.
Gilboa

G i l e a d

Mt. Ebal

Mt. Gerizim

S a m a r i a

Jordan

Joppa

River

Jericho

P l a t e a u   o f   T r a n s j o r d a n

Jerusalem

Bethlehem

Philistine Plain

Gath

J u d a h

Dead
Sea

a m m o n

Gaza

SHEPHELAH

Hebron

Gerar

Beer-sheba

N E G E B

M O A B

Don Pitcher

the
old
testament

Genesis

INTRODUCTION

The first five books of the Old Testament, the Pentateuch, were long thought to have been written by one man, Moses.[1] After they were canonized (that is, officially recognized as sacred texts) about 400 B.C., they were known as "the law of Moses," then simply as "the Law." To orthodox Jews these five books—Genesis, Exodus, Leviticus, Numbers, Deuteronomy—are still the most sacrosanct portion of the Bible. Since the seventeenth century, however, most biblical scholars have agreed that several men wrote the Pentateuch, and that the order in which it now appears is different from the order in which it was originally set down. At least three separate authors have been identified in Genesis, and—to give only one example—it is clear that the first chapter of Genesis was written approximately five centuries later than most of the second chapter.

The most important of the three authors of Genesis was also the earliest. Identified as J because of his use of "Jahveh" (or "Yahveh") for the name of God, he lived around 950 B.C., in that interlude when the Hebrew kingdom under Solomon briefly flourished. Essentially the story he tells is a nationalistic epic, and it formed the foundation and framework for his successors. In it, as in *The Aeneid*, a people under divine guidance fulfill their destiny. In three large movements J describes how the twelve tribes grew from Abraham's seed, how Joseph saved the world from starvation, and how Israel, after being rescued from Egypt by Moses, conquered Canaan, the land which God had promised to Abraham. J's narrative is full of suspense: note, for instance, how often the transmitter of the chosen seed is late in appearing or is threatened with death. Moreover, J's style is usually both simple and elevated, and he can deal equally well with the triumphant

---

[1] The division of the Pentateuch into "books" resulted from the fact that in ancient times it could not all be written on one roll of papyrus or parchment, but had to be split among five separate rolls. Other sections of the Bible were similarly divided into "books."

13

interventions of God or the pranks of a rustic Jacob. Using old stories
and legends that were being passed down by word of mouth among his
own people and among neighboring tribes, J was able to create a stirring
and unified epic. Even so, the over-all tone of his story, when he is
dealing with those distant events before Israel became a nation, is
idyllic and pastoral. The atmosphere in Genesis tends to be one of
peace and good will, and the Hebrew patriarchs usually settle conflicts
with their neighbors without recourse to arms.

The second author is called E because of his use of the word "Elohim"
for God. E probably lived in the Northern Kingdom of Israel shortly
before its conquest by the Assyrians in 721 B.C.[2] His concern was primarily with the religious history of his people, not with their rise to
nationhood. Almost certainly a priest, E expanded and modified J to
emphasize the origin and rise of certain rituals (see, for instance, the
incident in which Jacob wrestles with the angel; or, E's masterpiece, the
story of Abraham's willingness to sacrifice Isaac). More rhetorical than
J and more willing to let his protagonists behave emotionally, E added
to and somewhat altered the original saga, but he also enriched it.

The third major contributor (or, in this case, probably a group of
contributors) was also a priest, and as such he is regularly designated as
P. He lived in the fifth century, after the Jews had been conquered by
the Babylonians. To him and many of his contemporaries the tribal or
nationalistic God had, under the influence of the prophets, become the
one and only God, the Lord of all the world. Though Israel was still
His chosen people, their commonwealth was, after all its vicissitudes,
understandably more ideal than actual, more spiritual than political.
Thus it is to P that we owe the first chapter of Genesis, wherein a universal God creates a cosmos. But P also condenses the eight days of the
ancient Babylonian creation story to six, with a day added for rest and
worship. Here and elsewhere P and his fellow editors of the end of the
fifth century were concerned with reconciling the concept of a universal
God with that of an exclusively Jewish God. But these men, in combining the works J and E and adding bits of their own, managed to
compile a narrative that, though often inconsistent, is still exciting and,
ultimately, unified.[3]

Because Palestine was at the crossroads of the world, lying between
the old civilization of Egypt and the rising empires of the Tigris-

[2] Note, for example, that in chapter 37, below, Joseph's life is first saved by
Reuben, a northerner (the E source), then by Judah, a southerner (the J
source).
[3] Probably the "editorial" work on the Pentateuch began about 650 B.C. and
continued until about 400 B.C. Thus P and his colleagues were the last in
a long series of "editors."

Euphrates area, neither J nor his successors worked in isolation. The
story of creation is paralleled in Phoenician and Babylonian legends;
while the saga of the flood has many ancient counterparts, most of them
originating from a desire to explain the evident facts of geology. Equally
antique and widespread is the idea of a vanished golden age, a lost eden,
in which man was blissful and all creatures were vegetarians. Central to
this nostalgic belief was the dominant position of man, for whom the
earth was made, who showed through his power of giving names to
animals that he was the pinnacle of creation, and in whom God retained
an abiding and personal interest. Three other traits of Genesis are equally
common in ancient religions and literatures. One is the incorporation in
sacred or semi-sacred texts of localized oral stories which explain how a
place got its name or an area its characteristics (for instance, the tale of
Sodom and Gomorrah, which accounts for the bleak appearance, probably
caused by a volcano, of the region at the southern end of the Dead Sea).
The second is the use of stories about individuals to signify movements
involving relatively large groups and perhaps taking several centuries
(Abraham's journey westward, for example).⁴ The third common trait
is a fondness for certain etiological myths, for stories, that is, which
attempt to explain how a widespread trait or custom originated (why
most women hate snakes is, for instance, accounted for in chapter 3).

But other strands in Genesis serve the purpose of distinguishing the
Hebrews from their neighbors and from alien traditions. One such strand
is the emphasis on circumcision. Though this rite was widely practiced
among primitive religions, in the Pentateuch it becomes closely linked
with sabbatarianism and with certain dietary laws as a sign that the
chosen people are peculiarly close to their God. Another strand consists of stories intended to show that the non-Hebrew tribes are
inferior: Moab and Ammon, for instance, are the offspring of Lot's incest
with his daughters, and the Edomites are descended from the slow-
witted and short-sighted Esau. Esau's brother Jacob is, in contrast, wily
and self-reliant, and it is he who will transmit the chosen seed. There is,
in fact, a Herculean, as well as a shrewd, quality about Jacob: the sug-
gestion that he single-handedly set up a pillar to God at Bethel, that he
was able to remove a stone well-cover which normally took several men
to lift, and that he won his wrestling match with the angel. Also Joseph,
the next progenitor of the race, is, if not superhuman, able to become
the most important figure in Egypt: the man who not only determines
the country's agrarian and tax policies but also saves the world from

⁴ Jacob's blessing to his twelve sons is built up from a wide assortment of
once separate tribal "oracles" that look both forward and backward in time.

starvation. Consequently the Hebrew patriarchs, from Abraham through Joseph, are at once legendary and unique.

They also tend to be realistic. Joseph is heroic and magnanimous, but he is also vain and petty. The story of Simeon and Levi, who treacherously slay Hamor and Shechem and their people, is not glossed over or idealized. And Jacob's prophecy at the end of Genesis characterizes the twelve tribes of Israel in a manner that places honesty far above flattery. Even the cosmic event in which God unpredictably selects Abraham to be the father of the chosen people is handled matter-of-factly. Thus the miraculous elements which are prominent in Exodus and many later books of the Bible are relatively inconspicuous in this saga of the Hebrew patriarchs. Moreover, in Genesis, as in the Old Testament as a whole, there is no concept of personal immortality, no heaven or hell, to activate these racial heroes. Their righteousness is rewarded by earthly blessings and/or a feeling of harmony with God. Evil, on the other hand, is punished by earthly suffering, as in the case of Cain. One sign of righteousness, incidentally, is hospitality. In a nomadic society where water was scarce or in the apparent lawlessness of new cities this was a most important virtue: hence the many lovely scenes at wellheads, and hence Lot's willingness to sacrifice his daughters to secure the safety of his guests.

Arising from this relatively unsophisticated background, the Hebrew concept of God, whether the nationalistic and sometimes intimate God of J (chapters 2 and 3) or the transcendent universal God of P (chapter 1), contains many timeless elements. But the narrative of His dealings with the chosen people as told in Genesis has an anchorage in very ancient history. The eighteenth century before Christ was probably the period when Abraham (or the tribes for which he stands) moved westward along the Fertile Crescent. The next century in all likelihood witnessed the descent of Jacob and his family into Egypt, at a time when the Hyksos were in control of that country; and Joseph probably flourished around 1550 B.C. In any case, J and his successors, looking back through the mists of time, saw in these remote events the beginnings of a story that is still being told. ♣ ♣ ♣

Suggested Reading   (The books listed below and in the Suggested Readings in subsequent introductions are, of course, also relevant to other sections of the Bible, and to the Bible as a whole. I have tried, however, to subdivide most of the acknowledged great classics of Western literature, as well as some distinctive modern books, so that each appears with that section to which it is most closely related. In each case the order is chronological.)

Homer, *The Iliad*—the archetypal classical epic.

Ovid, *Metamorphoses; Fasti*—poems which illustrate the classical treatment of myth.

John Milton, *Paradise Lost*—the great Protestant epic about the fall of man.

George Bernard Shaw, *Back to Methuselah*—a modern reinterpretation of the cause and effect of man's fall.

Marc Connelly, *The Green Pastures*—a twentieth-century American play that retells parts of the Bible story in a way that is at once simple and sophisticated.

Thomas Mann, *Joseph and His Brothers*—a group of four novels which probe and expand the Joseph saga.

GENESIS

1 In the beginning God created the heaven and the earth. And the earth was without form, and void, and darkness was upon the face of the deep: and the spirit of God moved upon the face of the waters. And God said, "Let there be light": and there was light. And God saw the light, that it was good: and God divided the light from the darkness. And God called the light Day, and the darkness he called Night: and the evening and the morning were the first day.

And God said, "Let there be a firmament in the midst of the waters: and let it divide the waters from the waters." And God made the firmament, and divided the waters which were under the firmament from the waters which were above the firmament: and it was so. And God called the firmament Heaven: and the evening and the morning were the second day.

And God said, "Let the waters under the heaven be gathered together unto one place, and let the dry land appear": and it was so. And God called the dry land Earth, and the gathering together of the waters called he Seas: and God saw that it was good. And God said, "Let the earth bring forth grass, the herb yielding seed, and the fruit tree yielding fruit after his kind, whose seed is in itself, upon the earth: and it was so. And the earth brought forth grass, and herb yielding seed after his kind, and the tree yielding fruit, whose seed was in itself, after his kind: and God saw that it was good. And the evening and the morning were the third day.

And God said, "Let there be lights in the firmament of the heaven, to divide the day from the night: and let them be for signs and for seasons, and for days and years. And let them be for lights in the firmament of the heaven, to give light upon the earth": and it was so. And God made two great lights: the greater light to rule the day, and the lesser light to rule the night: he made the stars also. And God set them in the firmament of the heaven, to give light upon the earth: and to rule over the day, and over the night, and to divide the light from the darkness: and God saw that it was good. And the evening and the morning were the fourth day.

And God said, "Let the waters bring forth abundantly the moving creature that hath life, and fowl that may fly above the earth in the open firmament of heaven." And God created great whales, and every living creature that moveth, which the waters brought forth abundantly after their kind, and every winged fowl after his kind: and God saw that it was good. And God blessed them, saying, "Be fruitful, and multiply, and fill the waters in the seas, and let fowl multiply in the earth." And the evening and the morning were the fifth day.

And God said, "Let the earth bring forth the living creature after his kind, cattle, and creeping thing, and beast of the earth after his kind": and it was so. And God made the beast of the earth after his kind, and cattle after their kind, and every thing that creepeth upon the earth after his kind: and God saw that it was good.

And God said, "Let us make man in our image, after our likeness: and let them have dominion over the fish of the sea, and over the fowl of the air, and over the cattle, and over all the earth, and over every creeping thing that creepeth upon the earth." So God created man in his own image, in the image of God created he him; male and female created he them. And God blessed them, and God said unto them, "Be fruitful, and multiply, and replenish the earth, and subdue it, and have dominion over the fish of the sea, and over the fowl of the air, and over every living thing that moveth upon the earth."

And God said, "Behold, I have given you every herb bearing seed. which is upon the face of all the earth, and every tree, in the which is the fruit of a tree yielding seed; to you it shall be for meat: and to every beast of the earth, and to every fowl of the air, and to every thing that creepeth upon the earth, wherein there is life, I have given every green herb for meat": and it was so. And God saw every thing that he had made: and behold, it was very good. And the evening and the morning were the sixth day.

2 Thus the heavens and the earth were finished, and all the host of them. And on the seventh day God ended his work which he had made. And he rested on the seventh day from all his work which he had made. And God blessed the seventh day, and sanctified it: because that in it he had rested from all his work which God created and made.

These are the generations of the heavens and of the earth when they were created, in the day that the Lord God made the earth and the heavens, and every plant of the field before it was in the earth, and every herb of the field before it grew: for the Lord God had not caused it to rain upon the earth, and there was not a man to till the ground. But there went up a mist from the earth, and watered the whole face of the ground. And the Lord God formed man of the dust of the ground, and breathed into his nostrils the breath of life; and man became a living soul.

And the Lord God planted a garden eastward in Eden; and there he put the man whom he had formed. And out of the ground made the Lord God to grow every tree that is pleasant to the sight and good for food: the tree of life also in the midst of the garden, and the tree of knowledge of good and evil. And a river went out of Eden to water the garden, and from thence it was parted, and became into four heads. The name of the first is Pison: that is it which compasseth the whole land of Havilah, where there is gold. And the gold of that land is good: there is bdellium and the onyx stone. And the name of the second river is Gihon: the same is it that compasseth the whole land of Ethiopia. And the name of the third river is Hiddekel: that is it which goeth toward the east of Assyria: and the fourth river is Euphrates. And the Lord God took the man, and put him into the garden of Eden, to dress it and to keep it. And the Lord God commanded the man, saying, "Of every tree of the garden thou mayest freely eat. But of the tree of the knowledge of good and evil, thou shalt not eat of it: for in the day that thou eatest thereof thou shalt surely die."

And the Lord God said, "It is not good that the man should be alone: I will make him an help meet for him." And out of the ground the Lord God formed every beast of the field, and every fowl of the air, and brought them unto Adam, to see what he would call them: and whatsoever Adam called every living creature, that was the name thereof. And Adam gave names to all cattle, and to the fowl of the air, and to every beast of the field: but for Adam there was not found an help meet for him. And the Lord God caused a deep sleep to fall upon Adam, and he slept: and he took one of his ribs, and closed up the flesh instead thereof. And the rib which the Lord God had taken from man, made he a woman, and brought her unto the man. And Adam said, "This is now bone of my bones, and flesh of my flesh: she shall be called woman, because she was taken out of man." Therefore shall a man leave his father and his mother, and shall cleave unto his wife: and they shall be one flesh. And they were both naked, the man and his wife, and were not ashamed.

3 Now the serpent was more subtle than any beast of the field which the Lord God had made, and he said unto the woman, "Yea, hath God said, 'Ye shall not eat of every tree of the garden'?" And the woman said unto the serpent, "We may eat of the fruit of the trees of the garden: but of the fruit of the tree which is in the midst of the garden, God hath said, 'Ye shall not eat of it, neither shall ye touch it, lest ye die.'" And the serpent said unto the woman, "Ye shall not surely die. For God doth know that in the day ye eat thereof, then your eyes shall be opened: and ye shall be as gods, knowing good and evil." And when the woman saw that the tree was good for food, and that it was pleasant to the eyes, and a tree to be desired to make one wise, she took of the fruit thereof, and did eat, and gave also unto her husband with her, and he did eat. And the eyes of them both were opened, and they knew that they were naked, and they sewed fig leaves together, and made themselves aprons. And they heard the voice of the Lord God walking in the garden in the cool of the day: and Adam and his wife hid themselves from the presence of the Lord God, amongst the trees of the garden.

And the Lord God called unto Adam, and said unto him, "Where art thou?" And he said, "I heard thy voice in the garden: and I was afraid, because I was naked, and I hid myself." And he said, "Who told thee that thou wast naked? Hast thou eaten of the tree whereof I commanded thee that thou shouldst not eat?" And the man said, "The woman whom thou gavest to be with me, she gave me of the tree, and I did eat." And the Lord God said unto the woman, "What is this that thou hast done?" And the woman said, "The serpent beguiled me, and I did eat." And the Lord God said unto the serpent, "Because thou hast done this, thou art cursed above all cattle, and above every beast of the field: upon thy belly shalt thou go, and dust shalt thou eat, all the days of thy life. And I will put enmity between thee and the woman, and between thy seed and her seed: it shall bruise thy head, and thou shalt bruise his heel." Unto the woman he said, "I will greatly multiply thy sorrow and thy conception. In sorrow thou shalt bring forth children: and thy desire shall be to thy husband, and he shall rule over thee." And unto Adam he said, "Because thou hast hearkened unto the voice of thy wife, and hast eaten of the tree, of which I commanded thee, saying, 'Thou shalt not eat of it': cursed is the ground for thy sake: in sorrow shalt thou eat of it all the days of thy life. Thorns also and thistles shall it bring forth to thee: and thou shalt eat the herb of the field. In the sweat of thy face shalt thou eat bread, till thou return unto the ground: for out of it wast thou taken, for dust thou art, and unto dust shalt thou return." And Adam called his wife's name Eve, because she was the mother of all living. Unto Adam also, and to his wife, did the Lord God make coats of skins, and clothed them.

And the Lord God said, "Behold, the man is become as one of us, to know good and evil. And now, lest he put forth his hand, and take also of the tree of life, and eat and live for ever—": therefore the Lord God sent him forth from the garden of Eden, to till the ground from whence he was taken. So he drove out the man: and he placed at the east of the garden of Eden cherubim, and a flaming sword which turned every way, to keep the way of the tree of life.

4 And Adam knew[1] Eve his wife, and she conceived, and bare Cain, and said, "I have gotten a man from the Lord." And she again bare his brother Abel, and Abel was a keeper of sheep, but Cain

[1] "Knew" in the sense of having sexual intercourse.

was a tiller of the ground. And in process of time it came to pass, that Cain brought of the fruit of the ground an offering unto the Lord. And Abel, he also brought of the firstlings of his flock, and of the fat thereof: and the Lord had respect unto Abel and to his offering. But unto Cain and to his offering he had not respect: and Cain was very wroth, and his countenance fell. And the Lord said until Cain, "Why art thou wroth? And why is thy countenance fallen? If thou do well, shalt thou not be accepted? and if thou doest not well, sin lieth at the door: and unto thee shall be his desire, and thou shalt rule over him." And Cain talked with Abel his brother: and it came to pass when they were in the field, that Cain rose up against Abel his brother, and slew him.

And the Lord said unto Cain, "Where is Abel thy brother?" And he said, "I know not: am I my brother's keeper?" And he said "What hast thou done? the voice of thy brother's blood crieth unto me from the ground. And now art thou cursed from the earth, which hath opened her mouth to receive thy brother's blood from thy hand. When thou tillest the ground, it shall not henceforth yield unto thee her strength: a fugitive and a vagabond shalt thou be in the earth." And Cain said unto the Lord, "My punishment is greater than I can bear. Behold, thou hast driven me out this day from the face of the earth, and from thy face shall I be hid, and I shall be a fugitive, and a vagabond in the earth: and it shall come to pass, that every one that findeth me shall slay me." And the Lord said unto him, "Therefore whosoever slayeth Cain, vengeance shall be taken on him sevenfold." And the Lord set a mark upon Cain, lest any finding him should kill him.

And Cain went out from the presence of the Lord, and dwelt in the land of Nod,[2] on the east of Eden. And Cain knew his wife, and she conceived and bare Enoch, and he builded a city, and called the name of the city after the name of his son, Enoch. . . . And Adam knew his wife again, and she bare a son, and called his name Seth: "For God," said she, "hath appointed me another seed instead of Abel, whom Cain slew." And to Seth, to him also there was born a son, and he called his name Enos: then began men to call upon the name of the Lord. . . .

[2] *I.e.,* the land of wandering.

5 . . . And the days of Adam, after he had begotten Seth, were eight hundred years: and he begat sons and daughters. And all the days that Adam lived were nine hundred and thirty years: and he died. . . .

6 And it came to pass, when men began to multiply on the face of the earth, and daughters were born unto them, that the sons of God saw the daughters of men, that they were fair, and they took them wives of all which they chose. And the Lord said, "My spirit shall not always strive with men, for that he also is flesh: yet his days shall be an hundred and twenty years." There were giants in the earth in those days: and also after that, when the sons of God came in unto the daughters of men, and they bare children to them, the same became mighty men, which were of old, men of renown.

And God saw that the wickedness of men was great in the earth, and that every imagination of the thoughts of his heart was only evil continually. And it repented the Lord that he had made man on the earth, and it grieved him at his heart. And the Lord said, "I will destroy man, whom I have created, from the face of the earth: both man and beast, and the creeping thing, and the fowls of the air: for it repenteth me that I have made them." But Noah found grace in the eyes of the Lord.

These are the generations of Noah: Noah was a just man, and perfect in his generations, and Noah walked with God. And Noah begat three sons: Shem, Ham, and Japheth. The earth also was corrupt before God; and the earth was filled with violence. And God looked upon the earth, and behold, it was corrupt: for all flesh had corrupted his way upon the earth. And God said unto Noah, "The end of all flesh is come before me; for the earth is filled with violence through them; and behold, I will destroy them with the earth."

"Make thee an ark of gopher wood:[3] rooms shalt thou make in the ark, and shalt pitch it within and without with pitch. And this is the fashion which thou shalt make it of: the length of the ark shall be three hundred cubits,[4] the breadth of it fifty cubits, and the

[3] *I.e.*, cypress.
[4] The length of the forearm, from the elbow to the end of the middle finger (approximately 18 inches), equals one cubit.

height of it thirty cubits. A window shalt thou make to the ark, and
in a cubit shalt thou finish it above; and the door of the ark shalt
thou set in the side thereof: with lower, second, and third stories
shalt thou make it. And behold, I, even I do bring a flood of waters
upon the earth, to destroy all flesh wherein is the breath of life from
under heaven, and every thing that is in the earth shall die. But with
thee will I establish my covenant: and thou shalt come into the ark,
thou, and thy sons, and thy wife, and thy sons' wives with thee. And
of every living thing of all flesh, two of every sort shalt thou bring
into the ark, to keep them alive with thee: they shall be male and
female. Of fowls after their kind, and of cattle after their kind, of
every creeping thing of the earth after his kind, two of every sort
shall come unto thee, to keep them alive. And take thou unto thee of
all food that is eaten, and thou shalt gather it to thee; and it shall be
for food, for thee, and for them." Thus did Noah; according to all
that God commanded him, so did he.

7 And the Lord said unto Noah, "Come thou and all thy house
into the ark: for thee have I seen righteous before me in this
generation. Of every clean beast thou shalt take to thee by sevens,[5]
the male and his female: and of beasts that are not clean, by two, the
male and his female. Of fowls also of the air, by sevens, the
male and the female; to keep seed alive upon the face of all the
earth. For yet seven days, and I will cause it to rain upon the earth
forty days and forty nights: and every living substance that I have
made will I destroy from off the face of the earth." And Noah did
according unto all that the Lord commanded him. And Noah was
six hundred years old when the flood of waters was upon the earth.

And Noah went in, and his sons, and his wife, and his sons' wives
with him, into the ark, because of the waters of the flood. Of clean
beasts, and of beasts that are not clean, and of fowls, and of every
thing that creepeth upon the earth, there went in two and two unto
Noah into the ark, the male and the female, as God had commanded
Noah. And it came to pass after seven days, that the waters of the
flood were upon the earth.

In the six hundredth year of Noah's life, in the second month, the

---

[5] *I.e.*, seven pairs: probably in the J version there were fourteen of each kind
of "clean" animal; in P there were two of every kind.

seventeenth day of the month, the same day were all the fountains of the great deep broken up, and the windows of heaven were opened. And the rain was upon the earth forty days and forty nights. In the selfsame day entered Noah, and Shem, and Ham, and Japheth, the sons of Noah, and Noah's wife, and the three wives of his sons with them, into the ark, they, and every beast after his kind, and all the cattle after their kind, and every creeping thing that creepeth upon the earth after his kind, and every fowl after his kind, every bird of every sort. And they went in unto Noah into the ark, two and two of all flesh wherein is the breath of life. And they that went in, went in male and female of all flesh, as God had commanded him: and the Lord shut him in.

And the flood was forty days upon the earth, and the waters increased, and bare up the ark, and it was lifted up above the earth. And the waters prevailed, and were increased greatly upon the earth: and the ark went upon the face of the waters. And the waters prevailed exceedingly upon the earth, and all the high hills that were under the whole heaven were covered. Fifteen cubits upward did the waters prevail; and the mountains were covered. And all flesh died that moved upon the earth, both of fowl, and of cattle, and of beast, and of every creeping thing that creepeth upon the earth, and every man. All in whose nostrils was the breath of life, of all that was in the dry land, died. And every living substance was destroyed which was upon the face of the ground, both man and cattle, and the creeping things, and the fowl of the heaven; and they were destroyed from the earth: and Noah only remained alive, and they that were with him in the ark. And the waters prevailed upon the earth an hundred and fifty days.

8 And God remembered Noah, and every living thing, and all the cattle that was with him in the ark: and God made a wind to pass over the earth, and the waters assuaged. The fountains also of the deep and the windows of heaven were stopped, and the rain from heaven was restrained. And the waters returned from off the earth continually: and after the end of the hundred and fifty days the waters were abated. And the ark rested in the seventh month, on the seventeenth day of the month, upon the mountains of Ararat. And the waters decreased continually until the tenth month: in the tenth month, on the first day of the month, were the tops of the mountains seen.

And it came to pass at the end of forty days, that Noah opened the window of the ark which he had made. And he sent forth a raven, which went forth to and fro, until the waters were dried up from off the earth. Also he sent forth a dove from him, to see if the waters were abated from off the face of the ground. But the dove found no rest for the sole of her foot, and she returned unto him into the ark: for the waters were on the face of the whole earth. Then he put forth his hand, and took her, and pulled her in unto him, into the ark. And he stayed yet other seven days; and again he sent forth the dove out of the ark. And the dove came in to him in the evening, and lo, in her mouth was an olive leaf plucked off: so Noah knew that the waters were abated from off the earth. And he stayed yet other seven days, and sent forth the dove, which returned not again unto him any more.

And it came to pass in the six hundredth and one year, in the first month, the first day of the month, the waters were dried up from off the earth: and Noah removed the covering of the ark, and looked, and behold, the face of the ground was dry. And in the second month, on the seven and twentieth day of the month, was the earth dried.

And God spake unto Noah, saying, "Go forth of the ark, thou, and thy wife, and thy sons and thy sons' wives with thee: bring forth with thee every living thing that is with thee, of all flesh, both of fowl, and of cattle, and of every creeping thing that creepeth upon the earth, that they may breed abundantly in the earth, and be fruitful, and multiply upon the earth." And Noah went forth, and his sons, and his wife, and his sons' wives with him: every beast, every creeping thing, and every fowl, and whatsoever creepeth upon the earth, after their kinds, went forth out of the ark.

And Noah builded an altar unto the Lord, and took of every clean beast, and of every clean fowl, and offered burnt offerings on the altar. And the Lord smelled a sweet savour, and the Lord said in his heart, "I will not again curse the ground any more for man's sake; for the imagination of man's heart is evil from his youth: neither will I again smite any more every thing living, as I have done. While the earth remaineth, seedtime and harvest, and cold and heat, and summer and winter, and day and night shall not cease."

9 And God blessed Noah, and his sons, and said unto them, "Be fruitful and multiply, and replenish the earth. And the fear of you and the dread of you shall be upon every beast of the earth, and upon every fowl of the air, upon all that moveth upon the earth, and upon all the fishes of the sea; into your hand are they delivered. Every moving thing that liveth shall be meat for you; even as the green herb have I given you all things. But flesh with the life thereof, which is the blood thereof, shall you not eat. And surely your blood of your lives will I require: at the hand of every beast will I require it, and at the hand of man, at the hand of every man's brother will I require the life of man. Whoso sheddeth man's blood, by man shall his blood be shed: for in the image of God made he man. And you, be ye fruitful and multiply, bring forth abundantly in the earth, and multiply therein."

And God spake unto Noah, and to his sons with him, saying, "And I, behold, I establish my covenant with you and with your seed after you: and with every living creature that is with you, of the fowl, of the cattle, and of every beast of the earth with you, from all that go out of the ark, to every beast of the earth. And I will establish my covenant with you, neither shall all flesh be cut off any more by the waters of a flood, neither shall there any more be a flood to destroy the earth." And God said, "This is the token of the covenant which I make between me and you, and every living creature that is with you, for perpetual generations. I do set my bow in the cloud, and it shall be for a token of a covenant between me and the earth. And it shall come to pass, when I bring a cloud over the earth, that the bow shall be seen in the cloud. And I will remember my covenant, which is between me and you, and every living creature of all flesh: and the waters shall no more become a flood to destroy all flesh. And the bow shall be in the cloud; and I will look upon it, that I may remember the everlasting covenant between God and every living creature of all flesh that is upon the earth." And God said unto Noah, "This is the token of the covenant which I have established between me and all flesh that is upon the earth."

And the sons of Noah that went forth of the ark were Shem, and Ham, and Japheth: and Ham is the father of Canaan. These are the three sons of Noah: and of them was the whole earth overspread. And Noah began to be an husbandman, and he planted a vineyard.

And he drank of the vine, and was drunken, and he was uncovered within his tent. And Ham, the father of Canaan, saw the nakedness of his father, and told his two brethren without. And Shem and Japheth took a garment, and laid it upon both their shoulders, and went backward, and covered the nakedness of their father, and their faces were backward, and they saw not their father's nakedness. And Noah awoke from his wine, and knew what his younger son had done unto him. And he said, "Cursed be Canaan: a servant of servants shall he be unto his brethren." And he said, "Blessed be the Lord God of Shem, and Canaan shall be his servant. God shall enlarge Japheth, and he shall dwell in the tents of Shem, and Canaan shall be his servant." And Noah lived after the flood three hundred and fifty years. And all the days of Noah were nine hundred and fifty years, and he died.

10 Now these are the generations of the sons of Noah, Shem, Ham, and Japheth: and unto them were sons born after the flood. . . . And by these were the nations divided in the earth after the flood.

11 And the whole earth was of one language, and of one speech. And it came to pass, as they journeyed from the east, that they found a plain in the land of Shinar,[6] and they dwelt there. And they said one to another, "Go to, let us make brick, and burn them thoroughly." And they had brick for stone, and slime had they for mortar. And they said, "Go to, let us build us a city and a tower, whose top may reach unto heaven, and let us make us a name, lest we be scattered abroad upon the face of the whole earth." And the Lord came down to see the city and the tower, which the children of men builded. And the Lord said, "Behold, the people is one, and they have all one language: and this they begin to do: and now nothing will be restrained from them, which they have imagined to do. Go to, let us go down, and there confound their language, that they may not understand one another's speech." So the Lord scattered them abroad from thence upon the face of all the earth: and they left off to build the city. Therefore is the name of it called Babel, because the Lord did there confound the language of all the

---

[6] Babylonia.

earth: and from thence did the Lord scatter them abroad upon the face of all the earth. . . .

And Terah took Abram his son, and Lot the son of Haran his son's son, and Sarai his daughter in law, his son Abram's wife, and they went forth with them from Ur of the Chaldees, to go into the land of Canaan: and they came unto Haran, and dwelt there. And the days of Terah were two hundred and five years: and Terah died in Haran.

12 Now the Lord had said unto Abram, "Get thee out of thy country, and from thy kindred, and from thy father's house, unto a land that I will show thee. And I will make of thee a great nation, and I will bless thee, and make thy name great; and thou shalt be a blessing. And I will bless them that bless thee, and curse him that curseth thee: and in thee shall all families of the earth be blessed." So Abram departed, as the Lord had spoken unto him, and Lot went with him: and Abram was seventy and five years old when he departed out of Haran. And Abram took Sarai his wife, and Lot his brother's son, and all their substance that they had gathered, and the souls that they had gotten in Haran, and they went forth to go into the land of Canaan: and into the land of Canaan they came.

And Abram passed through the land, unto the place of Sichem, unto the plain of Moreh. And the Canaanite was then in the land. And the Lord appeared unto Abram, and said, "Unto thy seed will I give this land": and there builded he an altar unto the Lord, who appeared unto him. And he removed from thence unto a mountain on the east of Bethel, and pitched his tent, having Bethel on the west, and Hai on the east: and there he builded an altar unto the Lord, and called upon the name of the Lord. And Abram journeyed, going on still toward the south.

And there was a famine in the land, and Abram went down into Egypt to sojourn there: for the famine was grievous in the land. And it came to pass when he was come near to enter into Egypt, that he said unto Sarai his wife, "Behold now, I know that thou art a fair woman to look upon. Therefore it shall come to pass, when the Egyptians shall see thee, that they shall say, 'This is his wife': and they will kill me, but they will save thee alive. Say, I pray thee, thou art my sister, that it may be well with me for thy sake; and my soul shall live because of thee."

And it came to pass that, when Abram was come into Egypt, the Egyptians beheld the woman, that she was very fair. The princes also of Pharaoh saw her, and commended her before Pharaoh: and the woman was taken into Pharaoh's house. And he entreated Abram well for her sake: and he had sheep, and oxen, and he-asses, and menservants, and maidservants, and she-asses, and camels. And the Lord plagued Pharaoh and his house with great plagues, because of Sarai Abram's wife. And Pharaoh called Abram, and said, "What is this that thou hast done unto me? Why didst thou not tell me that she was thy wife? Why saidst thou, 'She is my sister'? so I might have taken her to me to wife: now therefore behold thy wife, take her, and go thy way." And Pharaoh commanded his men concerning him: and they sent him away, and his wife, and all that he had.

13 And Abram went up out of Egypt, he, and his wife, and all that he had, and Lot with him, into the south. And Abram was very rich in cattle, in silver, and in gold. And he went on his journeys from the south, even to Bethel, unto the place where his tent had been at the beginning, between Bethel and Hai: unto the place of the altar, which he had made there at the first: and there Abram called on the name of the Lord.

And Lot also, which went with Abram, had flocks, and herds, and tents. And the land was not able to bear them, that they might dwell together: for their substance was great, so that they could not dwell together. And there was a strife between the herdmen of Abram's cattle and the herdmen of Lot's cattle: and the Canaanite and the Perizzite dwelled then in the land. And Abram said unto Lot, "Let there be no strife, I pray thee, between me and thee, and between my herdmen and thy herdmen: for we be brethren. Is not the whole land before thee? Separate thyself, I pray thee, from me: if thou wilt take the left hand, then I will go to the right: or if thou depart to the right hand, then I will go to the left." And Lot lifted up his eyes, and beheld all the plain of Jordan, that it was well watered everywhere, before the Lord destroyed Sodom and Gomorrah, even as the garden of the Lord, like the land of Egypt, as thou comest unto Zoar. Then Lot chose him all the plain of Jordan: and Lot journeyed east; and they separated themselves the one from the other. Abram dwelled in the land of Canaan, and Lot dwelled in the cities of the plain, and pitched his tent toward Sodom. But the men of Sodom were wicked, and sinners before the Lord exceedingly.

And the Lord said unto Abram, after that Lot was separated from him, "Lift up now thine eyes, and look from the place where thou art, northward, and southward, and eastward, and westward. For all the land which thou seest, to thee will I give it, and to thy seed for ever. And I will make thy seed as the dust of the earth: so that if a man can number the dust of the earth, then shall thy seed also be numbered. Arise, walk through the land, in the length of it, and in the breadth of it: for I will give it unto thee." Then Abram removed his tent, and came and dwelt in the plain of Mamre, which is in Hebron, and built there an altar unto the Lord.

14 And it came to pass in the days of Amraphel king of Shinar, Arioch king of Ellasar, Chedorlaomer king of Elam, and Tidal king of nations: that these made war with Bera king of Sodom, and with Birsha king of Gomorrah, Shinab king of Admah, and Shemeber king of Zeboiim, and the king of Bela, which is Zoar. All these were joined together in the vale of Siddim, which is the Salt Sea. Twelve years they served Chedorlaomer, and in the thirteenth year they rebelled. And in the fourteenth year came Chedorlaomer, and the kings that were with him, and smote the Rephaim in Ashteroth Karnaim, and the Zuzim in Ham, and the Emim in Shaveh Kiriathaim, and the Horites in their Mount Seir, unto El-paran, which is by the wilderness. And they returned, and came to En-mishpat, which is Kadesh, and smote all the country of the Amalekites, and also the Amorites, that dwelt in Hazezon-tamar. And there went out the king of Sodom, and the king of Gomorrah, and the king of Admah, and the king of Zeboiim, and the king of Bela (the same is Zoar), and they joined battle with them in the vale of Siddim, with Chedorlaomer the king of Elam, and with Tidal king of nations, and Amraphel king of Shinar, and Arioch king of Ellasar; four kings with five. And the vale of Siddim was full of slime-pits: and the kings of Sodom and Gomorrah fled, and fell there: and they that remained fled to the mountain. And they took all the goods of Sodom and Gomorrah, and all their victuals, and went their way. And they took Lot, Abram's brother's son (who dwelt in Sodom), and his goods, and departed.

And there came one that had escaped, and told Abram the Hebrew, for he dwelt in the plain of Mamre the Amorite, brother of Eshcol, and brother of Aner: and these were confederate with Abram. And when Abram heard that his brother was taken captive, he armed his trained servants, born in his own house, three hundred and eighteen, and pursued them unto Dan. And he divided himself against them, he and his servants, by night, and smote them, and pursued them unto Hobah, which is on the left hand of Damascus. And he brought back all the goods, and also brought again his brother Lot, and his goods, and the women also, and the people.

And the king of Sodom went out to meet him (after his return from the slaughter of Chedorlaomer, and of the kings that were with him), at the valley of Shaveh, which is the king's dale. And Melchizedek king of Salem brought forth bread and wine: and he was the priest of the most high God. And he blessed him, and said, "Blessed be Abram of the most high God, possessor of heaven and earth, and blessed be the most high God, which hath delivered thine enemies into thy hand": and he gave him tithes[7] of all. And the king of Sodom said unto Abram, "Give me the persons, and take the goods to thyself." And Abram said to the king of Sodom, "I have lifted up mine hand unto the Lord, the most high God, the possessor of heaven and earth, that I will not take from a thread even to a shoe latchet, and that I will not take any thing that is thine, lest thou shouldest say, 'I have made Abram rich': save only that which the young men have eaten, and the portion of the men which went with me, Aner, Eshcol, and Mamre; let them take their portion."

15 After these things, the word of the Lord came unto Abram in a vision, saying, "Fear not, Abram: I am thy shield, and thy exceeding great reward." And Abram said, "Lord God, what wilt thou give me, seeing I go childless? and the steward of my house is this Eliezer of Damascus." And Abram said, "Behold, to me thou hast given no seed: and lo, one born in my house is mine heir." And behold, the word of the Lord came unto him, saying, "This shall not be thine heir: but he that shall come forth out of thy own bowels shall be thine heir." And he brought him forth abroad, and said, "Look now toward heaven, and tell[8] the stars, if thou be able to

[7] I.e., tenths.
[8] I.e., number.

number them." And he said unto him, "So shall thy seed be." And he believed in the Lord; and he counted it to him for righteousness. And he said unto him, "I am the Lord that brought thee out of Ur of the Chaldees, to give thee this land to inherit it." And he said, "Lord God, whereby shall I know that I shall inherit it?" And he said unto him, "Take me an heifer of three years old, and a she-goat of three years old, and a ram of three years old, and a turtle dove, and a young pigeon." And he took unto him all these, and divided them in the midst, and laid each piece one against another: but the birds divided he not. And when the fowls came down upon the carcasses, Abram drove them away. And when the sun was going down, a deep sleep fell upon Abram: and lo, an horror of great darkness fell upon him. And he said unto Abram, "Know of a surety that thy seed shall be a stranger in a land that is not theirs, and shall serve them, and they shall afflict them four hundred years. And also that nation whom they shall serve will I judge: and afterward shall they come out with great substance. And thou shalt go to thy fathers in peace; thou shalt be buried in a good old age. But in the fourth generation they shall come hither again: for the iniquity of the Amorites is not yet full." And it came to pass that when the sun went down, and it was dark, behold, a smoking furnace, and a burning lamp that passed between those pieces. In that same day the Lord made a covenant with Abram, saying, "Unto thy seed have I given this land from the river of Egypt unto the great river, the river Euphrates: the Kenites, and the Kenizzites, and the Kadmonites, and the Hittites, and the Perizzites, and the Rephaim, and the Amorites, and the Canaanites, and the Girgashites, and the Jebusites."

16 Now Sarai Abram's wife bare him no children: and she had an handmaid, an Egyptian, whose name was Hagar. And Sarai said unto Abram, "Behold now, the Lord hath restrained me from bearing: I pray thee go in unto my maid: it may be that I may obtain children by her": and Abram hearkened to the voice of Sarai. And Sarai Abram's wife took Hagar her maid, the Egyptian, after Abram had dwelt ten years in the land of Canaan, and gave her to her husband Abram, to be his wife.

And he went in unto Hagar, and she conceived: and when she saw that she had conceived, her mistress was despised in her eyes.

And Sarai said unto Abram, "My wrong be upon thee: I have given my maid into thy bosom, and when she saw that she had conceived, I was despised in her eyes: the Lord judge between me and thee." But Abram said unto Sarai, "Behold, thy maid is in thy hand; do to her as it pleaseth thee." And when Sarai dealt hardly with her, she fled from her face.

And the angel of the Lord found her by a fountain of water in the wilderness, by the fountain in the way to Shur: and he said, "Hagar, Sarai's maid, whence camest thou? and whither wilt thou go?" And she said, "I flee from the face of my mistress Sarai." And the angel of the Lord said unto her, "Return to thy mistress, and submit thyself under her hands." And the angel of the Lord said unto her, "I will multiply thy seed exceedingly, that it shall not be numbered for multitude." And the angel of the Lord said unto her, "Behold, thou art with child, and shalt bear a son, and shalt call his name Ishmael; because the Lord hath heard thy affliction. And he will be a wild man; his hand will be against every man, and every man's hand against him: and he shall dwell in the presence of all his brethren." And she called the name of the Lord that spake unto her, "Thou God seest me": for she said, "Have I also here looked after him that seeth me?" Wherefore the well was called Beer-lahai-roi: behold, it is between Kadesh and Bered.

And Hagar bare Abram a son: and Abram called his son's name, which Hagar bare, Ishmael. And Abram was fourscore and six years old when Hagar bare Ishmael to Abram.

17 And when Abram was ninety years old and nine, the Lord appeared to Abram, and said unto him, "I am the almighty God, walk before me, and be thou perfect. And I will make my covenant between me and thee, and will multiply thee exceedingly." And Abram fell on his face, and God talked with him, saying, "As for me, behold, my covenant is with thee, and thou shalt be a father of many nations. Neither shall thy name any more be called Abram, but thy name shall be Abraham: for a father of many nations have I made thee. And I will make thee exceeding fruitful, and I will make nations of thee, and kings shall come out of thee. And I will establish my covenant between me and thee, and thy seed after thee, in their generations for an everlasting covenant, to be a God unto thee, and to thy seed after thee. And I will give unto thee, and to thy seed after thee, the land wherein thou art a stranger, all the land of Canaan, for an everlasting possession, and I will be their God."

And God said unto Abraham, "Thou shalt keep my covenant therefore, thou, and thy seed after thee, in their generations. This is my covenant, which ye shall keep between me and you, and thy seed after thee: every man child among you shall be circumcised. And ye shall circumcise the flesh of your foreskin; and it shall be a token of the covenant betwixt me and you. And he that is eight days old shall be circumcised among you, every man child in your generations, he that is born in the house, or bought with money of any stranger, which is not of thy seed. He that is born in thy house, and he that is bought with thy money, must needs be circumcised: and my covenant shall be in your flesh for an everlasting covenant. And the uncircumcised man child whose flesh of his foreskin is not circumcised, that soul shall be cut off from his people: he hath broken my covenant."

And God said unto Abraham, "As for Sarai thy wife, thou shalt not call her name Sarai, but Sarah shall her name be. And I will bless her, and give thee a son also of her: yea I will bless her, and she shall be a mother of nations; kings of people shall be of her." Then Abraham fell upon his face, and laughed, and said in his heart, "Shall a child be born unto him that is an hundred years old? and shall Sarah that is ninety years old, bear?" And Abraham said unto God, "O that Ishmael might live before thee." And God said, "Sarah thy wife shall bear thee a son indeed, and thou shalt call his name Isaac: and I will establish my covenant with him for an everlasting covenant, and with his seed after him. And as for Ishmael, I have heard thee: behold, I have blessed him, and will make him fruitful, and will multiply him exceedingly: twelve princes shall he beget, and I will make him a great nation. But my covenant will I establish with Isaac, which Sarah shall bear unto thee at this set time in the next year." And he left off talking with him, and God went up from Abraham.

And Abraham took Ishmael his son, and all that were born in his house, and all that were bought with his money, every male among the men of Abraham's house, and circumcised the flesh of their foreskin, in the selfsame day, as God had said unto him. And Abraham

was ninety years old and nine when he was circumcised in the flesh
of his foreskin. And Ishmael his son was thirteen years old when he
was circumcised in the flesh of his foreskin. In the selfsame day was
Abraham circumcised, and Ishmael his son. And all the men of his
house, born in the house, and bought with money of the stranger,
were circumcised with him.

18 And the Lord appeared unto him in the plains of Mamre: and
he sat in the tent door, in the heat of the day. And he lifted
up his eyes and looked, and lo, three men stood by him: and when
he saw them, he ran to meet them from the tent door, and bowed
himself toward the ground, and said, "My Lord, if now I have found
favour in thy sight, pass not away, I pray thee, from thy servant:
let a little water, I pray you, be fetched, and wash your feet, and rest
yourselves under the tree: and I will fetch a morsel of bread; and
comfort ye your hearts, after that ye shall pass on: for therefore are
you come to your servant." And they said, "So do, as thou hast said."
And Abraham hastened into the tent, unto Sarah, and said, "Make
ready quickly three measures of fine meal, knead it, and make cakes
upon the hearth." And Abraham ran unto the herd, and fetched a
calf, tender and good, and gave it unto a young man: and he
hasted to dress it. And he took butter, and milk, and the calf
which he had dressed, and set it before them; and he stood by them
under the tree: and they did eat.

And they said unto him, "Where is Sarah thy wife?" And he said,
"Behold, in the tent." And he said, "I will certainly return unto thee
according to the time of your life; and lo, Sarah thy wife shall have
a son." And Sarah heard it in the tent door, which was behind him.
Now Abraham and Sarah were old, and well stricken in age: and
it ceased to be with Sarah after the manner of women. Therefore
Sarah laughed within herself, saying, "After I am waxed old shall I
have pleasure, my lord being old also?" And the Lord said unto
Abraham, "Wherefore did Sarah laugh, saying, 'Shall I of a surety
bear a child, which am old?' Is any thing too hard for the Lord? At
the time appointed will I return unto thee, according to the time of
life, and Sarah shall have a son." Then Sarah denied, saying, "I
laughed not": for she was afraid. And he said, "Nay, but thou didst
laugh."

And the men rose up from thence, and looked toward Sodom: and Abraham went with them, to bring them on the way. And the Lord said, "Shall I hide from Abraham that thing which I do; seeing that Abraham shall surely become a great and mighty nation, and all the nations of the earth shall be blessed in him? For I know him, that he will command his children, and his household after him, and they shall keep the way of the Lord, to do justice and judgment, that the Lord may bring upon Abraham that which he hath spoken of him." And the Lord said, "Because the cry of Sodom and Gomorrah is great, and because their sin is very grievous: I will go down now, and see whether they have done altogether according to the cry of it, which is come unto me: and if not, I will know." And the men turned their faces from thence, and went toward Sodom: but Abraham stood yet before the Lord.

And Abraham drew near, and said, "Wilt thou also destroy the righteous with the wicked? Peradventure there be fifty righteous within the city; wilt thou also destroy, and not spare the place for the fifty righteous that are therein? That be far from thee, to do after this manner, to slay the righteous with the wicked; and that the righteous should be as the wicked, that be far from thee: shall not the judge of all the earth do right?" And the Lord said, "If I find in Sodom fifty righteous within the city, then I will spare all the place for their sakes." And Abraham answered, and said, "Behold now, I have taken upon me to speak unto the Lord, which am but dust and ashes. Peradventure there shall lack five of the fifty righteous: wilt thou destroy all the city for lack of five?" And he said, "If I find there forty and five, I will not destroy it." And he spake unto him yet again, and said, "Peradventure there shall be forty found there." And he said, "I will not do it for forty's sake." And he said unto him, "Oh let not the Lord be angry, and I will speak: peradventure there shall thirty be found there." And he said, "I will not do it, if I find thirty there." And he said, "Behold now, I have taken upon me to speak unto the Lord: peradventure there shall be twenty found there." And he said, "I will not destroy it for twenty's sake." And he said, "Oh let not the Lord be angry, and I will speak yet but this once: peradventure ten shall be found there." And he said, "I will not destroy it for ten's sake." And the Lord went his way, as soon as he had left communing with Abraham: and Abraham returned unto his place.

19 And there came two angels to Sodom at even, and Lot sat in the gate of Sodom: and Lot seeing them rose up to meet them, and he bowed himself with his face toward the ground. And he said, "Behold now my lords, turn in, I pray you, into your servant's house, and tarry all night, and wash your feet, and ye shall rise up early and go on your ways." And they said, "Nay: but we will abide in the street all night." And he pressed upon them greatly, and they turned in unto him, and entered into his house: and he made them a feast, and did bake unleavened bread, and they did eat.

But before they lay down, the men of the city, even the men of Sodom, compassed the house round, both old and young, all the people from every quarter. And they called unto Lot, and said unto him, "Where are the men which came in to thee this night? bring them out unto us, that we may know them." And Lot went out at the door unto them, and shut the door after him, and said, "I pray you, brethren, do not so wickedly. Behold now, I have two daughters, which have not known man; let me, I pray you, bring them out unto you, and do ye to them as is good in your eyes: only unto these men do nothing: for therefore came they under the shadow of my roof." And they said, "Stand back." And they said again, "This one fellow came in to sojourn, and he will needs be a judge: now will we deal worse with thee than with them." And they pressed sore upon the man, even Lot, and came near to break the door. But the men put forth their hand, and pulled Lot into the house to them, and shut to the door. And they smote the men that were at the door of the house with blindness, both small and great: so that they wearied themselves to find the door.

And the men said unto Lot, "Hast thou here any besides? Son in law, and thy sons, and thy daughters, and whatsoever thou hast in the city, bring them out of this place. For we will destroy this place, because the cry of them is waxen great before the face of the Lord: and the Lord hath sent us to destroy it." And Lot went out, and spake unto his sons in law, which married his daughters, and said, "Up, get ye out of this place: for the Lord will destroy this city": but he seemed as one that mocked unto his sons in law.

And when the morning arose, then the angels hastened Lot, saying, "Arise, take thy wife, and thy two daughters, which are here, lest thou be consumed in the iniquity of the city." And while he lingered, the men laid hold upon his hand, and upon the hand of his wife, and upon the hand of his two daughters, the Lord being merciful unto him: and they brought him forth, and set him without the city.

And it came to pass, when they had brought them forth abroad, that he said, "Escape for thy life, look not behind thee, neither stay thou in all the plain: escape to the mountain, lest thou be consumed." And Lot said unto them, "Oh, not so, my Lord. Behold now, thy servant hath found grace in thy sight, and thou hast magnified thy mercy, which thou hast showed unto me in saving my life, and I cannot escape to the mountain, lest some evil take me, and I die. Behold now, this city is near to flee unto, and it is a little one. Oh, let me escape thither (is it not a little one?), and my soul shall live." And he said unto him, "See, I have accepted thee concerning this thing also, that I will not overthrow this city, for the which thou hast spoken. Haste thee, escape thither: for I cannot do any thing till thou be come thither": therefore the name of the city was called Zoar.

The sun was risen upon the earth when Lot entered into Zoar. Then the Lord rained upon Sodom and upon Gomorrah brimstone and fire from the Lord out of heaven. And he overthrew those cities, and all the plain, and all the inhabitants of the cities, and that which grew upon the ground. But his wife looked back from behind him, and she became a pillar of salt.

And Abraham got up early in the morning to the place where he stood before the Lord. And he looked toward Sodom and Gomorrah, and toward all the land of the plain, and beheld, and lo, the smoke of the country went up as the smoke of a furnace. And it came to pass, when God destroyed the cities of the plain, that God remembered Abraham, and sent Lot out of the midst of the overthrow, when he overthrew the cities in the which Lot dwelt.

And Lot went up out of Zoar, and dwelt in the mountain, and his two daughters with him: for he feared to dwell in Zoar, and he dwelt in a cave, he and his two daughters. And the firstborn said unto the younger, "Our father is old, and there is not a man in the earth to come in unto us after the manner of all the earth. Come, let us make our father drink wine, and we will lie with him, that we may preserve seed of our father." And they made their father drink wine that night, and the firstborn went in, and lay with her father: and he perceived not when she lay down, nor when she arose. And it came to pass on the morrow, that the firstborn said unto the younger, "Behold, I lay yesternight with my father: let us make him drink wine this night also, and go thou in, and lie with him, that we may preserve seed of our father." And they made their father drink wine that night also, and the younger arose, and lay with him: and he perceived not when she lay down, nor when she arose. Thus were both the daughters of Lot with child by their father. And the firstborn bare a son, and called his name Moab: the same is the father of the Moabites unto this day. And the younger, she also bare a son, and called his name Ben-ammi: the same is the father of the children of Ammon unto this day.

20 And Abraham journeyed from thence, toward the south country, and dwelled between Kadesh and Shur, and sojourned in Gerar. And Abraham said of Sarah his wife, "She is my sister": and Abimelech king of Gerar sent, and took Sarah. But God came to Abimelech in a dream by night, and said to him, "Behold, thou art but a dead man, for the woman which thou hast taken: for she is a man's wife." But Abimelech had not come near her: and he said, "Lord, wilt thou slay also a righteous nation? Said he not unto me, 'She is my sister'? and she, even she herself said, 'He is my brother': in the integrity of my heart and innocency of my hands have I done this." And God said unto him in a dream, "Yea, I know that thou didst this in the integrity of thy heart: for I also withheld thee from sinning against me, therefore suffered I thee not to touch her. Now therefore restore the man his wife: for he is a prophet, and he shall pray for thee, and thou shalt live: and if thou restore her not, know thou that thou shalt surely die, thou, and all that are thine." Therefore Abimelech rose early in the morning, and called all his servants, and told all these things in their ears: and the men were sore afraid. Then Abimelech called Abraham, and said unto him, "What hast thou done unto us? and what have I offended thee, that thou hast brought on me and on my kingdom a great sin? thou hast done deeds unto me that ought not to be done." And Abimelech said unto Abraham, "What sawest thou, that thou hast done this thing?" And Abraham said, "Because I thought, 'Surely the fear of God is not in this place: and they will slay me for my wife's sake.' And yet indeed she is my sister: she is the daughter of my father, but not the daughter of my mother; and she became my wife. And it came to pass when God caused me to wander from my father's house, that I said unto her, 'This is thy kindness which thou shalt show unto me; at every place whither we shall come, say of me, "He is my brother." ' " And Abimelech took sheep and oxen, and menservants, and womenservants, and gave them unto Abraham, and restored him Sarah his wife. And Abimelech said, "Behold, my land is before thee; dwell where it pleaseth thee." And unto Sarah he said, "Behold, I have given thy brother a thousand pieces of silver: behold, he is to thee a covering of the eyes, unto all that are with thee, and with all other": thus she was reproved.

So Abraham prayed unto God: and God healed Abimelech, and his wife, and his maidservants, and they bare children. For the Lord had fast closed up all the wombs of the house of Abimelech, because of Sarah Abraham's wife.

21 And the Lord visited Sarah as he had said, and the Lord did unto Sarah as he had spoken. For Sarah conceived, and bare Abraham a son in his old age, at the set time of which God had spoken to him. And Abraham called the name of his son that was born unto him, whom Sarah bare to him, Isaac. And Abraham circumcised his son Isaac, being eight days old, as God had commanded him. And Abraham was an hundred years old when his son Isaac was born unto him. And Sarah said, "God hath made me to laugh, so that all that hear will laugh with me." And she said, "Who would have said unto Abraham that Sarah should have given children suck? for I have borne him a son in his old age." And the child grew, and was weaned: and Abraham made a great feast the same day that Isaac was weaned.

And Sarah saw the son of Hagar the Egyptian, which she had borne unto Abraham, mocking. Wherefore she said unto Abraham, "Cast out this bondwoman and her son: for the son of this bondwoman shall not be heir with my son, even with Isaac." And the thing was very grievous in Abraham's sight, because of his son.

And God said unto Abraham, "Let it not be grievous in thy sight because of the lad, and because of thy bondwoman. In all that Sarah hath said unto thee, hearken unto her voice: for in Isaac shall thy seed be called. And also of the son of the bondwoman will I make a nation, because he is thy seed." And Abraham rose up early in the morning, and took bread, and a bottle of water, and gave it unto

Hagar (putting it on her shoulder), and the child, and sent her away: and she departed, and wandered in the wilderness of Beersheba. And the water was spent in the bottle, and she cast the child under one of the shrubs. And she went, and sat her down over against[9] him, a good way off, as it were a bowshot: for she said, "Let me not see the death of the child." And she sat over against him, and lifted up her voice, and wept. And God heard the voice of the lad, and the angel of God called to Hagar out of heaven, and said unto her, "What aileth thee, Hagar? fear not: for God hath heard the voice of the lad, where he is. Arise, lift up the lad, and hold him in thine hand: for I will make him a great nation." And God opened her eyes, and she saw a well of water, and she went, and filled the bottle with water, and gave the lad drink. And God was with the lad, and he grew, and dwelt in the wilderness, and became an archer. And he dwelt in the wilderness of Paran: and his mother took him a wife out of the land of Egypt.

And it came to pass at that time, that Abimelech and Phichol the chief captain of his host spake unto Abraham, saying, "God is with thee in all that thou doest. Now therefore swear unto me here by God, that thou wilt not deal falsely with me, nor with my son, nor with my son's son: but according to the kindness that I have done unto thee, thou shalt do unto me, and to the land wherein thou hast sojourned." And Abraham said, "I will swear." And Abraham reproved Abimelech because of a well of water, which Abimelech's servants had violently taken away. And Abimelech said, "I wot not who hath done this thing: neither didst thou tell me, neither yet heard I of it, but today." And Abraham took sheep and oxen, and gave them unto Abimelech: and both of them made a covenant. And Abraham set seven ewe lambs of the flock by themselves. And Abimelech said unto Abraham, "What mean these seven ewe lambs, which thou hast set by themselves?" And he said, "For these seven ewe lambs shalt thou take of my hand, that they may be a witness unto me, that I have digged this well." Wherefore he called that place Beer-sheba: because there they sware both of them. Thus they made a covenant at Beer-sheba: then Abimelech rose up, and Phichol the chief captain of his host, and they returned into the land of the Philistines.

[9] *I.e.*, opposite.

And Abraham planted a grove in Beer-sheba, and called there on the name of the Lord, the everlasting God. And Abraham sojourned in the Philistines' land many days.

22 And it came to pass after these things, that God did tempt Abraham, and said unto him, "Abraham:" and he said, "Behold, here I am." And he said, "Take now thy son, thine only son Isaac, whom thou lovest, and get thee into the land of Moriah; and offer him there for a burnt offering upon one of the mountains which I will tell thee of." And Abraham rose up early in the morning, and saddled his ass, and took two of his young men with him, and Isaac his son, and clave the wood for the burnt offering, and rose up, and went unto the place of which God had told him. Then on the third day Abraham lifted up his eyes, and saw the place afar off. And Abraham said unto his young men, "Abide you here with the ass, and I and the lad will go yonder and worship, and come again to you." And Abraham took the wood of the burnt offering, and laid it upon Isaac his son: and he took the fire in his hand, and a knife: and they went both of them together. And Isaac spake unto Abraham his father, and said, "My father": and he said, "Here am I, my son." And he said, "Behold the fire and the wood: but where is the lamb for a burnt offering?" And Abraham said, "My son, God will provide himself a lamb for a burnt offering": so they went both of them together. And they came to the place which God had told him of, and Abraham built an altar there, and laid the wood in order, and bound Isaac his son, and laid him on the altar upon the wood. And Abraham stretched forth his hand, and took the knife to slay his son. And the angel of the Lord called unto him out of heaven, and said, "Abraham, Abraham." And he said, "Here am I." And he said, "Lay not thine hand upon the lad, neither do thou any thing unto him: for now I know that thou fearest God, seeing thou hast not withheld thy son, thine only son from me." And Abraham lifted up his eyes, and looked, and behold, behind him a ram caught in a thicket by his horns: and Abraham went and took the ram, and offered him up for a burnt offering in the stead of his son. And Abraham called the name of that place Jehovah-jireh, as it is said to this day, "In the mount of the Lord it shall be seen."

And the angel of the Lord called unto Abraham out of heaven the second time, and said, "By myself have I sworn, saith the Lord, for because thou hast done this thing, and hast not withheld thy son, thine only son, that in blessing I will bless thee, and in multiplying I will multiply thy seed as the stars of the heaven, and as the sand which is upon the sea shore, and thy seed shall possess the gate of his enemies. And in thy seed shall all the nations of the earth be blessed, because thou hast obeyed my voice." So Abraham returned unto his young men, and they rose up, and went together to Beersheba, and Abraham dwelt at Beer-sheba. . . .

23 And Sarah was an hundred and seven and twenty years old: these were the years of the life of Sarah. And Sarah died in Kirjath-arba, the same is Hebron in the land of Canaan: and Abraham came to mourn for Sarah, and to weep for her.

And Abraham stood up from before his dead, and spake unto the sons of Heth, saying, "I am a stranger and a sojourner with you: give me a possession of a burying place with you, that I may bury my dead out of my sight." And the children of Heth answered Abraham, saying unto him, "Hear us, my lord, thou art a mighty prince amongst us: in the choice of our sepulchres bury thy dead: none of us shall withhold from thee his sepulchre, but that thou mayest bury thy dead." And Abraham stood up, and bowed himself to the people of the land, even to the children of Heth. And he communed with them, saying, "If it be your mind that I should bury my dead out of my sight, hear me, and entreat for me to Ephron the son of Zohar: that he may give me the cave of Machpelah, which he hath, which is in the end of his field: for as much money as it is worth he shall give it me for a possession of a burying place amongst you." And Ephron dwelt among the children of Heth. And Ephron the Hittite answered Abraham in the audience of the children of Heth, even of all that went in at the gate of his city, saying, "Nay, my lord, hear me: the field give I thee, and the cave that is therein, I give it thee, in the presence of the sons of my people give I it thee: bury thy dead." And Abraham bowed down himself before the people of the land. And he spake unto Ephron in the audience of the people of the land, saying, "But if thou wilt give it, I pray thee, hear me: I will give thee money for the field: take it of me, and I will bury my dead there." And Ephron answered Abraham, saying unto him, "My lord, hearken unto me: the land is worth four hundred shekels of silver: what is that betwixt me and thee? bury therefore thy dead." And Abraham hearkened unto Ephron, and Abraham weighed to Ephron the silver, which he had named, in the audience of the sons of Heth, four hundred shekels of silver, current money with the merchant.

And the field of Ephron, which was in Machpelah, which was before Mamre, the field, and the cave which was therein, and all the trees that were in the field, that were in all the borders round about, were made sure unto Abraham for a possession in the presence of the children of Heth, before all that went in at the gate of his city. And after this Abraham buried Sarah his wife in the cave of the field of Machpelah, before Mamre: the same is Hebron in the land of Canaan. And the field, and the cave that is therein, were made sure unto Abraham for a possession of a burying place by the sons of Heth.

24 And Abraham was old and well stricken in age: and the Lord had blessed Abraham in all things. And Abraham said unto his eldest servant of his house, that ruled over all that he had, "Put, I pray thee, thy hand under my thigh:[10] and I will make thee swear by the Lord, the God of heaven, and the God of the earth, that thou shalt not take a wife unto my son of the daughters of the Canaanites amongst whom I dwell. But thou shalt go unto my country, and to my kindred, and take a wife unto my son Isaac." And the servant said unto him, "Peradventure the woman will not be willing to follow me unto this land: must I needs bring thy son again unto the land from whence thou camest?" And Abraham said unto him, "Beware thou, that thou bring not my son thither again. The Lord God of heaven which took me from my father's house, and from the land of my kindred, and which spake unto me, and that sware unto me, saying, 'Unto thy seed will I give this land'; he shall send his angel before thee, and thou shalt take a wife unto my son from thence. And if the woman will not be willing to follow thee, then thou shalt be clear from this my oath: only bring not my son thither again." And the servant put his hand under the thigh of Abraham his master, and sware to him concerning that matter.

And the servant took ten camels, of the camels of his master, and departed (for all the goods of his master were in his hand), and he

[10] Probably an echo of the very ancient practice of swearing by the genital organs, themselves emblematic of the power of life.

arose, and went to Mesopotamia, unto the city of Nahor. And he made his camels to kneel down without the city, by a well of water, at the time of the evening, even the time that women go out to draw water. And he said, "O Lord, God of my master Abraham, I pray thee send me good speed this day, and show kindness unto my master Abraham. Behold, I stand here by the well of water; and the daughters of the men of the city come out to draw water. And let it come to pass, that the damsel to whom I shall say, 'Let down thy pitcher, I pray thee, that I may drink,' and she shall say, 'Drink, and I will give thy camels drink also'; let the same be she that thou hast appointed for thy servant Isaac: and thereby shall I know that thou hast showed kindness unto my master."

And it came to pass before he had done speaking, that behold, Rebekah came out, who was born to Bethuel, son of Milcah, the wife of Nahor, Abraham's brother, with her pitcher upon her shoulder. And the damsel was very fair to look upon, a virgin, neither had any man known her; and she went down to the well, and filled her pitcher, and came up. And the servant ran to meet her, and said, "Let me, I pray thee, drink a little water of thy pitcher." And she said, "Drink, my lord": and she hasted, and let down her pitcher upon her hand, and gave him drink. And when she had done giving him drink, she said, "I will draw water for thy camels also, until they have done drinking." And she hasted, and emptied her pitcher into the trough, and ran again unto the well to draw water, and drew for all his camels. And the man wondering at her held his peace, to wit, whether the Lord had made his journey prosperous or not. And it came to pass as the camels had done drinking, that the man took a golden earring, of half a shekel weight, and two bracelets for her hands, of ten shekels' weight of gold, and said, "Whose daughter art thou? tell me, I pray thee: is there room in thy father's house for us to lodge in?" And she said unto him, "I am the daughter of Bethuel the son of Milcah, which she bare unto Nahor": she said moreover unto him, "We have both straw and provender enough, and room to lodge in." And the man bowed down his head, and worshipped the Lord. And he said, "Blessed be the Lord God of my master Abraham, who hath not left destitute my master of his mercy and his truth: I being in the way, the Lord led me to the house of my master's brethren." And the damsel ran, and told them of her mother's house these things.

And Rebekah had a brother, and his name was Laban: and
Laban ran out unto the man, unto the well. And it came to pass
when he saw the earring, and bracelets upon his sister's hands,
and when he heard the words of Rebekah his sister, saying, "Thus
spake the man unto me," that he came unto the man; and behold,
he stood by the camels at the well. And he said, "Come in, thou
blessed of the Lord, wherefore standest thou without? for I have
prepared the house, and room for the camels."

And the man came into the house: and he ungirded his camels,
and gave straw and provender for the camels, and water to wash his
feet, and the men's feet that were with him. And there was set meat
before him to eat: but he said, "I will not eat until I have told mine
errand." And he said, "Speak on." And he said, "I am Abraham's
servant. And the Lord hath blessed my master greatly, and he is
become great: and he hath given him flocks, and herds, and silver,
and gold, and menservants, and maidservants, and camels, and
asses. And Sarah my master's wife bare a son to my master when
she was old: and unto him hath he given all that he hath. And my
master made me swear, saying, 'Thou shalt not take a wife to my
son of the daughters of the Canaanites, in whose land I dwell: but
thou shalt go unto my father's house, and to my kindred, and take
a wife unto my son.' And I said unto my master, 'Peradventure the
woman will not follow me.' And he said unto me, 'The Lord, before
whom I walk, will send his angel with thee, and prosper thy way:
and thou shalt take a wife for my son, of my kindred, and of my
father's house. Then shalt thou be clear from this my oath, when
thou comest to my kindred, and if they give not thee one, thou shalt
be clear from my oath.' And I came this day unto the well, and
said, 'O Lord God of my master Abraham, if now thou do prosper
my way which I go: behold, I stand by the well of water; and it
shall come to pass, that when the virgin cometh forth to draw water,
and I say to her, "Give me, I pray thee, a little water of thy pitcher
to drink"; and she say to me, "Both drink thou, and I will also draw
for thy camels": let the same be the woman whom the Lord hath
appointed out for my master's son.' And before I had done speaking
in mine heart, behold, Rebekah came forth, with her pitcher on her
shoulder; and she went down unto the well, and drew water: and I
said unto her, 'Let me drink, I pray thee.' And she made haste, and
let down her pitcher from her shoulder, and said, 'Drink, and I will

give thy camels drink also': so I drank, and she made the camels drink also. And I asked her, and said, 'Whose daughter art thou?' And she said, 'The daughter of Bethuel, Nahor's son, whom Milcah bare unto him': and I put the earring upon her face, and the bracelets upon her hands. And I bowed down my head, and worshipped the Lord, and blessed the Lord God of my master Abraham, which had led me in the right way to take my master's brother's daughter unto his son. And now if ye will deal kindly and truly with my master, tell me: and if not, tell me, that I may turn to the right hand, or to the left."

Then Laban and Bethuel answered and said, "The thing proceedeth from the Lord: we cannot speak unto thee bad or good. Behold, Rebekah is before thee, take her, and go, and let her be thy master's son's wife, as the Lord hath spoken." And it came to pass, that when Abraham's servant heard their words, he worshipped the Lord, bowing himself to the earth. And the servant brought forth jewels of silver, and jewels of gold, and raiment, and gave them to Rebekah: he gave also to her brother and to her mother precious things. And they did eat and drink, he and the men that were with him, and tarried all night, and they rose up in the morning, and he said, "Send me away unto my master." And her brother and her mother said, "Let the damsel abide with us a few days, at the least ten; after that, she shall go." And he said unto them, "Hinder me not, seeing the Lord hath prospered my way: send me away, that I may go to my master." And they said, "We will call the damsel, and inquire at her mouth." And they called Rebekah, and said unto her, "Wilt thou go with this man?" And she said, "I will go." And they sent away Rebekah their sister, and her nurse, and Abraham's servant, and his men. And they blessed Rebekah, and said unto her, "Thou art our sister, be thou the mother of thousands of millions, and let thy seed possess the gate of those which hate them."

And Rebekah arose, and her damsels, and they rode upon the camels, and followed the man: and the servant took Rebekah, and went his way. And Isaac came from the way of the well Lahai-roi, for he dwelt in the south country. And Isaac went out to meditate in the field at the eventide: and he lifted up his eyes, and saw, and behold, the camels were coming. And Rebekah lifted up her eyes, and when she saw Isaac, she lighted off the camel. For she had said unto the servant, "What man is this that walketh in the field to

meet us?" And the servant had said, "It is my master": therefore
she took a veil, and covered herself. And the servant told Isaac all
things that he had done. And Isaac brought her into his mother
Sarah's tent, and took Rebekah, and she became his wife, and he
loved her: and Isaac was comforted after his mother's death.

25 . . . And Abraham gave all that he had unto Isaac. But unto
the sons of the concubines which Abraham had, Abraham
gave gifts, and sent them away from Isaac his son (while he yet
lived) eastward, unto the east country. And these are the days of the
years of Abraham's life which he lived, an hundred threescore and
fifteen years. Then Abraham gave up the ghost, and died in a good
old age, an old man, and full of years, and was gathered to his
people. And his sons Isaac and Ishmael buried him in the cave of
Machpelah, in the field of Ephron the son of Zohar the Hittite,
which is before Mamre: the field which Abraham purchased of the
sons of Heth: there was Abraham buried, and Sarah his wife. And
it came to pass after the death of Abraham, that God blessed his son
Isaac, and Isaac dwelt by the well Lahai-roi. . . .

And Isaac was forty years old when he took Rebekah to wife, the
daughter of Bethuel the Syrian of Padan-aram, the sister to Laban
the Syrian. And Isaac entreated the Lord for his wife, because she
was barren: and the Lord was entreated of him, and Rebekah his
wife conceived. And the children struggled together within her; and
she said, "If it be so, why am I thus?" and she went to inquire of the
Lord. And the Lord said unto her, "Two nations are in thy womb,
and two manner of people shall be separated from thy bowels: and
the one people shall be stronger than the other people: and the
elder shall serve the younger."

And when her days to be delivered were fulfilled, behold, there
were twins in her womb. And the first came out red all over like an
hairy garment: and they called his name Esau. And after that came
his brother out, and his hand took hold on Esau's heel; and his name
was called Jacob: and Isaac was threescore years old when she bare
them. And the boys grew; and Esau was a cunning hunter, a man of
the field: and Jacob was a plain man, dwelling in tents. And Isaac
loved Esau, because he did eat of his venison: but Rebekah loved
Jacob.

And Jacob sod pottage:[11] and Esau came from the field, and he was faint. And Esau said to Jacob, "Feed me, I pray thee, with that same red pottage: for I am faint"; therefore was his name called Edom. And Jacob said, "Sell me this day thy birthright." And Esau said, "Behold, I am at the point to die: and what profit shall this birthright do to me?" And Jacob said, "Swear to me this day": and he sware unto him: and he sold his birthright unto Jacob. Then Jacob gave Esau bread and pottage of lentils; and he did eat and drink, and rose up, and went his way: thus Esau despised his birthright.

26 And there was a famine in the land, besides the first famine that was in the days of Abraham. And Isaac went unto Abimelech king of the Philistines, unto Gerar. And the Lord appeared unto him and said, "Go not down into Egypt; dwell in the land which I shall tell thee of. Sojourn in this land, and I will be with thee, and will bless thee: for unto thee, and unto thy seed, I will give all these countries, and I will perform the oath, which I sware unto Abraham thy father. And I will make thy seed to multiply as the stars of heaven, and will give unto thy seed all these countries: and in thy seed shall all the nations of the earth be blessed: because that Abraham obeyed my voice, and kept my charge, my commandments, my statutes, and my laws."

And Isaac dwelt in Gerar. And the men of the place asked him of his wife: and he said, "She is my sister": for he feared to say, "She is my wife": "lest," said he, "the men of the place should kill me for Rebekah"; because she was fair to look upon. And it came to pass when he had been there a long time, that Abimelech king of the Philistines looked out at a window, and saw, and behold, Isaac was sporting with Rebekah his wife. And Abimelech called Isaac and said, "Behold, of a surety she is thy wife: and how saidst thou, 'She is my sister'?" And Isaac said unto him, "Because I said, 'Lest I die for her.'" And Abimelech said, "What is this thou hast done unto us? one of the people might lightly have lain with thy wife, and thou shouldst have brought guiltiness upon us." And Abimelech charged all his people, saying, "He that toucheth this man or his wife shall surely be put to death." Then Isaac sowed in that land, and received in the same year an hundredfold: and the Lord blessed

[11] *I.e.*, Jacob boiled some food.

him. And the man waxed great, and went forward, and grew until he became very great. For he had possession of flocks, and possession of herds, and great store of servants, and the Philistines envied him. For all the wells which his father's servants had digged in the days of Abraham his father, the Philistines had stopped them, and filled them with earth. And Abimelech said unto Isaac, "Go from us: for thou art much mightier than we."

And Isaac departed thence, and pitched his tent in the valley of Gerar, and dwelt there. And Isaac digged again the wells of water, which they had digged in the days of Abraham his father: for the Philistines had stopped them after the death of Abraham, and he called their names after the names by which his father had called them. And Isaac's servants digged in the valley, and found there a well of springing water. And the herdmen of Gerar did strive with Isaac's herdmen, saying, "The water is ours"; and he called the name of the well Esek, because they strove with him. And they digged another well, and strove for that also: and he called the name of it Sitnah. And he removed from thence, and digged another well, and for that they strove not: and he called the name of it Rehoboth: and he said, "For now the Lord hath made room for us, and we shall be fruitful in the land." And he went up from thence to Beer-sheba. And the Lord appeared unto him the same night, and said, "I am the God of Abraham thy father: fear not, for I am with thee, and will bless thee, and multiply thy seed, for my servant Abraham's sake." And he builded an altar there, and called upon the name of the Lord, and pitched his tent there: and there Isaac's servants digged a well.

Then Abimelech went to him from Gerar, and Ahuzzath one of his friends, and Phichol the chief captain of his army. And Isaac said unto them, "Wherefore come ye to me, seeing ye hate me, and have sent me away from you?" And they said, "We saw certainly that the Lord was with thee: and we said, 'Let there be now an oath betwixt us, even betwixt us and thee, and let us make a covenant with thee, that thou wilt do us no hurt, as we have not touched thee, and as we have done unto thee nothing but good, and have sent thee away in peace: thou art now the blessed of the Lord.' " And he made them a feast, and they did eat and drink. And they rose up betimes[12] in the morning, and sware one to another:

12 *I.e.*, early.

and Isaac sent them away, and they departed from him in peace. And it came to pass the same day, that Isaac's servants came, and told him concerning the well which they had digged, and said unto him, "We have found water." And he called it Shebah: therefore the name of the city is Beer-sheba unto this day.

And Esau was forty years old when he took to wife Judith, the daughter of Beeri the Hittite, and Bashemath the daughter of Elon the Hittite: which were a grief of mind unto Isaac and to Rebekah.

27 And it came to pass that when Isaac was old, and his eyes were dim, so that he could not see, he called Esau his eldest son, and said unto him, "My son." And he said unto him, "Behold, here am I." And he said, "Behold now, I am old, I know not the day of my death. Now therefore take, I pray thee, thy weapons, thy quiver and thy bow, and go out to the field, and take me some venison. And make me savoury meat, such as I love, and bring it to me, that I may eat, that my soul may bless thee before I die." And Rebekah heard when Isaac spake to Esau his son: and Esau went to the field to hunt for venison, and to bring it.

And Rebekah spake unto Jacob her son, saying, "Behold, I heard thy father speak unto Esau thy brother, saying, 'Bring me venison, and make me savoury meat, that I may eat, and bless thee before the Lord, before my death.' Now therefore, my son, obey my voice, according to that which I command thee. Go now to the flock, and fetch me from thence two good kids of the goats, and I will make them savoury meat for thy father, such as he loveth. And thou shalt bring it to thy father, that he may eat, and that he may bless thee before his death." And Jacob said to Rebekah his mother, "Behold, Esau my brother is a hairy man, and I am a smooth man. My father peradventure will feel me, and I shall seem to him as a deceiver, and I shall bring a curse upon me, and not a blessing." And his mother said unto him, "Upon me be thy curse, my son: only obey my voice, and go fetch me them." And he went, and fetched, and brought them to his mother, and his mother made savoury meat, such as his father loved. And Rebekah took goodly raiment of her eldest son Esau, which were with her in the house, and put them upon Jacob her younger son: and she put the skins of the kids of the goats upon his hands, and upon the smooth of his neck. And she gave the savoury meat and the bread, which she had prepared, into the hand of her son Jacob.

And he came unto his father, and said, "My father": and he said, "Here am I: who art thou, my son?" And Jacob said unto his father, "I am Esau, thy firstborn; I have done according as thou badest me: arise, I pray thee, sit, and eat of my venison, that thy soul may bless me." And Isaac said unto his son, "How is it that thou hast found it so quickly, my son?" And he said, "Because the Lord thy God brought it to me." And Isaac said unto Jacob, "Come near, I pray thee, that I may feel thee, my son, whether thou be my very son Esau, or not." And Jacob went near unto Isaac his father: and he felt him, and said, "The voice is Jacob's voice, but the hands are the hands of Esau." And he discerned him not, because his hands were hairy, as his brother Esau's hands: so he blessed him. And he said, "Art thou my very son Esau?" And he said, "I am." And he said, "Bring it near to me, and I will eat of my son's venison, that my soul may bless thee." And he brought it near to him, and he did eat: and he brought him wine, and he drank. And his father Isaac said unto him, "Come near now, and kiss me, my son." And he came near, and kissed him: and he smelled the smell of his raiment, and blessed him, and said, "See, the smell of my son is as the smell of a field which the Lord hath blessed. Therefore God give thee of the dew of heaven, and the fatness of the earth, and plenty of corn and wine. Let people serve thee, and nations bow down to thee: be lord over thy brethren, and let thy mother's sons bow down to thee: cursed be every one that curseth thee, and blessed be he that blesseth thee."

And it came to pass, as soon as Isaac had made an end of blessing Jacob, and Jacob was yet scarce gone out from the presence of Isaac his father, that Esau his brother came in from his hunting. And he also had made savoury meat, and brought it unto his father, and said unto his father, "Let my father arise, and eat of his son's venison, that thy soul may bless me." And Isaac his father said unto him, "Who art thou?" And he said, "I am thy son, thy firstborn Esau." And Isaac trembled very exceedingly, and said, "Who? where is he that hath taken venison, and brought it me, and I have eaten of all before thou camest, and have blessed him? yea and he shall be blessed." And when Esau heard the words of his father, he cried with a great and exceeding bitter cry, and said unto his father,

"Bless me, even me also, O my father." And he said, "Thy brother came with subtlety, and hath taken away thy blessing." And he said, "Is not he rightly named Jacob? for he hath supplanted me these two times: he took away my birthright, and behold, now he hath taken away my blessing." And he said, "Hast thou not reserved a blessing for me?" And Isaac answered and said unto Esau, "Behold, I have made him thy lord, and all his brethren have I given to him for servants: and with corn and wine have I sustained him: and what shall I do now unto thee, my son?" And Esau said unto his father, "Hast thou but one blessing, my father? bless me, even me also, O my father." And Esau lifted up his voice, and wept. And Isaac his father answered, and said unto him, "Behold, thy dwelling shall be the fatness of the earth, and of the dew of heaven from above. And by thy sword shalt thou live, and shalt serve thy brother: and it shall come to pass when thou shalt have the dominion, that thou shalt break his yoke from off thy neck."

And Esau hated Jacob because of the blessing wherewith his father blessed him: and Esau said in his heart, "The days of mourning for my father are at hand; then will I slay my brother Jacob." And these words of Esau her elder son were told to Rebekah: and she sent and called Jacob her younger son, and said unto him, "Behold, thy brother Esau, as touching thee, doth comfort himself, purposing to kill thee. Now therefore, my son, obey my voice: and arise, flee thou to Laban my brother, to Haran. And tarry with him a few days, until thy brother's fury turn away; until thy brother's anger turn away from thee, and he forget that which thou hast done to him: then I will send, and fetch thee from thence: why should I be deprived also of you both in one day?" And Rebekah said to Isaac, "I am weary of my life because of the daughters of Heth: if Jacob take a wife of the daughters of Heth, such as these which are of the daughters of the land, what good shall my life do me?"

28 And Isaac called Jacob, and blessed him, and charged him, and said unto him, "Thou shalt not take a wife of the daughters of Canaan. Arise, go to Padan-aram, to the house of Bethuel thy mother's father, and take thee a wife from thence, of the daughters of Laban thy mother's brother. And God Almighty bless thee, and make thee fruitful, and multiply thee, that thou mayest be a multitude of people: and give thee the blessing of

Abraham, to thee and to thy seed with thee, that thou mayest inherit the land wherein thou art a stranger, which God gave unto Abraham." And Isaac sent away Jacob, and he went to Padan-aram unto Laban, son of Bethuel the Syrian, the brother of Rebekah, Jacob's and Esau's mother.

When Esau saw that Isaac had blessed Jacob, and sent him away to Padan-aram, to take him a wife from thence; and that as he blessed him, he gave him a charge, saying, "Thou shalt not take a wife of the daughters of Canaan"; and that Jacob obeyed his father and his mother, and was gone to Padan-aram; and Esau seeing that the daughters of Canaan pleased not Isaac his father; then went Esau unto Ishmael, and took unto the wives which he had, Mahalath the daughter of Ishmael Abraham's son, the sister of Nebajoth, to be his wife.

And Jacob went out from Beer-sheba, and went toward Haran. And he lighted upon a certain place, and tarried there all night, because the sun was set: and he took of the stones of that place, and put them for his pillows, and lay down in that place to sleep. And he dreamed, and behold, a ladder set up on the earth, and the top of it reached to heaven: and behold, the angels of God ascending and descending on it. And behold, the Lord stood above it, and said, "I am the Lord God of Abraham thy father, and the God of Isaac: the land whereon thou liest, to thee will I give it, and to thy seed. And thy seed shall be as the dust of the earth, and thou shalt spread abroad to the west, and to the east, and to the north, and to the south: and in thee, and in thy seed, shall all the families of the earth be blessed. And behold, I am with thee, and will keep thee in all places whither thou goest, and will bring thee again into this land: for I will not leave thee until I have done that which I have spoken to thee of."

And Jacob awaked out of his sleep, and he said, "Surely the Lord is in this place, and I knew it not." And he was afraid, and said, "How dreadful is this place? this is none other but the house of God, and this is the gate of heaven." And Jacob rose up early in the morning, and took the stone that he had put for his pillows, and set it up for a pillar, and poured oil upon the top of it. And he called the name of that place Bethel: but the name of that city was called Luz at the first. And Jacob vowed a vow, saying, "If God will be with me, and will keep me in this way that I go, and will give me bread to eat, and raiment to put on, so that I come again to my father's house in peace: then shall the Lord be my God. And this stone, which I have set for a pillar, shall be God's house: and of all that thou shalt give me I will surely give the tenth unto thee."

29 Then Jacob went on his journey, and came into the land of the people of the east. And he looked, and behold, a well in the field, and lo, there were three flocks of sheep lying by it: for out of that well they watered the flocks: and a great stone was upon the well's mouth. And thither were all the flocks gathered, and they rolled the stone from the well's mouth, and watered the sheep, and put the stone again upon the well's mouth in his place. And Jacob said unto them, "My brethren, whence be ye?" And they said, "Of Haran are we." And he said unto them, "Know ye Laban the son of Nahor?" And they said, "We know him." And he said unto them, "Is he well?" And they said, "He is well: and behold, Rachel his daughter cometh with the sheep." And he said, "Lo, it is yet high day, neither is it time that the cattle should be gathered together: water ye the sheep, and go and feed them." And they said, "We cannot, until all the flocks be gathered together, and till they roll the stone from the well's mouth: then we water the sheep."

And while he yet spake with them, Rachel came with her father's sheep: for she kept them. And it came to pass, when Jacob saw Rachel the daughter of Laban his mother's brother, and the sheep of Laban his mother's brother, that Jacob went near, and rolled the stone from the well's mouth, and watered the flock of Laban his mother's brother. And Jacob kissed Rachel, and lifted up his voice, and wept. And Jacob told Rachel that he was her father's brother,[13] and that he was Rebekah's son: and she ran and told her father. And it came to pass, when Laban heard the tidings of Jacob his sister's son, that he ran to meet him, and embraced him, and kissed him, and brought him to his house: and he told Laban all these things. And Laban said to him, "Surely thou art my bone and my flesh." And he abode with him the space of a month.

And Laban said unto Jacob, "Because thou art my brother, shouldest thou therefore serve me for nought? tell me, what shall thy wages be?" And Laban had two daughters: the name of the elder

[13] Here a synonym for nephew.

was Leah, and the name of the younger was Rachel. Leah was tender eyed:[14] but Rachel was beautiful and well-favoured. And Jacob loved Rachel, and said, "I will serve thee seven years for Rachel thy younger daughter." And Laban said, "It is better that I give her to thee than that I should give her to another man: abide with me." And Jacob served seven years for Rachel: and they seemed unto him but a few days, for the love he had to her.

And Jacob said unto Laban, "Give me my wife (for my days are fulfilled) that I may go in unto her." And Laban gathered together all the men of the place, and made a feast. And it came to pass in the evening, that he took Leah his daughter, and brought her to him, and he went in unto her. And Laban gave unto his daughter Leah, Zilpah his maid for a handmaid. And it came to pass, that in the morning, behold, it was Leah: and he said to Laban, "What is this thou hast done unto me? did not I serve with thee for Rachel? wherefore then hast thou beguiled me?" And Laban said, "It must not be so done in our country, to give the younger before the first-born. Fulfill her week, and we will give thee this also, for the service which thou shalt serve with me yet seven other years." And Jacob did so, and fulfilled her week: and he gave him Rachel his daughter to wife also. And Laban gave to Rachel his daughter Bilhah his handmaid to be her maid. And he went in also unto Rachel, and he loved also Rachel more than Leah, and served with him yet seven other years.

And when the Lord saw that Leah was hated, he opened her womb: but Rachel was barren. And Leah conceived, and bare a son, and she called his name Reuben: for she said, "Surely the Lord hath looked upon my affliction; now therefore my husband will love me." And she conceived again, and bare a son, and said, "Because the Lord hath heard that I was hated, he hath therefore given me this son also," and she called his name Simeon. And she conceived again, and bare a son, and said, "Now this time will my husband be joined unto me, because I have borne him three sons": therefore was his name called Levi. And she conceived again, and bare a son: and she said, "Now will I praise the Lord": therefore she called his name Judah, and left bearing.

[14] "Tender" in the sense of sore or weak.

30 And when Rachel saw that she bare Jacob no children, Rachel envied her sister, and said unto Jacob, "Give me children, or else I die." And Jacob's anger was kindled against Rachel, and he said, "Am I in God's stead, who hath withheld from thee the fruit of the womb?" And she said, "Behold my maid Bilhah: go in unto her, and she shall bear upon my knees, that I may also have children by her." And she gave him Bilhah her handmaid to wife: and Jacob went in unto her. And Bilhah conceived and bare Jacob a son. And Rachel said, "God hath judged me, and hath also heard my voice, and hath given me a son"; therefore called she his name Dan. And Bilhah Rachel's maid conceived again, and bare Jacob a second son. And Rachel said, "With great wrestlings have I wrestled with my sister, and I have prevailed": and she called his name Naphtali. When Leah saw that she had left bearing, she took Zilpah her maid, and gave her Jacob to wife. And Zilpah Leah's maid bare Jacob a son. And Leah said, "A troop cometh": and she called his name Gad. And Zilpah Leah's maid bare Jacob a second son. And Leah said, "Happy am I, for the daughters will call me blessed": and she called his name Asher.

And Reuben went in the days of wheat harvest, and found mandrakes[15] in the field, and brought them unto his mother Leah. Then Rachel said to Leah, "Give me, I pray thee, of thy son's mandrakes." And she said unto her, "Is it a small matter that thou hast taken my husband? and wouldst thou take away my son's mandrakes also?" And Rachel said, "Therefore he shall lie with thee tonight, for thy son's mandrakes." And Jacob came out of the field in the evening, and Leah went out to meet him, and said, "Thou must come in unto me: for surely I have hired thee with my son's mandrakes." And he lay with her that night. And God hearkened unto Leah, and she conceived, and bare Jacob the fifth son. And Leah said, "God hath given me my hire, because I have given my maiden to my husband": and she called his name Issachar. And Leah conceived again, and bare Jacob the sixth son. And Leah said, "God hath endued me with a good dowry: now will my husband dwell with me, because I have borne him six sons": and she called his name Zebulun. And afterwards she bare a daughter, and called her name Dinah.

[15] The herb mandrake was thought to promote fertility.

And God remembered Rachel, and God hearkened to her, and opened her womb. And she conceived, and bare a son, and said, "God hath taken away my reproach": and she called his name Joseph, and said, "The Lord shall add to me another son."

And it came to pass, when Rachel had borne Joseph, that Jacob said unto Laban, "Send me away, that I may go unto mine own place, and to my country. Give me my wives and my children, for whom I have served thee, and let me go: for thou knowest my service which I have done thee." And Laban said unto him, "I pray thee, if I have found favour in thine eyes, tarry: for I have learned by experience that the Lord hath blessed me for thy sake." And he said, "Appoint me thy wages, and I will give it." And he said unto him, "Thou knowest how I have served thee, and how thy cattle was with me. For it was little which thou hadst before I came, and it is now increased unto a multitude; and the Lord hath blessed thee since my coming: and now when shall I provide for mine own house also?" And he said, "What shall I give thee?" And Jacob said, "Thou shalt not give me anything; if thou wilt do this thing for me, I will again feed and keep thy flock. I will pass through all thy flock today, removing from thence all the speckled and spotted cattle, and all the brown cattle among the sheep, and the spotted and speckled among the goats, and of such shall be my hire. So shall my righteousness answer for me in time to come, when it shall come for my hire before thy face: every one that is not speckled and spotted amongst the goats, and brown amongst the sheep, that shall be counted stolen with me." And Laban said, "Behold, I would it might be according to thy word." And he removed that day the he-goats that were ring-streaked and spotted, and all the she-goats that were speckled and spotted, and every one that had some white in it, and all the brown amongst the sheep, and gave them into the hand of his sons. And he set three days' journey betwixt himself and Jacob: and Jacob fed the rest of Laban's flocks.

And Jacob took him rods of green poplar, and of the hazel and chestnut tree, and pilled[16] white streaks in them, and made the white appear which was in the rods. And he set the rods which he had pilled before the flocks in the gutters in the watering troughs when the flocks came to drink, that they should conceive when they came to drink. And the flocks conceived before the rods, and

[16] I.e., peeled.

brought forth cattle ring-streaked, speckled, and spotted. And Jacob did separate the lambs, and set the faces of the flocks toward the ring-streaked, and all the brown in the flock of Laban; and he put his own flocks by themselves, and put them not unto Laban's cattle. And it came to pass whensoever the stronger cattle did conceive, that Jacob laid the rods before the eyes of the cattle in the gutters, that they might conceive among the rods. But when the cattle were feeble, he put them not in; so the feebler were Laban's, and the stronger Jacob's. And the man increased exceedingly, and had much cattle, and maidservants, and menservants, and camels, and asses.

31 And he heard the words of Laban's sons, saying, "Jacob hath taken away all that was our father's; and of that which was our father's hath he gotten all this glory." And Jacob beheld the countenance of Laban, and behold, it was not toward him as before. And the Lord said unto Jacob, "Return unto the land of thy fathers, and to thy kindred; and I will be with thee." And Jacob sent and called Rachel and Leah to the field unto his flock, and said unto them, "I see your father's countenance, that it is not toward me as before: but the God of my father hath been with me. And ye know that with all my power I have served your father. And your father hath deceived me, and changed my wages ten times: but God suffered him not to hurt me. If he said thus, 'The speckled shall be thy wages,' then all the cattle bare speckled: and if he said thus, 'The ring-streaked shall be thy hire,' then bare all the cattle ring-streaked. Thus God hath taken away the cattle of your father, and given them to me. And it came to pass at the time that the cattle conceived, that I lifted up mine eyes and saw in a dream, and behold, the rams which leaped upon the cattle were ring-streaked, speckled, and grisled. And the angel of God spake unto me in a dream, saying, 'Jacob.' And I said, 'Here am I.' And he said, 'Lift up now thine eyes, and see, all the rams which leap upon the cattle are ring-streaked, speckled, and grisled: for I have seen all that Laban doeth unto thee. I am the God of Bethel, where thou anointedst the pillar, and where thou vowedst a vow unto me: now arise, get thee out from this land, and return unto the land of thy kindred.'" And Rachel and Leah answered, and said unto him, "Is there yet any portion or inheritance for us in our father's house? Are we not counted of him strangers? for he hath sold us, and hath quite devoured also our money. For all the riches which God hath taken from our father, that is ours, and our children's: now then whatsoever God hath said unto thee, do."

Then Jacob rose up, and set his sons and his wives upon camels. And he carried away all his cattle, and all his goods which he had gotten, the cattle of his getting, which he had gotten in Padan-aram, for to go to Isaac his father in the land of Canaan. And Laban went to shear his sheep: and Rachel had stolen the images[17] that were her father's. And Jacob stole away unawares to Laban the Syrian, in that he told him not that he fled. So he fled with all that he had, and he rose up and passed over the river, and set his face toward the mount Gilead. And it was told Laban on the third day, that Jacob was fled. And he took his brethren with him, and pursued after him seven days' journey, and they overtook him in the mount Gilead. And God came to Laban the Syrian in a dream by night, and said unto him, "Take heed that thou speak not to Jacob either good or bad."

Then Laban overtook Jacob. Now Jacob had pitched his tent in the mount: and Laban with his brethren pitched in the mount of Gilead. And Laban said to Jacob, "What hast thou done, that thou hast stolen away unawares to me, and carried away my daughters, as captives taken with the sword? Wherefore didst thou flee away secretly, and steal away from me, and didst not tell me, that I might have sent thee away with mirth, and with songs, with tabret,[18] and with harp, and hast not suffered me to kiss my sons and my daughters? thou hast now done foolishly in so doing. It is in the power of my hand to do you hurt: but the God of your father spake unto me yesternight, saying, 'Take thou heed that thou speak not to Jacob either good or bad.' And now though thou wouldest needs be gone, because thou sore longedst after thy father's house, yet wherefore hast thou stolen my gods?" And Jacob answered and said to Laban, "Because I was afraid: for I said, 'Peradventure thou wouldest take by force thy daughters from me.' With whomsoever thou findest thy gods, let him not live: before our brethren, discern thou what is thine with me, and take it to thee": for Jacob knew not that Rachel had stolen them. And Laban went into Jacob's tent, and into Leah's tent, and into the two maidservants' tents: but he found them not.

[17] I.e., Laban's household gods.
[18] A musical instrument similar to a tambourine.

Then went he out of Leah's tent, and entered into Rachel's tent. Now Rachel had taken the images, and put them in the camel's furniture, and sat upon them: and Laban searched all the tent, but found them not. And she said to her father, "Let it not displease my lord that I cannot rise up before thee; for the custom of women is upon me": and he searched, but found not the images.

And Jacob was wroth, and chode with Laban: and Jacob answered and said to Laban, "What is my trespass? what is my sin, that thou hast so hotly pursued after me? Whereas thou hast searched all my stuff, what hast thou found of all thy household stuff? set it here before my brethren, and thy brethren, that they may judge betwixt us both. This twenty years have I been with thee: thy ewes and thy she-goats have not cast their young,[19] and the rams of thy flocks have I not eaten. That which was torn of beasts I brought not unto thee: I bare the loss of it; of my hand didst thou require it, whether stolen by day, or stolen by night. Thus I was: in the day the drought consumed me, and the frost by night, and my sleep departed from mine eyes. Thus have I been twenty years in thy house: I served thee fourteen years for thy two daughters, and six years for thy cattle: and thou hast changed my wages ten times. Except the God of my father, the God of Abraham, and the fear of Isaac had been with me, surely thou hadst sent me away now empty: God hath seen mine affliction, and the labour of my hands, and rebuked thee yesternight."

And Laban answered and said unto Jacob, "These daughters are my daughters, and these children are my children, and these cattle are my cattle, and all that thou seest is mine: and what can I do this day unto these my daughters, or unto their children which they have borne? Now therefore come thou, let us make a covenant, I and thou: and let it be for a witness between me and thee." And Jacob took a stone, and set it up for a pillar. And Jacob said unto his brethren, "Gather stones": and they took stones, and made an heap, and they did eat there upon the heap. And Laban called it Jegar-sahadutha: but Jacob called it Galeed. And Laban said, "This heap is a witness between me and thee this day." Therefore was the name of it called Galeed, and Mizpah: for he said, "The Lord watch between me and thee when we are absent one from another. If thou shalt afflict my daughters, or if thou shalt take other wives

[19] I.e., have not miscarried.

besides my daughters, no man is with us; see, God is witness betwixt me and thee." And Laban said to Jacob, "Behold this heap, and behold this pillar, which I have cast betwixt me and thee. This heap be witness, and this pillar be witness, that I will not pass over this heap to thee, and that thou shalt not pass over this heap and this pillar unto me, for harm. The God of Abraham, and the God of Nahor, the God of their father, judge betwixt us." And Jacob sware by the fear of his father Isaac. Then Jacob offered sacrifice upon the mount, and called his brethren to eat bread, and they did eat bread, and tarried all night in the mount. And early in the morning Laban rose up and kissed his sons, and his daughters, and blessed them: and Laban departed, and returned unto his place.

32 And Jacob went on his way, and the angels of God met him. And when Jacob saw them, he said, "This is God's host": and he called the name of that place Mahanaim. And Jacob sent messengers before him to Esau his brother, unto the land of Seir, the country of Edom. And he commanded them, saying, "Thus shall ye speak unto my lord Esau, 'Thy servant Jacob saith thus, "I have sojourned with Laban, and stayed there until now. And I have oxen, and asses, flocks, and menservants, and womenservants: and I have sent to tell my lord, that I may find grace in thy sight." ' "

And the messengers returned to Jacob, saying, "We came to thy brother Esau, and also he cometh to meet thee, and four hundred men with him." Then Jacob was greatly afraid, and distressed, and he divided the people that was with him, and the flocks, and herds, and the camels, into two bands, and said, "If Esau come to the one company, and smite it, then the other company which is left shall escape."

And Jacob said, "O God of my father Abraham, and God of my father Isaac, the Lord which saidst unto me, 'Return unto thy country, and to thy kindred, and I will deal well with thee': I am not worthy of the least of all the mercies, and of all the truth, which thou hast showed unto thy servant: for with my staff I passed over this Jordan, and now I am become two bands. Deliver me, I pray thee, from the hand of my brother, from the hand of Esau: for I fear him, lest he will come and smite me, and the mother with the children. And thou saidst, 'I will surely do thee good, and make thy seed as the sand of the sea, which cannot be numbered for multitude.'"

And he lodged there that same night, and took of that which came to his hand a present for Esau his brother: two hundred she-goats, and twenty he-goats, two hundred ewes, and twenty rams, thirty milch camels with their colts, forty kine, and ten bulls, twenty she-asses, and ten foals. And he delivered them into the hand of his servants, every drove by themselves, and said unto his servants, "Pass over before me, and put a space betwixt drove and drove." And he commanded the foremost, saying, "When Esau my brother meeteth thee, and asketh thee, saying, 'Whose art thou? and whither goest thou? and whose are these before thee?' then thou shalt say, 'They be thy servant Jacob's: it is a present sent unto my lord Esau: and behold also, he is behind us.'" And so commanded he the second, and the third, and all that followed the droves, saying, "On this manner shall you speak unto Esau, when you find him. And say ye moreover, 'Behold, thy servant Jacob is behind us'": for he said, "I will appease him with the present that goeth before me, and afterward I will see his face; peradventure he will accept of me." So went the present over before him: and himself lodged that night in the company. And he rose up that night, and took his two wives, and his two womenservants, and his eleven sons, and passed over the ford Jabbok. And he took them, and sent them over the brook, and sent over that he had.

And Jacob was left alone: and there wrestled a man with him until the breaking of the day. And when he saw that he prevailed not against him, he touched the hollow of his thigh: and the hollow of Jacob's thigh was out of joint, as he wrestled with him. And he said, "Let me go, for the day breaketh": and he said, "I will not let thee go, except thou bless me." And he said unto him, "What is thy name?" And he said, "Jacob." And he said, "Thy name shall be called no more Jacob, but Israel: for as a prince hast thou power with God, and with men, and hast prevailed." And Jacob asked him, and said, "Tell me, I pray thee, thy name": and he said, "Wherefore is it that thou dost ask after my name?" And he blessed him there. And Jacob called the name of the place Peniel: "For I have seen God face to face, and my life is preserved." And as he passed over

Penuel, the sun rose upon him, and he halted upon his thigh.[20] Therefore the children of Israel eat not of the sinew which shrank, which is upon the hollow of the thigh, unto this day: because he touched the hollow of Jacob's thigh in the sinew that shrank.

33 And Jacob lifted up his eyes, and looked, and behold, Esau came, and with him four hundred men: and he divided the children unto Leah, and unto Rachel, and unto the two handmaids. And he put the handmaids and their children foremost, and Leah and her children after, and Rachel and Joseph hindermost. And he passed over before them, and bowed himself to the ground seven times, until he came near to his brother. And Esau ran to meet him, and embraced him, and fell on his neck, and kissed him, and they wept. And he lifted up his eyes, and saw the women and the children, and said, "Who are those with thee?" And he said, "The children which God hath graciously given thy servant." Then the handmaidens came near, they and their children, and they bowed themselves. And Leah also with her children came near, and bowed themselves: and after came Joseph near and Rachel, and they bowed themselves. And he said, "What meanest thou by all this drove which I met?" And he said, "These are to find grace in the sight of my lord." And Esau said, "I have enough: my brother, keep that thou hast unto thyself." And Jacob said, "Nay, I pray thee, if now I have found grace in thy sight, then receive my present at my hand: for therefore I have seen thy face, as though I had seen the face of God; and thou wast pleased with me. Take, I pray thee, my blessing that is brought to thee; because God hath dealt graciously with me, and because I have enough": and he urged him, and he took it.

And he said, "Let us take our journey, and let us go, and I will go before thee." And he said unto him, "My lord knoweth that the children are tender, and the flocks and herds with young are with me: and if men should over-drive them one day, all the flock will die. Let my lord, I pray thee, pass over before his servant, and I will lead on softly, according as the cattle that goeth before me, and the children, be able to endure, until I come unto my lord unto Seir." And Esau said, "Let me now leave with thee some of the folk that are with me." And he said, "What needeth it? let me find grace

[20] "Peniel" and "Penuel" are two forms of the same place-name. The phrase "halted upon his thigh" means that Jacob was limping.

in the sight of my lord." So Esau returned that day, on his way unto Seir. And Jacob journeyed to Succoth, and built him a house, and made booths for his cattle: therefore the name of the place is called Succoth.

And Jacob came to Shalem, a city of Shechem, which is in the land of Canaan, when he came from Padan-aram, and pitched his tent before the city. And he bought a parcel of a field where he had spread his tent, at the hand of the children of Hamor, Shechem's father, for an hundred pieces of money. And he erected there an altar, and called it El-Elohe-Israel.

34 And Dinah the daughter of Leah, which she bare unto Jacob, went out to see the daughters of the land. And when Shechem the son of Hamor the Hivite, prince of the country, saw her, he took her, and lay with her, and defiled her. And his soul clave unto Dinah the daughter of Jacob, and he loved the damsel, and spake kindly unto the damsel. And Shechem spake unto his father Hamor, saying, "Get me this damsel to wife." And Jacob heard that he had defiled Dinah his daughter (now his sons were with his cattle in the field), and Jacob held his peace until they were come.

And Hamor the father of Shechem went out unto Jacob to commune with him. And the sons of Jacob came out of the field when they heard it, and the men were grieved: and they were very wroth, because he had wrought folly in Israel in lying with Jacob's daughter; which thing ought not to be done. And Hamor communed with them, saying, "The soul of my son Shechem longeth for your daughter: I pray you give her him to wife. And make ye marriages with us, and give your daughters unto us, and take our daughters unto you. And ye shall dwell with us, and the land shall be before you: dwell and trade you therein, and get you possessions therein." And Shechem said unto her father, and unto her brethren, "Let me find grace in your eyes, and what ye shall say unto me I will give. Ask me never so much dowry and gift, and I will give according as ye shall say unto me: but give me the damsel to wife." And the sons of Jacob answered Shechem and Hamor his father deceitfully, and said, because he had defiled Dinah their sister: and they said unto them, "We cannot do this thing, to give our sister to one that is uncircumcised: for that were a reproach unto us. But in this will we consent unto you: if ye will be as we be, that every male of you be circumcised, then will we give our daughters unto you, and we will take your daughters to us, and we will dwell with you, and we will become one people. But if ye will not hearken unto us, to be circumcised, then will we take our daughter, and we will be gone." And their words pleased Hamor, and Shechem Hamor's son. And the young man deferred not to do the thing, because he had delight in Jacob's daughter: and he was more honourable than all the house of his father.

And Hamor and Shechem his son came unto the gate of their city, and communed with the men of their city, saying, "These men are peaceable with us, therefore let them dwell in the land, and trade therein: for the land, behold, it is large enough for them: let us take their daughters to us for wives, and let us give them our daughters. Only herein will the men consent unto us for to dwell with us to be one people, if every male among us be circumcised, as they are circumcised. Shall not their cattle, and their substance, and every beast of theirs be ours? only let us consent unto them, and they will dwell with us." And unto Hamor and unto Shechem his son hearkened all that went out of the gate of his city; and every male was circumcised, all that went out of the gate of his city.

And it came to pass on the third day when they were sore, that two of the sons of Jacob, Simeon and Levi, Dinah's brethren, took each man his sword and came upon the city boldly, and slew all the males. And they slew Hamor and Shechem his son with the edge of the sword, and took Dinah out of Shechem's house, and went out. The sons of Jacob came upon the slain, and spoiled the city, because they had defiled their sister. They took their sheep, and their oxen, and their asses, and that which was in the city, and that which was in the field. And all their wealth, and all their little ones, and their wives took they captive, and spoiled even all that was in the house. And Jacob said to Simeon and Levi, "Ye have troubled me to make me to stink among the inhabitants of the land, among the Canaanites, and the Perizzites: and I being few in number, they shall gather themselves together against me, and slay me, and I shall be destroyed, I and my house." And they said, "Should he deal with our sister as with an harlot?"

35 And God said unto Jacob, "Arise, go up to Bethel, and dwell there: and make there an altar unto God, that appeared unto thee when thou fleddest from the face of Esau thy brother." Then Jacob said unto his household, and to all that were with him, "Put away the strange gods that are among you, and be clean, and change your garments, and let us arise, and go up to Bethel, and I will make there an altar unto God, who answered me in the day of my distress, and was with me in the way which I went." And they gave unto Jacob all the strange gods which were in their hand, and all their earrings which were in their ears, and Jacob hid them under the oak which was by Shechem. And they journeyed: and the terror of God was upon the cities that were round about them, and they did not pursue after the sons of Jacob.

So Jacob came to Luz, which is in the land of Canaan (that is Bethel), he and all the people that were with him. And he built there an altar, and called the place El-beth-el, because there God appeared unto him, when he fled from the face of his brother. But Deborah Rebekah's nurse died, and she was buried beneath Bethel under an oak: and the name of it was called Allon-bachuth.

And God appeared unto Jacob again, when he came out of Padan-aram, and blessed him. And God said unto him, "Thy name is Jacob: thy name shall not be called any more Jacob, but Israel shall be thy name"; and he called his name Israel. And God said unto him, "I am God Almighty: be fruitful and multiply: a nation and a company of nations shall be of thee, and kings shall come out of thy loins. And the land which I gave Abraham, and Isaac, to thee I will give it, and to thy seed after thee will I give the land." And God went up from him in the place where he talked with him. And Jacob set up a pillar in the place where he talked with him, even a pillar of stone: and he poured a drink offering thereon, and he poured oil thereon. And Jacob called the name of the place where God spake with him Bethel.

And they journeyed from Bethel: and there was but a little way to come to Ephrath; and Rachel travailed, and she had hard labour. And it came to pass when she was in hard labour, that the midwife said unto her, "Fear not: thou shalt have this son also." And it came to pass, as her soul was in departing (for she died), that she called his name Ben-oni: but his father called him Benjamin. And Rachel died, and was buried in the way to Ephrath, which is Bethlehem. And Jacob set a pillar upon her grave: that is the pillar of Rachel's grave unto this day.

And Israel journeyed, and spread his tent beyond the tower of Edar. And it came to pass when Israel dwelt in that land, that Reuben went and lay with Bilhah his father's concubine: and Israel heard it. Now the sons of Jacob were twelve. The sons of Leah: Reuben, Jacob's firstborn, and Simeon, and Levi, and Judah, and Issachar, and Zebulun. The sons of Rachel: Joseph, and Benjamin. And the sons of Bilhah, Rachel's handmaid: Dan, and Naphtali. And the sons of Zilpah, Leah's handmaid: Gad, and Asher. These are the sons of Jacob, which were born to him in Padan-aram.

And Jacob came unto Isaac his father unto Mamre, unto the city of Arbah (which is Hebron) where Abraham and Isaac sojourned. And the days of Isaac were an hundred and fourscore years. And Isaac gave up the ghost, and died, and was gathered unto his people, being old and full of days: and his sons Esau and Jacob buried him . . . .

37 And Jacob dwelt in the land wherein his father was a stranger, in the land of Canaan. These are the generations of Jacob: Joseph, being seventeen years old, was feeding the flock with his brethren, and the lad was with the sons of Bilhah, and with the sons of Zilpah, his father's wives: and Joseph brought unto his father their evil report.[21] Now Israel loved Joseph more than all his children, because he was the son of his old age: and he made him a coat of many colours. And when his brethren saw that their father loved him more than all his brethren, they hated him, and could not speak peaceably unto him. And Joseph dreamed a dream, and he told it his brethren, and they hated him yet the more. And he said unto them, "Hear, I pray you, this dream which I have dreamed. For behold, we were binding sheaves in the field, and lo, my sheaf arose, and also stood upright; and behold, your sheaves stood round about, and made obeisance to my sheaf." And his brethren said to him, "Shalt thou indeed reign over us? or shalt thou indeed have dominion over us?" And they hated him yet the more, for his dreams, and for his words.

[21] I.e., an ill report of them.

And he dreamed yet another dream, and told it his brethren, and said, "Behold, I have dreamed a dream more: and behold, the sun and the moon, and the eleven stars made obeisance to me." And he told it to his father, and to his brethren: and his father rebuked him, and said unto him, "What is this dream that thou hast dreamed? Shall I, and thy mother, and thy brethren indeed come to bow down ourselves to thee to the earth?" And his brethren envied him: but his father observed [22] the saying.

And his brethren went to feed their father's flock in Shechem. And Israel said unto Joseph, "Do not thy brethren feed the flock in Shechem? Come, and I will send thee unto them": and he said to him, "Here am I." And he said to him, "Go, I pray thee, see whether it be well with thy brethren, and well with the flocks, and bring me word again": so he sent him out of the vale of Hebron, and he came to Shechem.

And a certain man found him, and behold, he was wandering in the field, and the man asked him, saying, "What seekest thou?" And he said, "I seek my brethren: tell me, I pray thee, where they feed their flocks." And the man said, "They are departed hence: for I heard them say, 'Let us go to Dothan.'" And Joseph went after his brethren, and found them in Dothan. And when they saw him afar off, even before he came near unto them, they conspired against him, to slay him. And they said one to another, "Behold, this dreamer cometh. Come now therefore, and let us slay him, and cast him into some pit, and we will say, 'Some evil beast hath devoured him': and we shall see what will become of his dreams." And Reuben heard it, and he delivered him out of their hands, and said, "Let us not kill him." And Reuben said unto them, "Shed no blood, but cast him into this pit that is in the wilderness, and lay no hand upon him"; that he might rid him out of their hands, to deliver him to his father again.

And it came to pass when Joseph was come unto his brethren, that they stripped Joseph out of his coat, his coat of many colours that was on him. And they took him, and cast him into a pit: and the pit was empty, there was no water in it. And they sat down to eat bread: and they lifted up their eyes and looked, and behold, a company of Ishmaelites came from Gilead, with their camels, bearing spicery and balm and myrrh, going to carry it down to Egypt.

[22] *I.e.*, remembered.

And Judah said unto his brethren, "What profit is it if we slay our brother, and conceal his blood? Come, and let us sell him to the Ishmaelites, and let not our hand be upon him: for he is our brother, and our flesh"; and his brethren were content. Then there passed by Midianites merchantmen; and they drew and lifted up Joseph out of the pit, and sold Joseph to the Ishmaelites for twenty pieces of silver: and they brought Joseph into Egypt.[23]

And Reuben returned unto the pit, and behold, Joseph was not in the pit: and he rent his clothes. And he returned unto his brethren and said, "The child is not, and I, whither shall I go?" And they took Joseph's coat, and killed a kid of the goats, and dipped the coat in the blood. And they sent the coat of many colours, and they brought it to their father, and said, "This have we found: know now whether it be thy son's coat or no." And he knew it, and said, "It is my son's coat: an evil beast hath devoured him; Joseph is without doubt rent in pieces." And Jacob rent his clothes, and put sackcloth upon his loins, and mourned for his son many days. And all his sons and all his daughters rose up to comfort him: but he refused to be comforted: and he said, "For I will go down into the grave unto my son, mourning"; thus his father wept for him. And the Midianites sold him into Egypt unto Potiphar, an officer of Pharaoh's, and captain of the guard.

38 And it came to pass at that time, that Judah went down from his brethren, and turned in to a certain Adullamite, whose name was Hirah: and Judah saw there a daughter of a certain Canaanite, whose name was Shuah: and he took her, and went in unto her. And she conceived, and bare a son, and he called his name Er. And she conceived again, and bare a son, and she called his name Onan. And she yet again conceived, and bare a son, and called his name Shelah: and he was at Chezib, when she bare him. And Judah took a wife for Er his firstborn, whose name was Tamar. And Er, Judah's firstborn, was wicked in the sight of the Lord, and the Lord slew him. And Judah said unto Onan, "Go in unto thy brother's wife, and marry her, and raise up seed to thy brother." And Onan knew that the seed should not be his; and it came to pass when he went in unto his brother's wife, that he spilled it on the

[23] An ancient editor, in fusing the accounts of J and E, made the Ishmaelites and the Midianites synonymous.

ground, lest that he should give seed to his brother. And the thing which he did displeased the Lord: wherefore he slew him also. Then said Judah to Tamar his daughter in law, "Remain a widow at thy father's house, till Shelah my son be grown" (for he said, "Lest peradventure he die also as his brethren did"): and Tamar went and dwelt in her father's house.

And in process of time the daughter of Shuah Judah's wife died: and Judah was comforted, and went up unto his sheep-shearers to Timnath, he and his friend Hirah the Adullamite. And it was told Tamar, saying, "Behold, thy father in law goeth up to Timnath to shear his sheep." And she put her widow's garments off from her, and covered her with a veil, and wrapped herself, and sat in an open place, which is by the way to Timnath: for she saw that Shelah was grown, and she was not given unto him to wife. When Judah saw her, he thought her to be an harlot: because she had covered her face. And he turned unto her by the way, and said, "Go to, I pray thee, let me come in unto thee" (for he knew not that she was his daughter in law): and she said, "What wilt thou give me, that thou mayest come in unto me?" And he said, "I will send thee a kid from the flock": and she said, "Wilt thou give me a pledge, till thou send it?" And he said, "What pledge shall I give thee?" And she said, "Thy signet, and thy bracelets, and thy staff that is in thine hand": and he gave it her, and came in unto her, and she conceived by him. And she arose and went away, and laid by her veil from her, and put on the garments of her widowhood. And Judah sent the kid by the hand of his friend the Adullamite, to receive his pledge from the woman's hand: but he found her not. Then he asked the men of that place, saying, "Where is the harlot that was openly by the wayside?" And they said, "There was no harlot in this place." And he returned to Judah, and said, "I cannot find her: and also the men of the place said that there was no harlot in this place." And Judah said, "Let her take it to her, lest we be shamed: behold, I sent this kid, and thou hast not found her."

And it came to pass about three months after, that it was told Judah, saying, "Tamar thy daughter in law hath played the harlot, and also behold, she is with child by whoredom": and Judah said, "Bring her forth, and let her be burnt." When she was brought forth, she sent to her father in law, saying, "By the man whose these are, am I with child": and she said, "Discern, I pray thee, whose are these, the signet, and bracelets, and staff." And Judah acknowledged them, and said, "She hath been more righteous than I: because that I gave her not to Shelah my son": and he knew her again no more.

And it came to pass in the time of her travail, that behold, twins were in her womb. And it came to pass when she travailed, that the one put out his hand, and the midwife took and bound upon his hand a scarlet thread, saying, "This came out first." And it came to pass as he drew back his hand, that behold, his brother came out: and she said, "How hast thou broken forth? this breach be upon thee": therefore his name was called Pharez. And afterward came out his brother, that had the scarlet thread upon his hand, and his name was called Zarah.

39 And Joseph was brought down to Egypt, and Potiphar, an officer of Pharaoh, captain of the guard, an Egyptian, bought him of the hand of the Ishmaelites, which had brought him down thither. And the Lord was with Joseph, and he was a prosperous man, and he was in the house of his master the Egyptian. And his master saw that the Lord was with him, and that the Lord made all that he did to prosper in his hand. And Joseph found grace in his sight, and he served him; and he made him overseer over his house, and all that he had he put into his hand. And it came to pass from the time that he had made him overseer in his house, and over all that he had, that the Lord blessed the Egyptian's house for Joseph's sake: and the blessing of the Lord was upon all that he had in the house, and in the field. And he left all that he had in Joseph's hand: and he knew not aught he had, save the bread which he did eat: and Joseph was a goodly person, and well-favoured.

And it came to pass after these things, that his master's wife cast her eyes upon Joseph, and she said, "Lie with me." But he refused, and said unto his master's wife, "Behold, my master wotteth not what is with me in the house, and he hath committed all that he hath to my hand. There is none greater in this house than I: neither hath he kept back any thing from me but thee, because thou art his wife: how then can I do this great wickedness, and sin against God?" And it came to pass, as she spake to Joseph day by day, that he hearkened not unto her, to lie by her, or to be with her. And it came to pass about this time, that Joseph went into the house to do his business, and there was none of the men of the house there within. And she caught him by his garment, saying, "Lie with me": and he left his garment in her hand, and fled, and got him out.

And it came to pass, when she saw that he had left his garment in her hand, and was fled forth, that she called unto the men of her house, and spake unto them, saying, "See, he hath brought in an Hebrew unto us, to mock us: he came in unto me to lie with me, and I cried with a loud voice. And it came to pass when he heard that I lifted up my voice and cried, that he left his garment with me, and fled, and got him out." And she laid up his garment by her, until her lord came home. And she spake unto him according to these words, saying, "The Hebrew servant which thou hast brought unto us came in unto me to mock me. And it came to pass as I lifted up my voice and cried, that he left his garment with me, and fled out." And it came to pass when his master heard the words of his wife, which she spake unto him, saying, "After this manner did thy servant to me," that his wrath was kindled. And Joseph's master took him, and put him into the prison, a place where the king's prisoners were bound: and he was there in the prison.

But the Lord was with Joseph, and showed him mercy, and gave him favour in the sight of the keeper of the prison. And the keeper of the prison committed to Joseph's hand all the prisoners that were in the prison, and whatsoever they did there, he was the doer of it: the keeper of the prison looked not to any thing that was under his hand, because the Lord was with him: and that which he did, the Lord made it to prosper.

40 And it came to pass after these things, that the butler of the king of Egypt, and his baker, had offended their lord the king of Egypt. And Pharaoh was wroth against two of his officers, against the chief of the butlers, and against the chief of the bakers. And he put them in ward in the house of the captain of the guard, into the prison, the place where Joseph was bound. And the captain of the guard charged Joseph with them, and he served them, and they continued a season in ward.

And they dreamed a dream both of them, each man his dream in one night, each man according to the interpretation of his dream, the butler and the baker of the king of Egypt, which were bound in the prison. And Joseph came in unto them in the morning, and looked upon them, and behold, they were sad. And he asked Pharaoh's officers that were with him in the ward of his lord's house, saying, "Wherefore look ye so sadly today?" And they said unto him, "We have dreamed a dream, and there is no interpreter of it." And Joseph said unto them, "Do not interpretations belong to God? tell me them, I pray you." And the chief butler told his dream to Joseph, and said to him, "In my dream, behold, a vine was before me: and in the vine were three branches, and it was as though it budded, and her blossoms shot forth; and the clusters thereof brought forth ripe grapes. And Pharaoh's cup was in my hand, and I took the grapes and pressed them into Pharaoh's cup: and I gave the cup into Pharaoh's hand." And Joseph said unto him, "This is the interpretation of it: the three branches are three days: yet within three days shall Pharaoh lift up thine head, and restore thee unto thy place, and thou shalt deliver Pharaoh's cup into his hand, after the former manner when thou wast his butler. But think on me when it shall be well with thee, and show kindness, I pray thee, unto me, and make mention of me unto Pharaoh, and bring me out of this house. For indeed I was stolen away out of the land of the Hebrews: and here also have I done nothing that they should put me into the dungeon."

When the chief baker saw that the interpretation was good, he said unto Joseph, "I also was in my dream, and behold, I had three white baskets on my head. And in the uppermost basket there was of all manner of bake-meats for Pharaoh, and the birds did eat them out of the basket upon my head." And Joseph answered, and said, "This is the interpretation thereof: the three baskets are three days: yet within three days shall Pharaoh lift up thy head from off thee, and shall hang thee on a tree, and the birds shall eat thy flesh from off thee."

And it came to pass the third day, which was Pharaoh's birthday, that he made a feast unto all his servants: and he lifted up the head of the chief butler and of the chief baker among his servants. And he restored the chief butler unto his butlership again, and he gave the cup into Pharaoh's hand. But he hanged the chief baker, as Joseph had interpreted to them. Yet did not the chief butler remember Joseph, but forgot him.

41 And it came to pass at the end of two full years, that Pharaoh dreamed: and behold, he stood by the river. And behold, there came up out of the river seven well-favoured kine and fat-fleshed, and they fed in a meadow. And behold, seven other kine came up after them out of the river, ill-favoured and lean-fleshed, and stood by the other kine, upon the brink of the river. And the ill-favoured and lean-fleshed kine did eat up the seven well-favoured and fat kine: so Pharaoh awoke. And he slept and dreamed the second time: and behold, seven ears of corn came up upon one stalk, rank[24] and good. And behold, seven thin ears and blasted with the east wind sprang up after them. And the seven thin ears devoured the seven rank and full ears: and Pharaoh awoke, and behold, it was a dream. And it came to pass in the morning, that his spirit was troubled, and he sent and called for all the magicians of Egypt, and all the wise men thereof: and Pharaoh told them his dream; but there was none that could interpret them unto Pharaoh.

Then spake the chief butler unto Pharaoh, saying, "I do remember my faults this day. Pharaoh was wroth with his servants, and put me in ward, in the captain of the guard's house, both me and the chief baker. And we dreamed a dream in one night, I and he: we dreamed each man according to the interpretation of his dream. And there was there with us a young man, an Hebrew, servant to the captain of the guard: and we told him, and he interpreted to us our dreams, to each man according to his dream he did interpret. And it came to pass, as he interpreted to us, so it was; me he restored unto mine office, and him he hanged."

Then Pharaoh sent and called Joseph, and they brought him hastily out of the dungeon: and he shaved himself, and changed his raiment, and came in unto Pharaoh. And Pharaoh said unto Joseph, "I have dreamed a dream, and there is none that can interpret it: and I have heard say of thee that thou canst understand a dream to interpret it." And Joseph answered Pharaoh, saying, "It is not in me: God shall give Pharaoh an answer of peace." And Pharaoh said unto Joseph, "In my dream, behold, I stood upon the bank of the river. And behold, there came up out of the river seven kine, fat-fleshed and well-favoured, and they fed in a meadow. And behold, seven

[24] I.e., luxuriant.

other kine came up after them, poor and very ill-favoured and lean-fleshed, such as I never saw in all the land of Egypt for badness. And the lean and the ill-favoured kine did eat up the first seven fat kine. And when they had eaten them up, it could not be known that they had eaten them, but they were still ill-favoured, as at the beginning: so I awoke. And I saw in my dream, and behold, seven ears came up in one stalk, full and good. And behold, seven ears, withered, thin, and blasted with the east wind, sprang up after them. And the thin ears devoured the seven good ears: and I told this unto the magicians, but there was none that could declare it to me."

And Joseph said unto Pharaoh, "The dream of Pharaoh is one; God hath showed Pharaoh what he is about to do. The seven good kine are seven years: and the seven good ears are seven years: the dream is one. And the seven thin and ill-favoured kine that came up after them are seven years; and the seven empty ears blasted with the east wind shall be seven years of famine. This is the thing which I have spoken unto Pharaoh: what God is about to do he showeth unto Pharaoh. Behold, there come seven years of great plenty throughout all the land of Egypt. And there shall arise after them seven years of famine, and all the plenty shall be forgotten in the land of Egypt: and the famine shall consume the land. And the plenty shall not be known in the land, by reason of that famine following: for it shall be very grievous. And for that the dream was doubled unto Pharaoh twice, it is because the thing is established by God: and God will shortly bring it to pass. Now therefore let Pharaoh look out a man discreet and wise, and set him over the land of Egypt. Let Pharaoh do this, and let him appoint officers over the land, and take up the fifth part of the land of Egypt in the seven plenteous years. And let them gather all the food of those good years that come, and lay up corn under the hand of Pharaoh, and let them keep food in the cities. And that food shall be for store to the land against the seven years of famine, which shall be in the land of Egypt, that the land perish not through the famine."

And the thing was good in the eyes of Pharaoh, and in the eyes of all his servants. And Pharaoh said unto his servants, "Can we find such a one as this is, a man in whom the spirit of God is?" And Pharaoh said unto Joseph, "Forasmuch as God hath showed thee all this, there is none so discreet and wise as thou art. Thou shalt be over

my house, and according unto thy word shall all my people be ruled:
only in the throne will I be greater than thou." And Pharaoh said
unto Joseph, "See, I have set thee over all the land of Egypt." And
Pharaoh took off his ring from his hand, and put it upon Joseph's
hand, and arrayed him in vestures of fine linen, and put a gold chain
about his neck. And he made him to ride in the second chariot which
he had: and they cried before him, "Bow the knee": and he made
him ruler over all the land of Egypt. And Pharaoh said unto Joseph,
"I am Pharaoh, and without thee shall no man lift up his hand or
foot in all the land of Egypt." And Pharaoh called Joseph's name
Zaphnath-paaneah, and he gave him to wife Asenath the daughter of
Poti-pherah, priest of On: and Joseph went out over all the land of
Egypt.

(And Joseph was thirty years old when he stood before Pharaoh
king of Egypt.) And Joseph went out from the presence of Pharaoh,
and went throughout all the land of Egypt. And in the seven
plenteous years the earth brought forth by handfuls. And he gathered
up all the food of the seven years, which were in the land of Egypt,
and laid up the food in the cities: the food of the field, which was
round about every city, laid he up in the same. And Joseph gathered
corn as the sand of the sea, very much, until he left numbering:
for it was without number. And unto Joseph were born two sons,
before the years of famine came: which Asenath the daughter of
Poti-pherah, priest of On, bare unto him. And Joseph called the
name of the firstborn Manasseh: "For God," said he, "hath made me
forget all my toil, and all my father's house." And the name of the
second called he Ephraim: "For God hath caused me to be fruitful
in the land of my affliction."

And the seven years of plenteousness, that was in the land of
Egypt, were ended. And the seven years of dearth began to come
according as Joseph had said, and the dearth was in all lands: but in
all the land of Egypt there was bread. And when all the land of
Egypt was famished, the people cried to Pharaoh for bread: and
Pharaoh said unto all the Egyptians, "Go unto Joseph: what he
saith to you, do." And the famine was over all the face of the earth;
and Joseph opened all the storehouses, and sold unto the Egyptians:
and the famine waxed sore in the land of Egypt. And all countries
came into Egypt to Joseph, for to buy corn, because that the famine
was so sore in all lands.

42 Now when Jacob saw that there was corn in Egypt, Jacob said unto his sons, "Why do ye look one upon another?" And he said, "Behold, I have heard that there is corn in Egypt: get you down thither and buy for us from thence, that we may live, and not die." And Joseph's ten brethren went down to buy corn in Egypt. But Benjamin, Joseph's brother, Jacob sent not with his brethren: for he said, "Lest peradventure mischief befall him." And the sons of Israel came to buy corn among those that came: for the famine was in the land of Canaan. And Joseph was the governor over the land, and he it was that sold to all the people of the land: and Joseph's brethren came, and bowed down themselves before him with their faces to the earth.

And Joseph saw his brethren, and he knew them, but made himself strange unto them, and spake roughly unto them; and he said unto them, "Whence come ye?" And they said, "From the land of Canaan, to buy food." And Joseph knew his brethren, but they knew not him. And Joseph remembered the dreams which he dreamed of them, and said unto them, "Ye are spies: to see the nakedness of the land you are come." And they said unto him, "Nay, my lord, but to buy food are thy servants come. We are all one man's sons; we are true men: thy servants are no spies." And he said unto them, "Nay: but to see the nakedness of the land you are come." And they said, "Thy servants are twelve brethren, the sons of one man in the land of Canaan: and behold, the youngest is this day with our father, and one is not." And Joseph said unto them, "That is it that I spake unto you, saying, 'Ye are spies.' Hereby ye shall be proved: by the life of Pharaoh ye shall not go forth hence, except your youngest brother come hither. Send one of you, and let him fetch your brother, and ye shall be kept in prison, that your words may be proved, whether there be any truth in you: or else by the life of Pharaoh surely ye are spies." And he put them all together into ward three days. And Joseph said unto them the third day, "This do, and live: for I fear God. If ye be true men, let one of your brethren be bound in the house of your prison: go ye, carry corn for the famine of your houses. But bring your youngest brother unto me, so shall your words be verified, and ye shall not die": and they did so.

And they said one to another, "We are verily guilty concerning our brother, in that we saw the anguish of his soul, when he besought

us, and we would not hear: therefore is this distress come upon us."
And Reuben answered them, saying, "Spake I not unto you, saying,
'Do not sin against the child,' and ye would not hear? therefore
behold also, his blood is required." [25] And they knew not that Joseph
understood them: for he spake unto them by an interpreter. And he
turned himself about from them and wept, and returned to them
again, and communed with them, and took from them Simeon, and
bound him before their eyes.

Then Joseph commanded to fill their sacks with corn, and to
restore every man's money into his sack, and to give them provision
for the way: and thus did he unto them. And they laded their asses
with the corn, and departed thence. And as one of them opened his
sack to give his ass provender in the inn, he espied his money: for
behold, it was in his sack's mouth. And he said unto his brethren,
"My money is restored, and lo, it is even in my sack": and their
heart failed them, and they were afraid, saying one to another,
"What is this that God hath done unto us?"

And they came unto Jacob their father, unto the land of Canaan,
and told him all that befell unto them, saying, "The man who is the
lord of the land spake roughly to us, and took us for spies of the
country. And we said unto him, 'We are true men; we are no spies.
We be twelve brethren, sons of our father: one is not, and the
youngest is this day with our father in the land of Canaan.' And
the man the lord of the country said unto us, 'Hereby shall I know
that ye are true men: leave one of your brethren here with me, and
take food for the famine of your households, and be gone. And
bring your youngest brother unto me: then shall I know that you
are no spies, but that you are true men: so will I deliver you your
brother, and ye shall traffic in the land.' "

And it came to pass as they emptied their sacks, that behold, every
man's bundle of money was in his sack: and when both they and
their father saw the bundles of money, they were afraid. And Jacob
their father said unto them, "Me have ye bereaved of my children:
Joseph is not, and Simeon is not, and ye will take Benjamin away:
all these things are against me." And Reuben spake unto his father,
saying, "Slay my two sons, if I bring him not to thee: deliver him
into my hand, and I will bring him to thee again." And he said, "My
son shall not go down with you, for his brother is dead, and he is

[25] *I.e.*, the time of reckoning for their presumed killing of Joseph.

left alone: if mischief befall him by the way in the which ye go, then shall ye bring down my gray hairs with sorrow to the grave."

43 And the famine was sore in the land. And it came to pass when they had eaten up the corn which they had brought out of Egypt, their father said unto them, "Go again, buy us a little food." And Judah spake unto him, saying, "The man did solemnly protest unto us, saying, 'Ye shall not see my face, except your brother be with you.' If thou wilt send our brother with us, we will go down and buy thee food. But if thou wilt not send him, we will not go down: for the man said unto us, 'Ye shall not see my face, except your brother be with you.'" And Israel said, "Wherefore dealt ye so ill with me, as to tell the man whether ye had yet a brother?" And they said, "The man asked us straitly of our state, and of our kindred, saying, 'Is your father yet alive? have ye another brother?' and we told him according to the tenor of these words: could we certainly know that he would say, 'Bring your brother down'?" And Judah said unto Israel his father, "Send the lad with me, and we will arise and go, that we may live, and not die, both we, and thou, and also our little ones. I will be surety for him; of my hand shalt thou require him: if I bring him not unto thee, and set him before thee, then let me bear the blame for ever. For except we had lingered, surely now we had returned this second time." And their father Israel said unto them, "If it must be so now, do this: take of the best fruits in the land in your vessels, and carry down the man a present, a little balm, and a little honey, spices, and myrrh, nuts, and almonds. And take double money in your hand, and the money that was brought again in the mouth of your sacks: carry it again in your hand; peradventure it was an oversight. Take also your brother, and arise, go again unto the man. And God Almighty give you mercy before the man, that he may send away your other brother, and Benjamin: if I be bereaved of my children, I am bereaved."

And the men took that present, and they took double money in their hand, and Benjamin, and rose up, and went down to Egypt, and stood before Joseph. And when Joseph saw Benjamin with them, he said to the ruler of his house, "Bring these men home, and slay, and make ready: for these men shall dine with me at noon." And the man did as Joseph bade: and the man brought the men into Joseph's house. And the men were afraid, because they were brought into Joseph's house, and they said, "Because of the money that was returned in our sacks at the first time are we brought in, that he may seek occasion against us, and fall upon us, and take us for bondmen, and our asses." And they came near to the steward of Joseph's house, and they communed with him at the door of the house, and said, "O sir, we came indeed down at the first time to buy food. And it came to pass when we came to the inn, that we opened our sacks, and behold, every man's money was in the mouth of his sack, our money in full weight: and we have brought it again in our hand. And other money have we brought down in our hands to buy food: we cannot tell who put our money in our sacks." And he said, "Peace be to you, fear not: your God, and the God of your father, hath given you treasure in your sacks: I had your money." And he brought Simeon out unto them. And the man brought the men into Joseph's house, and gave them water, and they washed their feet, and he gave their asses provender. And they made ready the present against Joseph came at noon: for they heard that they should eat bread there.

And when Joseph came home, they brought him the present which was in their hand into the house, and bowed themselves to him to the earth. And he asked them of their welfare, and said, "Is your father well, the old man of whom ye spake? Is he yet alive?" And they answered, "Thy servant our father is in good health, he is yet alive": and they bowed down their heads, and made obeisance. And he lifted up his eyes, and saw his brother Benjamin, his mother's son, and said, "Is this your younger brother, of whom ye spake unto me?" and he said, "God be gracious unto thee, my son." And Joseph made haste: for his bowels did yearn upon his brother: and he sought where to weep, and he entered into his chamber, and wept there. And he washed his face, and went out, and refrained himself, and said, "Set on bread." And they set on for him by himself, and for them by themselves, and for the Egyptians which did eat with him by themselves: because the Egyptians might not eat bread with the Hebrews: for that is an abomination unto the Egyptians. And they sat before him, the firstborn according to his birthright, and the youngest according to his youth: and the men marvelled one at another. And he took and sent messes unto them from before him: but Benjamin's mess was five times so much as any of theirs. And they drunk, and were merry with him.

44 And he commanded the steward of his house, saying, "Fill the men's sacks with food, as much as they can carry, and put every man's money in his sack's mouth. And put my cup, the silver cup, in the sack's mouth of the youngest, and his corn money": and he did according to the word that Joseph had spoken. As soon as the morning was light, the men were sent away, they, and their asses. And when they were gone out of the city, and not yet far off, Joseph said unto his steward, "Up, follow after the men; and when thou dost overtake them, say unto them, 'Wherefore have ye rewarded evil for good? Is not this it in which my lord drinketh? and whereby indeed he divineth? ye have done evil in so doing.' "

And he overtook them, and he spake unto them these same words. And they said unto him, "Wherefore saith my lord these words? God forbid that thy servants should do according to this thing. Behold, the money which we found in our sacks' mouths we brought again unto thee out of the land of Canaan: how then should we steal out of thy lord's house silver or gold? With whomsoever of thy servants it be found, both let him die, and we also will be my lord's bondmen." And he said, "Now also let it be according unto your words: he with whom it is found shall be my servant: and ye shall be blameless." Then they speedily took down every man his sack to the ground, and opened every man his sack. And he searched, and began at the eldest, and left at the youngest: and the cup was found in Benjamin's sack. Then they rent their clothes, and laded every man his ass, and returned to the city.

And Judah and his brethren came to Joseph's house (for he was yet there): and they fell before him on the ground. And Joseph said unto them, "What deed is this that ye have done? wot ye not that such a man as I can certainly divine?" And Judah said, "What shall we say unto my lord? what shall we speak? or how shall we clear ourselves? God hath found out the iniquity of thy servants behold, we are my lord's servants, both we, and he also with whom the cup is found." And he said, "God forbid that I should do so: but the man in whose hand the cup is found, he shall be my servant; and as for you, get you up in peace unto your father."

Then Judah came near unto him, and said, "Oh my lord, let thy servant, I pray thee, speak a word in my lord's ears, and let not thine anger burn against thy servant: for thou art even as Pharaoh. My lord asked his servants, saying, 'Have ye a father, or a brother?' And we said unto my lord, 'We have a father, an old man, and a child of his old age, a little one: and his brother is dead, and he alone is left of his mother, and his father loveth him.' And thou saidst unto thy servants, 'Bring him down unto me, that I may set mine eyes upon him.' And we said unto my lord, 'The lad cannot leave his father: for if he should leave his father, his father would die.' And thou saidst unto thy servants, 'Except your youngest brother come down with you, you shall see my face no more.' And it came to pass when we came up unto thy servant my father, we told him the words of my lord. And our father said, 'Go again, and buy us a little food.' And we said, 'We cannot go down: if our youngest brother be with us, then will we go down: for we may not see the man's face, except our youngest brother be with us.' And thy servant my father said unto us, 'Ye know that my wife bare me two sons. And the one went out from me, and I said, "Surely he is torn in pieces": and I saw him not since. And if ye take this also from me, and mischief befall him, ye shall bring down my gray hairs with sorrow to the grave.' Now therefore when I come to thy servant my father, and the lad be not with us (seeing that his life is bound up in the lad's life), it shall come to pass, when he seeth that the lad is not with us, that he will die, and thy servants shall bring down the gray hairs of thy servant our father with sorrow to the grave. For thy servant became surety for the lad unto my father, saying, 'If I bring him not unto thee, then I shall bear the blame to my father for ever.' Now therefore, I pray thee, let thy servant abide instead of the lad a bondman to my lord, and let the lad go up with his brethren. For how shall I go up to my father, and the lad be not with me, lest peradventure I see the evil that shall come on my father?"

45 Then Joseph could not refrain himself before all them that stood by him: and he cried, "Cause every man to go out from me"; and there stood no man with him, while Joseph made himself known unto his brethren. And he wept aloud: and the Egyptians and the house of Pharaoh heard. And Joseph said unto his brethren, "I am Joseph; doth my father yet live?" and his brethren could not answer him: for they were troubled at his presence. And Joseph said unto his brethren, "Come near to me, I pray you": and they came near; and he said, "I am Joseph your brother, whom ye sold into

Egypt. Now therefore be not grieved, nor angry with yourselves, that ye sold me hither: for God did send me before you to preserve life. For these two years hath the famine been in the land: and yet there are five years in the which there shall neither be earing[26] nor harvest. And God sent me before you to preserve you a posterity in the earth, and to save your lives by a great deliverance. So now it was not you that sent me hither, but God: and he hath made me a father to Pharaoh, and lord of all his house, and a ruler throughout all the land of Egypt. Haste you, and go up to my father, and say unto him, 'Thus saith thy son Joseph, "God hath made me lord of all Egypt; come down unto me, tarry not. And thou shalt dwell in the land of Goshen, and thou shalt be near unto me, thou, and thy children, and thy children's children, and thy flocks, and thy herds, and all that thou hast. And there will I nourish thee (for yet there are five years of famine), lest thou, and thy household, and all that thou hast, come to poverty."' And behold, your eyes see, and the eyes of my brother Benjamin, that it is my mouth that speaketh unto you. And you shall tell my father of all my glory in Egypt, and of all that you have seen, and ye shall haste and bring down my father hither." And he fell upon his brother Benjamin's neck, and wept: and Benjamin wept upon his neck. Moreover he kissed all his brethren, and wept upon them: and after that his brethren talked with him.

And the fame thereof was heard in Pharaoh's house, saying, "Joseph's brethren are come": and it pleased Pharaoh well, and his servants. And Pharaoh said unto Joseph, "Say unto thy brethren, 'This do ye, lade your beasts and go, get you unto the land of Canaan. And take your father, and your households, and come unto me; and I will give you the good of the land of Egypt, and ye shall eat the fat of the land.' Now thou art commanded, this do ye: take you wagons out of the land of Egypt for your little ones, and for your wives, and bring your father, and come. Also regard not your stuff: for the good of all the land of Egypt is yours." And the children of Israel did so: and Joseph gave them wagons, according to the commandment of Pharaoh, and gave them provision for the way. To all of them he gave each man changes of raiment; but to Benjamin he gave three hundred pieces of silver, and five changes of raiment. And to his father he sent after this manner: ten asses laden with the good

[26] *I.e.*, tilling.

things of Egypt, and ten she-asses laden with corn and bread and meat for his father by the way. So he sent his brethren away, and they departed: and he said unto them, "See that ye fall not out by the way."

And they went up out of Egypt, and came into the land of Canaan unto Jacob their father, and told him, saying, "Joseph is yet alive, and he is governor over all the land of Egypt." And Jacob's heart fainted, for he believed them not. And they told him all the words of Joseph, which he had said unto them: and when he saw the wagons which Joseph had sent to carry him, the spirit of Jacob their father revived. And Israel said, "It is enough; Joseph my son is yet alive: I will go and see him before I die."

46 And Israel took his journey with all that he had, and came to Beer-sheba, and offered sacrifices unto the God of his father Isaac. And God spake unto Israel in the visions of the night, and said, "Jacob, Jacob." And he said, "Here am I." And he said, "I am God, the God of thy father, fear not to go down into Egypt: for I will there make of thee a great nation. I will go down with thee into Egypt; and I will also surely bring thee up again: and Joseph shall put his hand upon thine eyes." And Jacob rose up from Beer-sheba: and the sons of Israel carried Jacob their father, and their little ones, and their wives, in the wagons which Pharaoh had sent to carry him. And they took their cattle, and their goods, which they had gotten in the land of Canaan, and came into Egypt, Jacob, and all his seed with him: his sons, and his sons' sons with him, his daughters, and his sons' daughters, and all his seed brought he with him into Egypt. . . . All the souls of the house of Jacob, which came into Egypt, were threescore and ten.

And he sent Judah before him unto Joseph, to direct his face unto Goshen, and they came into the land of Goshen. And Joseph made ready his chariot, and went up to meet Israel his father, to Goshen, and presented himself unto him: and he fell on his neck, and wept on his neck a good while. And Israel said unto Joseph, "Now let me die, since I have seen thy face, because thou art yet alive." And Joseph said unto his brethren, and unto his father's house, "I will go up, and show Pharaoh, and say unto him, 'My brethren, and my father's house, which were in the land of Canaan, are come unto me. And the men are shepherds, for their trade hath been to feed cattle:

and they have brought their flocks, and their herds, and all that they have.' And it shall come to pass when Pharaoh shall call you, and shall say, 'What is your occupation?' that ye shall say, 'Thy servants' trade hath been about cattle, from our youth even until now, both we, and also our fathers': that ye may dwell in the land of Goshen; for every shepherd is an abomination unto the Egyptians."

47 Then Joseph came and told Pharoah, and said, "My father and my brethren, and their flocks, and their herds, and all that they have, are come out of the land of Canaan: and behold, they are in the land of Goshen." And he took some of his brethren, even five men, and presented them unto Pharaoh. And Pharaoh said unto his brethren, "What is your occupation?" And they said unto Pharaoh, "Thy servants are shepherds, both we and also our fathers." They said moreover unto Pharaoh, "For to sojourn in the land are we come: for thy servants have no pasture for their flocks, for the famine is sore in the land of Canaan: now therefore we pray thee, let thy servants dwell in the land of Goshen." And Pharaoh spake unto Joseph, saying, "Thy father and thy brethren are come unto thee. The land of Egypt is before thee: in the best of the land make thy father and brethren to dwell, in the land of Goshen let them dwell: and if thou knowest any man of activity amongst them, then make them rulers over my cattle." And Joseph brought in Jacob his father, and set him before Pharaoh: and Jacob blessed Pharaoh. And Pharaoh said unto Jacob, "How old art thou?" And Jacob said unto Pharaoh, "The days of the years of my pilgrimage are an hundred and thirty years: few and evil have the days of the years of my life been, and have not attained unto the days of the years of the life of my fathers, in the days of their pilgrimage." And Jacob blessed Pharaoh, and went out from before Pharaoh.

And Joseph placed his father, and his brethren, and gave them a possession in the land of Egypt, in the best of the land, in the land of Rameses, as Pharaoh had commanded. And Joseph nourished his father and his brethren, and all his father's household, with bread, according to their families.

And there was no bread in all the land: for the famine was very sore, so that the land of Egypt and all the land of Canaan fainted by reason of the famine. And Joseph gathered up all the money that was found in the land of Egypt, and in the land of Canaan, for the corn which they bought: and Joseph brought the money into Pharaoh's house. And when money failed in the land of Egypt, and in the land of Canaan, all the Egyptians came unto Joseph, and said, "Give us bread: for why should we die in thy presence? for the money faileth." And Joseph said, "Give your cattle: and I will give you for your cattle, if money fail." And they brought their cattle unto Joseph: and Joseph gave them bread in exchange for horses, and for the flocks, and for the cattle of the herds, and for the asses, and he fed them with bread for all their cattle for that year.

When that year was ended, they came unto him the second year, and said unto him, "We will not hide it from my lord, how that our money is spent: my lord also had our herds of cattle: there is not aught left in the sight of my lord, but our bodies, and our lands. Wherefore shall we die before thine eyes, both we, and our land? buy us and our land for bread, and we and our land will be servants unto Pharaoh: and give us seed that we may live and not die, that the land be not desolate. And Joseph bought all the land of Egypt for Pharaoh: for the Egyptians sold every man his field, because the famine prevailed over them: so the land became Pharaoh's. And as for the people, he removed them to cities from one end of the borders of Egypt, even to the other end thereof. Only the land of the priests bought he not: for the priests had a portion assigned them of Pharaoh, and did eat their portion which Pharaoh gave them:[27] wherefore they sold not their lands. Then Joseph said unto the people, "Behold, I have bought you this day, and your land for Pharaoh: lo, here is seed for you, and ye shall sow the land. And it shall come to pass in the increase, that you shall give the fifth part unto Pharaoh, and four parts shall be your own, for seed of the field, and for your food, and for them of your households, and for food for your little ones." And they said, "Thou hast saved our lives: let us find grace in the sight of my lord, and we will be Pharaoh's servants." And Joseph made it a law over the land of Egypt unto this day, that Pharaoh should have the fifth part: except the land of the priests only, which became not Pharaoh's.

And Israel dwelt in the land of Egypt, in the country of Goshen, and they had possessions therein, and grew, and multiplied exceedingly. And Jacob lived in the land of Egypt seventeen years: so the whole age of Jacob was an hundred forty and seven years. And the

[27] *I.e.,* the priests lived on the allowance which Pharaoh granted them.

time drew nigh that Israel must die, and he called his son Joseph, and said unto him, "If now I have found grace in thy sight, put, I pray thee, thy hand under my thigh, and deal kindly and truly with me, bury me not, I pray thee, in Egypt. But I will lie with my fathers, and thou shalt carry me out of Egypt, and bury me in their burying place." And he said, "I will do as thou hast said." And he said, "Swear unto me." And he sware unto him. And Israel bowed himself upon the bed's head.

48 And it came to pass after these things, that one told Joseph, "Behold, thy father is sick": and he took with him his two sons, Manasseh and Ephraim. And one told Jacob, and said, "Behold, thy son Joseph cometh unto thee": and Israel strengthened himself, and sat upon the bed. And Jacob said unto Joseph, "God Almighty appeared unto me at Luz in the land of Canaan, and blessed me, and said unto me, 'Behold, I will make thee fruitful, and multiply thee, and I will make of thee a multitude of people, and will give this land to thy seed after thee, for an everlasting possession.' And now thy two sons, Ephraim and Manasseh, which were born unto thee in the land of Egypt, before I came unto thee into Egypt, are mine: as Reuben and Simeon, they shall be mine. And thy issue, which thou begettest after them, shall be thine, and shall be called after the name of their brethren in their inheritance. And as for me, when I came from Padan, Rachel died by me in the land of Canaan, in the way, when yet there was but a little way to come unto Ephrath: and I buried her there in the way of Ephrath, the same is Bethlehem."

And Israel beheld Joseph's sons, and said, "Who are these?" And Joseph said unto his father, "They are my sons, whom God hath given me in this place": and he said, "Bring them, I pray thee, unto me, and I will bless them." Now the eyes of Israel were dim for age, so that he could not see, and he brought them near unto him, and he kissed them, and embraced them. And Israel said unto Joseph, "I had not thought to see thy face: and lo, God hath showed me also thy seed." And Joseph brought them out from between his knees, and he bowed himself with his face to the earth. And Joseph took them both, Ephraim in his right hand toward Israel's left hand, and Manasseh in his left hand toward Israel's right hand, and brought them near unto him. And Israel stretched out his right hand, and laid it upon Ephraim's head who was the younger; and his left hand upon Manasseh's head, guiding his hands wittingly: for Manasseh was the firstborn.

And he blessed Joseph and said, "God before whom my fathers Abraham and Isaac did walk, the God which fed me all my life long unto this day, the Angel which redeemed me from all evil, bless the lads, and let my name be named on them, and the name of my fathers Abraham and Isaac, and let them grow into a multitude in the midst of the earth." And when Joseph saw that his father laid his right hand upon the head of Ephraim, it displeased him: and he held up his father's hand, to remove it from Ephraim's head unto Manasseh's head. And Joseph said unto his father, "Not so my father: for this is the firstborn; put thy right hand upon his head." And his father refused, and said, "I know it, my son, I know it: he also shall become a people, and he also shall be great: but truly his younger brother shall be greater than he; and his seed shall become a multitude of nations." And he blessed them that day, saying, "In thee shall Israel bless, saying, 'God make thee as Ephraim, and as Manasseh'": and he set Ephraim before Manasseh. And Israel said unto Joseph, "Behold, I die: but God shall be with you, and bring you again unto the land of your fathers. Moreover I have given to thee one portion above thy brethren, which I took out of the hand of the Amorite with my sword, and with my bow."

49 And Jacob called unto his sons, and said, "Gather yourselves together, that I may tell you that which shall befall you in the last days. Gather yourselves together, and hear, ye sons of Jacob, and hearken unto Israel your father.

"Reuben, thou art my firstborn, my might, and the beginning of my strength, the excellency of dignity, and the excellency of power: unstable as water, thou shalt not excel, because thou wentest up to thy father's bed: then defiledst thou it. He went up to my couch.

"Simeon and Levi are brethren, instruments of cruelty are in their habitations. O my soul, come not thou into their secret: unto their assembly mine honour be not thou united: for in their anger they slew a man, and in their self-will they digged down a wall. Cursed be their anger, for it was fierce; and their wrath, for it was cruel: I will divide them in Jacob, and scatter them in Israel.

"Judah, thou art he whom thy brethren shall praise: thy hand shall be in the neck of thine enemies, thy father's children shall bow down before thee. Judah is a lion's whelp: from the prey, my son, thou art gone up: he stooped down, he couched as a lion, and as an old lion: who shall rouse him up? The sceptre shall not depart from Judah, nor a lawgiver from between his feet, until Shiloh come: and unto him shall the gathering of the people be: binding his foal unto the vine, and his ass's colt unto the choice vine; he washed his garments in wine, and his clothes in the blood of grapes. His eyes shall be red with wine, and his teeth white with milk.

"Zebulun shall dwell at the haven of the sea, and he shall be for an haven of ships: and his border shall be unto Zidon.

"Issachar is a strong ass, couching down between two burdens. And he saw that rest was good, and the land that it was pleasant: and bowed his shoulder to bear, and became a servant unto tribute.

"Dan shall judge his people, as one of the tribes of Israel. Dan shall be a serpent by the way, an adder in the path, that biteth the horse heels, so that his rider shall fall backward. I have waited for thy salvation, O Lord.

"Gad, a troop shall overcome him: but he shall overcome at the last.

"Out of Asher his bread shall be fat, and he shall yield royal dainties.

"Naphtali is a hind let loose: he giveth goodly words.

"Joseph is a fruitful bough, even a fruitful bough by a well, whose branches run over the wall. The archers have sorely grieved him, and shot at him, and hated him. But his bow abode in strength, and the arms of his hands were made strong by the hands of the mighty God of Jacob: from thence is the shepherd, the stone of Israel, even by the God of thy father, who shall help thee, and by the Almighty, who shall bless thee with blessings of heaven above, blessings of the deep that lieth under, blessings of the breasts and of the womb. The blessings of thy father have prevailed above the blessings of my progenitors: unto the utmost bound of the everlasting hills, they shall be on the head of Joseph, and on the crown of the head of him that was separate from his brethren.

"Benjamin shall raven as a wolf: in the morning he shall devour the prey, and at night he shall divide the spoil."

All these are the twelve tribes of Israel, and this is it that their father spake unto them, and blessed them: every one according to his blessing he blessed them. And he charged them, and said unto

them, "I am to be gathered unto my people: bury me with my
fathers, in the cave that is in the field of Ephron the Hittite, in the
cave that is in the field of Machpelah, which is before Mamre, in the
land of Canaan, which Abraham bought with the field of Ephron
the Hittite for a possession of a burying place. (There they buried
Abraham and Sarah his wife, there they buried Isaac and Rebekah
his wife, and there I buried Leah.) The purchase of the field and
of the cave that is therein was from the children of Heth." And
when Jacob had made an end of commanding his sons, he gathered
up his feet into the bed, and yielded up the ghost, and was gathered
unto his people.

50 And Joseph fell upon his father's face, and wept upon him,
and kissed him. And Joseph commanded his servants the
physicians to embalm his father: and the physicians embalmed Israel.
And forty days were fulfilled for him (for so are fulfilled the days of
those which are embalmed), and the Egyptians mourned for him
threescore and ten days. And when the days of his mourning were
past, Joseph spake unto the house of Pharaoh, saying, "If now I have
found grace in your eyes, speak, I pray you, in the ears of Pharaoh,
saying, 'My father made me swear, saying, "Lo, I die: in my grave
which I have digged for me, in the land of Canaan, there shalt thou
bury me." Now therefore let me go up, I pray thee, and bury my
father, and I will come again.'" And Pharaoh said, "Go up, and
bury thy father, according as he made thee swear."

And Joseph went up to bury his father: and with him went up
all the servants of Pharaoh, the elders of his house, and all the elders
of the land of Egypt, and all the house of Joseph, and his
brethren, and his father's house: only their little ones, and their
flocks, and their herds, they left in the land of Goshen. And there
went up with him both chariots and horsemen: and it was a very
great company. And they came to the threshing floor of Atad, which
is beyond Jordan, and there they mourned with a great and very
sore lamentation: and he made a mourning for his father seven days.
And when the inhabitants of the land, the Canaanites, saw the
mourning in the floor of Atad, they said, "This is a grievous mourning to the Egyptians": wherefore the name of it was called, Abel-
mizraim, which is beyond Jordan. And his sons did unto him
according as he commanded them: for his sons carried him into the

land of Canaan, and buried him in the cave of the field of Mach-pelah, which Abraham bought with the field for a possession of a burying place of Ephron the Hittite, before Mamre. And Joseph returned into Egypt, he, and his brethren, and all that went up with him to bury his father, after he had buried his father.

And when Joseph's brethren saw that their father was dead, they said, "Joseph will peradventure hate us, and will certainly requite us all the evil which we did unto him." And they sent a messenger unto Joseph, saying, "Thy father did command before he died, saying, 'So shall ye say unto Joseph, "Forgive, I pray thee now, the trespass of thy brethren, and their sin: for they did unto thee evil" ': and now we pray thee, forgive the trespass of the servants of the God of thy father." And Joseph wept when they spake unto him. And his brethren also went and fell down before his face, and they said, "Behold, we be thy servants." And Joseph said unto them, "Fear not: for am I in the place of God? But as for you, ye thought evil against me, but God meant it unto good, to bring to pass, as it is this day, to save much people alive. Now therefore fear ye not: I will nourish you, and your little ones." And he comforted them, and spake kindly unto them.

And Joseph dwelt in Egypt, he, and his father's house: and Joseph lived an hundred and ten years. And Joseph saw Ephraim's children, of the third generation: the children also of Machir, the son of Manasseh, were brought up upon Joseph's knees. And Joseph said unto his brethren, "I die: and God will surely visit you, and bring you out of this land, unto the land which he sware to Abraham, to Isaac, and to Jacob." And Joseph took an oath of the children of Israel, saying, "God will surely visit you, and ye shall carry up my bones from hence." So Joseph died, being an hundred and ten years old: and they embalmed him, and he was put in a coffin, in Egypt.

exodus

INTRODUCTION

Exodus is central to the Old Testament, for it is in this book that Israel becomes a nation, welded together by Moses and equipped with a system of laws that will aid it in fulfilling its role in the divine scheme. The following selection is complete, except for genealogies, through verse 25 of chapter 21; it also includes chapter 32, the story of the golden calf, and it ends with the brief account in Deuteronomy of the death of Moses. The omitted sections are mainly legalistic and have little relevance to the Bible as literature.

As in Genesis, several authors contributed to Exodus. J is still predominant, and the central story continues to be the unfolding of God's nationalistic plan, the working out of His original promise to Abraham. E remains next in importance, and it is he who magnifies the already large figure of Moses—not primarily as a political chieftain but as an exalted religious leader. Then a new source appears in Exodus, whom we refer to as D—the Deuteronomist. A Jerusalem priest of the late seventh century B.C., D attempted to mediate between ritualistic Judaism and the teachings of the prophets by codifying morality and worship into a series of specific enactments. His hand dominates the end of chapter 21 as well as the portions of Exodus here omitted. P, coming two centuries later than D, is more evident in Exodus than in Genesis. The emphasis on the ceremonial aspects of the Passover as well as the sabbatarianism explicit in the story of the manna which fed the Jews are examples of his editing.[1] At the same time, Exodus is more unified

---

[1] In the account of the ten plagues there are many redundancies, overlappings, and inconsistencies. Most of them can be explained by the theory that J is primarily concerned with Moses as a human hero (his Moses appears alone before Pharaoh); E is more interested in the religious Moses (in his additions the rod, endowed with magic powers by God, is crucial); and in P's sections Aaron, who appears in none of the earlier sources, is given a large role, while God shows extra severity in hardening Pharaoh's heart and then punishing him and his people.

than Genesis, first because the events it covers are more homogeneous, second because the oral traditions behind them are less diverse than those from which the sagas of the patriarchs developed.

To J and E, and probably to D and P, the supreme moment in the history of Israel was the crossing of the Red Sea, an event that signified not only the birth of a nation but God's defeat of the world's strongest power. Yet Egyptian records, except for one or two veiled and indirect references to Hebrew slaves, fail to mention any such catastrophe. Almost certainly, however, an exodus of some oppressed groups from northern Egypt occurred in the thirteenth century, during the reign of Ramses II or of his son Merneptah. Thus certain tribal movements in the Near East were taking place at approximately the same time as the siege of Troy was demonstrating similar upheavals in the Greek archipelago. Just as Homer looked back on and glorified the past, so J and E wove together ancient stories to show the power of their God and the manifest destiny of their people. And some of these stories were very ancient. The God of Exodus—of the burning bush, the plagues, Mount Sinai— often seems the embodiment of a volcano. In a like manner, the incident in chapter 4 where Zipporah vicariously circumcises Moses harks back to a primitive myth in which the bride, to appease a hostile demon, offers him the foreskin of the bridegroom. (The antiquity of this story is underlined by the fact that she uses a stone knife, and that her act implies adult, not infant, circumcision.)

Yet, in all probability, Moses was an actual historic figure, a dynamic leader who delivered his people from slavery and established them as a self-conscious community, furnished with laws, an administrative hierarchy, and a fledgling army. In secular terms, there is a parallel between Moses and George Washington; in spiritual terms, Spinoza's characterization of Moses as a "God intoxicated" man is apt. At once a very human figure and a gigantic mediator between God and man, Moses dominates Exodus to such an extent that it is easy to understand why he was long thought to be the author of the entire Pentateuch. Further, his role as law-giver seemingly qualified him to compose the legal codes which fill Leviticus and Deuteronomy and which form a large part of The Book of Numbers.

To what extent the laws promulgated in Exodus are the revealed word of God, peculiarly Jewish, or a product of earlier Near Eastern codes raises complex problems. The ancient Babylonian Code of Hammurabi and the Assyrian and Hittite legal systems suggest that the Mosaic Code was similar to other ancient collections of law, though that of Hammurabi in particular was suited to a more sophisticated and urban society. All Near Eastern codes retained echoes of the eye-for-an-eye law of the desert, yet all were in the process of mitigating this law by allowing for monetary, rather than blood, compensation. The Ten Commandments themselves raise similar problems. Commandments five to nine deal with offenses condemned by almost every code, while the first four commandments attempt to purify Jewish worship from heathen contamination. Probably, therefore, regardless of the code's original indebtedness to Moses, the form in which it appears in Exodus is attributable to D, the Deuteronomist, seeking a compromise between the prophets' concern for right motives (note, in this connection, the tenth commandment) and the priests' stress on ritual observances.[2]

Another of the many problems raised by Exodus concerns the geography of the flight from Egypt and the Hebrews' subsequent wanderings. Probably the Red Sea can be identified with the Sea of Reeds (which is the correct translation of the Hebrew phrase) in the eastern section of the Nile delta; and there is increasing agreement that Mount Sinai was near the Gulf of Aqaba. The exact course of the Jews' wanderings in the wilderness remains a cloudy and much disputed issue. So, in fact, does the whole historicity of the exodus. Much ingenuity has been expended to explain the logic of such events as the plagues and the defeat of the Egyptian army. To J and E, however, the line between history and legend, between fact and hope, between natural and divine, was shadowy and largely meaningless. One of the oldest fragments in the Bible is the Song of Miriam, composed almost three centuries before J, five before E: "Sing ye to the Lord, for he hath triumphed gloriously: the horse and his rider hath he thrown into the sea." [3] But the question of whether this song celebrated an actual event or expressed a tribal longing is essentially irrelevant to the sweep and fervor of Exodus.

Suggested Reading

Homer, The Odyssey—a heroic story of wandering and of a self-reliant leader.

Virgil, The Aeneid—the epic of Rome's manifest destiny.

[2] Many scholars emphasize the influence on Moses of Jethro: that is, the influence of the Kenites on early Jewish institutions. Thus, for instance, the sabbath would be appropriate to a settled agricultural group, and it might well have been taken over by nomadic tribes who gradually absorbed—and were absorbed by—the inhabitants of the lands they occupied.

[3] Exodus, chapter 15, verse 21. The longer song which precedes it is a later author's attempt to recapture the tone and spirit of Miriam.

The Song of Roland—a chivalric romance about a medieval leader and his people.

James Joyce, *Ulysses*—an experimental modern novel, partly based on *The Odyssey*, centering around the theme of the quest for a father.

EXODUS

1 Now these are the names of the children of Israel, which came into Egypt, every man and his household came with Jacob. Reuben, Simeon, Levi, and Judah, Issachar, Zebulun, and Benjamin, Dan, and Naphtali, Gad, and Asher. And all the souls that came out of the loins of Jacob were seventy souls: for Joseph was in Egypt already. And Joseph died, and all his brethren, and all that generation.

And the children of Israel were fruitful, and increased abundantly, and multiplied, and waxed exceeding mighty, and the land was filled with them. Now there arose up a new king over Egypt, which knew not Joseph. And he said unto his people, "Behold, the people of the children of Israel are more and mightier than we. Come on, let us deal wisely with them, lest they multiply, and it come to pass that, when there falleth out any war, they join also unto our enemies, and fight against us, and so get them up out of the land." Therefore they did set over them taskmasters to afflict them with their burdens: and they built for Pharaoh treasure cities, Pithom and Raamses. But the more they afflicted them, the more they multiplied and grew: and they were grieved because of the children of Israel. And the Egyptians made the children of Israel to serve with rigour. And they made their lives bitter with hard bondage, in mortar, and in brick, and in all manner of service in the field: all their service wherein they made them serve was with rigour.

And the king of Egypt spake to the Hebrew midwives (of which the name of the one was Shiphrah, and the name of the other Puah), and he said, "When ye do the office of a midwife to the Hebrew women, and see them upon the stools, if it be a son, then ye shall kill him: but if it be a daughter, then she shall live." But the midwives feared God, and did not as the king of Egypt commanded them, but saved the men children alive. And the king of Egypt called for the midwives, and said unto them, "Why have ye done this thing, and have saved the men children alive?" And the midwives said unto

Pharaoh, "Because the Hebrew women are not as the Egyptian women: for they are lively, and are delivered ere the midwives come in unto them." Therefore God dealt well with the midwives: and the people multiplied and waxed very mighty. And it came to pass, because the midwives feared God, that he made them houses.[1] And Pharaoh charged all his people, saying, "Every son that is born, ye shall cast into the river, and every daughter ye shall save alive."

2 And there went a man of the house of Levi, and took to wife a daughter of Levi. And the woman conceived, and bare a son: and when she saw him that he was a goodly child, she hid him three months. And when she could not longer hide him, she took for him an ark of bulrushes, and daubed it with slime, and with pitch, and put the child therein, and she laid it in the flags by the river's brink. And his sister stood afar off, to wit what would be done to him.

And the daughter of Pharaoh came down to wash herself at the river, and her maidens walked along by the river side: and when she saw the ark among the flags, she sent her maid to fetch it. And when she had opened it, she saw the child: and behold, the babe wept. And she had compassion on him, and said, "This is one of the Hebrews' children." Then said his sister to Pharaoh's daughter, "Shall I go and call to thee a nurse of the Hebrew women, that she may nurse the child for thee?" And Pharaoh's daughter said to her, "Go." And the maid went and called the child's mother. And Pharaoh's daughter said unto her, "Take this child away, and nurse it for me, and I will give thee thy wages." And the woman took the child, and nursed it. And the child grew, and she brought him unto Pharaoh's daughter, and he became her son. And she called his name Moses: and she said, "Because I drew him out of the water."

And it came to pass in those days, when Moses was grown, that he went out unto his brethren, and looked on their burdens, and he spied an Egyptian smiting an Hebrew, one of his brethren. And he looked this way and that way, and when he saw that there was no man, he slew the Egyptian, and hid him in the sand. And when he went out the second day, behold, two men of the Hebrews strove together: and he said to him that did the wrong, "Wherefore smitest

[1] An ancient editorial insertion: God rewards the midwives by giving them families.

thou thy fellow?" And he said, "Who made thee a prince and a judge over us? intendest thou to kill me, as thou killedst the Egyptian?" And Moses feared, and said, "Surely this thing is known." Now when Pharaoh heard this thing, he sought to slay Moses. But Moses fled from the face of Pharaoh, and dwelt in the land of Midian: and he sat down by a well. Now the priest of Midian had seven daughters, and they came and drew water, and filled the troughs to water their father's flock. And the shepherds came and drove them away: but Moses stood up and helped them, and watered their flock. And when they came to Reuel [2] their father, he said, "How is it that you are come so soon today?" And they said, "An Egyptian delivered us out of the hand of the shepherds, and also drew water enough for us, and watered the flock." And he said unto his daughters, "And where is he? why is it that ye have left the man? Call him, that he may eat bread." And Moses was content to dwell with the man, and he gave Moses Zipporah his daughter. And she bare him a son, and he called his name Gershom: for he said, "I have been a stranger in a strange land."

And it came to pass in process of time, that the king of Egypt died, and the children of Israel sighed by reason of the bondage, and they cried, and their cry came up unto God, by reason of the bondage. And God heard their groaning, and God remembered his covenant with Abraham, with Isaac, and with Jacob. And God looked upon the children of Israel, and God had respect unto them.

3 Now Moses kept the flock of Jethro his father in law, the priest of Midian: and he led the flock to the backside of the desert, and came to the mountain of God, even to Horeb. And the angel of the Lord appeared unto him, in a flame of fire out of the midst of a bush, and he looked, and behold, the bush burned with fire, and the bush was not consumed. And Moses said "I will now turn aside, and see this great sight, why the bush is not burnt." And when the Lord saw that he turned aside to see, God called unto him out of the midst of the bush, and said, "Moses, Moses." And he said, "Here am I." And he said, "Draw not nigh hither: put off thy shoes from off thy feet, for the place whereon thou standest is holy ground." Moreover he said, "I am the God of thy father, the God of Abraham, the God

---

[2] Reuel was probably Jethro's father, and consequently Moses' future grandfather-in-law. (See the opening of chapter 3, below.)

of Isaac, and the God of Jacob." And Moses hid his face: for he was afraid to look upon God.

And the Lord said, "I have surely seen the affliction of my people which are in Egypt, and have heard their cry, by reason of their task-masters: for I know their sorrows, and I am come down to deliver them out of the hand of the Egyptians, and to bring them up out of that land, unto a good land and a large, unto a land flowing with milk and honey, unto the place of the Canaanites, and the Hittites, and the Amorites, and the Perizzites, and the Hivites, and the Jebu-sites. Now therefore behold, the cry of the children of Israel is come unto me: and I have also seen the oppression wherewith the Egyptians oppress them. Come now therefore, and I will send thee unto Pharaoh, that thou mayest bring forth my people the children of Israel out of Egypt."

And Moses said unto God, "Who am I, that I should go unto Pharaoh, and that I should bring forth the children of Israel out of Egypt?" And he said, "Certainly I will be with thee, and this shall be a token unto thee, that I have sent thee: when thou hast brought forth the people out of Egypt, ye shall serve God upon this moun-tain." And Moses said unto God, "Behold, when I come unto the children of Israel, and shall say unto them, 'The God of your fathers hath sent me unto you'; and they shall say to me, 'What is his name?' what shall I say unto them?" And God said unto Moses, "I AM THAT I AM": and he said, "Thus shalt thou say unto the children of Israel, 'I AM hath sent me unto you.' " And God said moreover unto Moses, "Thus shalt thou say unto the children of Israel, 'The Lord God of your fathers, the God of Abraham, the God of Isaac, and the God of Jacob, hath sent me unto you: this is my name for ever, and this is my memorial unto all generations.' Go and gather the elders of Israel together, and say unto them, 'The Lord God of your fathers, the God of Abraham, of Isaac, and of Jacob, appeared unto me, saying, "I have surely visited you, and seen that which is done to you in Egypt. And I have said, I will bring you up out of the affliction of Egypt, unto the land of the Canaanites, and the Hittites, and the Amorites, and the Perizzites, and the Hivites, and the Jebusites, unto a land flowing with milk and honey." ' And they shall hearken to thy voice: and thou shalt come, thou and the elders of Israel, unto the king of Egypt, and you shall say unto him, 'The Lord God of the Hebrews hath met with us: and now let us go (we beseech thee) three days' journey into the wilderness, that we may sacrifice to the Lord our God.'

"And I am sure that the king of Egypt will not let you go, no, not by a mighty hand. And I will stretch out my hand, and smite Egypt with all my wonders which I will do in the midst thereof: and after that he will let you go. And I will give this people favour in the sight of the Egyptians, and it shall come to pass that when ye go, ye shall not go empty: but every woman shall borrow of her neighbour, and of her that sojourneth in her house, jewels of silver, and jewels of gold, and raiment: and ye shall put them upon your sons, and upon your daughters, and ye shall spoil the Egyptians."

4 And Moses answered, and said, "But behold, they will not believe me, nor hearken unto my voice: for they will say, 'The Lord hath not appeared unto thee.'" And the Lord said unto him, "What is that in thine hand?" And he said, "A rod." And he said, "Cast it on the ground." And he cast it on the ground, and it became a serpent: and Moses fled from before it. And the Lord said unto Moses, "Put forth thine hand, and take it by the tail": and he put forth his hand, and caught it, and it became a rod in his hand: "That they may believe that the Lord God of their fathers, the God of Abraham, the God of Isaac, and the God of Jacob, hath appeared unto thee."

And the Lord said furthermore unto him, "Put now thine hand into thy bosom." And he put his hand into his bosom: and when he took it out, behold, his hand was leprous as snow. And he said, "Put thine hand into thy bosom again." And he put his hand into his bosom again, and plucked it out of his bosom, and behold, it was turned again as his other flesh. "And it shall come to pass, if they will not believe thee, neither hearken to the voice of the first sign, that they will believe the voice of the latter sign. And it shall come to pass, if they will not believe also these two signs, neither hearken unto thy voice, that thou shalt take of the water of the river, and pour it upon the dry land: and the water which thou takest out of the river shall become blood upon the dry land."

And Moses said unto the Lord, "O my Lord, I am not eloquent, neither heretofore, nor since thou hast spoken unto thy servant: but I am slow of speech, and of a slow tongue." And the Lord said unto him, "Who hath made man's mouth? or who maketh the dumb or

deaf, or the seeing, or the blind? have not I the Lord? Now therefore go, and I will be with thy mouth, and teach thee what thou
shalt say." And he said, "O my Lord, send, I pray thee, by the hand
of him whom thou wilt send." [3] And the anger of the Lord was
kindled against Moses, and he said, "Is not Aaron the Levite thy
brother? I know that he can speak well. And also behold, he cometh
forth to meet thee: and when he seeth thee, he will be glad in his
heart. And thou shalt speak unto him, and put words in his mouth,
and I will be with thy mouth, and with his mouth, and will teach
you what ye shall do. And he shall be thy spokesman unto the
people: and he shall be, even he shall be to thee instead of a mouth,
and thou shalt be to him instead of God. And thou shalt take this
rod in thine hand, wherewith thou shalt do signs."

And Moses went and returned to Jethro his father in law, and said
unto him, "Let me go, I pray thee, and return unto my brethren,
which are in Egypt, and see whether they be yet alive." And Jethro
said to Moses, "Go in peace." And the Lord said unto Moses in
Midian, "Go, return into Egypt: for all the men are dead which
sought thy life." And Moses took his wife, and his sons, and set them
upon an ass, and he returned to the land of Egypt. And Moses took
the rod of God in his hand. And the Lord said unto Moses, "When
thou goest to return into Egypt, see that thou do all those wonders
before Pharaoh, which I have put in thine hand: but I will harden
his heart, that he shall not let the people go. And thou shalt say
unto Pharaoh, 'Thus saith the Lord, "Israel is my son, even my firstborn. And I say unto thee, Let my son go, that he may serve me:
and if thou refuse to let him go, behold, I will slay thy son, even
thy firstborn." ' "

And it came to pass by the way in the inn, that the Lord met him,
and sought to kill him. Then Zipporah took a sharp stone, and cut
off the foreskin of her son, and cast it at his feet, and said, "Surely
a bloody husband art thou to me." So he let him go: then she said,
"A bloody husband thou art, because of the circumcision."

And the Lord said to Aaron, "Go into the wilderness to meet
Moses." And he went, and met him in the mount of God, and
kissed him. And Moses told Aaron all the words of the Lord, who
had sent him, and all the signs which he had commanded him.

And Moses and Aaron went, and gathered together all the elders

[3] *I.e.*, send some other person.

of the children of Israel. And Aaron spake all the words which the Lord had spoken unto Moses, and did the signs in the sight of the people. And the people believed: and when they heard that the Lord had visited the children of Israel, and that he had looked upon their affliction, then they bowed their heads and worshipped.

5 And afterward Moses and Aaron went in, and told Pharaoh, "Thus saith the Lord God of Israel, 'Let my people go, that they may hold a feast unto me in the wilderness.'" And Pharaoh said, "Who is the Lord, that I should obey his voice to let Israel go? I know not the Lord, neither will I let Israel go." And they said, "The God of the Hebrews hath met with us: let us go, we pray thee, three days' journey into the desert, and sacrifice unto the Lord our God, lest he fall upon us with pestilence, or with the sword." And the king of Egypt said unto them, "Wherefore do ye, Moses and Aaron, let⁴ the people from their works? get you unto your burdens." And Pharaoh said, "Behold, the people of the land now are many, and you make them rest from their burdens." And Pharaoh commanded the same day the taskmasters of the people, and their officers, saying, "Ye shall no more give the people straw to make brick, as heretofore: let them go and gather straw for themselves. And the tale⁵ of the bricks, which they did make heretofore, you shall lay upon them: you shall not diminish aught thereof: for they be idle; therefore they cry, saying, 'Let us go and sacrifice to our God.' Let there more work be laid upon the men, that they may labour therein, and let them not regard vain words."

And the taskmasters of the people went out, and their officers, and they spake to the people, saying, "Thus saith Pharaoh, 'I will not give you straw. Go ye, get you straw where you can find it: yet not aught of your work shall be diminished.'" So the people were scattered abroad throughout all the land of Egypt, to gather stubble instead of straw. And the taskmasters hasted them, saying, "Fulfill your works, your daily tasks, as when there was straw." And the officers of the children of Israel, which Pharaoh's taskmasters had set over them, were beaten, and demanded,⁶ "Wherefore have ye not ful-

---

⁴ *I.e.*, hinder.
⁵ *I.e.*, number.
⁶ *I.e.*, asked.

filled your task, in making brick both yesterday and today, as here-tofore?"

Then the officers of the children of Israel came and cried unto Pharaoh, saying, "Wherefore dealest thou thus with thy servants? There is no straw given unto thy servants, and they say to us, 'Make brick': and behold, thy servants are beaten: but the fault is in thine own people." But he said, "Ye are idle, ye are idle: therefore ye say, 'Let us go and do sacrifice to the Lord.' Go therefore now and work: for there shall no straw be given you, yet shall ye deliver the tale of bricks." And the officers of the children of Israel did see that they were in evil case, after it was said, "Ye shall not minish aught from your bricks of your daily task."

And they met Moses and Aaron, who stood in the way, as they came forth from Pharaoh. And they said unto them, "The Lord look upon you, and judge, because ye have made our savour to be abhorred in the eyes of Pharaoh, and in the eyes of his servants, to put a sword in their hand to slay us." And Moses returned unto the Lord, and said, "Lord, wherefore hast thou so evil entreated this people? why is it that thou hast sent me? For since I came to Pharaoh to speak in thy name, he hath done evil to this people, neither hast thou delivered thy people at all."

6 Then the Lord said unto Moses, "Now shalt thou see what I will do to Pharaoh: for with a strong hand shall he let them go, and with a strong hand shall he drive them out of his land." And God spake unto Moses, and said unto him, "I am the Lord. And I appeared unto Abraham, unto Isaac, and unto Jacob, by the name of God Almighty, but by my name JEHOVAH was I not known to them. And I have also established my covenant with them, to give them the land of Canaan, the land of their pilgrimage, wherein they were strangers. And I have also heard the groaning of the children of Israel, whom the Egyptians keep in bondage: and I have remembered my covenant. Wherefore say unto the children of Israel, 'I am the Lord, and I will bring you out from under the burdens of the Egyptians, and I will rid you out of their bondage: and I will redeem you with a stretched out arm, and with great judgments. And I will take you to me for a people, and I will be to you a God: and ye shall know that I am the Lord your God, which bringeth you out from under the burdens of the Egyptians. And I will bring you in unto

the land concerning the which I did swear to give it, to Abraham, to Isaac, and to Jacob, and I will give it you for an heritage: I am the Lord.'"

And Moses spake so unto the children of Israel: but they hearkened not unto Moses, for anguish of spirit, and for cruel bondage. And the Lord spake unto Moses, saying, "Go in, speak unto Pharaoh king of Egypt, that he let the children of Israel go out of his land." And Moses spake before the Lord, saying, "Behold, the children of Israel have not hearkened unto me: how then shall Pharaoh hear me, who am of uncircumcised lips?" And the Lord spake unto Moses and unto Aaron, and gave them a charge unto the children of Israel, and unto Pharaoh king of Egypt, to bring the children of Israel out of the land of Egypt. . . .

7 And the Lord said unto Moses, "See, I have made thee a god to Pharaoh, and Aaron thy brother shall be thy prophet. Thou shalt speak all that I command thee, and Aaron thy brother shall speak unto Pharaoh, that he send the children of Israel out of his land. And I will harden Pharaoh's heart, and multiply my signs and my wonders in the land of Egypt. But Pharaoh shall not hearken unto you, that I may lay my hand upon Egypt, and bring forth mine armies, and my people the children of Israel, out of the land of Egypt, by great judgments. And the Egyptians shall know that I am the Lord, when I stretch forth mine hand upon Egypt, and bring out the children of Israel from among them." And Moses and Aaron did as the Lord commanded them, so did they. And Moses was fourscore years old, and Aaron fourscore and three years old, when they spake unto Pharaoh.

And the Lord spake unto Moses, and unto Aaron, saying, "When Pharaoh shall speak unto you, saying, 'Show a miracle for you': then thou shalt say unto Aaron, 'Take thy rod and cast it before Pharaoh, and it shall become a serpent.'"

And Moses and Aaron went in unto Pharaoh, and they did so as the Lord had commanded: and Aaron cast down his rod before Pharaoh, and before his servants, and it became a serpent. Then Pharaoh also called the wise men and the sorcerers: now the magicians of Egypt, they also did in like manner with their enchantments. For they cast down every man his rod, and they became serpents: but Aaron's rod swallowed up their rods. And he hardened Pharaoh's heart, that he hearkened not unto them, as the Lord had said.

And the Lord said unto Moses, "Pharaoh's heart is hardened: he refuseth to let the people go. Get thee unto Pharaoh in the morning, lo, he goeth out unto the water, and thou shalt stand by the river's brink against[7] he come: and the rod which was turned to a serpent shalt thou take in thine hand. And thou shalt say unto him, 'The Lord God of the Hebrews hath sent me unto thee, saying, "Let my people go, that they may serve me in the wilderness": and behold, hitherto thou wouldest not hear.' Thus saith the Lord, 'In this thou shalt know that I am the Lord: behold, I will smite with the rod that is in my hand upon the waters which are in the river, and they shall be turned to blood. And the fish that is in the river shall die, and the river shall stink, and the Egyptians shall loathe to drink of the water of the river.' "

And the Lord spake unto Moses, "Say unto Aaron, 'Take thy rod, and stretch out thine hand upon the waters of Egypt, upon their streams, upon their rivers, and upon their ponds, and upon all their pools of water, that they may become blood, and that there may be blood throughout all the land of Egypt, both in vessels of wood, and in vessels of stone.' " And Moses and Aaron did so, as the Lord commanded: and he lifted up the rod and smote the waters that were in the river, in the sight of Pharaoh, and in the sight of his servants: and all the waters that were in the river were turned to blood. And the fish that was in the river died: and the river stank, and the Egyptians could not drink of the water of the river: and there was blood throughout all the land of Egypt. And the magicians of Egypt did so with their enchantments: and Pharaoh's heart was hardened, neither did he hearken unto them, as the Lord had said. And Pharaoh turned and went into his house, neither did he set his heart to this also. And all the Egyptians digged round about the river for water to drink: for they could not drink of the water of the river. And seven days were fulfilled after that the Lord had smitten the river.

8 And the Lord spake unto Moses, "Go unto Pharaoh, and say unto him, 'Thus saith the Lord, "Let my people go, that they may serve me." And if thou refuse to let them go, behold, I will

[7] I.e., until.

smite all thy borders with frogs. And the river shall bring forth frogs abundantly, which shall go up and come into thine house, and into thy bedchamber, and upon thy bed, and into the house of thy servants, and upon thy people, and into thine ovens, and into thy kneading troughs. And the frogs shall come up both on thee, and upon thy people, and upon all thy servants.' "

And the Lord spake unto Moses, "Say unto Aaron, 'Stretch forth thine hand with thy rod over the streams, over the rivers, and over the ponds, and cause frogs to come up upon the land of Egypt.' " And Aaron stretched out his hand over the waters of Egypt, and the frogs came up, and covered the land of Egypt. And the magicians did so with their enchantments, and brought up frogs upon the land of Egypt.

Then Pharaoh called for Moses, and Aaron, and said, "Entreat the Lord, that he may take away the frogs from me, and from my people: and I will let the people go, that they may do sacrifice unto the Lord." And Moses said unto Pharaoh, "Glory over me: when shall I entreat for thee, and for thy servants, and for thy people, to destroy the frogs from thee, and thy houses, that they may remain in the river only?" And he said, "Tomorrow." And he said, "Be it according to thy word: that thou mayest know that there is none like unto the Lord our God. And the frogs shall depart from thee, and from thy houses, and from thy servants, and from thy people; they shall remain in the river only." And Moses and Aaron went out from Pharaoh, and Moses cried unto the Lord because of the frogs which he had brought against Pharaoh. And the Lord did according to the word of Moses: and the frogs died out of the houses, out of the villages, and out of the fields. And they gathered them together upon heaps, and the land stank. But when Pharaoh saw that there was respite, he hardened his heart, and hearkened not unto them, as the Lord had said.

And the Lord said unto Moses, "Say unto Aaron, 'Stretch out thy rod, and smite the dust of the land, that it may become lice throughout all the land of Egypt.' " And they did so: for Aaron stretched out his hand with his rod, and smote the dust of the earth, and it became lice, in man and in beast: all the dust of the land became lice throughout all the land of Egypt. And the magicians did so with their enchantments to bring forth lice, but they could not: so there were lice upon man and upon beast. Then the magicians said unto Pharaoh, "This is the finger of God." And Pharaoh's heart was hardened, and he hearkened not unto them, as the Lord had said.

And the Lord said unto Moses, "Rise up early in the morning, and stand before Pharoah: lo, he cometh forth to the water, and say unto him, 'Thus saith the Lord, "Let my people go, that they may serve me. Else, if thou wilt not let my people go, behold, I will send swarms of flies upon thee, and upon thy servants, and upon thy people, and into thy houses: and the houses of the Egyptians shall be full of swarms of flies, and also the ground whereon they are. And I will sever in that day the land of Goshen in which my people dwell, that no swarms of flies shall be there, to the end thou mayest know that I am the Lord in the midst of the earth. And I will put a division between my people and thy people: tomorrow shall this sign be." ' " And the Lord did so: and there came a grievous swarm of flies into the house of Pharaoh, and into his servants' houses, and into all the land of Egypt: the land was corrupted by reason of the swarm of flies.

And Pharaoh called for Moses and for Aaron, and said, "Go ye, sacrifice to your God in the land." And Moses said, "It is not meet so to do; for we shall sacrifice the abomination[8] of the Egyptians to the Lord our God: lo, shall we sacrifice the abomination of the Egyptians before their eyes, and will they not stone us? We will go three days' journey into the wilderness, and sacrifice to the Lord our God, as he shall command us." And the Pharaoh said, "I will let you go that ye may sacrifice to the Lord your God in the wilderness: only you shall not go very far away: entreat for me." And Moses said, "Behold, I go out from thee, and I will entreat the Lord that the swarms of flies may depart from Pharaoh, from his servants, and from his people tomorrow: but let not Pharaoh deal deceitfully any more in not letting the people go to sacrifice to the Lord." And Moses went out from Pharaoh, and entreated the Lord: and the Lord did according to the word of Moses: and he removed the swarms of flies from Pharoah, from his servants, and from his people: there remained not one. And Pharaoh hardened his heart at this time also, neither would he let the people go.

[8] Apparently animal sacrifices would, at this time, have been offensive to the Egyptians.

9 Then the Lord said unto Moses, "Go in unto Pharaoh, and tell him, 'Thus saith the Lord God of the Hebrews, "Let my people go, that they may serve me. For if thou refuse to let them go, and wilt hold them still, behold, the hand of the Lord is upon thy cattle which is in the field, upon the horses, upon the asses, upon the camels, upon the oxen, and upon the sheep: there shall be a very grievous murrain.[9] And the Lord shall sever between the cattle of Israel and the cattle of Egypt, and there shall nothing die of all that is the children's of Israel." ' " And the Lord appointed a set time, saying, "Tomorrow the Lord shall do this thing in the land." And the Lord did that thing on the morrow; and all the cattle of Egypt died, but of the cattle of the children of Israel died not one. And Pharaoh sent, and behold, there was not one of the cattle of the Israelites dead. And the heart of Pharaoh was hardened, and he did not let the people go.

And the Lord said unto Moses and unto Aaron, "Take to you handfuls of ashes of the furnace, and let Moses sprinkle it toward the heaven, in the sight of Pharaoh: and it shall become small dust in all the land of Egypt, and shall be a boil breaking forth with blains[10] upon man, and upon beast, throughout all the land of Egypt." And they took ashes of the furnace, and stood before Pharaoh, and Moses sprinkled it up toward heaven: and it became a boil breaking forth with blains upon man and upon beast. And the magicians could not stand before Moses, because of the boils: for the boil was upon the magicians, and upon all the Egyptians. And the Lord hardened the heart of Pharaoh, and he hearkened not unto them, as the Lord had spoken unto Moses.

And the Lord said unto Moses, "Rise up early in the morning, and stand before Pharaoh, and say unto him, 'Thus saith the Lord God of the Hebrews, "Let my people go, that they may serve me. For I will at this time send all my plagues upon thine heart, and upon thy servants, and upon thy people: that thou mayest know that there is none like me in all the earth. For now I will stretch out my hand, that I may smite thee and thy people with pestilence, and thou shalt be cut off from the earth. And in very deed for this cause have I raised thee up, for to show in thee my power, and that my name

[9] A plague affecting cattle: similar to anthrax.
[10] Inflammatory sores.

may be declared throughout all the earth. As yet exaltest thou thyself against my people, that thou wilt not let them go? Behold, tomorrow about this time I will cause it to rain a very grievous hail, such as hath not been in Egypt, since the foundation thereof even until now. Send therefore now, and gather thy cattle, and all that thou hast in the field: for upon every man and beast which shall be found in the field, and shall not be brought home, the hail shall come down upon them, and they shall die." ' " He that feared the word of the Lord amongst the servants of Pharaoh made his servants and his cattle flee into the houses. And he that regarded not the word of the Lord left his servants and his cattle in the field.

And the Lord said unto Moses, "Stretch forth thine hand toward heaven, that there may be hail in all the land of Egypt, upon man and upon beast, and upon every herb of the field, throughout the land of Egypt." And Moses stretched forth his rod toward heaven, and the Lord sent thunder and hail, and the fire ran along upon the ground, and the Lord rained hail upon the land of Egypt. So there was hail, and fire mingled with the hail, very grievous, such as there was none like it in all the land of Egypt, since it became a nation. And the hail smote throughout all the land of Egypt all that was in the field, both man and beast: and the hail smote every herb of the field, and brake every tree of the field. Only in the land of Goshen where the children of Israel were, was there no hail.

And Pharaoh sent, and called for Moses and Aaron, and said unto them, "I have sinned this time: the Lord is righteous, and I and my people are wicked. Entreat the Lord (for it is enough) that there be no more mighty thunderings and hail, and I will let you go, and ye shall stay no longer." And Moses said unto him, "As soon as I am gone out of the city, I will spread abroad my hands unto the Lord, and the thunder shall cease, neither shall there be any more hail: that thou mayest know how that the earth is the Lord's. But as for thee and thy servants, I know that ye will not yet fear the Lord God." And the flax and the barley was smitten: for the barley was in the ear, and the flax was bolled:[11] but the wheat and the rye were not smitten: for they were not grown up. And Moses went out of the city from Pharaoh, and spread abroad his hands unto the Lord: and the thunders and hail ceased, and the rain was not poured upon the earth. And when Pharaoh saw that the rain and the hail and the

[11] *I.e.*, in bud.

thunders were ceased, he sinned yet more, and hardened his heart, he and his servants. And the heart of Pharaoh was hardened, neither would he let the children of Israel go, as the Lord had spoken by Moses.

10 And the Lord said unto Moses, "Go in unto Pharaoh: for I have hardened his heart, and the heart of his servants, that I might show these my signs before him: and that thou mayest tell in the ears of thy son, and of thy son's son, what things I have wrought in Egypt, and my signs which I have done amongst them, that ye may know how that I am the Lord." And Moses and Aaron came in unto Pharaoh, and said unto him, "Thus saith the Lord God of the Hebrews, 'How long wilt thou refuse to humble thyself before me? Let my people go, that they may serve me. Else, if thou refuse to let my people go, behold, tomorrow will I bring the locusts into thy coast. And they shall cover the face of the earth, that one cannot be able to see the earth, and they shall eat the residue of that which is escaped, which remaineth unto you from the hail, and shall eat every tree which groweth for you out of the field. And they shall fill thy houses, and the houses of all thy servants, and the houses of all the Egyptians, which neither thy fathers, nor thy fathers' fathers have seen, since the day that they were upon the earth unto this day.' " And he turned himself, and went out from Pharaoh. And Pharaoh's servants said unto him, "How long shall this man be a snare unto us? Let the men go, that they may serve the Lord their God: knowest thou not yet that Egypt is destroyed?" And Moses and Aaron were brought again unto Pharaoh: and he said unto them, "Go, serve the Lord your God: but who are they that shall go?" And Moses said, "We will go with our young, and with our old, with our sons and with our daughters, with our flocks and with our herds will we go: for we must hold a feast unto the Lord." And he said unto them, "Let the Lord be so with you, as I will let you go, and your little ones. Look to it, for evil is before you. Not so: go now ye that are men, and serve the Lord, for that you did desire." [12] And they were driven out from Pharaoh's presence.

[12] The Revised Standard Version thus gives Pharaoh's speech: "The Lord be with you, if ever I let you and your little ones go! Look, you have some evil purpose in mind. No! Go, the men among you, and serve the Lord, for that is what you desire."

And the Lord said unto Moses, "Stretch out thine hand over the land of Egypt for the locusts, that they may come up upon the land of Egypt, and eat every herb of the land, even all that the hail hath left." And Moses stretched forth his rod over the land of Egypt, and the Lord brought an east wind upon the land all that day, and all that night: and when it was morning, the east wind brought the locusts. And the locusts went up over all the land of Egypt, and rested in all the coasts of Egypt: very grievous were they: before them there were no such locusts as they, neither after them shall be such. For they covered the face of the whole earth, so that the land was darkened, and they did eat every herb of the land, and all the fruit of the trees which the hail had left, and there remained not any green thing in the trees, or in the herbs of the field, through all the land of Egypt.

Then Pharaoh called for Moses and Aaron in haste: and he said, "I have sinned against the Lord your God, and against you. Now therefore forgive, I pray thee, my sin only this once, and entreat the Lord your God, that he may take away from me this death only." And he went out from Pharaoh, and entreated the Lord. And the Lord turned a mighty strong west wind, which took away the locusts, and cast them into the Red Sea: there remained not one locust in all the coasts of Egypt. But the Lord hardened Pharaoh's heart, so that he would not let the children of Israel go.

And the Lord said unto Moses, "Stretch out thine hand toward heaven, that there may be darkness over the land of Egypt, even darkness which may be felt." And Moses stretched forth his hand toward heaven: and there was a thick darkness in all the land of Egypt three days. They saw not one another, neither rose any from his place for three days: but all the children of Israel had light in their dwellings.

And Pharaoh called unto Moses, and said, "Go ye, serve the Lord: only let your flocks and your herds be stayed: let your little ones also go with you." And Moses said, "Thou must give us also sacrifices, and burnt offerings, that we may sacrifice unto the Lord our God. Our cattle also shall go with us: there shall not an hoof be left behind: for thereof must we take to serve the Lord our God; and we know not with what we must serve the Lord, until we come thither."

But the Lord hardened Pharaoh's heart, and he would not let them go. And Pharaoh said unto him, "Get thee from me, take heed to thyself: see my face no more: for in that day thou seest my face, thou shalt die." And Moses said, "Thou hast spoken well, I will see thy face again no more."

11 And the Lord said unto Moses, "Yet will I bring one plague more upon Pharaoh, and upon Egypt; afterwards he will let you go hence: when he shall let you go, he shall surely thrust you out hence altogether. Speak now in the ears of the people, and let every man borrow of his neighbour, and every woman of her neighbour, jewels of silver, and jewels of gold." And the Lord gave the people favour in the sight of the Egyptians. Moreover the man Moses was very great in the land of Egypt, in the sight of Pharaoh's servants, and in the sight of the people. And Moses said, "Thus saith the Lord, 'About midnight will I go out into the midst of Egypt. And all the firstborn in the land of Egypt shall die, from the firstborn of Pharaoh that sitteth upon his throne, even unto the firstborn of the maidservant that is behind the mill, and all the firstborn of beasts. And there shall be a great cry throughout all the land of Egypt, such as there was none like it, nor shall be like it any more. But against any of the children of Israel shall not a dog move his tongue, against man or beast: that ye may know how that the Lord doth put a difference between the Egyptians and Israel. And all these thy servants shall come down unto me, and bow down themselves unto me, saying, "Get thee out, and all the people that follow thee": and after that I will go out.' " And he went out from Pharaoh in a great anger. And the Lord said unto Moses, "Pharaoh shall not hearken unto you, that my wonders may be multiplied in the land of Egypt." And Moses and Aaron did all these wonders before Pharaoh: and the Lord hardened Pharaoh's heart, so that he would not let the children of Israel go out of his land.

12 And the Lord spake unto Moses and Aaron in the land of Egypt, saying, "This month shall be unto you the beginning of months: it shall be the first month of the year to you.

"Speak ye unto all the congregation of Israel, saying, 'In the tenth day of this month they shall take to them every man a lamb, according to the house of their fathers, a lamb for an house. And if the household be too little for the lamb, let him and his neighbour next unto his house take it according to the number of the souls: every man according to his eating shall make your count for the lamb. Your lamb shall be without blemish, a male of the first year: ye shall take it out from the sheep or from the goats. And ye shall keep it up until the fourteenth day of the same month: and the whole assembly of the congregation of Israel shall kill it in the evening. And they shall take of the blood and strike it on the two side posts and on the upper door post of the houses wherein they shall eat it. And they shall eat the flesh in that night roast with fire, and unleavened bread, and with bitter herbs they shall eat it. Eat not of it raw, nor sodden at all with water, but roast with fire: his head, with his legs, and with the purtenance thereof. And ye shall let nothing of it remain until the morning: and that which remaineth of it until the morning ye shall burn with fire.

" 'And thus shall ye eat it: with your loins girded, your shoes on your feet, and your staff in your hand: and ye shall eat it in haste: it is the Lord's Passover. For I will pass through the land of Egypt this night, and will smite all the firstborn in the land of Egypt, both man and beast, and against all the gods of Egypt I will execute judgment: I am the Lord. And the blood shall be to you for a token upon the houses where you are: and when I see the blood, I will pass over you, and the plague shall not be upon you to destroy you, when I smite the land of Egypt. And this day shall be unto you for a memorial: and you shall keep it a feast to the Lord, throughout your generations: you shall keep it a feast by an ordinance for ever. Seven days shall ye eat unleavened bread, even the first day ye shall put away leaven out of your houses: for whosoever eateth leavened bread, from the first day until the seventh day, that soul shall be cut off from Israel. And in the first day there shall be an holy convocation, and in the seventh day there shall be an holy convocation to you: no manner of work shall be done in them, save that which every man must eat, that only may be done of you. And ye shall observe the feast of unleavened bread: for in this selfsame day have I brought your armies out of the land of Egypt; therefore shall ye observe this day in your generations by an ordinance for ever.

" 'In the first month, on the fourteenth day of the month at even, ye shall eat unleavened bread until the one and twentieth day of the month at even. Seven days shall there be no leaven found in your houses: for whosoever eateth that which is leavened, even that soul shall be cut off from the congregation of Israel, whether he be a stranger, or born in the land. Ye shall eat nothing leavened: in all your habitations shall ye eat unleavened bread.'"

Then Moses called for all the elders of Israel, and said unto them, "Draw out and take you a lamb, according to your families, and kill the Passover.[13] And ye shall take a bunch of hyssop, and dip it in the blood that is in the basin, and strike the lintel and the two side posts with the blood that is in the basin: and none of you shall go out at the door of his house until the morning. For the Lord will pass through to smite the Egyptians: and when he seeth the blood upon the lintel, and on the two side posts, the Lord will pass over the door, and will not suffer the destroyer to come in unto your houses to smite you. And ye shall observe this thing for an ordinance to thee and to thy sons for ever. And it shall come to pass when ye be come to the land, which the Lord will give you, according as he hath promised, that ye shall keep this service. And it shall come to pass, when your children shall say unto you, 'What mean ye by this service?' that ye shall say, 'It is the sacrifice of the Lord's Passover, who passed over the houses of the children of Israel in Egypt, when he smote the Egyptians, and delivered our houses.'" And the people bowed the head, and worshipped. And the children of Israel went away, and did as the Lord had commanded Moses and Aaron, so did they.

And it came to pass that at midnight the Lord smote all the firstborn in the land of Egypt, from the firstborn of Pharaoh that sat on his throne, unto the firstborn of the captive that was in the dungeon, and all the firstborn of cattle. And Pharaoh rose up in the night, he and all his servants, and all the Egyptians; and there was a great cry in Egypt: for there was not a house where there was not one dead.

And he called for Moses and Aaron by night, and said, "Rise up, and get you forth from amongst my people, both you and the children of Israel: and go, serve the Lord, as ye have said. Also take your flocks and your herds, as ye have said: and be gone, and bless me also." And the Egyptians were urgent upon the people that they might send them out of the land in haste: for they said, "We be all dead men." And the people took their dough before it was leavened, their kneading troughs being bound up in their clothes upon their shoulders. And the children of Israel did according to the word of

[13] *I.e.,* the Passover lamb.

Moses: and they borrowed of the Egyptians jewels of silver, and jewels of gold, and raiment. And the Lord gave the people favour in the sight of the Egyptians, so that they lent unto them such things as they required: and they spoiled the Egyptians.

And the children of Israel journeyed from Rameses to Succoth, about six hundred thousand on foot that were men, besides children. And a mixed multitude went up also with them, and flocks and herds, even very much cattle. And they baked unleavened cakes of the dough, which they brought forth out of Egypt; for it was not leavened: because they were thrust out of Egypt, and could not tarry, neither had they prepared for themselves any victual.

Now the sojourning of the children of Israel, who dwelt in Egypt, was four hundred and thirty years. And it came to pass at the end of the four hundred and thirty years, even the selfsame day it came to pass, that all the hosts of the Lord went out from the land of Egypt. It is a night to be much observed unto the Lord, for bringing them out from the land of Egypt: this is that night of the Lord to be observed of all the children of Israel, in their generations.

And the Lord said unto Moses and Aaron, "This is the ordinance of the Passover: there shall no stranger eat thereof. But every man's servant that is bought for money, when thou hast circumcised him, then shall he eat thereof. A foreigner and an hired servant shall not eat thereof. In one house shall it be eaten, thou shalt not carry forth aught of the flesh abroad out of the house, neither shall ye break a bone thereof. All the congregation of Israel shall keep it. And when a stranger shall sojourn with thee, and will keep the Passover to the Lord, let all his males be circumcised, and then let him come near, and keep it: and he shall be as one that is born in the land: for no uncircumcised person shall eat thereof. One law shall be to him that is homeborn, and unto the stranger that sojourneth among you." Thus did all the children of Israel: as the Lord commanded Moses and Aaron, so did they. And it came to pass the selfsame day, that the Lord did bring the children of Israel out of the land of Egypt by their armies.[14]

13 And the Lord spake unto Moses, saying, "Sanctify unto me all the firstborn, whatsoever openeth the womb, among the children of Israel, both of man and of beast: it is mine."

[14] I.e., in large numbers.

And Moses said unto the people, "Remember this day, in which ye came out from Egypt, out of the house of bondage: for by strength of hand the Lord brought you out from this place: there shall no leavened bread be eaten. This day came ye out, in the month Abib.[15]

"And it shall be when the Lord shall bring thee into the land of the Canaanites, and the Hittites, and the Amorites, and the Hivites, and the Jebusites, which he sware unto thy fathers to give thee, a land flowing with milk and honey, that thou shalt keep this service in this month. Seven days thou shalt eat unleavened bread, and in the seventh day shall be a feast to the Lord. Unleavened bread shall be eaten seven days: and there shall no leavened bread be seen with thee: neither shall there be leaven seen with thee in all thy quarters.

"And thou shalt show thy son in that day, saying, 'This is done because of that which the Lord did unto me, when I came forth out of Egypt. And it shall be for a sign unto thee, upon thine hand, and for a memorial between thine eyes, that the Lord's law may be in thy mouth: for with a strong hand hath the Lord brought thee out of Egypt. Thou shalt therefore keep this ordinance in his season from year to year.'

"And it shall be when the Lord shall bring thee into the land of the Canaanites as he sware unto thee, and to thy fathers, and shall give it thee: that thou shalt set apart unto the Lord all that openeth the matrix, and every firstling that cometh of a beast which thou hast, the males shall be the Lord's. And every firstling of an ass thou shalt redeem with a lamb: and if thou wilt not redeem it, then thou shalt break his neck, and all the first born of man amongst thy children shalt thou redeem.

"And it shall be when thy son asketh thee in time to come, saying, 'What is this?' that thou shalt say unto him, 'By strength of hand the Lord brought us out from Egypt, from the house of bondage. And it came to pass when Pharaoh would hardly let us go, that the Lord slew all the firstborn in the land of Egypt, both the firstborn of man, and the firstborn of beast: therefore I sacrifice to the Lord all that openeth the matrix, being males: but all the firstborn of my children I redeem. And it shall be for a token upon thine hand, and for frontlets between thine eyes. For by strength of hand the Lord brought us forth out of Egypt.' "

[15] The Hebrew month of Nisan: *i.e.*, March-April.

And it came to pass when Pharaoh had let the people go, that God led them not through the way of the land of the Philistines, although that was near: for God said, "Lest peradventure the people repent when they see war, and they return to Egypt": but God led the people about through the way of the wilderness of the Red Sea: and the children of Israel went up harnessed[16] out of the land of Egypt. And Moses took the bones of Joseph with him: for he had straitly sworn the children of Israel, saying, "God will surely visit you, and ye shall carry up my bones away hence with you."

And they took their journey from Succoth, and encamped in Etham, in the edge of the wilderness. And the Lord went before them by day in a pillar of cloud to lead them the way; and by night in a pillar of fire, to give them light; to go by day and night. He took not away the pillar of the cloud by day, nor the pillar of fire by night, from before the people.

14 And the Lord spake unto Moses, saying, "Speak unto the children of Israel, that they turn and encamp before Pi-hahiroth, between Migdol and the sea, over against Baal-zephon: before it shall ye encamp by the sea. For Pharaoh will say of the children of Israel, 'They are entangled in the land, the wilderness hath shut them in.' And I will harden Pharaoh's heart, that he shall follow after them, and I will be honoured upon Pharaoh, and upon all his host, that the Egyptians may know that I am the Lord." And they did so.

And it was told the king of Egypt, that the people fled: and the heart of Pharaoh and of his servants was turned against the people, and they said, "Why have we done this, that we have let Israel go from serving us?" And he made ready his chariot, and took his people with him. And he took six hundred chosen chariots, and all the chariots of Egypt, and captains over every one of them. And the Lord hardened the heart of Pharaoh king of Egypt, and he pursued after the children of Israel: and the children of Israel went out with an high hand. But the Egyptians pursued after them (all the horses and chariots of Pharaoh, and his horsemen, and his army) and overtook them encamping by the sea, beside Pi-hahiroth, before Baal-zephon.

[16] "Harnessed" here means either equipped for battle, or in groups of fives and fifties.

And when Pharaoh drew nigh, the children of Israel lifted up their eyes, and behold, the Egyptians marched after them, and they were sore afraid: and the children of Israel cried out unto the Lord. And they said unto Moses, "Because there were no graves in Egypt, hast thou taken us away to die in the wilderness? Wherefore hast thou dealt thus with us, to carry us forth out of Egypt? Is not this the word that we did tell thee in Egypt, saying, 'Let us alone, that we may serve the Egyptians?' For it had been better for us to serve the Egyptians, than that we should die in the wilderness."

And Moses said unto the people, "Fear ye not, stand still, and see the salvation of the Lord, which he will show to you today: for the Egyptians whom ye have seen today, ye shall see them again no more for ever. The Lord shall fight for you, and ye shall hold your peace."

And the Lord said unto Moses, "Wherefore criest thou unto me? Speak unto the children of Israel, that they go forward: but lift thou up thy rod, and stretch out thine hand over the sea, and divide it: and the children of Israel shall go on dry ground through the midst of the sea. And I, behold, I will harden the hearts of the Egyptians, and they shall follow them: and I will get me honour upon Pharaoh, and upon all his host, upon his chariots, and upon his horsemen. And the Egyptians shall know that I am the Lord, when I have gotten me honour upon Pharaoh, upon his chariots, and upon his horsemen."

And the angel of God, which went before the camp of Israel, removed and went behind them, and the pillar of the cloud went from before their face, and stood behind them. And it came between the camp of the Egyptians and the camp of Israel, and it was a cloud and darkness to them, but it gave light by night to these: so that the one came not near the other all the night. And Moses stretched out his hand over the sea, and the Lord caused the sea to go back by a strong east wind all that night, and made the sea dry land, and the waters were divided. And the children of Israel went into the midst of the sea upon the dry ground, and the waters were a wall unto them on their right hand, and on their left.

And the Egyptians pursued, and went in after them, to the midst of the sea, even all Pharaoh's horses, his chariots, and his horsemen. And it came to pass, that in the morning watch the Lord looked unto the host of the Egyptians, through the pillar of fire and of the cloud, and troubled the host of the Egyptians, and took off their chariot wheels, that they drave them heavily: so that the Egyptians said, "Let us flee from the face of Israel: for the Lord fighteth for them against the Egyptians."

And the Lord said unto Moses, "Stretch out thine hand over the sea, that the waters may come again upon the Egyptians, upon their chariots, and upon their horsemen." And Moses stretched forth his hand over the sea, and the sea returned to his strength when the morning appeared: and the Egyptians fled against it: and the Lord overthrew the Egyptians in the midst of the sea. And the waters returned, and covered the chariots, and the horsemen, and all the host of Pharaoh that came into the sea after them: there remained not so much as one of them. But the children of Israel walked upon dry land, in the midst of the sea, and the waters were a wall unto them on their right hand, and on their left. Thus the Lord saved Israel that day out of the hand of the Egyptians: and Israel saw the Egyptians dead upon the sea shore. And Israel saw that great work which the Lord did upon the Egyptians: and the people feared the Lord, and believed the Lord, and his servant Moses.

15 Then sang Moses and the children of Israel this song unto the Lord, and spake, saying, "I will sing unto the Lord: for he hath triumphed gloriously, the horse and his rider hath he thrown into the sea.

The Lord is my strength and song, and he is become my salvation: he is my God, and I will prepare him an habitation, my father's God, and I will exalt him.

The Lord is a man of war: the Lord is his name.

Pharaoh's chariots and his host hath he cast into the sea: his chosen captains also are drowned in the Red Sea.

The depths have covered them: they sank into the bottom as a stone.

Thy right hand, O Lord, is become glorious in power, thy right hand, O Lord, hath dashed in pieces the enemy.

And in the greatness of thine excellency thou hast overthrown them that rose up against thee: thou sentest forth thy wrath, which consumed them as stubble.

And with the blast of thy nostrils the waters were gathered together: the floods stood upright as an heap, and the depths were congealed in the heart of the sea.

The enemy said, 'I will pursue, I will overtake, I will divide the spoil: my lust shall be satisfied upon them: I will draw my sword, mine hand shall destroy them.'

Thou didst blow with thy wind, the sea covered them, they sank as lead in the mighty waters.

Who is like unto thee, O Lord, amongst the gods? who is like thee, glorious in holiness, fearful in praises, doing wonders!

Thou stretchedst out thy right hand, the earth swallowed them.

Thou in thy mercy hast led forth the people which thou hast redeemed: thou hast guided them in thy strength unto thy holy habitation.

The people shall hear, and be afraid: sorrow shall take hold on the inhabitants of Palestina,

Then the dukes of Edom shall be amazed: the mighty men of Moab, trembling shall take hold upon them: all the inhabitants of Canaan shall melt away.

Fear and dread shall fall upon them, by the greatness of thine arm then shall be as still as a stone, till thy people pass over, O Lord, till the people pass over, which thou hast purchased.

Thou shalt bring them in, and plant them in the mountain of thine inheritance, in the place, O Lord, which thou hast made for thee to dwell in, in the sanctuary, O Lord, which thy hands have established.

The Lord shall reign for ever and ever.

For the horse of Pharaoh went in with his chariots and with his horsemen into the sea, and the Lord brought again the waters of the sea upon them: but the children of Israel went on dry land in the midst of the sea."

And Miriam the prophetess, the sister of Aaron, took a timbrel in her hand, and all the women went out after her, with timbrels and with dances. And Miriam answered them, "Sing ye to the Lord, for he hath triumphed gloriously: the horse and his rider hath he thrown into the sea." So Moses brought Israel from the Red Sea, and they went out into the wilderness of Shur: and they went three days in the wilderness, and found no water.

And when they came to Marah, they could not drink of the waters of Marah, for they were bitter: therefore the name of it was called Marah. And the people murmured against Moses, saying, "What shall we drink?" And he cried unto the Lord: and the Lord showed him a tree, which when he had cast into the waters, the waters were made sweet: there he made for them a statute and an ordinance, and there he proved[17] them, and said, "If thou wilt diligently hearken to the voice of the Lord thy God, and wilt do that which is right in his sight, and wilt give ear to his commandments, and keep all his statutes, I will put none of these diseases upon thee, which I have brought upon the Egyptians: for I am the Lord that healeth thee."

And they came to Elim, where were twelve wells of water, and threescore and ten palm trees, and they encamped there by the waters.

16 And they took their journey from Elim, and all the congregation of the children of Israel came unto the wilderness of Sin, which is between Elim and Sinai, on the fifteenth day of the second month after their departing out of the land of Egypt. And the whole congregation of the children of Israel murmured against Moses and Aaron in the wilderness. And the children of Israel said unto them, "Would to God we had died by the hand of the Lord in the land of Egypt, when we sat by the flesh pots, and when we did eat bread to the full: for ye have brought us forth into this wilderness, to kill this whole assembly with hunger."

Then said the Lord unto Moses, "Behold, I will rain bread from heaven for you: and the people shall go out, and gather a certain rate every day, that I may prove them, whether they will walk in my law, or no. And it shall come to pass, that on the sixth day they shall prepare that which they bring in, and it shall be twice as much as they gather daily." And Moses and Aaron said unto all the children of Israel, "At even, then ye shall know that the Lord hath brought you out from the land of Egypt. And in the morning, then ye shall see the glory of the Lord, for that he heareth your murmurings against the Lord: and what are we, that ye murmur against us?" And Moses said, "This shall be when the Lord shall give you in the evening flesh to eat, and in the morning bread to the full: for that the Lord heareth your murmurings which ye murmur against him; and what are we? your murmurings are not against us, but against the Lord."

And Moses spake unto Aaron, "Say unto all the congregation of

17 *I.e.,* tested.

the children of Israel, 'Come near before the Lord: for he hath heard your murmurings.'" And it came to pass as Aaron spake unto the whole congregation of the children of Israel, that they looked toward the wilderness, and behold, the glory of the Lord appeared in the cloud.

And the Lord spake unto Moses, saying, "I have heard the murmurings of the children of Israel: speak unto them, saying, 'At even ye shall eat flesh, and in the morning ye shall be filled with bread: and ye shall know that I am the Lord your God.'" And it came to pass, that at even the quails came up, and covered the camp: and in the morning the dew lay round about the host. And when the dew that lay was gone up, behold, upon the face of the wilderness there lay a small round thing, as small as the hoar frost on the ground. And when the children of Israel saw it, they said one to another, "It is manna": for they wist not what it was. And Moses said unto them, "This is the bread which the Lord hath given you to eat.

"This is the thing which the Lord hath commanded: 'Gather of it every man according to his eating: an omer[18] for every man, according to the number of your persons, take ye every man for them which are in his tents.'" And the children of Israel did so, and gathered, some more, some less. And when they did mete it with an omer, he that gathered much had nothing over, and he that gathered little had no lack: they gathered every man according to his eating. And Moses said, "Let no man leave of it till the morning." Notwithstanding they hearkened not unto Moses, but some of them left of it until the morning, and it bred worms, and stank: and Moses was wroth with them. And they gathered it every morning, every man according to his eating: and when the sun waxed hot it melted.

And it came to pass that on the sixth day they gathered twice as much bread, two omers for one man: and all the rulers of the congregation came and told Moses. And he said unto them, "This is that which the Lord hath said, 'Tomorrow is the rest of the holy sabbath unto the Lord: bake that which you will bake today, and seethe[19] that ye will seethe, and that which remaineth over lay up for you to be kept until the morning.'" And they laid it up till the morning, as Moses bade: and it did not stink, neither was there any worm

[18] Approximately 7 pints.
[19] *I.e.,* boil.

therein. And Moses said, "Eat that today, for today is a sabbath unto the Lord: today ye shall not find it in the field. Six days ye shall gather it, but on the seventh day, which is the sabbath, in it there shall be none."

And it came to pass, that there went out some of the people on the seventh day for to gather, and they found none. And the Lord said unto Moses, "How long refuse ye to keep my commandments and my laws? See, for that the Lord hath given you the sabbath, therefore he giveth you on the sixth day the bread of two days: abide ye every man in his place: let no man go out of his place on the seventh day." So the people rested on the seventh day. And the house of Israel called the name thereof manna: and it was like coriander seed, white: and the taste of it was like wafers made with honey.

And Moses said, "This is the thing which the Lord commandeth: 'Fill an omer of it to be kept for your generations, that they may see the bread wherewith I have fed you in the wilderness, when I brought you forth from the land of Egypt.'" And Moses said unto Aaron, "Take a pot, and put an omer full of manna therein, and lay it up before the Lord, to be kept for your generations." As the Lord commanded Moses, so Aaron laid it up before the testimony,[20] to be kept. And the children of Israel did eat manna forty years, until they came to a land inhabited: they did eat manna, until they came unto the borders of the land of Canaan. Now an omer is the tenth part of an ephah.

17 And all the congregation of the children of Israel journeyed from the wilderness of Sin, after their journeys, according to the commandment of the Lord, and pitched in Rephidim: and there was no water for the people to drink. Wherefore the people did chide with Moses and said, "Give us water that we may drink." And Moses said unto them, "Why chide you with me? Wherefore do ye tempt the Lord?" And the people thirsted there for water, and the people murmured against Moses, and said, "Wherefore is this that thou hast brought us up out of Egypt, to kill us and our children and our cattle with thirst?" And Moses cried unto the Lord, saying, "What shall I do unto this people? they be almost ready to stone me." And the Lord said unto Moses, "Go on before the people, and take with

[20] I.e., the ark or sacred box in which certain holy objects were kept. (See the Introduction to the Saul-David story.)

thee of the elders of Israel; and thy rod, wherewith thou smotest the river, take in thine hand, and go. Behold, I will stand before thee there, upon the rock in Horeb, and thou shalt smite the rock, and there shall come water out of it, that the people may drink." And Moses did so, in the sight of the elders of Israel. And he called the name of the place Massah, and Meribah, because of the chiding of the children of Israel and because they tempted the Lord, saying, "Is the Lord amongst us, or not?"

Then came Amalek, and fought with Israel in Rephidim. And Moses said unto Joshua, "Choose us out men, and go out, fight with Amalek: tomorrow I will stand on the top of the hill, with the rod of God in mine hand." So Joshua did as Moses had said to him, and fought with Amalek: and Moses, Aaron, and Hur went up to the top of the hill. And it came to pass when Moses held up his hand, that Israel prevailed: and when he let down his hand, Amalek prevailed. But Moses' hands were heavy, and they took a stone, and put it under him, and he sat thereon: and Aaron and Hur stayed up his hands, the one on the one side, and the other on the other side, and his hands were steady until the going down of the sun. And Joshua discomfited Amalek, and his people, with the edge of the sword. And the Lord said unto Moses, "Write this for a memorial in a book, and rehearse it in the ears of Joshua: for I will utterly put out the remembrance of Amalek from under heaven." And Moses built an altar, and called the name of it Jehovah-nissi: for he said, "Because the Lord hath sworn that the Lord will have war with Amalek from generation to generation."

18 When Jethro the priest of Midian, Moses' father in law, heard of all that God had done for Moses, and for Israel his people, and that the Lord had brought Israel out of Egypt: then Jethro Moses' father in law took Zipporah Moses' wife, after he had sent her back, and her two sons, of which the name of the one was Gershom; for he said, "I have been an alien in a strange land": and the name of the other was Eliezer; "For the God of my father," said he, "was mine help, and delivered me from the sword of Pharaoh." And Jethro Moses' father in law came with his sons and his wife unto Moses into the wilderness, where he encamped at the mount of God. And he said unto Moses, "I thy father in law Jethro am come unto thee, and thy wife, and her two sons with her."

And Moses went out to meet his father in law, and did obeisance, and kissed him: and they asked each other of their welfare, and they came into the tent. And Moses told his father in law all that the Lord had done unto Pharaoh and to the Egyptians for Israel's sake, and all the travail that had come upon them by the way, and how the Lord delivered them. And Jethro rejoiced for all the goodness which the Lord had done to Israel, whom he had delivered out of the hand of the Egyptians. And Jethro said, "Blessed be the Lord, who hath delivered you out of the hand of the Egyptians, and out of the hand of Pharaoh, who hath delivered the people from under the hand of the Egyptians. Now I know that the Lord is greater than all gods: for in the thing wherein they dealt proudly he was above them." And Jethro, Moses' father in law, took a burnt offering and sacrifices for God: and Aaron came, and all the elders of Israel, to eat with Moses' father in law before God.

And it came to pass on the morrow, that Moses sat to judge the people: and the people stood by Moses, from the morning unto the evening. And when Moses' father in law saw all that he did to the people, he said, "What is this thing that thou doest to the people? Why sittest thou thyself alone, and all the people stand by thee from morning unto even?" And Moses said unto his father in law, "Because the people come unto me to inquire of God. When they have a matter, they come unto me, and I judge between one and another, and I make them know the statutes of God and his laws." And Moses' father in law said unto him, "The thing that thou doest is not good. Thou wilt surely wear away, both thou, and this people that is with thee: for this thing is too heavy for thee; thou art not able to perform it thyself alone. Hearken now unto my voice, I will give thee counsel, and God shall be with thee: be thou for the people to God-ward, that thou mayest bring the causes unto God: and thou shalt teach them ordinances and laws, and shalt show them the way wherein they must walk, and the work that they must do. Moreover thou shalt provide out of all the people able men, such as fear God, men of truth, hating covetousness, and place such over them, to be rulers of thousands, and rulers of hundreds, rulers of fifties, and rulers of tens. And let them judge the people at all seasons: and it shall be that every great matter they shall bring unto thee, but every small matter they shall judge: so shall it be easier for thyself, and they shall bear the burden with thee. If thou shalt do this thing, and

God command thee so, then thou shalt be able to endure, and all this people shall also go to their place in peace." So Moses hearkened to the voice of his father in law, and did all that he had said. And Moses chose able men out of all Israel, and made them heads over the people, rulers of thousands, rulers of hundreds, rulers of fifties, and rulers of tens. And they judged the people at all seasons: the hard causes they brought unto Moses, but every small matter they judged themselves.

And Moses let his father in law depart, and he went his way into his own land.

19 In the third month when the children of Israel were gone forth out of the land of Egypt, the same day came they into the wilderness of Sinai. For they were departed from Rephidim, and were come to the desert of Sinai, and had pitched in the wilderness, and there Israel camped before the mount. And Moses went up unto God: and the Lord called unto him out of the mountain, saying, "Thus shalt thou say to the house of Jacob, and tell the children of Israel: 'Ye have seen what I did unto the Egyptians, and how I bare you on eagles' wings, and brought you unto myself. Now therefore, if ye will obey my voice indeed, and keep my covenant, then ye shall be a peculiar treasure unto me above all people: for all the earth is mine. And ye shall be unto me a kingdom of priests, and an holy nation.' These are the words which thou shalt speak unto the children of Israel."

And Moses came and called for the elders of the people, and laid before their faces all these words which the Lord commanded him. And all the people answered together, and said, "All that the Lord hath spoken we will do." And Moses returned the words of the people unto the Lord. And the Lord said unto Moses, "Lo, I come unto thee in a thick cloud, that the people may hear when I speak with thee, and believe thee for ever": and Moses told the words of the people unto the Lord.

And the Lord said unto Moses, "Go unto the people, and sanctify them today and tomorrow, and let them wash their clothes. And be ready against the third day: for the third day the Lord will come down in the sight of all the people, upon mount Sinai. And thou shalt set bounds unto the people round about, saying, 'Take heed to yourselves, that ye go not up into the mount, or touch the border of it: whosoever toucheth the mount shall be surely put to death. There shall not a hand touch it, but he shall surely be stoned, or shot through; whether it be beast or man, it shall not live': when the trumpet soundeth long, they shall come up to the mount."

And Moses went down from the mount unto the people, and sanctified the people; and they washed their clothes. And he said unto the people, "Be ready against the third day: come not at your wives."

And it came to pass on the third day in the morning, that there were thunders and lightnings, and a thick cloud upon the mount, and the voice of the trumpet exceeding loud, so that all the people that was in the camp trembled. And Moses brought forth the people out of the camp to meet with God, and they stood at the nether part of the mount. And mount Sinai was altogether on a smoke, because the Lord descended upon it in fire: and the smoke thereof ascended as the smoke of a furnace, and the whole mount quaked greatly. And when the voice of the trumpet sounded long, and waxed louder and louder, Moses spake, and God answered him by a voice. And the Lord came down upon mount Sinai, on the top of the mount: and the Lord called Moses up to the top of the mount, and Moses went up. And the Lord said unto Moses, "Go down, charge the people, lest they break through unto the Lord to gaze, and many of them perish. And let the priests also, which come near to the Lord, sanctify themselves, lest the Lord break forth upon them." And Moses said unto the Lord, "The people cannot come up to mount Sinai: for thou chargedst us, saying, 'Set bounds about the mount, and sanctify it.'" And the Lord said unto him, "Away, get thee down, and thou shalt come up, thou, and Aaron with thee: but let not the priests and the people break through, to come up unto the Lord, lest he break forth upon them." So Moses went down unto the people, and spake unto them.

20 And God spake all these words, saying, "I am the Lord thy God, which have brought thee out of the land of Egypt, out of the house of bondage:

Thou shalt have no other gods before me.

Thou shalt not make unto thee any graven image, or any likeness of any thing that is in heaven above, or that is in the earth beneath, or that is in the water under the earth. Thou shalt not bow down to them, nor serve them: for I the Lord thy God am a jealous God, visiting the iniquity of the fathers upon the children, unto the third and fourth generation of them that hate me: and showing mercy unto thousands of them that love me, and keep my commandments.

Thou shalt not take the name of the Lord thy God in vain: for the Lord will not hold him guiltless that taketh his name in vain.

Remember the sabbath day, to keep it holy. Six days shalt thou labour, and do all thy work: but the seventh day is the sabbath of the Lord thy God: in it thou shalt not do any work, thou, nor thy son, nor thy daughter, thy manservant, nor thy maidservant, nor thy cattle, nor thy stranger that is within thy gates: for in six days the Lord made heaven and earth, the sea, and all that in them is, and rested the seventh day: wherefore the Lord blessed the sabbath day, and hallowed it.

Honour thy father and thy mother: that thy days may be long upon the land, which the Lord thy God giveth thee.

Thou shalt not kill.

Thou shalt not commit adultery.

Thou shalt not steal.

Thou shalt not bear false witness against thy neighbour.

Thou shalt not covet thy neighbour's house, thou shalt not covet thy neighbour's wife, nor his manservant, nor his maidservant, nor his ox, nor his ass, nor any thing that is thy neighbour's."

And all the people saw the thunderings, and the lightnings, and the noise of the trumpet, and the mountain smoking: and when the people saw it, they removed, and stood afar off. And they said unto Moses, "Speak thou with us, and we will hear: but let not God speak with us, lest we die." And Moses said unto the people, "Fear not: for God is come to prove you, and that his fear may be before your faces, that ye sin not." And the people stood afar off, and Moses drew near unto the thick darkness where God was.

And the Lord said unto Moses, "Thus thou shalt say unto the children of Israel, 'Ye have seen that I have talked with you from heaven. Ye shall not make with me gods of silver, neither shall ye make unto you gods of gold. An altar of earth thou shalt make unto me, and shalt sacrifice thereon thy burnt offerings, and thy peace offerings, thy sheep, and thine oxen: in all places where I record my name I will come unto thee, and I will bless thee. And if thou wilt make me an altar of stone, thou shalt not build it of hewn stone:

for if thou lift up thy tool upon it, thou hast polluted it. Neither shalt thou go up by steps unto mine altar, that thy nakedness be not discovered thereon.' "

21 "Now these are the judgments which thou shalt set before them. 'If thou buy an Hebrew servant, six years he shall serve, and in the seventh he shall go out free for nothing. If he came in by himself, he shall go out by himself: if he were married, then his wife shall go out with him. If his master have given him a wife, and she have borne him sons or daughters, the wife and her children shall be her master's, and he shall go out by himself. And if the servant shall plainly say, "I love my master, my wife, and my children, I will not go out free": then his master shall bring him unto the judges, he shall also bring him to the door, or unto the door post, and his master shall bore his ear through with an awl, and he shall serve him for ever.

'And if a man sell his daughter to be a maidservant, she shall not go out as the menservants do. If she please not her master, who hath betrothed her to himself, then shall he let her be redeemed: to sell her unto a strange nation he shall have no power, seeing he hath dealt deceitfully with her. And if he have betrothed her unto his son, he shall deal with her after the manner of daughters. If he take him another wife, her food, her raiment, and her duty of marriage shall he not diminish. And if he do not these three unto her, then shall she go out free without money.

'He that smiteth a man, so that he die, shall be surely put to death. And if a man lie not in wait, but God deliver him into his hands, then I will appoint thee a place whither he shall flee: but if a man come presumptuously upon his neighbour to slay him with guile, thou shalt take him from mine altar, that he may die.

'And he that smiteth his father, or his mother, shall be surely put to death.

'And he that stealeth a man, and selleth him, or if he be found in his hand, he shall surely be put to death.

'And he that curseth his father or his mother, shall surely be put to death.

'And if men strive together, and one smite another with a stone, or with his fist, and he die not, but keepeth his bed: if he rise again, and walk abroad upon his staff, then shall he that smote him be quit: only he shall pay for the loss of his time, and shall cause him to be thoroughly healed.

'And if a man smite his servant, or his maid, with a rod, and he die under his hand, he shall be surely punished: notwithstanding, if he continue a day or two, he shall not be punished, for he is his money.

'If men strive, and hurt a woman with child, so that her fruit depart from her, and yet no mischief follow, he shall be surely punished, according as the woman's husband will lay upon him, and he shall pay as the judges determine.

'And if any mischief follow, then thou shalt give life for life, eye for eye, tooth for tooth, hand for hand, foot for foot, burning for burning, wound for wound, stripe for stripe.' ". . .

32 And when the people saw that Moses delayed to come down out of the mount, the people gathered themselves together unto Aaron, and said unto him, "Up, make us gods which shall go before us: for as for this Moses, the man that brought us up out of the land of Egypt, we wot not what is become of him." And Aaron said unto them, "Break off the golden earrings which are in the ears of your wives, of your sons, and of your daughters, and bring them unto me." And all the people brake off the golden earrings which were in their ears, and brought them unto Aaron. And he received them at their hand, and fashioned it with a graving tool, after he had made it a molten calf: and they said, "These be thy gods, O Israel, which brought thee up out of the land of Egypt." And when Aaron saw it, he built an altar before it, and Aaron made proclamation, and said, "Tomorrow is a feast to the Lord." And they rose up early on the morrow, and offered burnt offerings, and brought peace offerings: and the people sat down to eat and to drink, and rose up to play.

And the Lord said unto Moses, "Go, get thee down: for thy people which thou broughtest out of the land of Egypt have corrupted themselves. They have turned aside quickly out of the way which I commanded them: they have made them a molten calf, and have worshipped it, and have sacrificed thereunto, and said, 'These be thy gods, O Israel, which have brought thee up out of the land of Egypt.'" And the Lord said unto Moses, "I have seen this people, and behold, it is a stiffnecked people. Now therefore let me alone, that my wrath may wax hot against them, and that I may consume them: and I will make of thee a great nation." And Moses besought the Lord his God, and said, "Lord, why doth thy wrath wax hot against thy people, which thou hast brought forth out of the land of Egypt, with great power, and with a mighty hand? Wherefore should the Egyptians speak and say, 'For mischief did he bring them out, to slay them in the mountains, and to consume them from the face of the earth'? Turn from thy fierce wrath, and repent of this evil against thy people. Remember Abraham, Isaac, and Israel thy servants, to whom thou swarest by thine own self, and saidst unto them, 'I will multiply your seed as the stars of heaven: and all this land that I have spoken of will I give unto your seed, and they shall inherit it for ever.' " And the Lord repented of the evil which he thought to do unto his people.

And Moses turned, and went down from the mount, and the two tables of the testimony were in his hand: the tables were written on both their sides; on the one side, and on the other were they written. And the tables were the work of God; and the writing was the writing of God, graven upon the tables. And when Joshua heard the noise of the people as they shouted, he said unto Moses, "There is a noise of war in the camp." And he said, "It is not the voice of them that shout for mastery, neither is it the voice of them that cry for being overcome: but the noise of them that sing do I hear."

And it came to pass, as soon as he came nigh unto the camp, that he saw the calf, and the dancing: and Moses' anger waxed hot, and he cast the tables out of his hands, and brake them beneath the mount. And he took the calf which they had made, and burnt it in the fire, and ground it to powder, and strewed it upon the water, and made the children of Israel drink of it. And Moses said unto Aaron, "What did this people unto thee, that thou hast brought so great a sin upon them?" And Aaron said, "Let not the anger of my lord wax hot: thou knowest the people, that they are set on mischief. For they said unto me, 'Make us gods which shall go before us: for as for this Moses, the man that brought us up out of the land of Egypt, we wot not what is become of him.' And I said unto them, 'Whosoever hath any gold, let them break it off': so they gave it me: then I cast it into the fire, and there came out this calf."

And when Moses saw that the people were naked (for Aaron had made them naked unto their shame amongst their enemies), then Moses stood in the gate of the camp, and said, "Who is on the Lord's side? let him come unto me. And all the sons of Levi gathered themselves together unto him. And he said unto them, "Thus saith the Lord God of Israel, 'Put every man his sword by his side, and go in and out from gate to gate throughout the camp, and slay every man his brother, and every man his companion, and every man his neighbour.'" And the children of Levi did according to the word of Moses; and there fell of the people that day about three thousand men. For Moses had said, "Consecrate yourselves today to the Lord, even every man upon his son, and upon his brother, that he may bestow upon you a blessing this day."

And it came to pass on the morrow, that Moses said unto the people, "Ye have sinned a great sin: and now I will go up unto the Lord; peradventure I shall make an atonement for your sin." And Moses returned unto the Lord, and said, "Oh, this people have sinned a great sin, and have made them gods of gold. Yet now, if thou wilt forgive their sin; and if not, blot me, I pray thee, out of thy book, which thou hast written." And the Lord said unto Moses, "Whosoever hath sinned against me, him will I blot out of my book. Therefore now go, lead the people unto the place of which I have spoken unto thee: behold, mine angel shall go before thee; nevertheless in the day when I visit, I will visit their sin upon them." And the Lord plagued the people, because they made the calf, which Aaron made.

DEUTERONOMY

34 And Moses went up from the plains of Moab, unto the mountain of Nebo, to the top of Pisgah, that is over against Jericho: and the Lord showed him all the land of Gilead, unto Dan, and all Naphtali, and the land of Ephraim, and Manasseh, and all the land of Judah, unto the utmost sea, and the south, and the plain of the valley of Jericho, the city of palm trees, unto Zoar. And the Lord said unto him, "This is the land which I sware unto Abraham, unto Isaac, and unto Jacob, saying, 'I will give it unto thy seed': I have caused thee to see it with thine eyes, but thou shalt not go over thither." [1]

So Moses the servant of the Lord died there in the land of Moab, according to the word of the Lord. And he buried him in a valley in the land of Moab, over against Beth-peor: but no man knoweth of his sepulchre unto this day.

And Moses was an hundred and twenty years old when he died: his eye was not dim, nor his natural force abated.

And the children of Israel wept for Moses in the plains of Moab thirty days: so the days of weeping and mourning for Moses were ended.

And Joshua the son of Nun was full of the spirit of wisdom: for Moses had laid his hands upon him, and the children of Israel hearkened unto him, and did as the Lord commanded Moses.

And there arose not a prophet since in Israel like unto Moses, whom the Lord knew face to face: in all the signs and the wonders which the Lord sent him to do in the land of Egypt, to Pharaoh, and to all his servants, and to all his land, and in all that mighty hand, and in all the great terror, which Moses showed in the sight of all Israel.

---

[1] A possible explanation of why God does not let Moses enter the promised land is contained in The Book of Numbers, chapter 20. Here Moses' method of getting water out of a rock implies a slight deviation from absolute obedience to God, and this, in turn, provokes God's anger.

samson

INTRODUCTION

The Book of Judges[1] continues the history of the Hebrews begun in the Pentateuch. Its concern is with events between the death of Joshua and the crowning of Saul as king: from about 1225 to 1025 B.C. During this time the Philistines, a group originating in the Aegean, occupied the leading coastal cities of Palestine and dominated the hinterlands. Not only were the conquests of Joshua threatened, but so was the very existence of Israel. The story of Saul and David tells of the eventual repulse of the Philistines by a briefly unified nation; much of Judges deals with localized and essentially ineffectual uprisings against them. Thus Samson, who can be dated around 1100 B.C., is partly a symbol of this abortive resistance. (At the end of his career his people are actually no closer to liberation than they were at its beginning.) But Samson is not so much a figure from history as he is the hero of a folk tale. His story, largely written by J, comes from pre-literary oral traditions: not the sagas of bards sung in aristocratic houses, but from rustic tales told around a campfire. Like other simple folk heroes, Samson is strong, lusty, endowed with a rough sense of humor, and easily victimized by scheming women. In J's hands he retains all these characteristics of a Hebrew Paul Bunyan, but he is also given heroic qualities of a more epic sort, qualities which link him, even if remotely, with a Moses or an Achilles. ✿ ✿ ✿

Suggested Reading

Beowulf—the Anglo-Saxon epic of a strong man.

John Milton, *Samson Agonistes*—a classical-Puritan drama about the death of Samson.

[1] The noun "judge" did not designate a legal personage but a leader similar to a king, except that he could not found a dynasty.

135

JUDGES

13 And the children of Israel did evil again in the sight of the Lord, and the Lord delivered them into the hand of the Philistines forty years.

And there was a certain man of Zorah, of the family of the Danites, whose name was Manoah, and his wife was barren, and bare not. And the angel of the Lord appeared unto the woman, and said unto her, "Behold now, thou art barren, and bearest not: but thou shalt conceive, and bear a son. Now therefore beware, I pray thee, and drink not wine nor strong drink, and eat not any unclean thing. For lo, thou shalt conceive, and bear a son, and no razor shall come on his head: for the child shall be a Nazarite[1] unto God from the womb: and he shall begin to deliver Israel out of the hand of the Philistines."

Then the woman came, and told her husband, saying, "A man of God came unto me, and his countenance was like the countenance of an angel of God, very terrible: but I asked him not whence he was, neither told he me his name: but he said unto me, 'Behold, thou shalt conceive, and bear a son; and now, drink no wine nor strong drink, neither eat any unclean thing: for the child shall be a Nazarite to God from the womb to the day of his death.' "

Then Manoah entreated the Lord, and said, "O my Lord, let the man of God which thou didst send come again unto us, and teach us what we shall do unto the child that shall be born." And God hearkened to the voice of Manoah; and the angel of God came again unto the woman as she sat in the field: but Manoah her husband was not with her. And the woman made haste, and ran, and showed her husband, and said unto him, "Behold, the man hath appeared unto me that came unto me the other day." And Manoah arose, and went after his wife, and came to the man, and said unto him, "Art thou the man that spakest unto the woman?" And he said, "I am." And Manoah said, "Now let thy words come to pass. How shall we order the child, and how shall we do unto him?" And the angel of the Lord said unto Manoah, "Of all that I said unto the woman, let her beware. She may not eat of any thing that cometh of the vine,

---

[1] *I.e.*, one who is set apart, dedicated to the Lord.

neither let her drink wine or strong drink, nor eat any unclean thing: all that I commanded her, let her observe."

And Manoah said unto the angel of the Lord. "I pray thee, let us detain thee, until we shall have made ready a kid for thee." And the angel of the Lord said unto Manoah, "Though thou detain me, I will not eat of thy bread: and if thou wilt offer a burnt offering, thou must offer it unto the Lord": for Manoah knew not that he was an angel of the Lord. And Manoah said unto the angel of the Lord, "What is thy name, that when thy sayings come to pass we may do thee honour?" And the angel of the Lord said unto him, "Why askest thou thus after my name, seeing it is secret?" So Manoah took a kid, with a meat offering, and offered it upon a rock unto the Lord: and the angel did wondrously, and Manoah and his wife looked on. For it came to pass, when the flame went up toward heaven from off the altar, that the angel of the Lord ascended in the flame of the altar: and Manoah and his wife looked on it, and fell on their faces to the ground. (But the angel of the Lord did no more appear to Manoah and to his wife.) Then Manoah knew that he was an angel of the Lord. And Manoah said unto his wife, "We shall surely die, because we have seen God." But his wife said unto him, "If the Lord were pleased to kill us, he would not have received a burnt offering and a meat offering at our hands, neither would he have showed us all these things, nor would as at this time have told us such things as these."

And the woman bare a son, and called his name Samson: and the child grew, and the Lord blessed him. And the spirit of the Lord began to move him at times in the camp of Dan, between Zorah and Eshtaol.

14 And Samson went down to Timnath, and saw a woman in Timnath, of the daughters of the Philistines. And he came up, and told his father and his mother, and said, "I have seen a woman in Timnath of the daughters of the Philistines: now therefore get her for me to wife." Then his father and his mother said unto him, "Is there never a woman among the daughters of thy brethren, or among all my people, that thou goest to take a wife of the uncircumcised Philistines?" And Samson said unto his father, "Get her for me, for she pleaseth me well." But his father and mother knew not that it was of the Lord, that he sought an occasion against the Philistines: for at that time the Philistines had dominion over Israel.

Then went Samson down, and his father and his mother, to Timnath, and came to the vineyards of Timnath: and behold, a young lion roared against him. And the spirit of the Lord came mightily upon him, and he rent him as he would have rent a kid, and he had nothing in his hand: but he told not his father or his mother what he had done. And he went down, and talked with the woman; and she pleased Samson well.

And after a time he returned to take her, and he turned aside to see the carcass of the lion: and behold, there was a swarm of bees and honey in the carcass of the lion. And he took thereof in his hands, and went on eating, and came to his father and mother, and he gave them, and they did eat: but he told not them that he had taken the honey out of the carcass of the lion.

So his father went down unto the woman, and Samson made there a feast: for so used the young men to do. And it came to pass when they saw him, that they brought thirty companions to be with him. And Samson said unto them, "I will now put forth a riddle unto you: if you can certainly declare it me within the seven days of the feast, and find it out, then I will give you thirty sheets, and thirty change of garments: but if ye cannot declare it me, then shall ye give me thirty sheets, and thirty change of garments." And they said unto him, "Put forth thy riddle, that we may hear it." And he said unto them, "Out of the eater came forth meat, and out of the strong came forth sweetness."

And they could not in three days expound the riddle. And it came to pass on the seventh day, that they said unto Samson's wife, "Entice thy husband, that he may declare unto us the riddle, lest we burn thee and thy father's house with fire: have ye called us to take that we have? is it not so?" And Samson's wife wept before him, and said, "Thou dost but hate me, and lovest me not: thou hast put forth a riddle unto the children of my people, and hast not told it me." And he said unto her, "Behold, I have not told it my father nor my mother, and shall I tell it thee?" And she wept before him the seven days, while the feast lasted: and it came to pass on the seventh day, that he told her, because she lay sore upon him: and she told the riddle to the children of her people. And the men of the city said unto him on the seventh day before the sun went down,

"What is sweeter than honey? and what is stronger than a lion?" And he said unto them, "If ye had not plowed with my heifer, ye had not found out my riddle."

And the Spirit of the Lord came upon him, and he went down to Ashkelon, and slew thirty men of them, and took their spoil, and gave change of garments unto them which expounded the riddle; and his anger was kindled, and he went up to his father's house. But Samson's wife was given to his companion, whom he had used as his friend.

15 But it came to pass within a while after, in the time of wheat harvest, that Samson visited his wife with a kid, and he said, "I will go in to my wife into the chamber." But her father would not suffer him to go in. And her father said, "I verily thought that thou hadst utterly hated her, therefore I gave her to thy companion: is not her younger sister fairer than she? take her, I pray thee, instead of her." And Samson said concerning them, "Now shall I be more blameless than the Philistines, though I do them a displeasure?" And Samson went and caught three hundred foxes, and took firebrands, and turned tail to tail, and put a firebrand in the midst between two tails. And when he had set the brands on fire, he let them go into the standing corn of the Philistines, and burnt up both the shocks, and also the standing corn, with the vineyards and olives. Then the Philistines said, "Who hath done this?" And they answered, "Samson, the son in law of the Timnite, because he had taken his wife and given her to his companion." And the Philistines came up, and burnt her and her father with fire. And Samson said unto them, "Though ye have done this, yet will I be avenged of you, and after that I will cease." And he smote them hip and thigh with a great slaughter; and he went down and dwelt in the top of the rock Etam.

Then the Philistines went up, and pitched in Judah, and spread themselves in Lehi. And the men of Judah said, "Why are ye come up against us?" And they answered, "To bind Samson are we come up, to do to him as he hath done to us." Then three thousand men of Judah went to the top of the rock Etam, and said to Samson, "Knowest thou not that the Philistines are rulers over us? What is this that thou hast done unto us?" And he said unto them, "As they did unto me, so have I done unto them." And they said unto him,

"We are come down to bind thee, that we may deliver thee into the hand of the Philistines." And Samson said unto them, "Swear unto me that ye will not fall upon me yourselves." And they spake unto him, saying, "No: but we will bind thee fast, and deliver thee into their hand: but surely we will not kill thee." And they bound him with two new cords, and brought him up from the rock.

And when he came unto Lehi, the Philistines shouted against him: and the spirit of the Lord came mightily upon him, and the cords that were upon his arms became as flax that was burnt with fire, and his bands loosed from off his hands. And he found a new jawbone of an ass, and put forth his hand, and took it, and slew a thousand men therewith. And Samson said, "With the jawbone of an ass, heaps upon heaps, with the jaw of an ass have I slain a thousand men." And it came to pass when he had made an end of speaking, that he cast away the jawbone out of his hand, and called that place Ramath-lehi.

And he was sore athirst, and called on the Lord, and said, "Thou hast given this great deliverance into the hand of thy servant: and now shall I die for thirst, and fall into the hand of the uncircumcised?" But God clave a hollow place that was in the jaw, and there came water thereout, and when he had drunk, his spirit came again, and he revived: wherefore he called the name thereof En-hakkore, which is in Lehi unto this day. And he judged Israel in the days of the Philistines twenty years.

16 Then went Samson to Gaza, and saw there an harlot, and went in unto her. And it was told the Gazites, saying, "Samson is come hither." And they compassed him in, and laid wait for him all night in the gate of the city, and were quiet all the night, saying, "In the morning, when it is day, we shall kill him." And Samson lay till midnight, and arose at midnight, and took the doors of the gate of the city, and the two posts, and went away with them, bar and all, and put them upon his shoulders, and carried them up to the top of a hill that is before Hebron.

And it came to pass afterward, that he loved a woman in the valley of Sorek, whose name was Delilah. And the lords of the Philistines came up unto her, and said unto her, "Entice him, and see wherein his great strength lieth, and by what means we may prevail against him, that we may bind him, to afflict him: and we will give thee every one of us eleven hundred pieces of silver."

And Delilah said to Samson, "Tell me, I pray thee, wherein thy great strength lieth, and wherewith thou mightest be bound, to afflict thee." And Samson said unto her, "If they bind me with seven green withes that were never dried, then shall I be weak, and be as another man." Then the lords of the Philistines brought up to her seven green withes which had not been dried, and she bound him with them. Now there were men lying in wait, abiding with her in the chamber: and she said unto him, "The Philistines be upon thee, Samson." And he brake the withes, as a thread of tow is broken when it toucheth the fire: so his strength was not known. And Delilah said unto Samson, "Behold, thou hast mocked me, and told me lies: now tell me, I pray thee, wherewith thou mightest be bound." And he said unto her, "If they bind me fast with new ropes that never were occupied, then shall I be weak, and be as another man." Delilah therefore took new ropes, and bound him therewith, and said unto him, "The Philistines be upon thee, Samson." (And there were liers in wait abiding in the chamber.) And he brake them from off his arms, like a thread. And Delilah said unto Samson, "Hitherto thou hast mocked me, and told me lies: tell me wherewith thou mightest be bound." And he said unto her, "If thou weavest the seven locks of my head with the web." And she fastened it with the pin, and said unto him, "The Philistines be upon thee, Samson." And he awaked out of his sleep, and went away with the pin of the beam, and with the web.

And she said unto him, "How canst thou say, 'I love thee,' when thine heart is not with me? Thou hast mocked me these three times, and hast not told me wherein thy great strength lieth." And it came to pass, when she pressed him daily with her words, and urged him, so that his soul was vexed unto death, that he told her all his heart, and said unto her, "There hath not come a razor upon mine head: for I have been a Nazarite unto God from my mother's womb: if I be shaven, then my strength will go from me, and I shall become weak, and be like any other man." And when Delilah saw that he had told her all his heart, she sent and called for the lords of the Philistines, saying, "Come up this once, for he hath showed me all his heart." Then the lords of the Philistines came up unto her, and brought money in their hand. And she made him sleep upon her knees, and she called for a man, and she caused him to shave off the seven locks of his head, and she began to afflict him, and his strength went from him. And she said, "The Philistines be upon thee, Samson." And he awoke out of his sleep, and said, "I will go out as at other times before, and shake myself." And he wist not that the Lord was departed from him.

But the Philistines took him, and put out his eyes, and brought him down to Gaza, and bound him with fetters of brass, and he did grind in the prison house. Howbeit the hair of his head began to grow again, after he was shaven. Then the lords of the Philistines gathered them together, for to offer a great sacrifice unto Dagon their god, and to rejoice: for they said, "Our god hath delivered Samson our enemy into our hand." And when the people saw him, they praised their god: for they said, "Our god hath delivered into our hands our enemy, and the destroyer of our country, which slew many of us." And it came to pass when their hearts were merry, that they said, "Call for Samson, that he may make us sport." And they called for Samson out of the prison house, and he made them sport, and they set him between the pillars. And Samson said unto the lad that held him by the hand, "Suffer me, that I may feel the pillars whereupon the house standeth, that I may lean upon them."

Now the house was full of men and women, and all the lords of the Philistines were there: and there were upon the roof about three thousand men and women, that beheld while Samson made sport. And Samson called unto the Lord, and said, "O Lord God, remember me, I pray thee, and strengthen me, I pray thee, only this once, O God, that I may be at once avenged of the Philistines, for my two eyes." And Samson took hold of the two middle pillars, upon which the house stood, and on which it was borne up, of the one with his right hand, and of the other with his left. And Samson said, "Let me die with the Philistines": and he bowed himself with all his might: and the house fell upon the lords, and upon all the people that were therein. So the dead which he slew at his death were more than they which he slew in his life. Then his brethren, and all the house of his father, came down, and took him, and brought him up, and buried him between Zorah and Eshtaol, in the burying place of Manoah his father: and he judged Israel twenty years.

Ruth

INTRODUCTION

Though placed immediately after Judges in most versions of the Bible, The Book of Ruth is relatively late, having been written around 400 B.C. But the unknown author deliberately gave his tale an archaic flavor and set it in the ancient days of the judges. Basically Ruth is a short story, an idyllic piece of fiction, not a slice of history; no real unpleasantness mars its tranquil surface. It is even likely that the author was what we would now call a liberal, for he seems opposed to that form of racial prejudice which prohibits mixed marriages. After all, it is Ruth, a Moabitess, who is the great-grandmother of David—and David, next to Moses, was Israel's greatest hero. ♣ ♣ ♣

Suggested Reading

Boccaccio, *The Decameron,* and Chaucer, *The Canterbury Tales*— varied and dynamic medieval collections of short stories.

Gustave Flaubert, *Madame Bovary*—a nineteenth-century French novel in which a young woman coming into an established society behaves very differently from Ruth.

RUTH

1 Now it came to pass in the days when the judges ruled, that there was a famine in the land: and a certain man of Bethlehem-Judah went to sojourn in the country of Moab, he, and his wife, and his two sons. And the name of the man was Elimelech, and the name of his wife Naomi, and the name of his two sons Mahlon and Chilion, Ephrathites of Bethlehem-Judah: and they came into the country of Moab, and continued there. And Elimelech Naomi's husband died, and she was left, and her two sons. And they took

143

them wives of the women of Moab: the name of the one was Orpah, and the name of the other Ruth: and they dwelled there about ten years. And Mahlon and Chilion died also both of them, and the woman was left[1] of her two sons and her husband.

Then she arose with her daughters in law, that she might return from the country of Moab: for she had heard in the country of Moab how that the Lord had visited his people in giving them bread. Wherefore she went forth out of the place where she was, and her two daughters in law with her: and they went on the way to return unto the land of Judah. And Naomi said unto her two daughters in law, "Go, return each to her mother's house: the Lord deal kindly with you, as ye have dealt with the dead, and with me. The Lord grant you that you may find rest, each of you in the house of her husband." Then she kissed them, and they lifted up their voice and wept. And they said unto her, "Surely we will return with thee, unto thy people."

And Naomi said, "Turn again, my daughters: why will you go with me? Are there yet any more sons in my womb, that they may be your husbands? Turn again, my daughters, go your way, for I am too old to have an husband: if I should say, 'I have hope, if I should have a husband also tonight, and should also bear sons': would ye tarry for them till they were grown? would ye stay for them from having husbands? nay, my daughters: for it grieveth me much for your sakes that the hand of the Lord is gone out against me." And they lifted up their voice and wept again: and Orpah kissed her mother in law, but Ruth clave unto her. And she said, "Behold, thy sister in law is gone back unto her people, and unto her gods: return thou after thy sister in law." And Ruth said, "Entreat me not to leave thee, or to return from following after thee: for whither thou goest, I will go; and where thou lodgest, I will lodge: thy people shall be my people, and thy God my God: where thou diest, will I die, and there will I be buried: the Lord do so to me, and more also, if aught but death part thee and me." When she saw that she was steadfastly minded to go with her, then she left speaking unto her.

So they two went until they came to Bethlehem: and it came to pass when they were come to Bethlehem, that all the city was moved about them, and they said, "Is this Naomi?" And she said unto them, "Call me not Naomi; call me Mara: for the Almighty hath dealt

[1] I.e., bereft.

very bitterly with me. I went out full, and the Lord hath brought me home again empty: why then call ye me Naomi, seeing the Lord hath testified against me, and the Almighty hath afflicted me?" So Naomi returned, and Ruth the Moabitess her daughter in law with her, which returned out of the country of Moab: and they came to Bethlehem in the beginning of barley harvest.

2 And Naomi had a kinsman of her husband's, a mighty man of wealth, of the family of Elimelech, and his name was Boaz. And Ruth the Moabitess said unto Naomi, "Let me now go to the field, and glean ears of corn after him, in whose sight I shall find grace." And she said unto her, "Go, my daughter." And she went, and came, and gleaned in the field after the reapers: and her hap was to light on a part of the field belonging unto Boaz, who was of the kindred of Elimelech.

And behold, Boaz came from Bethlehem, and said unto the reapers, "The Lord be with you"; and they answered him, "The Lord bless thee." Then said Boaz unto his servant that was set over the reapers, "Whose damsel is this?" And the servant that was set over the reapers answered and said, "It is the Moabitish damsel that came back with Naomi out of the country of Moab: and she said, 'I pray you, let me glean and gather after the reapers amongst the sheaves': so she came, and hath continued even from the morning until now, that she tarried a little in the house." Then said Boaz unto Ruth, "Hearest thou not, my daughter? Go not to glean in another field, neither go from hence, but abide here fast by my maidens. Let thine eyes be on the field that they do reap, and go thou after them: have I not charged the young men, that they shall not touch thee? and when thou art athirst, go into the vessels, and drink of that which the young men have drawn."

Then she fell on her face, and bowed herself to the ground, and said unto him, "Why have I found grace in thine eyes, that thou shouldest take knowledge of me, seeing I am a stranger?" And Boaz answered and said unto her, "It hath fully been showed me all that thou hast done unto thy mother in law since the death of thine husband: and how thou hast left thy father and thy mother, and the land of thy nativity, and art come unto a people which thou knewest not heretofore. The Lord recompense thy work, and a full reward be given thee of the Lord God of Israel, under whose wings thou art come to trust." Then she said, "Let me find favour in thy sight, my lord, for that thou hast comforted me, and for that thou hast spoken friendly unto thine handmaid, though I be not like unto one of thine handmaidens." And Boaz said unto her, "At mealtime come thou hither, and eat of the bread, and dip thy morsel in the vinegar." And she sat beside the reapers: and he reached her parched corn, and she did eat, and was sufficed, and left. And when she was risen up to glean, Boaz commanded his young men, saying, "Let her glean even among the sheaves, and reproach her not. And let fall also some of the handfuls of purpose for her, and leave them that she may glean them, and rebuke her not." So she gleaned in the field until even, and beat out that she had gleaned: and it was about an ephah of barley.

And she took it up, and went into the city: and her mother in law saw what she had gleaned; and she brought forth, and gave to her that she had reserved, after she was sufficed. And her mother in law said unto her, "Where hast thou gleaned today? and where wroughtest thou? blessed be he that did take knowledge of thee." And she showed her mother in law with whom she had wrought, and said, "The man's name with whom I wrought today is Boaz." And Naomi said unto her daughter in law, "Blessed be he of the Lord, who hath not left off his kindness to the living and to the dead." And Naomi said unto her, "The man is near of kin unto us, one of our next kinsmen." And Ruth the Moabitess said, "He said unto me also, 'Thou shalt keep fast by my young men, until they have ended all my harvest.'" And Naomi said unto Ruth her daughter in law, "It is good, my daughter, that thou go out with his maidens, that they meet thee not in any other field." So she kept fast by the maidens of Boaz to glean, unto the end of barley harvest, and of wheat harvest, and dwelt with her mother in law.

3 Then Naomi her mother in law said unto her, "My daughter, shall I not seek rest for thee, that it may be well with thee? And now is not Boaz of our kindred, with whose maidens thou wast? Behold, he winnoweth barley tonight in the threshing floor. Wash thyself therefore, and anoint thee, and put thy raiment upon thee, and get thee down to the floor: but make not thyself known unto the man, until he shall have done eating and drinking. And it shall be when he lieth down, that thou shalt mark the place where he shall

lie, and thou shalt go in, and uncover his feet, and lay thee down, and he will tell thee what thou shalt do." And she said unto her, "All that thou sayest unto me I will do."

And she went down unto the floor, and did according to all that her mother in law bade her. And when Boaz had eaten and drunk, and his heart was merry, he went to lie down at the end of the heap of corn: and she came softly, and uncovered his feet, and laid her down. And it came to pass at midnight, that the man was afraid, and turned himself: and behold, a woman lay at his feet. And he said, "Who art thou?" And she answered, "I am Ruth thine handmaid: spread therefore thy skirt over thine handmaid, for thou art a near kinsman." And he said, "Blessed be thou of the Lord, my daughter: for thou hast showed more kindness in the latter end than at the beginning, inasmuch as thou followedst not young men, whether poor or rich. And now, my daughter, fear not, I will do to thee all that thou requirest: for all the city of my people doth know that thou art a virtuous woman. And now it is true that I am thy near kinsman: howbeit there is a kinsman nearer than I. Tarry this night, and it shall be in the morning, that if he will perform unto thee the part of a kinsman, well; let him do the kinsman's part; but if he will not do the part of a kinsman to thee, then will I do the part of a kinsman to thee, as the Lord liveth: lie down until the morning."

And she lay at his feet until the morning: and she rose up before one could know another. And he said, "Let it not be known that a woman came into the floor." Also he said, "Bring the veil that thou hast upon thee, and hold it." And when she held it, he measured six measures of barley, and laid it on her: and she went into the city. And when she came to her mother in law, she said, "Who art thou, my daughter?" And she told her all that the man had done to her. And she said, "These six measures of barley gave he me, for he said to me, 'Go not empty unto thy mother in law.'" Then said she, "Sit still, my daughter, until thou know how the matter will fall: for the man will not be in rest, until he have finished the thing this day."

4 Then went Boaz up to the gate, and sat him down there: and behold, the kinsman of whom Boaz spake came by, unto whom he said, "Ho, such a one: turn aside, sit down here." And he turned aside, and sat down. And he took ten men of the elders of the city, and said, "Sit ye down here." And they sat down. And he said unto

the kinsman, "Naomi, that is come again out of the country of Moab, selleth a parcel of land, which was our brother Elimelech's. And I thought to advertise[2] thee, saying, 'Buy it before the inhabitants, and before the elders of my people.' If thou wilt redeem it, redeem it, but if thou wilt not redeem it, then tell me, that I may know: for there is none to redeem it besides thee; and I am after thee." And he said, "I will redeem it." Then said Boaz, "What day thou buyest the field of the hand of Naomi, thou must buy it also of Ruth the Moabitess, the wife of the dead, to raise up the name of the dead upon his inheritance."

And the kinsman said, "I cannot redeem it for myself, lest I mar mine own inheritance: redeem thou my right to thyself, for I cannot redeem it." Now this was the manner in former time in Israel, concerning redeeming and concerning changing, for to confirm all things: a man plucked off his shoe, and gave it to his neighbour: and this was a testimony in Israel. Therefore the kinsman said unto Boaz, "Buy it for thee": so he drew off his shoe.

And Boaz said unto the elders, and unto all the people, "Ye are witnesses this day, that I have bought all that was Elimelech's, and all that was Chilion's, and Mahlon's, of the hand of Naomi. Moreover, Ruth the Moabitess, the wife of Mahlon, have I purchased to be my wife, to raise up the name of the dead upon his inheritance, that the name of the dead be not cut off from among his brethren, and from the gate of his place: ye are witnesses this day." And all the people that were in the gate, and the elders, said, "We are witnesses: the Lord make the woman that is come into thine house like Rachel and like Leah, which two did build the house of Israel: and do thou worthily in Ephratah, and be famous in Bethlehem. And let thy house be like the house of Pharez (whom Tamar bare unto Judah), of the seed which the Lord shall give thee of this young woman."

So Boaz took Ruth, and she was his wife: and when he went in unto her, the Lord gave her conception, and she bare a son. And the women said unto Naomi, "Blessed be the Lord, which hath not left thee this day without a kinsman, that his name may be famous in Israel: and he shall be unto thee a restorer of thy life, and a nourisher of thine old age: for thy daughter in law which loveth

[2] *I.e.*, inform.

thee, which is better to thee than seven sons, hath borne him." And Naomi took the child, and laid it in her bosom, and became nurse unto it. And the women her neighbours gave it a name, saying, "There is a son born to Naomi"; and they called his name Obed: he is the father of Jesse, the father of David. . . .

saul and david

INTRODUCTION

The story of Saul and David in the two books of Samuel and in the beginning of The First Book of the Kings is one of the literary high points of the Bible. It is a unified history written five hundred years before Herodotus, as well as, in many respects, an artistic epic that predates Homer by two centuries. But the original story, like so much of the Old Testament, underwent a series of additions and changes; consequently, if one reads it in full, he gets a garbled, inconsistent account. The following selection, therefore, attempts to weed out the larger blocks of interpolated material so that it can be read in somewhat the same form in which it was first composed almost three thousand years ago.[1]

The original author was a contemporary of J, living in the time of Solomon. (A few scholars attribute the Saul-David story to J.) When a young man he was, almost certainly, an eyewitness to the later events he narrates; and one tenable theory identifies him with Ahimaaz, the son of David's priest Zadok. (This Ahimaaz's name has been italicized the few times it appears, in order to show why he might be a logical candidate.) The author, whatever his name, was a man of genius. His style is simple, rapid, vivid. He is objective and impartial. David is the hero of his story, but the author is honest in detailing David's faults; and when Nathan denounces the king for murdering Uriah, the author's moral indignation anticipates that of the prophets. Proud of his nation's accomplishments and convinced that God was with Israel, he nevertheless wrote his history of recent events with such control and realism that we can still be swept up in it.

For approximately two centuries after 950 B.C. this history and J's narrative contained in Genesis, Exodus, and Judges formed the backbone of Israel's cultural heritage, and these works helped to give the fledgling nation a sense of pride and unity. During the next two

[1] Following, in general, the selection made by Pfeiffer for *The Hebrew Iliad*.

centuries, however, various editors who viewed the establishment of the monarchy under Saul as a disaster tampered with the story. They made Saul a villain, exaggerated the importance of Samuel, repainted David as almost faultless, and inserted many moralizing interludes.

The actual background of the Saul-David story is a continuation of the one adumbrated in Judges. Around 1025 B.C. the struggles against the Philistines became more intense, less localized. The desperateness of the situation promoted a sense of national unity among the Israelite tribes and, as a result, Saul became king of a temporary confederation. Though he was defeated by the militarily stronger Philistines, he paved the way for later victories. David, avoiding pitched battles and employing guerrilla tactics, finally routed the invaders, and those who survived were absorbed in the melting pot that was ancient Palestine. David then made Jerusalem the capital city of his kingdom, itself now a union between Israel in the north and Judah in the south. After his death around 970 B.C. his son Solomon, by a series of palace intrigues, took over the throne and with oriental splendor ruled his small empire. It was at this pinnacle of Hebrew history, a moment analogous to the period in England immediately following the defeat of the Spanish Armada, that J and his colleagues wrote their proud and exhilarating narratives.

Of all the heroes of Hebrew history Saul and David are probably the most vivid. We can still see Saul: intensely emotional—even manic-depressive—quick tempered, prone to prophetic trances, dedicated to his people, battling hard against overwhelming odds, frustrated and irritated by the man who came to comfort him.[2] Yet he was a ruler who, unlike David, never faced serious rebellion. David is equally human: devious, clever, exhibitionistic and, at the same time, brave, loyal, thoughtful. He was a leader plagued by family troubles and national rebellions, but still great enough to become Israel's first real king—as well as the model for later messianic hopes. Nor are the minor personages merely two-dimensional: Jonathan, for instance, is plausible as son and friend; the handsome, unstable, ambitious Absalom is worthy to evoke his father's grief; Joab, the dogged guardian of the monarchy, can still be heard, speaking gruffly and forthrightly.

Though in the background the figure of the Lord looms very large and terrible, explicit religion occupies only a small place in this story. We see it most clearly in the references to the "ark" or the "ephod," a sacred box containing lots which could be consulted by those anxious to see what action God recommended. This box was guarded by priests

[2] David's lament over the fallen Saul, which is almost certainly authentic, is moving, virile, honest. Read carefully, it tells much about both men.

who "read" the answer which the "oracles"—perhaps a primitive form of dice—provided. And Ahimaaz, the son of one of these priests, may well qualify as the first great historian of the Western world. ♣ ♣ ♣

Suggested Reading

Aeschylus, Sophocles, Euripides: Plays—tragic irony in Greek classical drama.

Aristotle, *Poetics*—a classical Greek definition of the hero.

John Dryden, *Absalom and Achitophel*—a witty retelling of part of the David story so that it applies to the politics of Restoration England.

Thomas Hardy, *The Mayor of Casterbridge*—a novel based on the Saul-David story but set in early nineteenth-century England.

William Faulkner, *Absalom, Absalom!*—a novel, centering around the American Civil War, which harks back, in part, to David's family troubles.

I SAMUEL

9 Now there was a man of Benjamin whose name was Kish, the son of Abiel, the son of Zeror, the son of Bechorath, the son of Aphiah, a Benjamite, a mighty man of power. And he had a son whose name was Saul, a choice young man, and a goodly: and there was not among the children of Israel a goodlier person than he: from his shoulders and upward he was higher than any of the people. And the asses of Kish, Saul's father, were lost; and Kish said to Saul his son, "Take now one of the servants with thee, and arise, go seek the asses." And he passed through mount Ephraim, and passed through the land of Shalisha, but they found them not; then they passed through the land of Shalim, and there they were not; and he passed through the land of the Benjamites, but they found them not. And when they were come to the land of Zuph, Saul said to his servant that was with him, "Come, and let us return, lest my father leave caring for the asses and take thought for us."

And he said unto him, "Behold now, there is in this city a man of God, and he is an honourable man; all that he sayeth cometh surely to pass: now let us go thither; peradventure he can show us our way that we should go." Then said Saul to his servant, "But behold, if we go, what shall we bring the man? for the bread is spent in our vessels, and there is not a present to bring to the man of God: what have we?" And the servant answered Saul again, and said, "Behold, I have here at hand the fourth part of a shekel of silver; that will I give to the man of God to tell us our way." (Beforetime in Israel, when a man went to inquire of God, thus he spake: "Come, and let us go to the seer"; for he that is now called a prophet was beforetime called a seer.) Then said Saul to his servant, "Well said: come, let us go": so they went unto the city where the man of God was.

And as they went up the hill to the city, they found young maidens going out to draw water, and said unto them, "Is the seer here?" And they answered them, and said, "He is: behold, he is before you, make haste now: for he came today to the city; for there is a sacrifice of the people today in the high place. As soon as ye be come into the city, ye shall straightway find him, before he go up to the high place to eat: for the people will not eat until he come, because he doth bless the sacrifice; and afterwards they eat that be bidden. Now therefore get you up, for about this time ye shall find him." And they went up into the city: and when they were come into the city, behold, Samuel came out against them, for to go up to the high place.

Now the Lord had told Samuel in his ear a day before Saul came, saying, "Tomorrow about this time I will send thee a man out of the land of Benjamin, and thou shalt anoint him to be captain over my people Israel, that he may save my people out of the hand of the Philistines: for I have looked upon my people, because their cry is come unto me." And when Samuel saw Saul, the Lord said unto him, "Behold the man whom I spake to thee of: this same shall reign over my people." Then Saul drew near to Samuel in the gate, and said, "Tell me, I pray thee, where the seer's house is." And Samuel answered Saul, and said, "I am the seer: go up before me into the high place, for ye shall eat with me today, and tomorrow I will let thee go, and will tell thee all that is in thine heart. And as for thine asses that were lost three days ago, set not thy mind on them, for they are found. And on whom is all the desire of Israel? is it not on thee, and on all thy father's house?" And Saul answered, and said, "Am not I a Benjamite, of the smallest of the tribes of Israel? and my family the least of all the familes of the tribe of Benjamin? Wherefore then speakest thou so to me?"

And Samuel took Saul, and his servant, and brought them into the parlor, and made them sit in the chiefest place among them that were bidden, which were about thirty persons. And Samuel said unto the cook, "Bring the portion which I gave thee, of which I said unto thee, 'Set it by thee.'" And the cook took up the shoulder, and that which was upon it, and set it before Saul; and Samuel said, "Behold, that which is left, set it before thee, and eat: for unto this time hath it been kept for thee, since I said, 'I have invited the people.'" So Saul did eat with Samuel that day.

And when they were come down from the high place into the city, Samuel communed with Saul upon the top of the house. And they arose early: and it came to pass, about the spring of the day, that Samuel called Saul to the top of the house, saying, "Up, that I may send thee away." And Saul arose, and they went out both of them, he and Samuel, abroad. And as they were going down to the end of the city, Samuel said to Saul, "Bid the servant pass on before us (and he passed on), but stand thou still a while, that I may show thee the word of God."

10 Then Samuel took a vial of oil, and poured it upon his head, and kissed him, and said, "Is it not because the Lord hath anointed thee to be captain over his inheritance? When thou art departed from me today, then thou shalt find two men by Rachel's sepulchre in the border of Benjamin, at Zelzah: and they will say unto thee, 'The asses which thou wentest to seek are found: and lo, thy father hath left the care of the asses, and sorroweth for you, saying, "What shall I do for my son?"' Then shalt thou go on forward from thence, and thou shalt come to the plain of Tabor, and there shall meet thee three men, going up to God to Bethel, one carrying three kids, and another carrying three loaves of bread, and another carrying a bottle of wine. And they will salute thee, and give thee two loaves of bread, which thou shalt receive of their hands. After that thou shalt come to the hill of God, where is the garrison of the Philistines: and it shall come to pass when thou art come thither to the city, that thou shalt meet a company of prophets coming down from the high place, with a psaltery, and a tabret, and a pipe, and a harp before them, and they shall prophesy. And the spirit of the Lord will come upon thee, and thou shalt prophesy with them, and shalt be turned into another man. And let it be when these signs are come unto thee, that thou do as occasion serve thee, for God is with thee. And thou shalt go down before me to Gilgal, and behold, I will come down unto thee, to offer burnt offerings, and to sacrifice sacrifices of peace offerings: seven days shalt thou tarry, till I come to thee, and show thee what thou shalt do."

And it was so that when he turned his back to go from Samuel, God gave him another heart: and all those signs came to pass that day. And when they came thither to the hill, behold, a company of the prophets met him, and the spirit of God came upon him, and he prophesied among them. And it came to pass when all that knew him beforetime saw that, behold, he prophesied among the prophets, then the people said one to another, "What is this that is come unto the son of Kish? Is Saul also among the prophets?" And one of the same place answered, and said, "But who is their father?" Therefore it became a proverb: "Is Saul also among the prophets?" And when he had made an end of prophesying, he came to the high place.

And Saul's uncle said unto him, and to his servant, "Whither went ye?" And he said, "To seek the asses: and when we saw that they were nowhere, we came to Samuel." And Saul's uncle said, "Tell me, I pray thee, what Samuel said unto you." And Saul said unto his uncle, "He told us plainly that the asses were found." But of the matter of the kingdom, whereof Samuel spake, he told him not.

And Samuel called the people together unto the Lord to Mizpeh, and said unto the children of Israel, "Thus saith the Lord God of Israel, 'I brought up Israel out of Egypt, and delivered you out of the hand of the Egyptians, and out of the hand of all kingdoms, and of them that oppressed you.' And ye have this day rejected your God, who himself saved you out of all your adversities and your tribulations: and ye have said unto him, 'Nay, but set a king over us.' Now therefore present yourselves before the Lord by your tribes, and by your thousands."

And when Samuel had caused all the tribes of Israel to come near, the tribe of Benjamin was taken. When he had caused the tribe of Benjamin to come near by their families, the family of Matri was taken, and Saul the son of Kish was taken: and when they sought him, he could not be found. Therefore they inquired of the Lord further, if the man should yet come thither: and the Lord answered, "Behold, he hath hid himself among the stuff." And they ran, and fetched him thence, and when he stood among the people, he was higher than any of the people from his shoulders and upward. And Samuel said to all the people, "See ye him whom the Lord hath chosen, that there is none like him among all the people?" And all the people shouted, and said, "God save the king." Then Samuel told the people the manner of the kingdom, and wrote it in a book, and laid it up before the Lord; and Samuel sent all the people away, every man to his house.

And Saul also went home to Gibeah, and there went with him a band of men, whose hearts God had touched. But the children of Belial said, "How shall this man save us?" And they despised him, and brought him no presents: but he held his peace.

11 Then Nahash the Ammonite came up, and encamped against Jabesh Gilead: and all the men of Jabesh said unto Nahash, "Make a covenant with us, and we will serve thee." And Nahash the Ammonite answered them, "On this condition will I make a covenant with you, that I may thrust out all your right eyes, and lay it for a reproach upon all Israel." And the elders of Jabesh said unto him, "Give us seven days' respite, that we may send messengers unto all the coasts of Israel: and then, if there be no man to save us, we will come out to thee."

Then came the messengers to Gibeah of Saul, and told the tidings in the ears of the people: and all the people lifted up their voices, and wept. And behold, Saul came after the herd out of the field, and Saul said, "What aileth the people that they weep?" And they told him the tidings of the men of Jabesh. And the spirit of God came upon Saul when he heard those tidings and his anger was kindled greatly. And he took a yoke of oxen, and hewed them in pieces, and sent them throughout all the coasts of Israel by the hands of messengers, saying, "Whosoever cometh not forth after Saul and after Samuel, so shall it be done unto his oxen": and the fear of the Lord fell on the people, and they came out with one consent. And when he numbered them in Bezek, the children of Israel were three hundred thousand, and the men of Judah thirty thousand.

And they said unto the messengers that came, "Thus shall ye say unto the men of Jabesh Gilead, 'Tomorrow, by that time the sun be hot, ye shall have help.'" And the messengers came, and showed it to the men of Jabesh, and they were glad. Therefore the men of Jabesh said, "Tomorrow we will come out unto you, and ye shall do with us all that seemeth good unto you." And it was so on the morrow, that Saul put the people in three companies, and they came into the midst of the host in the morning watch, and slew the Ammonites, until the heat of the day: and it came to pass, that they which remained were scattered, so that two of them were not left together.

And the people said unto Samuel, "Who is he that said, 'Shall Saul reign over us?' Bring the men, that we may put them to death." And Saul said, "There shall not a man be put to death this day: for today the Lord hath wrought salvation in Israel." Then said Samuel to the people, "Come, and let us go to Gilgal, and renew the kingdom there." And all the people went to Gilgal, and there they made Saul king before the Lord in Gilgal: and there they sacrificed sacrifices of peace offerings before the Lord: and there Saul and all the men of Israel rejoiced greatly.

13 Saul reigned one year, and when he had reigned two years over Israel, Saul chose him three thousand men of Israel: whereof two thousand were with Saul in Michmash and in mount Bethel, and a thousand were with Jonathan in Gibeah of Benjamin: and the rest of the people he sent every man to his tent. And Jonathan smote the garrison of the Philistines that was in Geba, and the Philistines heard of it: and Saul blew the trumpet throughout all the land, saying, "Let the Hebrews hear." And all Israel heard say that Saul had smitten a garrison of the Philistines, and that Israel also was had in abomination with the Philistines: and the people were called together after Saul to Gilgal. And the Philistines gathered themselves together to fight with Israel, thirty thousand chariots, and six thousand horsemen, and people as the sand which is on the seashore in multitude, and they came up, and pitched in Michmash, eastward from Beth-aven. When the men of Israel saw that they were in a strait (for the people were distressed), then the people did hide themselves in caves, and in thickets, and in rocks, and in high places, and in pits. And some of the Hebrews went over Jordan, to the land of Gad and Gilead; as for Saul, he was yet in Gilgal, and all the people followed him trembling. . . .

And Samuel arose, and gat him up from Gilgal, unto Gibeah of Benjamin; and Saul numbered the people that were present with him, about six hundred men. And Saul and Jonathan his son, and the people that were present with them, abode in Gibeah of Benjamin: but the Philistines encamped in Michmash. And the spoilers came out of the camp of the Philistines, in three companies: one company turned unto the way that leadeth to Ophrah, unto the land of Shual; and another company turned the way to Bethoron; and another company turned to the way of the border, that looketh to the valley of Zeboim toward the wilderness.

Now there was no smith found throughout all the land of Israel: for the Philistines said, "Lest the Hebrews make them swords or spears." But all the Israelites went down to the Philistines, to sharpen every man his share[1] and his coulter, and his axe, and his mattock. Yet they had a file for the mattocks, and for the coulters, and for the forks, and for the axes, and to sharpen the goads. So it came to pass in the day of battle that there was neither sword nor spear found in the hand of any of the people that were with Saul and Jonathan: but with Saul and with Jonathan his son was there found. And the garrison of the Philistines went out to the passage of Michmash.

14 Now it came to pass upon a day, that Jonathan the son of Saul said unto the young man that bare his armour, "Come, and let us go over to the Philistines' garrison, that is on the other side": but he told not his father. And Saul tarried in the uttermost part of Gibeah, under a pomegranate tree, which is in Migron: and the people that were with him were about six hundred men. And Ahiah the son of Ahitub, Ichabod's brother, the son of Phinehas, the son of Eli, the Lord's priest in Shiloh, wearing an ephod: and the people knew not that Jonathan was gone.

And between the passages, by which Jonathan sought to go over unto the Philistines' garrison, there was a sharp rock on the one side, and a sharp rock on the other side: and the name of the one was Bozez, and the name of the other Seneh. The forefront of the one was situate northward over against Michmash, and the other southward over against Gibeah. And Jonathan said to the young man that bare his armour, "Come, and let us go over unto the garrison of these uncircumcised; it may be that the Lord will work for us: for there is no restraint to the Lord to save by many or by few." And his armour-bearer said unto him, "Do all that is in thine heart: turn

[1] *I.e.,* plowshare.

thee, behold, I am with thee according to thy heart." Then said Jonathan, "Behold, we will pass over unto these men, and we will discover ourselves unto them. If they say thus unto us, 'Tarry until we come to you': then we will stand still in our place, and will not go up unto them. But if they say thus, 'Come up unto us': then we will go up: for the Lord hath delivered them into our hand: and this shall be a sign unto us."

And both of them discovered themselves unto the garrison of the Philistines: and the Philistines said, 'Behold, the Hebrews come forth out of the holes, where they had hid themselves." And the men of the garrison answered Jonathan and his armour-bearer, and said, "Come up to us, and we will show you a thing." And Jonathan said unto his armour-bearer, "Come up after me; for the Lord hath delivered them into the hand of Israel." And Jonathan climbed up upon his hands, and upon his feet, and his armour-bearer after him: and they fell before Jonathan; and his armour-bearer slew after him. And that first slaughter, which Jonathan and his armour-bearer made, was about twenty men, within as it were an half acre of land, which a yoke of oxen might plow. And there was trembling in the host, in the field, and among all the people: the garrison and the spoilers, they also trembled, and the earth quaked: so it was a very great trembling.

And the watchmen of Saul in Gibeah of Benjamin looked: and behold, the multitude melted away, and they went on beating down one another. Then said Saul unto the people that were with him, "Number now, and see who is gone from us." And when they had numbered, behold, Jonathan and his armour-bearer were not there. And Saul said unto Ahiah, "Bring hither the ark of God": (for the ark of God was at that time with the children of Israel).

And it came to pass while Saul talked unto the priest, that the noise that was in the host of the Philistines went on, and increased: and Saul said unto the priest, "Withdraw thine hand." And Saul and all the people that were with him assembled themselves, and they came to the battle, and behold, every man's sword was against his fellow, and there was a very great discomfiture. Moreover, the Hebrews that were with the Philistines before that time, which went up with them into the camp from the country round about, even they also turned to be with the Israelites that were with Saul and Jonathan. Likewise all the men of Israel, which had hid themselves in mount Ephraim, when they heard that the Philistines fled, even they also followed hard after them in the battle. So the Lord saved Israel that day: and the battle passed over unto Beth-aven.

And the men of Israel were distressed that day; for Saul had adjured the people, saying, "Cursed be the man that eateth any food until evening, that I may be avenged on mine enemies": so none of the people tasted any food. And all they of the land came to a wood, and there was honey upon the ground. And when the people were come into the wood, behold, the honey dropped, but no man put his hand to his mouth: for the people feared the oath. But Jonathan heard not when his father charged the people with the oath; wherefore he put forth the end of the rod that was in his hand, and dipped it in an honeycomb, and put his hand to his mouth, and his eyes were enlightened. Then answered one of the people, and said, "Thy father straitly charged the people with an oath, saying, 'Cursed be the man that eateth any food this day.'" And the people were faint. Then said Jonathan, "My father hath troubled the land: see, I pray you, how mine eyes have been enlightened, because I tasted a little of this honey: how much more, if haply the people had eaten freely today of the spoil of their enemies which they found? for had there not been now a much greater slaughter among the Philistines?" And they smote the Philistines that day from Michmash to Aijalon: and the people were very faint. And the people flew upon the spoil, and took sheep, and oxen, and calves, and slew them on the ground, and the people did eat them with the blood.

Then they told Saul, saying, "Behold, the people sin against the Lord, in that they eat with the blood." And he said, "Ye have transgressed: roll a great stone unto me this day." And Saul said, "Disperse yourselves among the people, and say unto them, 'Bring me hither every man his ox, and every man his sheep, and slay them here, and eat, and sin not against the Lord in eating with the blood.'" And all the people brought every man his ox with him that night, and slew them there. And Saul built an altar unto the Lord: the same was the first altar that he built unto the Lord.

And Saul said, "Let us go down after the Philistines by night, and spoil them until the morning light, and let us not leave a man of them." And they said, "Do whatsoever seemeth good unto thee." Then said the priest, "Let us draw near hither unto God." And Saul asked counsel of God: "Shall I go down after the Philistines? Wilt thou deliver them into the hand of Israel?" But he answered him not that day. And Saul said, "Draw ye near hither, all the chief of the people: and know and see wherein this sin hath been this day. For as the Lord liveth, which saveth Israel, though it be in Jonathan my son, he shall surely die." But there was not a man among all the people that answered him. Then said he unto all Israel, "Be ye on one side, and I and Jonathan my son will be on the other side." And the people said unto Saul, "Do what seemeth good unto thee." Therefore Saul said unto the Lord God of Israel, "Give a perfect lot." And Saul and Jonathan were taken: but the people escaped. And Saul said, "Cast lots between me and Jonathan my son." And Jonathan was taken. Then Saul said to Jonathan, "Tell me what thou hast done." And Jonathan told him, and said, "I did but taste a little honey with the end of the rod that was in mine hand, and lo, I must die." And Saul answered, "God do so, and more also: for thou shalt surely die, Jonathan." And the people said unto Saul, "Shall Jonathan die, who hath wrought this great salvation in Israel? God forbid: as the Lord liveth, there shall not one hair of his head fall to the ground: for he hath wrought with God this day." So the people rescued Jonathan, that he died not. Then Saul went up from following the Philistines: and the Philistines went to their own place.

So Saul took the kingdom over Israel, and fought against all his enemies on every side, against Moab, and against the children of Ammon, and against Edom, and against the kings of Zobah, and against the Philistines: and whithersoever he turned himself, he vexed them. And he gathered an host, and smote the Amalekites, and delivered Israel out of the hands of them that spoiled them. Now the sons of Saul were Jonathan and Ishui and Melchishua: and the names of his two daughters were these: the name of the first-born Merab, and the name of the younger Michal: and the name of Saul's wife was Ahinoam, the daughter of Ahimaaz:[2] and the name of the captain of his host was Abner, the son of Ner, Saul's uncle. And Kish was the father of Saul, and Ner the father of Abner was the son of Abiel. And there was sore war against the Philistines all the days of Saul: and when Saul saw any strong man, or any valiant man, he took him unto him.

[2] This is not the same Ahimaaz who appears at the end of the Saul-David story and perhaps wrote it.

16 . . . But the spirit of the Lord departed from Saul, and an evil spirit from the Lord troubled him. And Saul's servants said unto him, "Behold now, an evil spirit from God troubleth thee. Let our lord now command thy servants, which are before thee, to seek out a man, who is a cunning player on an harp: and it shall come to pass when the evil spirit from God is upon thee, that he shall play with his hand, and thou shalt be well." And Saul said unto his servants, "Provide me now a man that can play well, and bring him to me." Then answered one of the servants, and said, "Behold, I have seen a son of Jesse the Bethlehemite, that is cunning in playing, and a mighty valiant man, and a man of war, and prudent in matters, and a comely person, and the Lord is with him."

Wherefore Saul sent messengers unto Jesse, and said, "Send me David thy son, which is with the sheep." And Jesse took an ass laden with bread, and a bottle of wine, and a kid, and sent them by David his son unto Saul. And David came to Saul, and stood before him: and he loved him greatly, and he became his armour-bearer. And Saul sent to Jesse, saying, "Let David, I pray thee, stand before me: for he hath found favour in my sight." And it came to pass, when the evil spirit from God was upon Saul, that David took an harp, and played with his hand: so Saul was refreshed, and was well, and the evil spirit departed from him.

17 Now the Philistines gathered together their armies to battle, and were gathered together at Shochoh, which belongeth to Judah, and pitched between Shochoh and Azekah, in Ephes-dammim. And Saul and the men of Israel were gathered together, and pitched by the valley of Elah, and set the battle in array against the Philistines. And the Philistines stood on a mountain on the one side, and Israel stood on a mountain on the other side: and there was a valley between them.

And there went out a champion out of the camp of the Philistines, named Goliath, of Gath: whose height was six cubits and a span. And he had an helmet of brass upon his head, and he was armed with a coat of mail: and the weight of the coat was five thousand shekels of brass. And he had greaves of brass upon his legs, and a target of brass between his shoulders. And the staff of his spear was like a weaver's beam, and his spear's head weighed six hundred shekels of iron: and one bearing a shield went before him. And he stood and cried unto the armies of Israel, and said unto them, "Why are ye come out to set your battle in array? am not I a Philistine, and you servants to Saul? choose you a man for you, and let him come down to me. If he be able to fight with me, and to kill me, then will we be your servants: but if I prevail against him, and kill him, then shall ye be our servants, and serve us." And the Philistine said, "I defy the armies of Israel this day; give me a man, that we may fight together." When Saul and all Israel heard those words of the Philistine, they were dismayed, and greatly afraid.

Now David was the son of that Ephrathite of Bethlehem-Judah whose name was Jesse, and he had eight sons: and the man went among men for an old man in the days of Saul. And the three eldest sons of Jesse went, and followed Saul to the battle: and the names of his three sons that went to the battle were Eliab, the firstborn, and next unto him Abinadab, and the third, Shammah. And David was the youngest: and the three eldest followed Saul. But David went and returned from Saul to feed his father's sheep at Bethlehem. And the Philistine drew near, morning and evening, and presented himself forty days. And Jesse said unto David his son, "Take now for thy brethren an ephah of this parched corn, and these ten loaves, and run to the camp to thy brethren. And carry these ten cheeses unto the captain of their thousand, and look how thy brethren fare, and take their pledge." Now Saul, and they, and all the men of Israel were in the valley of Elah, fighting with the Philistines.

And David rose up early in the morning, and left the sheep with a keeper, and took, and went, as Jesse had commanded him; and he came to the trench, as the host was going forth to the fight, and shouted for the battle. For Israel and the Philistines had put the battle in array, army against army. And David left his carriage in the hand of the keeper of the carriage, and ran into the army, and came and saluted his brethren. And as he talked with them, behold, there came up the champion (the Philistine of Gath, Goliath by name) out of the armies of the Philistines, and spake according to the same words: and David heard them. And all the men of Israel, when they saw the man, fled from him, and were sore afraid. And the men of Israel said, "Have ye seen this man that is come up? Surely to defy Israel is he come up: and it shall be, that the man who killeth him, the king will enrich him with great riches, and will give him his daughter, and make his father's house free in Israel." And David spake to the men that stood by him, saying, "What shall be done to the man that killeth this Philistine, and taketh away the reproach from Israel? for who is this uncircumcised Philistine, that he should defy the armies of the living God?" And the people answered him after this manner, saying, "So shall it be done to the man that killeth him."

And Eliab his eldest brother heard when he spake unto the men, and Eliab's anger was kindled against David, and he said, "Why camest thou down hither? and with whom hast thou left those few sheep in the wilderness? I know thy pride, and the naughtiness of thine heart; for thou art come down that thou mightest see the battle." And David said, "What have I now done? Is there not a cause?" And he turned from him toward another, and spake after the same manner: and the people answered him again after the former manner. And when the words were heard which David spake, they rehearsed them before Saul: and he sent for him.

And David said to Saul, "Let no man's heart fail because of him: thy servant will go and fight with this Philistine." And Saul said to David, "Thou art not able to go against this Philistine, to fight with him: for thou art but a youth, and he a man of war from his youth." And David said unto Saul, "Thy servant kept his father's sheep, and there came a lion, and a bear, and took a lamb out of the flock: and I went after him, and smote him, and delivered it out of his mouth: and when he arose against me, I caught him by his beard, and smote him, and slew him. Thy servant slew both the lion and the bear: and this uncircumcised Philistine shall be as one of them, seeing he hath defied the armies of the living God." David said moreover, "The Lord that delivered me out of the paw of the lion, and out of the paw of the bear, he will deliver me out of the hand of this Philistine." And Saul said unto David, "Go, and the Lord be with thee."

And Saul armed David with his armour, and he put an helmet of brass upon his head, also he armed him with a coat of mail. And David girded his sword upon his armour, and he assayed to go, for he had not proved it: and David said unto Saul, "I cannot go with these: for I have not proved them." And David put them off him. And he took his staff in his hand, and chose him five smooth stones out of the brook, and put them in a shepherd's bag which he had, even in a scrip; and his sling was in his hand: and he drew near to the Philistine. And the Philistine came on and drew near unto David, and the man that bare the shield went before him. And when the Philistine looked about, and saw David, he disdained him: for he was but a youth, and ruddy, and of a fair countenance. And the Philistine said unto David, "Am I a dog, that thou comest to me with staves?" And the Philistine cursed David by his gods. And the Philistine said to David, "Come to me, and I will give thy flesh unto the fowls of the air, and to the beasts of the field." Then said David to the Philistine, "Thou comest to me with a sword, and with a spear, and with a shield: but I come to thee in the name of the Lord of hosts, the God of the armies of Israel, whom thou hast defied. This day will the Lord deliver thee into mine hand, and I will smite thee, and take thine head from thee, and I will give the carcasses of the host of the Philistines this day unto the fowls of the air, and to the wild beasts of the earth, that all the earth may know that there is a God in Israel. And all this assembly shall know that the Lord saveth not with sword and spear (for the battle is the Lord's), and he will give you into our hands."

And it came to pass when the Philistine arose, and came, and drew nigh to meet David, that David hasted, and ran toward the army to meet the Philistine. And David put his hand in his bag, and took thence a stone, and slang it, and smote the Philistine in his forehead, that the stone sunk into his forehead, and he fell upon his face to the earth. So David prevailed over the Philistine with a sling and with a stone, and smote the Philistine, and slew him; but there was no sword in the hand of David. Therefore David ran and stood upon the Philistine, and took his sword, and drew it out of the sheath thereof, and slew him, and cut off his head therewith. And when the Philistines saw their champion was dead, they fled. And the men of Israel and of Judah arose, and shouted, and pursued the Philistines, until thou come to the valley, and to the gates of Ekron: and the wounded of the Philistines fell down by the way to Shaaraim, even unto Gath, and unto Ekron. And the children of Israel returned from chasing after the Philistines, and they spoiled their tents. And David took the head of the Philistine, and brought it to Jerusalem, but he put his armour in his tent.

And when Saul saw David go forth against the Philistine, he said unto Abner the captain of the host, "Abner, whose son is this youth?" And Abner said, "As thy soul liveth, O king, I cannot tell." And the

king said, "Inquire thou whose son the stripling is." And as David
returned from the slaughter of the Philistine, Abner took him, and
brought him before Saul, with the head of the Philistine in his hand.
And Saul said to him, "Whose son art thou, thou young man?" And
David answered, "I am the son of thy servant Jesse, the Bethlehemite."

18 And it came to pass when he had made an end of speaking
unto Saul, that the soul of Jonathan was knit with the soul of
David, and Jonathan loved him as his own soul. And Saul took him
that day, and would let him go no more home to his father's house.
Then Jonathan and David made a covenant, because he loved him
as his own soul. And Jonathan stripped himself of the robe that was
upon him, and gave it to David, and his garments, even to his sword,
and to his bow, and to his girdle.

And David went out whithersoever Saul sent him, and behaved
himself wisely: and Saul set him over the men of war, and he was
accepted in the sight of all the people, and also in the sight of Saul's
servants. And it came to pass as they came, when David was
returned from the slaughter of the Philistine, that the women came
out of all cities of Israel, singing and dancing, to meet king Saul,
with tabrets, with joy, and with instruments of music. And the
women answered one another as they played, and said, "Saul hath
slain his thousands, and David his ten thousands." And Saul was
very wroth, and the saying displeased him, and he said, "They have
ascribed unto David ten thousands, and to me they have ascribed but
thousands: and what can he have more but the kingdom?" And Saul
eyed David from that day and forward.

And it came to pass on the morrow, that the evil spirit from God
came upon Saul, and he prophesied in the midst of the house: and
David played with his hand, as at other times: and there was a
javelin in Saul's hand. And Saul cast the javelin; for he said, "I will
smite David even to the wall with it": and David avoided out of his
presence twice.

And Saul was afraid of David, because the Lord was with him,
and was departed from Saul. Therefore Saul removed him from him,
and made him his captain over a thousand, and he went out and
came in before the people. And David behaved himself wisely in all
his ways; and the Lord was with him. Wherefore when Saul saw

that he behaved himself very wisely, he was afraid of him. But all Israel and Judah loved David, because he went out and came in before them.

And Saul said to David, "Behold, my elder daughter Merab, her will I give thee to wife: only be thou valiant for me, and fight the Lord's battles": for Saul said, "Let not mine hand be upon him, but let the hand of the Philistines be upon him." And David said unto Saul, "Who am I? and what is my life, or my father's family in Israel, that I should be son in law to the king?" But it came to pass at the time when Merab Saul's daughter should have been given to David, that she was given unto Adriel the Meholathite to wife. And Michal Saul's daughter loved David: and they told Saul, and the thing pleased him. And Saul said, "I will give him her, that she may be a snare to him, and that the hand of the Philistines may be against him." Wherefore Saul said to David, "Thou shalt this day be my son in law, in the one of the twain."

And Saul commanded his servants, saying, "Commune with David secretly, and say, 'Behold, the king hath delight in thee, and all his servants love thee: now therefore be the king's son in law.'" And Saul's servants spake those words in the ears of David. And David said, "Seemeth it to you a light thing to be a king's son in law, seeing that I am a poor man, and lightly esteemed?" And the servants of Saul told him, saying, "On this manner spake David." And Saul said, "Thus shall ye say to David, 'The king desireth not any dowry, but an hundred foreskins of the Philistines, to be avenged of the king's enemies.'" But Saul thought to make David fall by the hand of the Philistines. And when his servants told David these words, it pleased David well to be the king's son in law: and the days were not expired. Wherefore David arose and went, he and his men, and slew of the Philistines two hundred men; and David brought their foreskins, and they gave them in full tale to the king, that he might be the king's son in law: and Saul gave him Michal his daughter to wife.

And Saul saw and knew that the Lord was with David, and that Michal Saul's daughter loved him. And Saul was yet the more afraid of David; and Saul became David's enemy continually. Then the princes of the Philistines went forth: and it came to pass after they went forth, that David behaved himself more wisely than all the servants of Saul, so that his name was much set by.

19 And Saul spake to Jonathan his son, and to all his servants, that they should kill David. But Jonathan Saul's son delighted much in David, and Jonathan told David, saying, "Saul my father seeketh to kill thee. Now therefore, I pray thee, take heed to thyself until the morning, and abide in a secret place, and hide thyself: and I will go out and stand beside my father in the field where thou art, and I will commune with my father of thee, and what I see, that I will tell thee."

And Jonathan spake good of David unto Saul his father, and said unto him, "Let not the king sin against his servant, against David: because he hath not sinned against thee, and because his works have been to thee-ward very good. For he did put his life in his hand, and slew the Philistine, and the Lord wrought a great salvation for all Israel: thou sawest it, and didst rejoice. Wherefore then wilt thou sin against innocent blood, to slay David without a cause?" And Saul hearkened unto the voice of Jonathan; and Saul sware, "As the Lord liveth, he shall not be slain." And Jonathan called David, and Jonathan showed him all those things: and Jonathan brought David to Saul, and he was in his presence, as in times past.

And there was war again, and David went out, and fought with the Philistines, and slew them with a great slaughter, and they fled from him. And the evil spirit from the Lord was upon Saul, as he sat in his house with his javelin in his hand: and David played with his hand. And Saul sought to smite David even to the wall with the javelin: but he slipped away out of Saul's presence, and he smote the javelin into the wall: and David fled, and escaped that night. Saul also sent messengers unto David's house, to watch him, and to slay him in the morning: and Michal David's wife told him, saying, "If thou save not thy life tonight, tomorrow thou shalt be slain."

So Michal let David down through a window: and he went and fled, and escaped. And Michal took an image, and laid it in the bed, and put a pillow of goats' hair for his bolster, and covered it with a cloth. And when Saul sent messengers to take David, she said, "He is sick." And Saul sent the messengers again to see David, saying, "Bring him up to me in the bed, that I may slay him." And when the messengers were come in, behold, there was an image in the bed, with a pillow of goats' hair for his bolster. And Saul said unto Michal, "Why hast thou deceived me so, and sent away mine enemy, that he is escaped?" And Michal answered Saul, "He said unto me, 'Let me go; why should I kill thee?'"

So David fled, and escaped, and came to Samuel to Ramah, and told him all that Saul had done to him: and he and Samuel went and dwelt in Naioth. And it was told Saul, saying, "Behold, David is at Naioth in Ramah." And Saul sent messengers to take David: and when they saw the company of the prophets prophesying, and Samuel standing as appointed over them, the spirit of God was upon the messengers of Saul, and they also prophesied. And when it was told Saul, he sent other messengers, and they prophesied likewise: and Saul sent messengers again the third time, and they prophesied also. Then went he also to Ramah, and came to a great well that is in Sechu: and he asked, and said, "Where are Samuel and David?" And one said, "Behold, they be at Naioth in Ramah." And he went thither to Naioth in Ramah: and the spirit of God was upon him also, and he went on, and prophesied until he came to Naioth in Ramah. And he stripped off his clothes also, and prophesied before Samuel in like manner, and lay down naked all that day, and all that night. Wherefore they say, "Is Saul also among the prophets?"

20 And David fled from Naioth in Ramah, and came and said before Jonathan, "What have I done? what is mine iniquity? and what is my sin before thy father, that he seeketh my life?" And he said unto him, "God forbid, thou shalt not die; behold, my father will do nothing, either great or small, but that he will show it me: and why should my father hide this thing from me? it is not so." And David sware moreover, and said, "Thy father certainly knoweth that I have found grace in thine eyes, and he saith, 'Let not Jonathan know this, lest he be grieved': but truly, as the Lord liveth, and as thy soul liveth, there is but a step between me and death." Then said Jonathan unto David, "Whatsoever thy soul desireth, I will even do it for thee." And David said unto Jonathan, "Behold, tomorrow is the new moon, and I should not fail to sit with the king at meat: but let me go, that I may hide myself in the field unto the third day at even. If thy father at all miss me, then say, 'David earnestly asked leave of me that he might run to Bethlehem his city: for there is a yearly sacrifice there for all the family.' If he say thus, 'It is well,' thy servant shall have peace: but if he be very wroth, then be sure that evil is determined by him. Therefore thou shalt deal kindly with thy servant, for thou hast brought thy servant into a covenant of the Lord with thee: notwithstanding, if there be in me iniquity, slay me thyself: for why shouldest thou bring me to thy father?" And Jonathan said, "Far be it from thee: for if I knew certainly that evil were determined by my father to come upon thee, then would not I tell it thee?" Then said David to Jonathan, "Who shall tell me? or what if thy father answer thee roughly?"

And Jonathan said unto David, "Come, and let us go out into the field." And they went out both of them into the field. And Jonathan said unto David, "O Lord God of Israel, when I have sounded my father about tomorrow any time, or the third day, and behold, if there be good toward David, and I then send not unto thee, and show it thee; the Lord do so and much more to Jonathan: but if it please my father to do thee evil, then I will show it thee, and send thee away, that thou mayest go in peace, and the Lord be with thee, as he hath been with my father. And thou shalt not only, while yet I live, show me the kindness of the Lord, that I die not: but also thou shalt not cut off thy kindness from my house for ever: no not when the Lord hath cut off the enemies of David, every one from the face of the earth." So Jonathan made a covenant with the house of David, saying, "Let the Lord even require it at the hand of David's enemies." And Jonathan caused David to swear again, because he loved him: for he loved him as he loved his own soul. Then Jonathan said to David, "Tomorrow is the new moon: and thou shalt be missed, because thy seat will be empty. And when thou hast stayed three days, then thou shalt go down quickly, and come to the place where thou didst hide thyself when the business was in hand, and shalt remain by the stone Ezel. And I will shoot three arrows on the side thereof, as though I shot at a mark. And behold, I will send a lad, saying, 'Go, find out the arrows.' If I expressly say unto the lad, 'Behold, the arrows are on this side of thee, take them': then come thou, for there is peace to thee, and no hurt, as the Lord liveth. But if I say thus unto the young man, 'Behold, the arrows are beyond thee'; go thy way, for the Lord hath sent thee away. And as touching the matter which thou and I have spoken of, behold, the Lord be between thee and me for ever."

So David hid himself in the field: and when the new moon was come, the king sat him down to eat meat. And the king sat upon his seat, as at other times, even upon a seat by the wall: and

Jonathan arose, and Abner sat by Saul's side, and David's place was empty. Nevertheless, Saul spake not any thing that day: for he thought, "Something hath befallen him, he is not clean; surely he is not clean." And it came to pass on the morrow, which was the second day of the month, that David's place was empty: and Saul said unto Jonathan his son, "Wherefore cometh not the son of Jesse to meat, neither yesterday nor today?" And Jonathan answered Saul, "David earnestly asked leave of me to go to Bethlehem. And he said, 'Let me go, I pray thee, for our family hath a sacrifice in the city, and my brother, he hath commanded me to be there: and now, if I have found favour in thine eyes, let me get away, I pray thee, and see my brethren.' Therefore he cometh not unto the king's table." Then Saul's anger was kindled against Jonathan, and he said unto him, "Thou son of the perverse rebellious woman, do not I know that thou hast chosen the son of Jesse to thine own confusion, and unto the confusion of thy mother's nakedness? For as long as the son of Jesse liveth upon the ground, thou shalt not be established, nor thy kingdom: wherefore now send and fetch him unto me, for he shall surely die." And Jonathan answered Saul his father, and said unto him, "Wherefore shall he be slain? what hath he done?" And Saul cast a javelin at him to smite him, whereby Jonathan knew that it was determined of his father to slay David. So Jonathan arose from the table in fierce anger, and did eat no meat the second day of the month: for he was grieved for David, because his father had done him shame.

And it came to pass in the morning, that Jonathan went out into the field, at the time appointed with David, and a little lad with him. And he said unto his lad, "Run, find out now the arrows which I shoot." And as the lad ran, he shot an arrow beyond him. And when the lad was come to the place of the arrow which Jonathan had shot, Jonathan cried after the lad, and said, "Is not the arrow beyond thee?" And Jonathan cried after the lad, "Make speed, haste, stay not." And Jonathan's lad gathered up the arrows, and came to his master. But the lad knew not any thing: only Jonathan and David knew the matter. And Jonathan gave his artillery unto his lad, and said unto him, "Go, carry them to the city."

And as soon as the lad was gone, David arose out of a place toward the south, and fell on his face to the ground, and bowed himself three times: and they kissed one another, and wept one with another, until David exceeded. And Jonathan said to David, "Go in peace, forasmuch as we have sworn both of us in the name of the Lord, saying, 'The Lord be between me and thee, and between my seed and thy seed for ever.'" And he arose, and departed: and Jonathan went into the city.

21 Then came David to Nob, to Ahimelech the priest, and Ahimelech was afraid at the meeting of David, and said unto him, "Why art thou alone, and no man with thee?" And David said unto Ahimelech the priest, "The king hath commanded me a business, and hath said unto me, 'Let no man know any thing of the business whereabout I send thee, and what I have commanded thee': and I have appointed my servants to such and such a place. Now therefore what is under thine hand? give me five loaves of bread in mine hand, or what there is present." And the priest answered David, and said, "There is no common bread under mine hand, but there is hallowed bread; if the young men have kept themselves at least from women." And David answered the priest, and said unto him, "Of a truth women have been kept from us about these three days, since I came out, and the vessels of the young men are holy, and the bread is in a manner common, yea, though it were sanctified this day in the vessel." So the priest gave him hallowed bread; for there was no bread there but the shewbread, that was taken from before the Lord, to put hot bread in the day when it was taken away. Now a certain man of the servants of Saul was there that day, detained before the Lord, and his name was Doeg, an Edomite, the chiefest of the herdmen that belonged to Saul.

And David said unto Ahimelech, "And is there not here under thine hand spear or sword? for I have neither brought my sword nor my weapons with me, because the king's business required haste." And the priest said, "The sword of Goliath the Philistine, whom thou slewest in the valley of Elah, behold, it is here wrapped in a cloth behind the ephod: if thou wilt take that, take it; for there is no other save that here." And David said, "There is none like that, give it me."

And David arose, and fled that day, for fear of Saul, and went to Achish the king of Gath. And the servants of Achish said unto him, "Is not this David the king of the land? did they not sing one to another of him in dances, saying, 'Saul hath slain his thousands, and

David his ten thousands'?" And David laid up these words in his heart, and was sore afraid of Achish the king of Gath. And he changed his behaviour before them, and feigned himself mad in their hands, and scrabbled on the doors of the gate, and let his spittle fall down upon his beard. Then said Achish unto his servants, "Lo, you see the man is mad: wherefore then have ye brought him to me? Have I need of mad men, that ye have brought this fellow to play the mad man in my presence? Shall this fellow come into my house?"

22 David therefore departed thence, and escaped to the cave Adullam: and when his brethren and all his father's house heard it, they went down thither to him. And every one that was in distress, and every one that was in debt, and every one that was discontented, gathered themselves unto him, and he became a captain over them: and there were with him about four hundred men.

And David went thence to Mizpeh of Moab; and he said unto the king of Moab, "Let my father and my mother, I pray thee, come forth, and be with you, till I know what God will do for me." And he brought them before the king of Moab: and they dwelt with him all the while that David was in the hold.[3] And the prophet Gad said unto David, "Abide not in the hold; depart, and get thee into the land of Judah." Then David departed, and came into the forest of Hareth.

When Saul heard that David was discovered, and the men that were with him (now Saul abode in Gibeah under a tree in Ramah, having his spear in his hand, and all his servants were standing about him): then Saul said unto his servants that stood about him, "Hear now, ye Benjamites: will the son of Jesse give every one of you fields, and vineyards, and make you all captains of thousands, and captains of hundreds: that all of you have conspired against me, and there is none that showeth me that my son hath made a league with the son of Jesse, and there is none of you that is sorry for me, or showeth unto me that my son hath stirred up my servant against me, to lie in wait, as at this day?"

Then answered Doeg the Edomite (which was set over the servants of Saul), and said, "I saw the son of Jesse coming to Nob, to

[3] *I.e.,* stronghold.

Ahimelech the son of Ahitub. And he inquired of the Lord for him, and gave him victuals, and gave him the sword of Goliath the Philistine." Then the king sent to call Ahimelech the priest, the son of Ahitub, and all his father's house, the priests that were in Nob: and they came all of them to the king. And Saul said, "Hear now thou son of Ahitub." And he answered, "Here I am, my lord." And Saul said unto him, "Why have ye conspired against me, thou and the son of Jesse, in that thou hast given him bread, and a sword, and hast inquired of God for him, that he should rise against me, to lie in wait, as at this day?" Then Ahimelech answered the king, and said, "And who is so faithful among all thy servants as David, which is the king's son in law, and goeth at thy bidding, and is honourable in thine house? Did I then begin to inquire of God for him? be it far from me: let not the king impute any thing unto his servant, nor to all the house of my father: for thy servant knew nothing of all this, less or more." And the king said, "Thou shalt surely die, Ahimelech, thou, and all thy father's house."

And the king said unto the footmen that stood about him, "Turn and slay the priests of the Lord, because their hand also is with David, and because they knew when he fled, and did not show it to me." But the servants of the king would not put forth their hand to fall upon the priests of the Lord. And the king said to Doeg, "Turn thou and fall upon the priests." And Doeg the Edomite turned, and fell upon the priests, and slew on that day fourscore and five persons that did wear a linen ephod.[4] And Nob, the city of the priests, smote he with the edge of the sword, both men and women, children and sucklings, and oxen and asses, and sheep, with the edge of the sword.

And one of the sons of Ahimelech the son of Ahitub, named Abiathar, escaped and fled after David: and Abiathar showed David that Saul had slain the Lord's priests. And David said unto Abiathar, "I knew it that day, when Doeg the Edomite was there, that he would surely tell Saul: I have occasioned the death of all the persons of thy father's house. Abide thou with me, fear not: for he that seeketh my life seeketh thy life: but with me thou shalt be in safeguard."

[4] The correct meaning probably is: "fourscore and five persons qualified to bear the ephod."

23 Then they told David, saying, "Behold, the Philistines fight against Keilah, and they rob the threshingfloors." Therefore David inquired of the Lord, saying, "Shall I go and smite these Philistines?" And the Lord said unto David, "Go, and smite the Philistines, and save Keilah." And David's men said unto him, "Behold, we be afraid here in Judah: how much more then if we come to Keilah against the armies of the Philistines?" Then David inquired of the Lord yet again. And the Lord answered him, and said, "Arise, go down to Keilah: for I will deliver the Philistines into thine hand." So David and his men went to Keilah, and fought with the Philistines, and brought away their cattle, and smote them with a great slaughter. So David saved the inhabitants of Keilah. And it came to pass when Abiathar the son of Ahimelech fled to David to Keilah, that he came down with an ephod in his hand.

And it was told Saul that David was come to Keilah: and Saul said, "God hath delivered him into mine hand: for he is shut in, by entering into a town that hath gates and bars." And Saul called all the people together to war, to go down to Keilah, to besiege David and his men.

And David knew that Saul secretly practiced mischief against him, and he said to Abiathar the priest, "Bring hither the ephod." Then said David, "O Lord God of Israel, thy servant hath certainly heard that Saul seeketh to come to Keilah, to destroy the city for my sake. Will the men of Keilah deliver me up into his hand? will Saul come down, as thy servant hath heard? O Lord God of Israel, I beseech thee, tell thy servant." And the Lord said, "He will come down." Then said David, "Will the men of Keilah deliver me, and my men, into the hand of Saul?" And the Lord said, "They will deliver thee up."

Then David and his men, which were about six hundred, arose, and departed out of Keilah, and went whithersoever they could go: and it was told Saul that David was escaped from Keilah, and he forbare to go forth. And David abode in the wilderness in strongholds, and remained in a mountain in the wilderness of Ziph: and Saul sought him every day, but God delivered him not into his hand. And David saw that Saul was come out to seek his life: and David was in the wilderness of Ziph in a wood.

And Jonathan Saul's son arose, and went to David into the wood, and strengthened his hand in God. And he said unto him, "Fear not; for the hand of Saul my father shall not find thee, and thou shalt be king over Israel, and I shall be next unto thee: and that also Saul my father knoweth." And they two made a covenant before the Lord: and David abode in the wood, and Jonathan went to his house.

Then came up the Ziphites to Saul to Gibeah, saying, "Doth not David hide himself with us in strongholds in the wood, in the hill of Hachilah, which is on the south of Jeshimon? Now therefore, O king, come down according to all the desire of thy soul to come down, and our part shall be to deliver him into the king's hand." And Saul said, "Blessed be ye of the Lord, for ye have compassion on me. Go, I pray you, prepare yet, and know and see his place where his haunt is, and who hath seen him there: for it is told me that he dealeth very subtly. See therefore, and take knowledge of all the lurking places where he hideth himself, and come ye again to me with the certainty, and I will go with you: and it shall come to pass, if he be in the land, that I will search him out throughout all the thousands of Judah." And they arose, and went to Ziph before Saul: but David and his men were in the wilderness of Maon, in the plain on the south of Jeshimon. Saul also and his men went to seek him. And they told David: wherefore he came down into a rock, and abode in the wilderness of Maon: and when Saul heard that, he pursued after David in the wilderness of Maon. And Saul went on this side of the mountain, and David and his men on that side of the mountain: and David made haste to get away for fear of Saul: for Saul and his men compassed David and his men round about to take them.

But there came a messenger unto Saul, saying, "Haste thee, and come: for the Philistines have invaded the land." Wherefore Saul returned from pursuing after David, and went against the Philistines; therefore they called that place Sela-hammahlekoth. And David went up from thence, and dwelt in strongholds at En-gedi.

24 And it came to pass when Saul was returned from following the Philistines, that it was told him, saying, "Behold, David is in the wilderness of En-gedi." Then Saul took three thousand chosen men out of all Israel, and went to seek David and his men upon the rocks of the wild goats. And he came to the sheepcotes by the way, where was a cave, and Saul went in to cover his feet: and

David and his men remained in the sides of the cave. And the men of David said unto him, "Behold the day of which the Lord said unto thee, 'Behold, I will deliver thine enemy into thine hand, that thou mayest do to him as it shall seem good unto thee.'" Then David arose, and cut off the skirt of Saul's robe privily. And it came to pass afterward, that David's heart smote him, because he had cut off Saul's skirt. And he said unto his men, "The Lord forbid that I should do this thing unto my master, the Lord's anointed, to stretch forth mine hand against him, seeing he is the anointed of the Lord." So David stayed his servants with these words, and suffered them not to rise against Saul. But Saul rose up out of the cave, and went on his way. David also arose afterward, and went out of the cave, and cried after Saul, saying, "My lord the king." And when Saul looked behind him, David stooped with his face to the earth, and bowed himself.

And David said to Saul, "Wherefore hearest thou men's words, saying, 'Behold, David seeketh thy hurt'? Behold, this day thine eyes have seen how that the Lord had delivered thee today into mine hand in the cave: and some bade me kill thee, but mine eye spared thee, and I said, 'I will not put forth mine hand against my lord, for he is the Lord's anointed.' Moreover, my father, see, yea, see the skirt of thy robe in my hand: for in that I cut off the skirt of thy robe, and killed thee not, know thou and see that there is neither evil nor transgression in mine hand, and I have not sinned against thee; yet thou huntest my soul, to take it. The Lord judge between me and thee, and the Lord avenge me of thee: but mine hand shall not be upon thee. As saith the proverb of the ancients, 'Wickedness proceedeth from the wicked': but mine hand shall not be upon thee. After whom is the king of Israel come out? after whom dost thou pursue? after a dead dog, after a flea. The Lord therefore be judge, and judge between me and thee, and see, and plead my cause, and deliver me out of thine hand."

And it came to pass when David had made an end of speaking these words unto Saul, that Saul said, "Is this thy voice, my son David?" And Saul lifted up his voice, and wept. And he said to David, "Thou art more righteous than I: for thou hast rewarded me good, whereas I have rewarded thee evil. And thou hast showed this day how thou hast dealt well with me: forasmuch as when the Lord had delivered me into thine hand, thou killedst me not. For if a man find his enemy, will he let him go well away? wherefore the Lord reward thee good, for that thou hast done unto me this day. And now behold, I know well that thou shalt surely be king, and that the kingdom of Israel shall be established in thine hand. Swear now therefore unto me by the Lord that thou wilt not cut off my seed after me, and that thou wilt not destroy my name out of my father's house." And David sware unto Saul, and Saul went home: but David and his men got them up into the hold.

25 And Samuel died, and all the Israelites were gathered together, and lamented him, and buried him in his house at Ramah. And David arose, and went down to the wilderness of Paran. And there was a man in Maon, whose possessions were in Carmel, and the man was very great, and he had three thousand sheep, and a thousand goats: and he was shearing his sheep in Carmel. Now the name of the man was Nabal, and the name of his wife Abigail: and she was a woman of good understanding, and of a beautiful countenance: but the man was churlish and evil in his doings, and he was of the house of Caleb.

And David heard in the wilderness that Nabal did shear his sheep. And David sent out ten young men, and David said unto the young men, "Get you up to Carmel, and go to Nabal, and greet him in my name; and thus shall ye say to him that liveth in prosperity, 'Peace be both to thee, and peace be to thine house, and peace be unto all that thou hast. And now, I have heard that thou hast shearers: now thy shepherds which were with us, we hurt them not, neither was there aught missing unto them, all the while they were in Carmel. Ask thy young men, and they will show thee. Wherefore let the young men find favour in thine eyes (for we come in a good day): give, I pray thee, whatsoever cometh to thine hand unto thy servants, and to thy son David.' " And when David's young men came, they spake to Nabal according to all those words in the name of David, and ceased.

And Nabal answered David's servants, and said, "Who is David? and who is the son of Jesse? There be many servants nowadays that break away every man from his master. Shall I then take my bread and my water, and my flesh that I have killed for my shearers, and give it unto men, whom I know not whence they be?" So David's young men turned their way, and went again, and came and told him all those sayings. And David said unto his men, "Gird you on every man his sword." And they girded on every man his sword, and David also girded on his sword: and there went up after David about four hundred men, and two hundred abode by the stuff.

But one of the young men told Abigail, Nabal's wife, saying, "Behold, David sent messengers out of the wilderness to salute our master: and he railed on them. But the men were very good unto us, and we were not hurt, neither missed we any thing as long as we were conversant with them, when we were in the fields. They were a wall unto us both by night and day, all the while we were with them keeping sheep. Now therefore know and consider what thou wilt do: for evil is determined against our master, and against all his household: for he is such a son of Belial that a man cannot speak to him."

Then Abigail made haste, and took two hundred loaves, and two bottles of wine, and five sheep ready dressed, and five measures of parched corn, and a hundred clusters of raisins, and two hundred cakes of figs, and laid them on asses. And she said unto her servants, "Go on before me, behold, I come after you": but she told not her husband Nabal. And it was so as she rode on the ass, that she came down by the covert of the hill, and behold, David and his men came down against her, and she met them. (Now David had said, "Surely in vain have I kept all that this fellow hath in the wilderness, so that nothing was missed of all that pertained unto him: and he hath requited me evil for good. So and more also do God unto the enemies of David, if I leave of all that pertain to him by the morning light any that pisseth against the wall.") And when Abigail saw David, she hasted, and lighted off the ass, and fell before David on her face, and bowed herself to the ground, and fell at his feet, and said, "Upon me, my lord, upon me let this iniquity be, and let thine handmaid, I pray thee, speak in thine audience, and hear the words of thine handmaid. Let not my lord, I pray thee, regard this man of Belial, even Nabal: for as his name is, so is he:[5] Nabal is his name, and folly is with him: but I thine handmaid saw not the young men of my lord, whom thou didst send. Now therefore, my lord, as the Lord liveth, and as thy soul liveth, seeing the Lord hath withholden thee from coming to shed blood, and from avenging thyself with

[5] "Nabal" means fool.

thine own hand: now let thine enemies, and they that seek evil to my lord, be as Nabal. And now this blessing which thine handmaid hath brought unto my lord, let it even be given unto the young men that follow my lord." . . .

And David said to Abigail, "Blessed be the Lord God of Israel, which sent thee this day to meet me. And blessed be thy advice, and blessed be thou, which hast kept me this day from coming to shed blood, and from avenging myself with mine own hand. For in very deed, as the Lord God of Israel liveth, which hath kept me back from hurting thee, except thou hadst hasted and come to meet me, surely there had not been left unto Nabal, by the morning light, any that pisseth against the wall." So David received of her hand that which she had brought him, and said unto her, "Go up in peace to thine house; see, I have hearkened to thy voice, and have accepted thy person."

And Abigail came to Nabal, and behold, he held a feast in his house like the feast of a king; and Nabal's heart was merry within him, for he was very drunken: wherefore she told him nothing, less or more, until the morning light. But it came to pass in the morning, when the wine was gone out of Nabal, and his wife had told him these things, that his heart died within him, and he became as a stone. And it came to pass about ten days after, that the Lord smote Nabal, that he died.

And when David heard that Nabal was dead, he said, "Blessed be the Lord, that hath pleaded the cause of my reproach from the hand of Nabal, and hath kept his servant from evil: for the Lord hath returned the wickedness of Nabal upon his own head." And David sent, and communed with Abigail, to take her to him to wife. And when the servants of David were come to Abigail to Carmel, they spake unto her, saying, "David sent us unto thee, to take thee to him to wife." And she arose, and bowed herself on her face to the earth, and said, "Behold, let thine handmaid be a servant to wash the feet of the servants of my lord." And Abigail hasted, and rose, and rode upon an ass, with five damsels of hers that went after her; and she went after the messengers of David, and became his wife. David also took Ahinoam of Jezreel, and they were also both of them his wives. But Saul had given Michal his daughter, David's wife, to Phalti the son of Laish, which was of Gallim.

26 And the Ziphites came unto Saul to Gibeah, saying, "Doth not David hide himself in the hill of Hachilah, which is before Jeshimon?" Then Saul arose, and went down to the wilderness of Ziph, having three thousand chosen men of Israel with him, to seek David in the wilderness of Ziph. And Saul pitched in the hill of Hachilah, which is before Jeshimon, by the way: but David abode in the wilderness, and he saw that Saul came after him into the wilderness. David therefore sent out spies, and understood that Saul was come in very deed.

And David arose, and came to the place where Saul had pitched: and David beheld the place where Saul lay, and Abner the son of Ner the captain of his host: and Saul lay in the trench, and the people pitched round about him. Then answered David, and said to Ahimelech the Hittite, and to Abishai the son of Zeruiah brother to Joab, saying, "Who will go down with me to Saul to the camp?" And Abishai said, "I will go down with thee." So David and Abishai came to the people by night, and behold, Saul lay sleeping within the trench, and his spear stuck in the ground at his bolster: but Abner and the people lay round about him. Then said Abishai to David, "God hath delivered thine enemy into thine hand this day: now therefore let me smite him, I pray thee, with the spear, even to the earth at once, and I will not smite him the second time." And David said to Abishai, "Destroy him not: for who can stretch forth his hand against the Lord's anointed, and be guiltless?" David said furthermore, "As the Lord liveth, the Lord shall smite him, or his day shall come to die, or he shall descend into battle, and perish. The Lord forbid that I should stretch forth mine hand against the Lord's anointed: but I pray thee, take thou now the spear that is at his bolster, and the cruse of water, and let us go." So David took the spear and the cruse of water from Saul's bolster; and they got them away, and no man saw it, nor knew it, neither awaked: for they were all asleep, because a deep sleep from the Lord was fallen upon them.

Then David went over to the other side, and stood on the top of a hill afar off (a great space being between them): and David cried to the people, and to Abner the son of Ner, saying, "Answerest thou not, Abner?" Then Abner answered, and said, "Who art thou that criest to the king?" And David said to Abner, "Art not thou a valiant man? and who is like to thee in Israel? Wherefore then hast thou not kept thy lord the king? for there came one of the people in, to destroy the king thy lord. This thing is not good that thou hast done: as the Lord liveth, ye are worthy to die, because ye have not kept your master the Lord's anointed: and now see where the king's spear is, and the cruse of water that was at his bolster." And Saul knew David's voice, and said, "Is this thy voice, my son David?" And David said, "It is my voice, my lord, O king." And he said, "Wherefore doth my lord thus pursue after his servant? for what have I done? or what evil is in mine hand? Now therefore, I pray thee, let my lord the king hear the words of his servant: if the Lord have stirred thee up against me, let him accept an offering: but if they be the children of men, cursed be they before the Lord: for they have driven me out this day from abiding in the inheritance of the Lord, saying. 'Go, serve other gods.' Now therefore, let not my blood fall to the earth before the face of the Lord: for the king of Israel is come out to seek a flea, as when one doth hunt a partridge in the mountains."

Then said Saul, "I have sinned: return, my son David, for I will no more do thee harm, because my soul was precious in thine eyes this day: behold, I have played the fool, and have erred exceedingly." And David answered, and said, "Behold the king's spear, and let one of the young men come over and fetch it. The Lord render to every man his righteousness, and his faithfulness: for the Lord delivered thee into my hand today, but I would not stretch forth mine hand against the Lord's anointed. And behold, as thy life was much set by this day in mine eyes: so let my life be much set by in the eyes of the Lord, and let him deliver me out of all tribulation." Then Saul said to David, "Blessed be thou, my son David: thou shalt both do great things, and also shalt still prevail." So David went on his way, and Saul returned to his place.

27 And David said in his heart, "I shall now perish one day by the hand of Saul: there is nothing better for me than that I should speedily escape into the land of the Philistines; and Saul shall despair of me, to seek me any more in any coast of Israel: so shall I escape out of his hand." And David arose, and he passed over with the six hundred men that were with him, unto Achish, the son of Maoch, king of Gath. And David dwelt with Achish at Gath, he and his men, every man with his household, even David with his two wives, Ahinoam the Jezreelitess, and Abigail the Carmelitess, Nabal's wife. And it was told Saul that David was fled to Gath, and he sought no more again for him.

And David said unto Achish, "If I have now found grace in thine eyes, let them give me a place in some town in the country, that I may dwell there: for why should thy servant dwell in the royal city with thee?" Then Achish gave him Ziklag that day: wherefore Ziklag pertaineth unto the kings of Judah unto this day. And the time that David dwelt in the country of the Philistines was a full year and four months.

And David and his men went up and invaded the Geshurites, and the Gezrites, and the Amalekites: for those nations were of old the inhabitants of the land, as thou goest to Shur, even unto the land of Egypt. And David smote the land, and left neither man nor woman alive, and took away the sheep, and the oxen, and the asses, and the camels, and the apparel, and returned, and came to Achish. And Achish said, "Whither have ye made a road[6] today?" And David said, "Against the south of Judah, and against the south of the Jerahmeel-ites, and against the south of the Kenites." And David saved neither man nor woman alive, to bring tidings to Gath, saying, "Lest they should tell on us, saying, 'So did David, and so will be his manner all the while he dwelleth in the country of the Philistines.'" And Achish believed David, saying, "He hath made his people Israel utterly to abhor him, therefore he shall be my servant for ever."

28 And it came to pass in those days, that the Philistines gathered their armies together for warfare, to fight with Israel: and Achish said unto David, "Know thou assuredly, that thou shalt go out with me to battle, thou, and thy men." And David said to Achish, "Surely thou shalt know what thy servant can do." And Achish said to David, "Therefore will I make thee keeper of mine head for ever."

Now Samuel was dead, and all Israel had lamented him, and buried him in Ramah, even in his own city: and Saul had put away those that had familiar spirits, and the wizards, out of the land. And the Philistines gathered themselves together, and came and pitched in Shunem: and Saul gathered all Israel together, and they pitched in Gilboa. And when Saul saw the host of the Philistines, he was

6 *I.e.*, a raid.

afraid, and his heart greatly trembled. And when Saul inquired of
the Lord, the Lord answered him not, neither by dreams, nor by
Urim,[7] nor by prophets.

Then said Saul unto his servants, "Seek me a woman that hath a
familiar spirit, that I may go to her, and inquire of her." And his
servants said to him, "Behold, there is a woman that hath a familiar
spirit at Endor." And Saul disguised himself, and put on other
raiment, and he went, and two men with him, and they came to the
woman by night, and he said, "I pray thee, divine unto me by the
familiar spirit, and bring me him up whom I shall name unto thee."
And the woman said unto him, "Behold, thou knowest what Saul
hath done, how he hath cut off those that have familiar spirits, and
the wizards, out of the land: wherefore then layest thou a snare for
my life, to cause me to die?" And Saul sware to her by the Lord, saying, "As the Lord liveth, there shall be no punishment happen to
thee for this thing." Then said the woman, "Whom shall I bring up
unto thee?" And he said, "Bring me up Samuel." And when the
woman saw Samuel, she cried with a loud voice; and the woman
spake to Saul, saying, "Why hast thou deceived me? for thou art
Saul." And the king said unto her, "Be not afraid: for what sawest
thou?" And the woman said unto Saul, "I saw gods ascending out of
the earth." And he said unto her, "What form is he of?" And she
said, "An old man cometh up, and he is covered with a mantle." And
Saul perceived that it was Samuel, and he stooped with his face to
the ground, and bowed himself.

And Samuel said to Saul, "Why hast thou disquieted me, to bring
me up?" And Saul answered, "I am sore distressed; for the Philistines
make war against me, and God is departed from me, and answereth
me no more, neither by prophets, nor by dreams: therefore I have
called thee, that thou mayest make known unto me what I shall do."
Then said Samuel, "Wherefore then dost thou ask of me, seeing the
Lord is departed from thee, and is become thine enemy? And the
Lord hath done to him, as he spake by me: for the Lord hath rent
the kingdom out of thine hand, and given it to thy neighbour, even
to David: because thou obeyedst not the voice of the Lord, nor exe-
cutedst his fierce wrath upon Amalek, therefore hath the Lord done
this thing unto thee this day. Moreover, the Lord will also deliver
Israel with thee into the hand of the Philistines: and tomorrow shalt

[7] A form of lots used for divination.

thou and thy sons be with me: the Lord also shall deliver the host
of Israel into the hand of the Philistines." Then Saul fell straightway
all along on the earth, and was sore afraid, because of the words of
Samuel, and there was no strength in him: for he had eaten no
bread all the day, nor all the night.

And the woman came unto Saul, and saw that he was sore
troubled, and said unto him, "Behold, thine handmaid hath obeyed
thy voice, and I have put my life in my hand, and have hearkened
unto thy words which thou spakest unto me. Now therefore, I pray
thee, hearken thou also unto the voice of thine handmaid, and let
me set a morsel of bread before thee; and eat, that thou mayest have
strength, when thou goest on thy way." But he refused, and said, "I
will not eat." But his servants together with the woman compelled
him; and he hearkened unto their voice: so he arose from the earth,
and sat upon the bed. And the woman had a fat calf in the house,
and she hasted, and killed it, and took flour and kneaded it, and did
bake unleavened bread thereof. And she brought it before Saul, and
before his servants, and they did eat: then they arose up, and went
away that night.

29 Now the Philistines gathered together all their armies to
Aphek: and the Israelites pitched by a fountain which is in
Jezreel. And the lords of the Philistines passed on by hundreds, and
by thousands: but David and his men passed on in the rearward
with Achish. Then said the princes of the Philistines, "What do
these Hebrews here?" And Achish said unto the princes of the
Philistines, "Is not this David, the servant of Saul the king of Israel,
which hath been with me these days, or these years, and I have
found no fault in him since he fell unto me, unto this day?" And the
princes of the Philistines were wroth with him, and the princes of
the Philistines said unto him, "Make this fellow return, that he may
go again to his place which thou hast appointed him, and let him
not go down with us to battle, lest in the battle he be an adversary
to us: for wherewith should he reconcile himself unto his master?
should it not be with the heads of these men? Is not this David, of
whom they sang one to another in dances, saying, 'Saul slew his
thousands, and David his ten thousands'?"

Then Achish called David, and said unto him, "Surely, as the
Lord liveth, thou hast been upright, and thy going out and thy

coming in with me in the host is good in my sight: for I have not found evil in thee since the day of thy coming unto me unto this day: nevertheless, the lords favour thee not. Wherefore now return and go in peace, that thou displease not the lords of the Philistines."

And David said unto Achish, "But what have I done? and what hast thou found in thy servant so long as I have been with thee unto this day, that I may not go fight against the enemies of my lord the king?" And Achish answered, and said to David, "I know that thou art good in my sight, as an angel of God: notwithstanding, the princes of the Philistines have said, 'He shall not go up with us to the battle.' Wherefore now rise up early in the morning, with thy master's servants that are come with thee: and as soon as ye be up early in the morning, and have light, depart." So David and his men rose up early to depart in the morning, to return into the land of the Philistines; and the Philistines went up to Jezreel.

30 And it came to pass when David and his men were come to Ziklag on the third day, that the Amalekites had invaded the south and Ziklag, and smitten Ziklag, and burnt it with fire, and had taken the women captives that were therein; they slew not any either great or small, but carried them away, and went on their way. So David and his men came to the city, and behold, it was burnt with fire, and their wives, and their sons, and their daughters were taken captives. Then David and the people that were with him lifted up their voice, and wept, until they had no more power to weep. And David's two wives were taken captives, Ahinoam the Jezreelitess, and Abigail the wife of Nabal the Carmelite. And David was greatly distressed: for the people spake of stoning him, because the soul of all the people was grieved, every man for his sons, and for his daughters: but David encouraged himself in the Lord his God.

And David said to Abiathar the priest, Ahimelech's son, "I pray thee, bring me hither the ephod": and Abiathar brought thither the ephod to David. And David inquired at the Lord, saying, "Shall I pursue after this troop? shall I overtake them?" And he answered him, "Pursue, for thou shalt surely overtake them, and without fail recover all." So David went, he and the six hundred men that were with him, and came to the brook Besor, where those that were left behind stayed. But David pursued, he and four hundred men (for two hundred abode behind, which were so faint that they could not go over the brook Besor).

And they found an Egyptian in the field, and brought him to David, and gave him bread, and he did eat, and they made him drink water. And they gave him a piece of a cake of figs, and two clusters of raisins: and when he had eaten, his spirit came again to him: for he had eaten no bread, nor drunk any water, three days and three nights. And David said unto him, "To whom belongest thou? and whence art thou?" And he said, "I am a young man of Egypt, servant to an Amalekite, and my master left me, because three days ago I fell sick. We made an invasion upon the south of the Cherethites, and upon the coast which belongeth to Judah, and upon the south of Caleb, and we burnt Ziklag with fire." And David said to him, "Canst thou bring me down to this company?" And he said, "Swear unto me by God that thou wilt neither kill me, nor deliver me into the hands of my master, and I will bring thee down to this company."

And when he had brought him down, behold, they were spread abroad upon all the earth, eating and drinking, and dancing, because of all the great spoil that they had taken out of the land of the Philistines, and out of the land of Judah. And David smote them from the twilight, even unto the evening of the next day: and there escaped not a man of them, save four hundred young men which rode upon camels, and fled. And David recovered all that the Amalekites had carried away: and David rescued his two wives. And there was nothing lacking to them, neither small nor great, neither sons nor daughters, neither spoil, nor any thing that they had taken to them: David recovered all. And David took all the flocks, and all the herds, which they drave before those other cattle, and said, "This is David's spoil."

And David came to the two hundred men which were so faint that they could not follow David, whom they had made also to abide at the brook Besor: and they went forth to meet David, and to meet the people that were with him: and when David came near to the people, he saluted them. Then answered all the wicked men, and men of Belial, of those that went with David, and said, "Because they went not with us, we will not give them aught of the spoil that we have recovered, save to every man his wife and his children, that they may lead them away, and depart." Then said David, "Ye shall not do so, my brethren, with that which the Lord hath given us, who hath preserved us, and delivered the company that came against us into our hand. For who will hearken unto you in this matter? But as his part is that goeth down to the battle, so shall his part be that tarrieth by the stuff: they shall part alike." And it was so from that day forward, that he made it a statute, and an ordinance for Israel, unto this day. And when David came to Ziklag, he sent of the spoil unto the elders of Judah, even to his friends, saying, "Behold, a present for you, of the spoil of the enemies of the Lord.". . .

31 Now the Philistines fought against Israel: and the men of Israel fled from before the Philistines, and fell down slain in mount Gilboa. And the Philistines followed hard upon Saul, and upon his sons, and the Philistines slew Jonathan, and Abinadab, and Malchishua, Saul's sons. And the battle went sore against Saul, and the archers hit him, and he was sore wounded of the archers. Then said Saul unto his armour-bearer, "Draw thy sword, and thrust me through therewith, lest these uncircumcised come and thrust me through, and abuse me." But his armour-bearer would not, for he was sore afraid: therefore Saul took a sword, and fell upon it. And when his armour-bearer saw that Saul was dead, he fell likewise upon his sword, and died with him. So Saul died, and his three sons, and his armour-bearer, and all his men, that same day together.

And when the men of Israel that were on the other side of the valley, and they that were on the other side Jordan, saw that the men of Israel fled, and that Saul and his sons were dead, they forsook the cities and fled, and the Philistines came and dwelt in them. And it came to pass on the morrow when the Philistines came to strip the slain, that they found Saul and his three sons fallen in mount Gilboa. And they cut off his head, and stripped off his armour, and sent into the land of the Philistines round about, to publish it in the house of their idols, and among the people. And they put his armour in the house of Ashtaroth: and they fastened his body to the wall of Beth-shan.

And when the inhabitants of Jabesh-gilead heard of that which the Philistines had done to Saul, all the valiant men arose, and went all night, and took the body of Saul and the bodies of his sons from the wall of Beth-shan, and came to Jabesh, and burnt them there.

And they took their bones, and buried them under a tree at Jabesh, and fasted seven days.

II SAMUEL

1 Now it came to pass after the death of Saul, when David was returned from the slaughter of the Amalekites, and David had abode two days in Ziklag, it came even to pass on the third day, that behold, a man came out of the camp from Saul with his clothes rent, and earth upon his head: and so it was when he came to David, that he fell to the earth, and did obeisance. And David said unto him, "From whence comest thou?" And he said unto him, "Out of the camp of Israel am I escaped." And David said unto him, "How went the matter? I pray thee, tell me." And he answered that "The people are fled from the battle, and many of the people also are fallen and dead, and Saul and Jonathan his son are dead also." And David said unto the young man that told him, "How knowest thou that Saul and Jonathan his son be dead?" And the young man that told him said, "As I happened by chance upon mount Gilboa, behold, Saul leaned upon his spear: and lo, the chariots and horsemen followed hard after him. And when he looked behind him, he saw me, and called unto me: and I answered, 'Here am I.' And he said unto me, 'Who art thou?' And I answered him, 'I am an Amalekite.' He said unto me again, 'Stand, I pray thee, upon me, and slay me: for anguish is come upon me, because my life is yet whole in me.' So I stood upon him, and slew him, because I was sure that he could not live after that he was fallen: and I took the crown that was upon his head, and the bracelet that was on his arm, and have brought them hither unto my lord." Then David took hold on his clothes, and rent them, and likewise all the men that were with him. And they mourned and wept, and fasted until even, for Saul and for Jonathan his son, and for the people of the Lord, and for the house of Israel, because they were fallen by the sword.

And David said unto the young man that told him, "Whence art thou?" And he answered, "I am the son of a stranger, an Amalekite." And David said unto him, "How wast thou not afraid to stretch forth thine hand to destroy the Lord's anointed?" And David called one of the young men, and said, "Go near, and fall upon him." And he smote him, that he died. And David said unto him, "Thy blood be upon thy head: for thy mouth hath testified against thee, saying, 'I have slain the Lord's anointed.'"

And David lamented with this lamentation over Saul, and over Jonathan his son (also he bade them teach the children of Judah the use of the bow: behold, it is written in the Book of Jasher):

"The beauty of Israel is slain upon thy high places: how are the mighty fallen!

Tell it not in Gath, publish it not in the streets of Askalon: lest the daughter of the Philistines rejoice, lest the daughters of the uncircumcised triumph.

Ye mountains of Gilboa, let there be no dew, neither let there be rain upon you, nor fields of offerings: for there the shield of the mighty is vilely cast away, the shield of Saul, as though he had not been anointed with oil.

From the blood of the slain, from the fat of the mighty, the bow of Jonathan turned not back, and the sword of Saul returned not empty.

Saul and Jonathan were lovely and pleasant in their lives, and in their death they were not divided: they were swifter than eagles, they were stronger than lions.

Ye daughters of Israel, weep over Saul, who clothed you in scarlet, with other delights, who put on ornaments of gold upon your apparel.

How are the mighty fallen in the midst of battle! O Jonathan, thou wast slain in thine high places.

I am distressed for thee, my brother Jonathan, very pleasant hast thou been unto me: thy love to me was wonderful, passing the love of women.

How are the mighty fallen, and the weapons of war perished!"

2 And it came to pass after this, that David inquired of the Lord, saying, "Shall I go up into any of the cities of Judah?" And the Lord said unto him, "Go up." And David said, "Whither shall I go up?" And he said, "Unto Hebron." So David went up thither, and his two wives also, Ahinoam the Jezreelitess, and Abigail Nabal's wife the Carmelite. And his men that were with him did David bring up, every man with his household: and they dwelt in the cities of Hebron. And the men of Judah came, and there they anointed

David king over the house of Judah: and they told David, saying that the men of Jabesh-gilead were they that buried Saul.

And David sent messengers unto the men of Jabesh-gilead, and said unto them, "Blessed be ye of the Lord, that ye have showed this kindness unto your lord, even unto Saul, and have buried him. And now the Lord show kindness and truth unto you: and I also will requite you this kindness, because ye have done this thing. Therefore now let your hands be strengthened, and be ye valiant: for your master Saul is dead, and also the house of Judah have anointed me king over them."

But Abner the son of Ner, captain of Saul's host, took Ishbosheth the son of Saul, and brought him over to Mahanaim. And he made him king over Gilead, and over the Ashurites, and over Jezreel, and over Ephraim, and over Benjamin, and over all Israel. Ishbosheth Saul's son was forty years old when he began to reign over Israel, and reigned two years: but the house of Judah followed David. (And the time that David was king in Hebron over the house of Judah was seven years and six months.)

And Abner the son of Ner, and the servants of Ishbosheth the son of Saul, went out from Mahanaim to Gibeon. And Joab the son of Zeruiah, and the servants of David, went out, and met together by the pool of Gibeon: and they sat down, the one on the one side of the pool, and the other on the other side of the pool. And Abner said to Joab, "Let the young men now arise, and play before us." And Joab said, "Let them arise." Then there arose and went over by number twelve of Benjamin, which pertained to Ishbosheth the son of Saul, and twelve of the servants of David. And they caught every one his fellow by the head, and thrust his sword in his fellow's side, so they fell down together: wherefore that place was called Helkath-hazzurim, which is in Gibeon. And there was a very sore battle that day: and Abner was beaten, and the men of Israel, before the servants of David.

And there were three sons of Zeruiah there, Joab, and Abishai, and Asahel: and Asahel was as light of foot as a wild roe. And Asahel pursued after Abner, and in going he turned not to the right hand nor to the left from following Abner. Then Abner looked behind him, and said, "Art thou Asahel?" And he answered, "I am." And Abner said to him, "Turn thee aside to thy right hand, or to thy left, and lay thee hold on one of the young men, and take thee his armour." But Asahel would not turn aside from following of him. And Abner said again to Asahel, "Turn thee aside from following me: wherefore should I smite thee to the ground? how then should I hold up my face to Joab thy brother?" Howbeit he refused to turn aside: wherefore Abner with the hinder end of the spear smote him under the fifth rib, that the spear came out behind him, and he fell down there, and died in the same place: and it came to pass, that as many as came to the place where Asahel fell down and died, stood still. Joab also and Abishai pursued after Abner: and the sun went down when they were come to the hill of Ammah, that lieth before Giah by the way of the wilderness of Gibeon.

And the children of Benjamin gathered themselves together after Abner, and became one troop, and stood on the top of a hill. Then Abner called to Joab, and said, "Shall the sword devour for ever? Knowest thou not that it will be bitterness in the latter end? How long shall it be then, ere thou bid the people return from following their brethren?" And Joab said, "As God liveth, unless thou hadst spoken, surely then in the morning the people had gone up every one from following his brother." So Joab blew a trumpet, and all the people stood still, and pursued after Israel no more, neither fought they any more. And Abner and his men walked all that night through the plain, and passed over Jordan, and went through all Bithron, and they came to Mahanaim. And Joab returned from following Abner; and when he had gathered all the people together, there lacked of David's servants nineteen men, and Asahel. But the servants of David had smitten of Benjamin and of Abner's men, so that three hundred and threescore men died. And they took up Asahel, and buried him in the sepulchre of his father, which was in Bethlehem: and Joab and his men went all night, and they came to Hebron at break of day.

3 Now there was long war between the house of Saul and the house of David: but David waxed stronger and stronger, and the house of Saul waxed weaker and weaker. And unto David were sons born in Hebron: and his firstborn was Amnon, of Ahinoam the Jezreelitess. And his second, Chileab, of Abigail the wife of Nabal the Carmelite; and the third, Absalom, the son of Maacah the daughter of Talmai king of Geshur; and the fourth, Adonijah, the son of Haggith; and the fifth, Shephatiah, the son of Abital; and the sixth,

Ithream by Eglah David's wife: these were born to David in Hebron.

And it came to pass while there was war between the house of Saul and the house of David, that Abner made himself strong for the house of Saul. And Saul had a concubine, whose name was Rizpah, the daughter of Aiah: and Ishbosheth said to Abner, "Wherefore hast thou gone in unto my father's concubine?" Then was Abner very wroth for the words of Ishbosheth, and said, "Am I a dog's head, which against Judah do show kindness this day unto the house of Saul thy father, to his brethren, and to his friends, and have not delivered thee into the hand of David, that thou chargest me today with a fault concerning this woman? So do God to Abner, and more also, except, as the Lord hath sworn to David, even so I do to him: to translate the kingdom from the house of Saul, and to set up the throne of David over Israel, and over Judah, from Dan even to Beer-sheba." And he could not answer Abner a word again, because he feared him.

And Abner sent messengers to David on his behalf, saying, "Whose is the land?" saying also, "Make thy league with me, and behold, my hand shall be with thee, to bring about all Israel unto thee." And he said, "Well, I will make a league with thee: but one thing I require of thee, that is, thou shalt not see my face, except thou first bring Michal Saul's daughter, when thou comest to see my face." And David sent messengers to Ishbosheth Saul's son, saying, "Deliver me my wife Michal, which I espoused to me for an hundred foreskins of the Philistines." And Ishbosheth sent, and took her from her husband, even from Phaltiel the son of Laish. And her husband went with her along weeping behind her to Bahurim: then said Abner unto him, "Go, return." And he returned.

And Abner had communication with the elders of Israel, saying, "Ye sought for David in times past, to be king over you. Now then do it, for the Lord hath spoken of David, saying, 'By the hand of my servant David I will save my people Israel out of the hand of the Philistines, and out of the hand of all their enemies.'" And Abner also spake in the ears of Benjamin: and Abner went also to speak in the ears of David in Hebron all that seemed good to Israel, and that seemed good to the whole house of Benjamin. So Abner came to David to Hebron, and twenty men with him: and David made Abner and the men that were with him a feast. And Abner said unto David, "I will arise, and go, and will gather all Israel unto my lord the king, that they may make a league with thee, and that thou mayest reign over all that thine heart desireth." And David sent Abner away, and he went in peace.

And behold, the servants of David and Joab came from pursuing a troop, and brought in a great spoil with them: (but Abner was not with David in Hebron, for he had sent him away, and he was gone in peace). When Joab and all the host that was with him were come, they told Joab, saying, "Abner the son of Ner came to the king, and he hath sent him away, and he is gone in peace." Then Joab came to the king, and said, "What hast thou done? behold, Abner came unto thee, why is it that thou hast sent him away, and he is quite gone? Thou knowest Abner the son of Ner, that he came to deceive thee, and to know thy going out, and thy coming in, and to know all that thou doest." And when Joab was come out from David, he sent messengers after Abner, which brought him again from the well of Sirah; but David knew it not. And when Abner was returned to Hebron, Joab took him aside in the gate to speak with him quietly, and smote him there under the fifth rib, that he died, for the blood of Asahel his brother.

And afterward when David heard it, he said, "I and my kingdom are guiltless before the Lord for ever from the blood of Abner the son of Ner: let it rest on the head of Joab, and on all his father's house, and let there not fail from the house of Joab one that hath an issue, or that is a leper, or that leaneth on a staff, or that falleth on the sword, or that lacketh bread." So Joab and Abishai his brother slew Abner, because he had slain their brother Asahel at Gibeon in the battle.

And David said to Joab, and to all the people that were with him, "Rend your clothes, and gird you with sackcloth, and mourn before Abner." And king David himself followed the bier. And they buried Abner in Hebron, and the king lifted up his voice, and wept at the grave of Abner; and all the people wept. And the king lamented over Abner, and said, "Died Abner as a fool dieth? Thy hands were not bound, nor thy feet put into fetters: as a man falleth before wicked men, so fellest thou." And all the people wept again over him. And when all the people came to cause David to eat meat while it was yet day, David sware, saying, "So do God to me, and more also, if I taste bread or aught else, till the sun be down." And all the people took notice of it, and it pleased them: as whatsoever the king

did pleased all the people. For all the people, and all Israel, understood that day that it was not of the king to slay Abner the son of
Ner. And the king said unto his servants, "Know ye not that there
is a prince and a great man fallen this day in Israel? And I am this
day weak, though anointed king, and these men the sons of
Zeruiah be too hard for me: the Lord shall reward the doer of evil,
according to his wickedness."

4 And when Saul's son heard that Abner was dead in Hebron, his
hands were feeble, and all the Israelites were troubled. And
Saul's son had two men that were captains of bands: the name of
the one was Baanah, and the name of the other Rechab, the sons of
Rimmon a Beerothite, of the children of Benjamin: (for Beeroth also
was reckoned of Benjamin: and the Beerothites fled to Gittaim, and
were sojourners there until this day). And Jonathan, Saul's son, had
a son that was lame of his feet. He was five years old when the
tidings came of Saul and Jonathan out of Jezreel, and his nurse took
him up, and fled: and it came to pass as she made haste to flee, that
he fell, and became lame, and his name was Mephibosheth. And the
sons of Rimmon the Beerothite, Rechab and Baanah, went, and came
about the heat of the day to the house of Ishbosheth, who lay on a
bed at noon. And they came thither into the midst of the house, as
though they would have fetched wheat, and they smote him under
the fifth rib, and Rechab and Baanah his brother escaped. For when
they came into the house, he lay on his bed in his bedchamber, and
they smote him, and slew him, and beheaded him, and took his
head, and got them away through the plain all night. And they
brought the head of Ishbosheth unto David to Hebron, and said to
the king, "Behold the head of Ishbosheth the son of Saul, thine
enemy, which sought thy life, and the Lord hath avenged my lord
the king this day of Saul and of his seed."

And David answered Rechab and Baanah his brother, the sons of
Rimmon the Beerothite, and said unto them, "As the Lord liveth,
who hath redeemed my soul out of all adversity, when one told me,
saying, 'Behold, Saul is dead' (thinking to have brought good tidings),
I took hold of him, and slew him in Ziklag, who thought that I
would have given him a reward for his tidings: how much more,
when wicked men have slain a righteous person, in his own house,
upon his bed? Shall I not therefore now require his blood of your

hand, and take you away from the earth?" And David commanded his young men, and they slew them, and cut off their hands and their feet, and hanged them up over the pool in Hebron: but they took the head of Ishbosheth, and buried it in the sepulchre of Abner, in Hebron.

5 Then came all the tribes of Israel to David unto Hebron, and spake, saying, "Behold, we are thy bone and thy flesh. Also in time past when Saul was king over us, thou wast he that leddest out and broughtest in Israel: and the Lord said to thee, 'Thou shalt feed my people Israel, and thou shalt be a captain over Israel.' " So all the elders of Israel came to the king to Hebron, and king David made a league with them in Hebron before the Lord: and they anointed David king over Israel.

David was thirty years old when he began to reign, and he reigned forty years. In Hebron he reigned over Judah seven years and six months: and in Jerusalem he reigned thirty and three years over all Israel and Judah. And the king and his men went to Jerusalem, unto the Jebusites, the inhabitants of the land: which spake unto David, saying, "Except thou take away the blind and the lame, thou shalt not come in hither": thinking, "David cannot come in hither." Nevertheless David took the stronghold of Zion: the same is the city of David. And David said on that day, "Whosoever getteth up to the gutter, and smiteth the Jebusites, and the lame, and the blind, that are hated of David's soul, he shall be chief and captain": wherefore they said, "The blind and the lame shall not come into the house." So David dwelt in the fort, and called it the city of David, and David built round about from Millo and inward. And David went on, and grew great, and the Lord God of hosts was with him.

And Hiram king of Tyre sent messengers to David, and cedar trees, and carpenters, and masons: and they built David an house. And David perceived that the Lord had established him king over Israel, and that he had exalted his kingdom for his people Israel's sake.

And David took him more concubines and wives out of Jerusalem, after he was come from Hebron: and there were yet sons and daughters born to David. And these be the names of those that were born unto him in Jerusalem: Shammuah, and Shobab, and Nathan, and Solomon, Ibhar also, and Elishua, and Nepheg, and Japhia, and Elishama, and Eliada, and Eliphalet.

But when the Philistines heard that they had anointed David king over Israel, all the Philistines came up to seek David, and David heard of it, and went down to the hold. The Philistines also came, and spread themselves in the valley of Rephaim. And David inquired of the Lord, saying, "Shall I go up to the Philistines? wilt thou deliver them into mine hand?" And the Lord said unto David, "Go up: for I will doubtless deliver the Philistines into thine hand." And David came to Baal-perazim, and David smote them there, and said, "The Lord hath broken forth upon mine enemies before me, as the breach of waters." Therefore he called the name of that place Baal-perazim. And there they left their images, and David and his men burned them. And the Philistines came up yet again, and spread themselves in the valley of Rephaim. And when David inquired of the Lord, he said, "Thou shalt not go up: but fetch a compass behind them, and come upon them over against the mulberry trees. And let it be when thou hearest the sound of a going in the tops of the mulberry trees, that then thou shalt bestir thyself: for then shall the Lord go out before thee, to smite the host of the Philistines." And David did so, as the Lord had commanded him; and smote the Philistines from Geba until thou come to Gazer.

6 Again, David gathered together all the chosen men of Israel, thirty thousand: and David arose and went with all the people that were with him from Baale of Judah, to bring up from thence the ark of God, whose name is called by the name of the Lord of hosts that dwelleth between the cherubim. And they set the ark of God upon a new cart, and brought it out of the house of Abinadab that was in Gibeah: and Uzzah and Ahio, the sons of Abinadab, drave the new cart. And they brought it out of the house of Abinadab which was at Gibeah, accompanying the ark of God; and Ahio went before the ark. And David and all the house of Israel played before the Lord on all manner of instruments made of fir wood, even on harps, and on psalteries, and on timbrels, and on cornets, and on cymbals.

And when they came to Nachon's threshing floor, Uzzah put forth his hand to the ark of God, and took hold of it, for the oxen shook it. And the anger of the Lord was kindled against Uzzah, and God smote him there for his error, and there he died by the ark of God. And David was displeased, because the Lord had made a breach upon Uzzah: and he called the name of the place Perez-uzzah to this day. And David was afraid of the Lord that day, and said, "How shall the ark of the Lord come to me?" So David would not remove the ark of the Lord unto him into the city of David: but David carried it aside into the house of Obed-edom the Gittite. And the ark of the Lord continued in the house of Obed-edom the Gittite three months: and the Lord blessed Obed-edom, and all his household.

And it was told king David, saying, "The Lord hath blessed the house of Obed-edom, and all that pertaineth unto him, because of the ark of God. So David went, and brought up the ark of God from the house of Obed-edom, into the city of David, with gladness. And it was so, that when they that bare the ark of the Lord had gone six paces, he sacrificed oxen and fatlings. And David danced before the Lord with all his might, and David was girded with a linen ephod. So David and all the house of Israel brought up the ark of the Lord with shouting, and with the sound of the trumpet. And as the ark of the Lord came into the city of David, Michal Saul's daughter looked through a window, and saw king David leaping and dancing before the Lord, and she despised him in her heart.

And they brought in the ark of the Lord, and set it in his place, in the midst of the tabernacle that David had pitched for it: and David offered burnt offerings and peace offerings before the Lord. And as soon as David had made an end of offering burnt offerings and peace offerings, he blessed the people in the name of the Lord of hosts. And he dealt among all the people, even among the whole multitude of Israel, as well to the women as men, to every one a cake of bread, and a good piece of flesh, and a flagon of wine: so all the people departed every one to his house.

Then David returned to bless his household: and Michal the daughter of Saul came out to meet David, and said, "How glorious was the king of Israel today, who uncovered himself today in the eyes of the handmaids of his servants, as one of the vain fellows shamelessly uncovereth himself!" And David said unto Michal, "It was before the Lord, which chose me before thy father, and before all his house, to appoint me ruler over the people of the Lord, over Israel: therefore will I play before the Lord. And I will yet be more vile than thus, and will be base in mine own sight: and of the maid-servants which thou hast spoken of, of them shall I be had in honour.". . .

9 And David said, "Is there yet any that is left of the house of Saul, that I may show him kindness for Jonathan's sake?" And there was of the house of Saul a servant whose name was Ziba: and when they had called him unto David, the king said unto him, "Art thou Ziba?" And he said, "Thy servant is he." And the king said, "Is there not yet any of the house of Saul, that I may show the kindness of God unto him?" And Ziba said unto the king, "Jonathan hath yet a son, which is lame on his feet." And the king said unto him, "Where is he?" And Ziba said unto the king, "Behold, he is in the house of Machir, the son of Ammiel, in Lo-debar."

Then king David sent, and fetched him out of the house of Machir, the son of Ammiel, from Lo-debar. Now when Mephibo-sheth, the son of Jonathan, the son of Saul, was come unto David, he fell on his face, and did reverence. And David said, "Mephibo-sheth!" And he answered, "Behold thy servant." And David said unto him, "Fear not; for I will surely show thee kindness, for Jonathan thy father's sake, and will restore thee all the land of Saul thy father, and thou shalt eat bread at my table continually." And he bowed himself, and said, "What is thy servant, that thou shouldest look upon such a dead dog as I am?"

Then the king called to Ziba, Saul's servant, and said unto him, "I have given unto thy master's son all that pertained to Saul and to all his house. Thou therefore, and thy sons, and thy servants, shall till the land for him, and thou shalt bring in the fruits, that thy master's son may have food to eat: but Mephibosheth thy master's son shall eat bread alway at my table." Now Ziba had fifteen sons, and twenty servants. Then said Ziba unto the king, "According to all that my lord the king hath commanded his servant, so shall thy servant do." "As for Mephibosheth," said the king, "he shall eat at my table, as one of the king's sons." And Mephibosheth had a young son, whose name was Micha: and all that dwelt in the house of Ziba were servants unto Mephibosheth. So Mephibosheth dwelt in Jerusalem: for he did eat continually at the king's table, and was lame on both his feet.

10 And it came to pass after this, that the king of the children of Ammon died, and Hanun his son reigned in his stead. Then said David, "I will show kindness unto Hanun the son of Nahash, as his father showed kindness unto me." And David sent to comfort him by the hand of his servants, for his father: and David's servants came into the land of the children of Ammon. And the princes of the children of Ammon said unto Hanun their lord, "Thinkest thou that David doth honour thy father, that he hath sent comforters unto thee? Hath not David rather sent his servants unto thee to search the city, and to spy it out, and to overthrow it?" Wherefore Hanun took David's servants, and shaved off the one half of their beards, and cut off their garments in the middle, even to their buttocks, and sent them away. When they told it unto David, he sent to meet them, because the men were greatly ashamed: and the king said, "Tarry at Jericho until your beards be grown, and then return."

And when the children of Ammon saw that they stank before David, the children of Ammon sent, and hired the Syrians of Bethrehob, and the Syrians of Zoba, twenty thousand footmen, and of king Maacah a thousand men, and of Ishtob twelve thousand men. And when David heard of it, he sent Joab, and all the host of the mighty men. And the children of Ammon came out, and put the battle in array at the entering in of the gate: and the Syrians of Zoba and of Rehob, and Ishtob, and Maacah, were by themselves in the field. When Joab saw that the front of the battle was against him, before and behind, he chose of all the choice men of Israel, and put them in array against the Syrians. And the rest of the people he delivered into the hand of Abishai his brother, that he might put them in array against the children of Ammon. And he said, "If the Syrians be too strong for me, then thou shalt help me: but if the children of Ammon be too strong for thee, then I will come and help thee. Be of good courage, and let us play the men, for our people, and for the cities of our God: and the Lord do that which seemeth him good." And Joab drew nigh, and the people that were with him, unto the battle against the Syrians: and they fled before him. And when the children of Ammon saw that the Syrians were fled, then fled they also before Abishai, and entered into the city: so Joab returned from the children of Ammon, and came to Jerusalem.

And when the Syrians saw that they were smitten before Israel, they gathered themselves together. And Hadarezer sent, and brought out the Syrians that were beyond the river, and they came to Helam, and Shobach the captain of the host of Hadarezer went before them. And when it was told David, he gathered all Israel together, and passed over Jordan, and came to Helam: and the Syrians set themselves in array against David, and fought with him. And the Syrians fled before Israel, and David slew the men of seven hundred chariots of the Syrians, and forty thousand horsemen, and smote Shobach the captain of their host, who died there. And when all the kings that were servants to Hadarezer saw that they were smitten before Israel, they made peace with Israel, and served them: so the Syrians feared to help the children of Ammon any more.

11 And it came to pass, that after the year was expired, at the time when kings go forth to battle, that David sent Joab, and his servants with him, and all Israel; and they destroyed the children of Ammon, and besieged Rabbah: but David tarried still at Jerusalem.

And it came to pass in an eveningtide, that David arose from off his bed, and walked upon the roof of the king's house: and from the roof he saw a woman washing herself; and the woman was very beautiful to look upon. And David sent and inquired after the woman. And one said, "Is not this Bathsheba the daughter of Eliam, the wife of Uriah the Hittite?" And David sent messengers, and took her; and she came in unto him, and he lay with her (for she was purified from her uncleanness), and she returned unto her house. And the woman conceived, and sent and told David, and said, "I am with child."

And David sent to Joab, saying, "Send me Uriah the Hittite." And Joab sent Uriah to David. And when Uriah was come unto him, David demanded of him how Joab did, and how the people did, and how the war prospered. And David said to Uriah, "Go down to thy house, and wash thy feet." And Uriah departed out of the king's house, and there followed him a mess of meat from the king. But Uriah slept at the door of the king's house, with all the servants of his lord, and went not down to his house. And when they had told David, saying, "Uriah went not down unto his house," David said unto Uriah, "Camest thou not from thy journey? why then didst thou not go down unto thine house?" And Uriah said unto David, "The ark, and Israel, and Judah abide in tents; and my lord Joab, and the servants of my lord, are encamped in the open fields; shall I then go into mine house, to eat and to drink, and to lie with my wife? As thou livest, and as thy soul liveth, I will not do this thing." And David said to Uriah, "Tarry here today also, and tomorrow I will let thee depart." So Uriah abode in Jerusalem that day, and the morrow. And when David had called him, he did eat and drink before him, and he made him drunk: and at even he went out to lie on his bed with the servants of his lord, but went not down to his house.

And it came to pass in the morning, that David wrote a letter to Joab, and sent it by the hand of Uriah. And he wrote in the letter, saying, "Set ye Uriah in the forefront of the hottest battle, and retire ye from him, that he may be smitten, and die." And it came to pass when Joab observed the city, that he assigned Uriah unto a place where he knew that valiant men were. And the men of the city went out, and fought with Joab: and there fell some of the people of the servants of David, and Uriah the Hittite died also.

Then Joab sent, and told David all the things concerning the war: and charged the messenger, saying, "When thou hast made an end of telling the matters of the war unto the king, and if so be that the king's wrath arise, and he say unto thee, 'Wherefore approached ye so nigh unto the city when ye did fight? knew ye not that they would shoot from the wall? Who smote Abimelech the son of Jerubbesheth? did not a woman cast a piece of millstone upon him from the wall, that he died in Thebez? why went ye nigh the wall?' then say thou, 'Thy servant Uriah the Hittite is dead also.'"

So the messenger went, and came and showed David all that Joab had sent him for. And the messenger said unto David, "Surely the men prevailed against us, and came out unto us into the field, and we were upon them even unto the entering of the gate. And the shooters shot from off the wall upon thy servants, and some of the king's servants be dead, and thy servant Uriah the Hittite is dead also." Then David said unto the messenger, "Thus shalt thou say unto Joab, 'Let not this thing displease thee: for the sword devoureth one as well as another: make thy battle more strong against the city, and overthrow it'; and encourage thou him."

And when the wife of Uriah heard that Uriah her husband was dead, she mourned for her husband. And when the mourning was past,

David sent, and fetched her to his house, and she became his wife, and bare him a son: but the thing that David had done displeased the Lord.

12 And the Lord sent Nathan unto David: and he came unto him, and said unto him, "There were two men in one city; the one rich, and the other poor. The rich man had exceeding many flocks and herds. But the poor man had nothing save one little ewe lamb, which he had bought and nourished up: and it grew up together with him, and with his children; it did eat of his own meat, and drank of his own cup, and lay in his bosom, and was unto him as a daughter. And there came a traveller unto the rich man, and he spared to take of his own flock, and of his own herd, to dress for the wayfaring man that was come unto him, but took the poor man's lamb, and dressed it for the man that was come to him." And David's anger was greatly kindled against the man, and he said to Nathan, "As the Lord liveth, the man that hath done this thing shall surely die. And he shall restore the lamb fourfold, because he did this thing, and because he had no pity."

And Nathan said to David, "Thou art the man. Thus saith the Lord God of Israel, 'I anointed thee king over Israel, and I delivered thee out of the hand of Saul, and I gave thee thy master's house, and thy master's wives into thy bosom, and gave thee the house of Israel and of Judah, and if that had been too little, I would moreover have given unto thee such and such things. Wherefore hast thou despised the commandment of the Lord, to do evil in his sight? thou hast killed Uriah the Hittite with the sword, and hast taken his wife to be thy wife, and hast slain him with the sword of the children of Ammon. Now therefore the sword shall never depart from thine house, because thou hast despised me, and hast taken the wife of Uriah the Hittite to be thy wife.' Thus saith the Lord, 'Behold, I will raise up evil against thee out of thine own house, and I will take thy wives before thine eyes, and give them unto thy neighbour, and he shall lie with thy wives in the sight of this sun. For thou didst it secretly: but I will do this thing before all Israel, and before the sun.'" And David said unto Nathan, "I have sinned against the Lord." And Nathan said unto David, "The Lord also hath put away thy sin, thou shalt not die. Howbeit, because by this deed thou hast given great occasion to the enemies of the Lord to blaspheme, the child also that is born unto thee shall surely die."

And Nathan departed unto his house: and the Lord struck the child that Uriah's wife bare unto David, and it was very sick. David therefore besought God for the child, and David fasted, and went in, and lay all night upon the earth. And the elders of his house arose, and went to him, to raise him up from the earth: but he would not, neither did he eat bread with them. And it came to pass on the seventh day, that the child died: and the servants of David feared to tell him that the child was dead: for they said, "Behold, while the child was yet alive, we spake unto him, and he would not hearken unto our voice: how will he then vex himself, if we tell him that the child is dead?" But when David saw that his servants whispered, David perceived that the child was dead: therefore David said unto his servants, "Is the child dead?" And they said, "He is dead." Then David arose from the earth and washed and anointed himself, and changed his apparel, and came into the house of the Lord, and worshipped: then he came to his own house, and when he required, they set bread before him, and he did eat. Then said his servants unto him, "What thing is this that thou hast done? thou didst fast and weep for the child, while it was alive, but when the child was dead, thou didst rise and eat bread." And he said, "While the child was yet alive, I fasted and wept: for I said, 'Who can tell whether God will be gracious to me, that the child may live?' But now he is dead, wherefore should I fast? Can I bring him back again? I shall go to him, but he shall not return to me."

And David comforted Bathsheba his wife, and went in unto her, and lay with her: and she bare a son, and he called his name Solomon, and the Lord loved him. And he sent by the hand of Nathan the prophet, and he called his name Jedidiah, because of the Lord.

And Joab fought against Rabbah of the children of Ammon, and took the royal city. And Joab sent messengers to David, and said, "I have fought against Rabbah, and have taken the city of waters. Now therefore, gather the rest of the people together, and encamp against the city, and take it: lest I take the city, and it be called after my name." And David gathered all the people together, and went to Rabbah, and fought against it, and took it. And he took their king's crown from off his head (the weight whereof was a talent of gold,

with the precious stones) and it was set on David's head, and
he brought forth the spoil of the city in great abundance. And he
brought forth the people that were therein, and put them under
saws, and under harrows of iron, and under axes of iron, and made
them pass through the brick-kiln. And thus did he unto all the cities
of the children of Ammon. So David and all the people returned
unto Jerusalem.

13 And it came to pass after this, that Absalom the son of David
had a fair sister, whose name was Tamar: and Amnon the son
of David loved her. And Amnon was so vexed, that he fell sick for
his sister Tamar: for she was a virgin, and Amnon thought it hard
for him to do any thing to her. But Amnon had a friend, whose
name was Jonadab, the son of Shimeah, David's brother: and
Jonadab was a very subtle man. And he said unto him, "Why art
thou, being a king's son, lean from day to day? Wilt thou not tell
me?" And Amnon said unto him, "I love Tamar my brother
Absalom's sister." And Jonadab said unto him, "Lay thee down on
thy bed, and make thyself sick: and when thy father cometh to see
thee, say unto him, 'I pray thee, let my sister Tamar come, and give
me meat, and dress the meat in my sight, that I may see it, and eat
it at her hand.'"

So Amnon lay down, and made himself sick: and when the king
was come to see him, Amnon said unto the king, "I pray thee, let
Tamar my sister come, and make me a couple of cakes in my sight,
that I may eat at her hand." Then David sent home to Tamar, saying, "Go now to thy brother Amnon's house, and dress him meat."
So Tamar went to her brother Amnon's house (and he was laid
down), and she took flour, and kneaded it, and made cakes in his
sight, and did bake the cakes. And she took a pan, and poured them
out before him, but he refused to eat: and Amnon said, "Have out
all men from me." And they went out every man from him. And
Amnon said unto Tamar, "Bring the meat into the chamber, that I
may eat of thine hand." And Tamar took the cakes which she had
made, and brought them into the chamber to Amnon her brother.
And when she had brought them unto him to eat, he took hold of
her, and said unto her, "Come lie with me, my sister." And she
answered him, "Nay, my brother, do not force me: for no such thing
ought to be done in Israel; do not thou this folly. And I, whither

shall I cause my shame to go? and as for thee, thou shalt be as one of the fools in Israel: now therefore, I pray thee, speak unto the king, for he will not withhold me from thee." Howbeit he would not hearken unto her voice, but being stronger than she, forced her, and lay with her.

Then Amnon hated her exceedingly, so that the hatred wherewith he hated her was greater than the love wherewith he had loved her: and Amnon said unto her, "Arise, be gone." And she said unto him, "There is no cause: this evil in sending me away is greater than the other that thou didst unto me." But he would not hearken unto her. Then he called his servant that ministered unto him, and said, "Put now this woman out from me, and bolt the door after her." And she had a garment of diverse colours upon her, for with such robes were the king's daughters that were virgins apparelled. Then his servant brought her out, and bolted the door after her.

And Tamar put ashes on her head, and rent her garment of diverse colours that was on her, and laid her hand on her head, and went on, crying. And Absalom her brother said unto her, "Hath Amnon thy brother been with thee? But hold now thy peace, my sister: he is thy brother, regard not this thing." So Tamar remained desolate in her brother Absalom's house. But when king David heard of all these things, he was very wroth. And Absalom spake unto his brother Amnon neither good nor bad: for Absalom hated Amnon, because he had forced his sister Tamar.

And it came to pass after two full years, that Absalom had sheep-shearers in Baal-hazor, which is beside Ephraim: and Absalom invited all the king's sons. And Absalom came to the king, and said, "Behold now, thy servant hath sheep-shearers; let the king, I beseech thee, and his servants, go with thy servant." And the king said to Absalom, "Nay, my son, let us not all now go, lest we be chargeable unto thee." And he pressed him: howbeit he would not go, but blessed him. Then said Absalom, "If not, I pray thee, let my brother Amnon go with us." And the king said unto him, "Why should he go with thee?" But Absalom pressed him, that he let Amnon and all the king's sons go with him.

Now Absalom had commanded his servants, saying, "Mark ye now when Amnon's heart is merry with wine, and when I say unto you, 'Smite Amnon,' then kill him, fear not: have not I commanded you? Be courageous, and be valiant." And the servants of Absalom did unto Amnon as Absalom had commanded. Then all the king's sons arose, and every man gat him up upon his mule, and fled. And it came to pass, while they were in the way, that tidings came to David, saying, "Absalom hath slain all the king's sons, and there is not one of them left." Then the king arose, and tare his garments, and lay on the earth: and all his servants stood by with their clothes rent. And Jonadab, the son of Shimeah David's brother, answered and said, "Let not my lord suppose that they have slain all the young men the king's sons; for Amnon only is dead: for by the appointment of Absalom this hath been determined, from the day that he forced his sister Tamar. Now therefore let not my lord the king take the thing to his heart, to think that all the king's sons are dead: for Amnon only is dead."

But Absalom fled: and the young man that kept the watch lifted up his eyes, and looked, and behold, there came much people by the way of the hillside behind him. And Jonadab said unto the king, "Behold, the king's sons come: as thy servant said, so it is." And it came to pass as soon as he had made an end of speaking, that behold, the king's sons came, and lifted up their voice, and wept; and the king also and all his servants wept very sore.

But Absalom fled, and went to Talmai the son of Ammihud king of Geshur: and David mourned for his son every day. So Absalom fled, and went to Geshur, and was there three years. And the soul of king David longed to go forth unto Absalom: for he was comforted concerning Amnon, seeing he was dead.

14 Now Joab the son of Zeruiah perceived that the king's heart was toward Absalom. And Joab sent to Tekoah, and fetched thence a wise woman, and said unto her, "I pray thee, feign thyself to be a mourner, and put on now mourning apparel, and anoint not thyself with oil, but be as a woman that had a long time mourned for the dead: and come to the king, and speak on this manner unto him": so Joab put the words in her mouth.

And when the woman of Tekoah spake to the king, she fell on her face to the ground, and did obeisance, and said, "Help, O king." And the king said unto her, "What aileth thee?" And she answered, "I am indeed a widow woman, and mine husband is dead. And thy handmaid had two sons, and they two strove together in the field, and there was none to part them, but the one smote the other, and slew him. And behold, the whole family is risen against thine hand-maid, and they said, 'Deliver him that smote his brother, that we may kill him, for the life of his brother whom he slew, and we will destroy the heir also': and so they shall quench my coal which is left, and shall not leave to my husband neither name nor remainder upon the earth." And the king said unto the woman, "Go to thine house, and I will give charge concerning thee." And the woman of Tekoah said unto the king, "My lord, O king, the iniquity be on me, and on my father's house: and the king and his throne be guiltless." And the king said, "Whosoever saith aught unto thee, bring him to me, and he shall not touch thee any more." Then said she, "I pray thee, let the king remember the Lord thy God, that thou wouldst not suffer the revengers of blood to destroy any more, lest they destroy my son." And he said, "As the Lord liveth, there shall not one hair of thy son fall to the earth." Then the woman said, "Let thine handmaid, I pray thee, speak one word unto my lord the king." And he said, "Say on."

And the woman said, "Wherefore then hast thou thought such a thing against the people of God? For the king doth speak this thing as one which is faulty, in that the king doth not fetch home again his banished. For we must needs die, and are as water spilt on the ground, which cannot be gathered up again: neither doth God re-spect any person, yet doth he devise means, that his banished be not expelled from him. Now therefore that I am come to speak of this thing unto my lord the king, it is because the people have made me afraid: and thy handmaid said, 'I will now speak unto the king; it may be that the king will perform the request of his handmaid. For the king will hear, to deliver his handmaid out of the hand of the man that would destroy me and my son together out of the in-heritance of God.' Then thine handmaid said, 'The word of my lord the king shall now be comfortable': for as an angel of God, so is my lord the king to discern good and bad: therefore the Lord thy God will be with thee." Then the king answered and said unto the woman, "Hide not from me, I pray thee, the thing that I shall ask thee." And the woman said, "Let my lord the king now speak." And the king said, "Is not the hand of Joab with thee in all this?" And the woman answered and said, "As thy soul liveth, my lord the king, none can turn to the right hand or to the left from aught that my lord the king hath spoken: for thy servant Joab, he bade me, and he put all these words in the mouth of thine handmaid: to fetch about this form of speech hath thy servant Joab done this thing: and my lord is wise, according to the wisdom of an angel of God, to know all things that are in the earth."

And the king said unto Joab, "Behold now, I have done this thing: go therefore, bring the young man Absalom again." And Joab fell to the ground on his face, and bowed himself, and thanked the king: and Joab said, "Today thy servant knoweth that I have found grace in thy sight, my lord, O king, in that the king hath fulfilled the request of his servant." So Joab arose, and went to Geshur, and brought Absalom to Jerusalem. And the king said, "Let him turn to his own house, and let him not see my face." So Absalom returned to his own house, and saw not the king's face.

But in all Israel there was none to be so much praised as Absalom for his beauty: from the sole of his foot even to the crown of his head, there was no blemish in him. And when he polled his head, (for it was at every year's end that he polled it: because the hair was heavy on him, therefore he polled it) he weighed the hair of his head at two hundred shekels after the king's weight. And unto Absalom there were born three sons, and one daughter, whose name was Tamar: she was a woman of a fair countenance.

So Absalom dwelt two full years in Jerusalem, and saw not the king's face. Therefore Absalom sent for Joab, to have sent him to the king, but he would not come to him: and when he sent again the second time, he would not come. Therefore he said unto his servants, "See, Joab's field is near mine, and he hath barley there: go, and set it on fire": and Absalom's servants set the field on fire. Then Joab arose, and came to Absalom unto his house, and said unto him, "Wherefore have thy servants set my field on fire?" And Absalom answered Joab, "Behold, I sent unto thee, saying, 'Come hither, that I may send thee to the king, to say, "Wherefore am I come from Geshur? It had been good for me to have been there still": now therefore let me see the king's face: and if there be any iniquity in me, let him kill me.'" So Joab came to the king, and told him: and when he had called for Absalom, he came to the king, and bowed himself on his face to the ground before the king: and the king kissed Absalom.

15 And it came to pass after this, that Absalom prepared him chariots and horses, and fifty men to run before him. And Absalom rose up early, and stood beside the way of the gate: and it was so, that when any man that had a controversy came to the king for judgment, then Absalom called unto him, and said, "Of what city art thou?" And he said, "Thy servant is of one of the tribes of Israel." And Absalom said unto him, "See, thy matters are good and right, but there is no man deputed of the king to hear thee." Absalom said moreover, "Oh that I were made judge in the land, that every man which hath any suit or cause might come unto me, and I would do him justice." And it was so, that when any man came nigh to him, to do him obeisance, he put forth his hand, and took him, and kissed him. And on this manner did Absalom to all Israel that came to the king for judgment: so Absalom stole the hearts of the men of Israel.

And it came to pass after forty years, that Absalom said unto the king, "I pray thee, let me go and pay my vow which I have vowed unto the Lord in Hebron. For thy servant vowed a vow while I abode at Geshur in Syria, saying, 'If the Lord shall bring me again indeed to Jerusalem, then I will serve the Lord.'" And the king said unto him, "Go in peace." So he arose, and went to Hebron.

But Absalom sent spies throughout all the tribes of Israel, saying, "As soon as ye hear the sound of the trumpet, then ye shall say, 'Absalom reigneth in Hebron.'" And with Absalom went two hundred men out of Jerusalem, that were called, and they went in their simplicity, and they knew not any thing. And Absalom sent for Ahithophel the Gilonite, David's counsellor, from his city, even from Giloh, while he offered sacrifices: and the conspiracy was strong; for the people increased continually with Absalom.

And there came a messenger to David, saying, "The hearts of the men of Israel are after Absalom." And David said unto all his servants that were with him at Jerusalem, "Arise, and let us flee; for we shall not else escape from Absalom: make speed to depart, lest he overtake us suddenly, and bring evil upon us, and smite the city with the edge of the sword." And the king's servants said unto the king, "Behold, thy servants are ready to do whatsoever my lord the king shall appoint." And the king went forth, and all his household after him: and the king left ten women, which were concubines, to keep the house. And the king went forth, and all the people after him, and tarried in a place that was far off. And all his servants passed on beside him: and all the Cherethites, and all the Pelethites, and all the Gittites, six hundred men which came after him from Gath, passed on before the king.

Then said the king to Ittai the Gittite, "Wherefore goest thou also with us? Return to thy place, and abide with the king: for thou art a stranger, and also an exile. Whereas thou camest but yesterday, should I this day make thee go up and down with us? Seeing I go whither I may, return thou, and take back thy brethren: mercy and truth be with thee." And Ittai answered the king, and said, "As the Lord liveth, and as my lord the king liveth, surely in what place my lord the king shall be, whether in death or life, even there also will thy servant be." And David said to Ittai, "Go and pass over." And Ittai the Gittite passed over, and all his men, and all the little ones that were with him. And all the country wept with a loud voice, and all the people passed over: the king also himself passed over the brook Kidron, and all the people passed over, toward the way of the wilderness.

And lo, Zadok also, and all the Levites were with him, bearing the ark of the covenant of God, and they set down the ark of God; and Abiathar went up, until all the people had done passing out of the city. And the king said unto Zadok, "Carry back the ark of God into the city: if I shall find favour in the eyes of the Lord, he will bring me again, and show me both it and his habitation. But if he thus say, 'I have no delight in thee': behold, here am I, let him do to me as seemeth good unto him." The king said also unto Zadok the priest, "Art not thou a seer? Return into the city in peace, and your two sons with you, *Ahimaaz* thy son, and Jonathan the son of Abiathar. See, I will tarry in the plain of the wilderness, until there come word from you to certify me." Zadok therefore and Abiathar carried the ark of God again to Jerusalem; and they tarried there. And David went up by the ascent of mount Olivet, and wept as he went up, and had his head covered, and he went barefoot, and all the people that was with him covered every man his head, and they went up, weeping as they went up.

And one told David, saying, "Ahithophel is among the conspirators with Absalom." And David said, "O Lord, I pray thee turn the counsel of Ahithophel into foolishness." And it came to pass, that when David was come to the top of the mount, where he worshipped God, behold, Hushai the Archite came to meet him, with his coat rent, and earth upon his head: unto whom David said, "If thou passest on with me, then thou shalt be a burden unto me. But if thou return to the city, and say unto Absalom, 'I will be thy servant, O king: as I have been thy father's servant hitherto, so will I now also be thy servant': then mayest thou for me defeat the counsel of Ahithophel. And hast thou not there with thee Zadok and Abiathar the priests? therefore it shall be, that what thing soever thou shalt hear out of the king's house, thou shalt tell it to Zadok and Abiathar the priests. Behold, they have there with them their two sons, *Ahimaaz* Zadok's son, and Jonathan Abiathar's son: and by them ye shall send unto me every thing that ye can hear." So Hushai David's friend came into the city, and Absalom came into Jerusalem.

16 And when David was a little past the top of the hill, behold, Ziba the servant of Mephibosheth met him with a couple of asses saddled, and upon them two hundred loaves of bread, and an hundred bunches of raisins, and an hundred of summer fruits, and a bottle of wine. And the king said unto Ziba, "What meanest thou by these?" And Ziba said, "The asses be for the king's household to ride on, and the bread and summer fruit for the young men to eat, and the wine, that such as be faint in the wilderness may drink." And the king said, "And where is thy master's son?" And Ziba said unto the king, "Behold, he abideth at Jerusalem: for he said, 'Today shall the house of Israel restore me the kingdom of my father.'" Then said the king to Ziba, "Behold, thine are all that pertained unto Mephibosheth." And Ziba said, "I humbly beseech thee that I may find grace in thy sight, my lord, O king."

And when King David came to Bahurim, behold, thence came out a man of the family of the house of Saul, whose name was Shimei the son of Gera: he came forth, and cursed still as he came. And he cast stones at David, and at all the servants of King David: and all the people, and all the mighty men were on his right hand, and on his left. And thus said Shimei when he cursed, "Come out, come out, thou bloody man, and thou man of Belial. The Lord hath returned upon thee all the blood of the house of Saul, in whose stead thou hast reigned, and the Lord hath delivered the kingdom into the hand of Absalom thy son: and behold, thou art taken in thy mischief, because thou art a bloody man."

Then said Abishai the son of Zeruiah unto the king, "Why should this dead dog curse my lord the king? let me go over, I pray thee, and take off his head." And the king said, "What have I to do with you, ye sons of Zeruiah? So let him curse, because the Lord hath said unto him, 'Curse David.' Who shall then say, 'Wherefore hast thou done so?'" And David said to Abishai, and to all his servants, "Behold, my son, which came forth of my bowels, seeketh my life: how much more now may this Benjamite do it? let him alone, and let him curse; for the Lord hath bidden him. It may be that the Lord will look on mine affliction, and that the Lord will requite me good for his cursing this day." And as David and his men went by the way, Shimei went along on the hill's side over against him, and cursed as he went, and threw stones at him, and cast dust. And the king, and all the people that were with him, came weary, and refreshed themselves there.

And Absalom, and all the people the men of Israel, came to Jerusalem, and Ahithophel with him. And it came to pass when Hushai the Archite, David's friend, was come unto Absalom, that Hushai said unto Absalom, "God save the king, God save the king." And Absalom said to Hushai, "Is this thy kindness to thy friend? Why wentest thou not with thy friend?" And Hushai said unto Absalom, "Nay, but whom the Lord, and this people, and all the men of Israel choose, his will I be, and with him will I abide. And again, whom should I serve? should I not serve in the presence of his son? As I have served in thy father's presence, so will I be in thy presence."

Then said Absalom to Ahithophel, "Give counsel among you what we shall do." And Ahithophel said unto Absalom, "Go in unto thy father's concubines, which he hath left to keep the house, and all Israel shall hear that thou art abhorred of thy father: then shall the hands of all that are with thee be strong." So they spread Absalom a tent upon the top of the house, and Absalom went in unto his father's concubines, in the sight of all Israel. And the counsel of Ahithophel, which he counselled in those days, was as if a man had inquired at the oracle of God: so was all the counsel of Ahithophel, both with David and with Absalom.

17 Moreover Ahithophel said unto Absalom, "Let me now choose out twelve thousand men, and I will arise and pursue after David this night. And I will come upon him while he is weary and weak-handed, and will make him afraid: and all the people that are with him shall flee, and I will smite the king only. And I will bring back all the people unto thee: the man whom thou seekest is as if all returned: so all the people shall be in peace." And the saying pleased Absalom well, and all the elders of Israel.

Then said Absalom, "Call now Hushai the Archite also, and let us hear likewise what he saith." And when Hushai was come to Absalom, Absalom spake unto him, saying, "Ahithophel hath spoken after this manner: shall we do after his saying? if not, speak thou." And Hushai said unto Absalom, "The counsel that Ahithophel hath given is not good at this time. For," said Hushai, "thou knowest thy father and his men, that they be mighty men, and they be chafed in their minds, as a bear robbed of her whelps in the field: and thy father is a man of war, and will not lodge with the people. Behold, he is hid now in some pit, or in some other place: and it will come to pass, when some of them be overthrown at the first, that whoso-ever heareth it will say, 'There is a slaughter among the people that follow Absalom.' And he also that is valiant, whose heart is as the heart of a lion, shall utterly melt: for all Israel knoweth that thy father is a mighty man, and they which be with him are valiant men. Therefore I counsel that all Israel be generally gathered unto thee, from Dan even to Beer-sheba, as the sand that is by the sea for multitude, and that thou go to battle in thine own person. So shall we come upon him in some place where he shall be found, and we will light upon him as the dew falleth on the ground: and of him and of all the men that are with him, there shall not be left so much as one. Moreover, if he be gotten into a city, then shall all Israel bring ropes to that city, and we will draw it into the river, until there be not one small stone found there." And Absalom and all the men of Israel said, "The counsel of Hushai the Archite is better than the counsel of Ahithophel": for the Lord had appointed to defeat the good counsel of Ahithophel, to the intent that the Lord might bring evil upon Absalom.

Then said Hushai unto Zadok and to Abiathar the priests, "Thus and thus did Ahithophel counsel Absalom and the elders of Israel, and thus have I counselled. Now therefore send quickly, and tell David, saying, 'Lodge not this night in the plains of the wilderness, but speedily pass over, lest the king be swallowed up, and all the people that are with him.'" Now Jonathan and *Ahimaaz* stayed by En-rogel (for they might not be seen to come into the city): and a wench went and told them: and they went, and told king David. Nevertheless, a lad saw them, and told Absalom: but they went both of them away quickly, and came to a man's house in Bahurim, which had a well in his court, whither they went down. And the woman took and spread a covering over the well's mouth, and spread ground corn thereon; and the thing was not known. And when Absalom's servants came to the woman to the house, they said, "Where is *Ahimaaz* and Jonathan?" And the woman said unto them, "They be gone over the brook of water." And when they had sought, and could not find them, they returned to Jerusalem. And it came to pass after they had departed, that they came up out of the well, and went and told king David, and said unto David, "Arise, and pass quickly over the water: for thus hath Ahithophel counselled against you." Then David arose, and all the people that were with him, and they passed over Jordan: by the morning light there lacked not one of them that was not gone over Jordan.

And when Ahithophel saw that his counsel was not followed, he saddled his ass, and arose, and gat him home to his house, to his city, and put his household in order, and hanged himself, and died, and was buried in the sepulchre of his father.

Then David came to Mahanaim: and Absalom passed over Jordan, he and all the men of Israel with him. And Absalom made Amasa captain of the host instead of Joab: which Amasa was a man's son whose name was Ithra, an Israelite, that went in to Abigail the daughter of Nahash, sister to Zeruiah Joab's mother. So Israel and Absalom pitched in the land of Gilead.

And it came to pass when David was come to Mahanaim, that Shobi the son of Nahash of Rabbah of the children of Ammon, and Machir the son of Ammiel of Lodebar, and Barzillai the Gileadite of Rogelim, brought beds, and basins, and earthen vessels, and wheat, and barley, and flour, and parched corn, and beans, and lentils, and parched pulse, and honey, and butter, and sheep, and cheese of kine for David, and for the people that were with him, to eat: for they said, "The people is hungry, and weary, and thirsty in the wilderness."

18 And David numbered the people that were with him, and set captains of thousands and captains of hundreds over them. And David sent forth a third part of the people under the hand of Joab, and a third part under the hand of Abishai the son of Zeruiah, Joab's brother, and a third part under the hand of Ittai the Gittite: and the king said unto the people, "I will surely go forth with you myself also." But the people answered, "Thou shalt not go forth: for if we flee away, they will not care for us, neither if half of us die will they care for us: but now thou art worth ten thousand of us: therefore now it is better that thou succor us out of the city." And the king said unto them, "What seemeth you best I will do." And the king stood by the gate side, and all the people came out by hundreds, and by thousands. And the king commanded Joab, and Abishai, and Ittai, saying, "Deal gently for my sake with the young man, even with Absalom." And all the people heard when the king gave all the captains charge concerning Absalom.

So the people went out into the field against Israel: and the battle was in the wood of Ephraim, where the people of Israel were slain before the servants of David, and there was there a great slaughter that day of twenty thousand men. For the battle was there scattered over the face of all the country: and the wood devoured more people that day than the sword devoured.

And Absalom met the servants of David; and Absalom rode upon a mule, and the mule went under the thick boughs of a great oak, and his head caught hold of the oak, and he was taken up between the heaven and the earth; and the mule that was under him went away. And a certain man saw it, and told Joab, and said, "Behold, I saw Absalom hanged in an oak." And Joab said unto the man that told him, "And behold, thou sawest him, and why didst thou not smite him there to the ground? and I would have given thee ten shekels of silver, and a girdle." And the man said unto Joab, "Though I should receive a thousand shekels of silver in mine hand, yet would I not put forth mine hand against the king's son: for in our hearing the king charged thee, and Abishai, and Ittai, saying, 'Beware that none touch the young man Absalom.' Otherwise, I should have wrought falsehood against mine own life: for there is no matter hid from the king, and thou thyself wouldest have set thyself against me." Then said Joab, "I may not tarry thus with thee." And he took three darts in his hand, and thrust them through the heart of Absalom, while he was yet alive in the midst of the oak. And ten young men that bare Joab's armour compassed about and smote Absalom, and slew him. And Joab blew the trumpet, and the people returned from pursuing after Israel: for Joab held back the people. And they took Absalom, and cast him into a great pit in the wood, and laid a very great heap of stones upon him: and all Israel fled every one to his tent.

Now Absalom in his lifetime had taken and reared up for himself a pillar, which is in the king's dale: for he said, "I have no son to keep my name in remembrance." And he called the pillar after his own name, and it is called unto this day Absalom's place.

Then said *Ahimaaz* the son of Zadok, "Let me now run, and bear the king tidings, how that the Lord hath avenged him of his enemies." And Joab said unto him, "Thou shalt not bear tidings this day, but thou shalt bear tidings another day: but this day thou shalt bear no tidings, because the king's son is dead." Then said Joab to Cushi, "Go tell the king what thou hast seen." And Cushi bowed himself unto Joab, and ran. Then said *Ahimaaz* the son of Zadok yet again to Joab, "But howsoever, let me, I pray thee, also run after Cushi." And Joab said, "Wherefore wilt thou run, my son, seeing that thou hast no tidings ready?" "But howsoever," said he, "let me run." And he said unto him, "Run." Then *Ahimaaz* ran by the way of the plain, and overran Cushi.

And David sat between the two gates: and the watchman went up to the roof over the gate unto the wall, and lifted up his eyes, and looked, and behold, a man running alone. And the watchman cried, and told the king. And the king said, "If he be alone, there is tidings in his mouth." And he came apace, and drew near. And the watchman saw another man running: and the watchman called unto the porter, and said, "Behold, another man running alone." And the king said, "He also bringeth tidings." And the watchman said, "Me thinketh the running of the foremost is like the running of *Ahimaaz* the son of Zadok." And the king said, "He is a good man, and cometh with good tidings." And *Ahimaaz* called, and said unto the king, "All is well." And he fell down to the earth, upon his face before the king, and said, "Blessed be the Lord thy God which hath delivered up the men that lifted up their hand against my lord the king." And the king said, "Is the young man Absalom safe?" And *Ahimaaz* answered, "When Joab sent the king's servant, and me thy servant, I saw a great tumult, but I knew not what it was." And the king said unto him, "Turn aside and stand here." And he turned aside, and stood still. And behold, Cushi came, and Cushi said, "Tidings my lord the king: for the Lord hath avenged thee this day of all them that rose up against thee." And the king said unto Cushi, "Is the young man Absalom safe?" And Cushi answered, "The enemies of my lord the king, and all that rise against thee to do thee hurt, be as that young man is."

And the king was much moved, and went up to the chamber over the gate, and wept: and as he went, thus he said, "O my son Absalom! my son, my son Absalom! would God I had died for thee, O Absalom, my son, my son!"

I KINGS

1 Now king David was old, and stricken in years, and they covered him with clothes, but he gat no heat. Wherefore his servants said unto him, "Let there be sought for my lord the king a young virgin, and let her stand before the king, and let her cherish him, and let her lie in thy bosom, that my lord the king may get heat." So they sought for a fair damsel throughout all the coasts of Israel, and found Abishag a Shunammite, and brought her to the king. And the damsel was very fair, and cherished the king, and ministered to him: but the king knew her not.

Then Adonijah the son of Haggith exalted himself, saying, "I will be king": and he prepared him chariots and horsemen, and fifty men to run before him. And his father had not displeased him at any time in saying, "Why hast thou done so?" And he also was a very goodly man, and his mother bare him after Absalom. And he conferred with Joab the son of Zeruiah, and with Abiathar the priest: and they following Adonijah, helped him. But Zadok the priest, and Benaiah the son of Jehoiada, and Nathan the prophet, and Shimei, and Rei, and the mighty men which belonged to David, were not with Adonijah. And Adonijah slew sheep, and oxen, and fat cattle, by the stone of Zoheleth, which is by En-rogel, and called all his brethren the king's sons, and all the men of Judah the king's servants. But

Nathan the prophet, and Benaiah, and the mighty men, and Solomon his brother, he called not.

Wherefore Nathan spake unto Bathsheba the mother of Solomon, saying, "Hast thou not heard that Adonijah the son of Haggith doth reign, and David our lord knoweth it not? Now therefore come, let me, I pray thee, give thee counsel, that thou mayest save thine own life, and the life of thy son Solomon. Go, and get thee in unto king David, and say unto him, 'Didst not thou, my lord, O king, swear unto thine handmaid, saying, "Assuredly Solomon thy son shall reign after me, and he shall sit upon my throne"? why then doth Adonijah reign?' Behold, while thou yet talkest there with the king, I also will come in after thee, and confirm thy words."

And Bathsheba went in unto the king into the chamber: and the king was very old, and Abishag the Shunammite ministered unto the king. And Bathsheba bowed, and did obeisance unto the king: and the king said, "What wouldest thou?" And she said unto him, "My lord, thou swarest by the Lord thy God unto thine handmaid, saying, 'Assuredly Solomon thy son shall reign after me, and he shall sit upon my throne.' And now behold, Adonijah reigneth; and now, my lord the king, thou knowest it not. And he hath slain oxen, and fat cattle, and sheep in abundance, and hath called all the sons of the king, and Abiathar the priest, and Joab the captain of the host: but Solomon thy servant hath he not called. And thou, my lord, O king, the eyes of all Israel are upon thee, that thou shouldest tell them who shall sit on the throne of my lord the king after him. Otherwise it shall come to pass, when my lord the king shall sleep with his fathers, that I and my son Solomon shall be counted offenders."

And lo, while she yet talked with the king, Nathan the prophet also came in. And they told the king, saying, "Behold Nathan the prophet." And when he was come in before the king, he bowed himself before the king with his face to the ground. And Nathan said, "My lord O king, hast thou said, 'Adonijah shall reign after me, and he shall sit upon my throne'? For he is gone down this day, and hath slain oxen, and fat cattle, and sheep in abundance, and hath called all the king's sons, and the captains of the host, and Abiathar the priest: and behold, they eat and drink before him, and say, 'God save king Adonijah.' But me, even me thy servant, and Zadok the priest, and Benaiah the son of Jehoiada, and thy servant Solomon, hath he not called. Is this thing done by my lord the king, and thou hast not showed it unto thy servant, who should sit on the throne of my lord the king after him?"

Then king David answered, and said, "Call me Bathsheba." And she came into the king's presence, and stood before the king. And the king sware, and said, "As the Lord liveth, that hath redeemed my soul out of all distress, even as I sware unto thee by the Lord God of Israel, saying, 'Assuredly Solomon thy son shall reign after me, and he shall sit upon my throne in my stead'; even so will I certainly do this day." Then Bathsheba bowed with her face to the earth, and did reverence to the king, and said, "Let my lord king David live for ever."

And king David said, "Call me Zadok the priest, and Nathan the prophet, and Benaiah the son of Jehoiada." And they came before the king. The king also said unto them, 'Take with you the servants of your lord, and cause Solomon my son to ride upon mine own mule, and bring him down to Gihon. And let Zadok the priest, and Nathan the prophet anoint him there king over Israel: and blow ye with the trumpet, and say, 'God save king Solomon.' Then ye shall come up after him, that he may come and sit upon my throne; for he shall be king in my stead: and I have appointed him to be ruler over Israel, and over Judah." And Benaiah the son of Jehoiada answered the king, and said, "Amen: the Lord God of my lord the king say so too. As the Lord hath been with my lord the king, even so be he with Solomon, and make his throne greater than the throne of my lord king David." So Zadok the priest, and Nathan the prophet, and Benaiah the son of Jehoiada, and the Cherethites, and the Pelethites, went down, and caused Solomon to ride upon king David's mule, and brought him to Gihon. And Zadok the priest took an horn of oil out of the tabernacle, and anointed Solomon: and they blew the trumpet, and all the people said, "God save king Solomon." And all the people came up after him, and the people piped with pipes, and rejoiced with great joy, so that the earth rent with the sound of them.

And Adonijah and all the guests that were with him heard it as they had made an end of eating. And when Joab heard the sound of the trumpet, he said, "Wherefore is this noise of the city, being in an uproar?" And while he yet spake, behold, Jonathan the son of Abiathar the priest came, and Adonijah said unto him, "Come in, for thou art a valiant man, and bringest good tidings." And Jonathan answered, and said to Adonijah, "Verily our lord king David hath made Solomon king. And the king hath sent with him Zadok the priest, and Nathan the prophet, and Benaiah the son of Jehoiada, and the Cherethites, and the Pelethites, and they have caused him to ride upon the king's mule. And Zadok the priest and Nathan the prophet have anointed him king in Gihon: and they are come up from thence rejoicing, so that the city rang again: this is the noise that ye have heard. And also Solomon sitteth on the throne of the kingdom. And moreover, the king's servants came to bless our lord king David, saying, 'God make the name of Solomon better than thy name, and make his throne greater than thy throne.' And the king bowed himself upon the bed. And also thus said the king, 'Blessed be the Lord God of Israel, which hath given one to sit on my throne this day, mine eyes even seeing it.'" And all the guests that were with Adonijah were afraid, and rose up, and went every man his way.

And Adonijah feared because of Solomon, and arose, and went, and caught hold on the horns of the altar. And it was told Solomon, saying, "Behold, Adonijah feareth king Solomon: for lo, he hath caught hold on the horns of the altar, saying, 'Let king Solomon swear unto me today that he will not slay his servant with the sword.'" And Solomon said, "If he will show himself a worthy man, there shall not an hair of him fall to the earth: but if wickedness shall be found in him, he shall die." So king Solomon sent, and they brought him down from the altar, and he came and bowed himself to king Solomon: and Solomon said unto him, "Go to thine house."

2 Now the days of David drew nigh, that he should die, and he charged Solomon his son, saying, "I go the way of all the earth: be thou strong therefore, and show thyself a man. And keep the charge of the Lord thy God, to walk in his ways, to keep his statutes, and his commandments, and his judgments, and his testimonies, as it is written in the law of Moses, that thou mayest prosper in all that thou doest, and whithersoever thou turnest thyself: that the Lord may continue his word which he spake concerning me, saying, 'If thy children take heed to their way, to walk before me in truth, with all their heart, and with all their soul, there shall not fail thee (said he) a man on the throne of Israel.' Moreover thou knowest also what Joab the son of Zeruiah did to me, and what he did to the two captains of the hosts of Israel, unto Abner the son of Ner, and unto Amasa the son of Jether, whom he slew, and shed the blood of war in peace, and put the blood of war upon his girdle that was about his loins, and in his shoes that were on his feet. Do therefore according to thy wisdom, and let not his hoar head go down to the grave in peace. But show kindness unto the sons of Barzillai the Gileadite, and let them be of those that eat at thy table: for so they came to me when I fled because of Absalom thy brother. And behold, thou hast with thee Shimei the son of Gera, a Benjamite of Bahurim, which cursed me with a grievous curse in the day when I went to Mahanaim: but he came down to meet me at Jordan, and I sware to him by the Lord, saying, 'I will not put thee to death with the sword.' Now therefore hold him not guiltless: for thou art a wise man, and knowest what thou oughtest to do unto him, but his hoar head bring thou down to the grave with blood." So David slept with his fathers, and was buried in the city of David. And the days that David reigned over Israel were forty years: seven years reigned he in Hebron, and thirty and three years reigned he in Jerusalem.

Then sat Solomon upon the throne of David his father, and his kingdom was established greatly. . . .

ISAIAH

INTRODUCTION

The Law did much to mold the form of Judaism; the prophets did much to shape its spirit, as well as the spirit of Christianity. For roughly three centuries beginning about 750 B.C. a series of inspired men preached a religion of righteousness, and their words established much of the foundation for Western morality. These men are here represented only by the writings of two authors, First and Second Isaiah. Since, however, all the prophets were explicitly concerned with moral problems, and since they deliberately mingled gloom and hope—even if in varying ratios—a small sample can illustrate the impact and fervor of their combined message.

The immediate predecessors of the prophets were men susceptible to mystic states who traveled around Palestine arousing religious enthusiasm, foretelling the future, and practising clairvoyance (as Samuel did in the case of Saul's lost asses). In the ninth century B.C. the semi-legendary Elijah combined miracles with preaching, and in the middle of the next century Amos, the first of the great prophets, undertook his short-lived mission. Declaring that the Lord's jurisdiction extended over all nations, he spiritualized and moralized the concept of God, and in so doing he anticipated Micah's famous summary: "What doth the Lord require of thee but to do justly, and to love mercy, and to walk humbly with thy God?" In the decade after Amos, Hosea lightened the general tone of doom typical of most of the prophets by inserting a message of divine love, utilizing the metaphor of a marriage between God and His people. But the scroll labeled at the top with the name Isaiah is the most influential and representative of all Hebrew prophetic writings. This scroll is itself a small library—the work of several hands, many generations, and much re-editing and textual corruption. (Since papyrus or parchment was too valuable to waste, any blank space at the end of one group of writings was filled in by another collection. Thus the sixty-six chapters that comprise this "book" can be divided into three parts: First Isaiah, chapters 1-39; Second Isaiah, chapters 40-55; Third Isaiah, chapters 56-66. Very early copies of parts of such a scroll are among the recent Dead Sea discoveries.)

First Isaiah lived from about 770 to 700 B.C. Influenced by Amos, he preached an international God of justice unconcerned with ritual. But as a Jerusalem aristocrat he was also acutely aware of the spread of wealth among the Jewish upper classes during the reign of Uzziah (780-740), and of the political disaster encroaching from the north. Isaiah's fears—moral and political—were justified: by 720 the Southern Kingdom of Judah had become a tributary to Assyria, and the Northern Kingdom of Israel had been conquered by this new colossus of the north. Though many of the leading Israelites were deported, Isaiah continued to recommend submission to, not revolt against, the conquerors, whom he viewed as a divine instrument for punishing a recalcitrant people. He also preached repentance and complete reliance on God. If one trusts wholly in God, then he will be saved, and thus a small remnant can survive. This remnant, interested not in wealth and ritual but in righteousness, will restore Israel; and this potentially regenerated nation is the only hope amid a dismal present. One of the reasons for the immediate popularity of Isaiah was this hope of a collective messiah, of a purified remnant—a hope that could offer some cheer to a beaten and dispersed people. Even so, the major burden of First Isaiah's message is one of pessimism: the political and religious regeneration of Israel is a remote event that will affect only a few, and before it occurs the vast majority must be scourged and afflicted. (Note, for instance, the despair, at once personal and national, of the end of chapter 6.) Despite much garbling of the text, Isaiah's intense sincerity shines through, as does the vigor of his style and the force of his convictions.

Second Isaiah lived some two hundred years after his namesake. In the generation before him Jeremiah, the most mystical and autobiographical of the prophets, had been close to despair, while Ezekiel, with a zeal that bordered on fanaticism, had occasionally relieved the gloom with flashes of apocalyptic hope. Such a ray of hope seemed more than ever necessary. In 598 B.C. Nebuchadnezzar captured Jerusalem and deported the leading Jews to the newly risen empire of Babylonia. In 587 Jerusalem was destroyed and a second group deported, and in 581 a third group was forced into exile. It was during the immediately ensuing period, the "Babylonian Captivity," that Second Isaiah wrote. In a style that is rhetorical and singing he delivered a message of rhapsodic joy. Israel's sufferings were drawing to a close, and a new dawn was about to dispel the dark night. With an enthusiasm sometimes bordering on incoherence he told his discouraged audience that their God was faithful and loving, and that He would soon restore His people. Almost certainly Second Isaiah's picture of the suffering servant was intended to be a personification of Israel: the Jews, by their sufferings, have vicariously atoned for the sins of the human race. Combining Amos's God of justice, Hosea's God of love, and First Isaiah's enlarged God of Israel, Second Isaiah saw God as entirely monotheistic and international. And to him God's people were chosen in the sense that their pangs and their righteousness qualified them to lead the world to a New Jerusalem. At once influenced and repelled by The Book of Job, Second Isaiah found in God's cosmic power a new covenant of hope.

Third Isaiah, who is not represented in this selection, was one or more fifth-century authors who essentially restated the message of Second Isaiah. Around 460 B.C. Malachi, among the last of the Hebrew prophets, returned to a more pessimistic note. Palestine had been under Persian domination for almost a century, and the new day had not yet dawned. Perhaps that fact best explains why the words of both Isaiahs still have particular relevance in the darkling world of today. ♣ ♣ ♣

Suggested Reading

John Bunyan, *Pilgrim's Progress*—a seventeenth-century prose allegory written by a type of Puritan prophet.

William Blake, "Prophetical Books"—Romantic poems that are consciously prophetic.

D. H. Lawrence, novels and short stories—works by a twentieth-century writer, steeped in the Bible, who often speaks with the voice of an Old Testament prophet.

ISAIAH

1 The vision of Isaiah the son of Amoz, which he saw concerning Judah and Jerusalem in the days of Uzziah, Jotham, Ahaz, and Hezekiah, kings of Judah. Hear, O heavens, and give ear, O earth: for the Lord hath spoken: "I have nourished and brought up children, and they have rebelled against me. The ox knoweth his owner, and the ass his master's crib: but Israel doth not know, my people doth not consider." Ah sinful nation, a people laden with iniquity, a seed of evildoers, children that are corrupters: they have forsaken the Lord, they have provoked the Holy One of Israel unto anger, they are gone away backward.

Why should ye be stricken any more? ye will revolt more and more: the whole head is sick, and the whole heart faint. From the sole of the foot, even unto the head, there is no soundness in it; but wounds, and bruises, and putrifying sores: they have not been closed, neither bound up, neither mollified with ointment. Your country is desolate, your cities are burnt with fire: your land, strangers devour it in your presence, and it is desolate, as overthrown by strangers. And the daughter of Zion is left as a cottage in a vineyard, as a lodge in a garden of cucumbers, as a besieged city. Except the Lord of hosts had left unto us a very small remnant, we should have been as Sodom, and we should have been like unto Gomorrah.

Hear the word of the Lord, ye rulers of Sodom, give ear unto the law of our God, ye people of Gomorrah. "To what purpose is the multitude of your sacrifices unto me?" saith the Lord. "I am full of the burnt offerings of rams, and the fat of fed beasts, and I delight not in the blood of bullocks, or of lambs, or of he-goats. When ye come to appear before me, who hath required this at your hand, to tread my courts? Bring no more vain oblations, incense is an abomination unto me: the new moons, and sabbaths, the calling of assemblies, I cannot away with; it is iniquity, even the solemn meeting. Your new moons and your appointed feasts my soul hateth: they are a trouble unto me, I am weary to bear them. And when ye spread forth your hands, I will hide mine eyes from you; yea, when ye make many prayers, I will not hear: your hands are full of blood.

"Wash ye, make you clean, put away the evil of your doings from before mine eyes, cease to do evil, learn to do well, seek judgment, relieve the oppressed, judge the fatherless, plead for the widow. Come now, and let us reason together," saith the Lord: "though your sins be as scarlet, they shall be as white as snow; though they be red like crimson, they shall be as wool. If ye be willing and obedient, ye shall eat the good of the land. But if ye refuse and rebel, ye shall be devoured with the sword: for the mouth of the Lord hath spoken it."

How is the faithful city become an harlot? it was full of judgment, righteousness lodged in it; but now murderers. Thy silver is become dross, thy wine mixed with water. Thy princes are rebellious and companions of thieves: every one loveth gifts, and followeth after rewards: they judge not the fatherless, neither doth the cause of the widow come unto them. Therefore saith the Lord, the Lord of hosts, the Mighty One of Israel, "Ah, I will ease me of mine adversaries, and avenge me of mine enemies. And I will turn my hand upon thee, and purely purge away thy dross, and take away all thy tin. And I will restore thy judges as at the first, and thy counsellors as at the beginning: afterward thou shalt be called the city of righteousness, the faithful city." Zion shall be redeemed with judgment, and her converts with righteousness.

And the destruction of the transgressors and of the sinners shall be together: and they that forsake the Lord shall be consumed. For they shall be ashamed of the oaks which ye have desired, and ye shall be confounded for the gardens that ye have chosen. For ye shall be as an oak whose leaf fadeth, and as a garden that hath no water. And the strong shall be as tow, and the maker of it as a spark, and they shall both burn together, and none shall quench them.

2 The word that Isaiah, the son of Amoz, saw concerning Judah and Jerusalem. And it shall come to pass in the last days, that the mountain of the Lord's house shall be established in the top of the mountains, and shall be exalted above the hills; and all nations shall flow unto it. And many people shall go and say, "Come ye and let us go up to the mountain of the Lord, to the house of the God of Jacob, and he will teach us of his ways, and we will walk in his paths": for out of Zion shall go forth the law, and the word of the Lord from Jerusalem. And he shall judge among the nations, and shall rebuke many people: and they shall beat their swords into plowshares, and their spears into pruning hooks: nation shall not lift up sword against nation, neither shall they learn war any more. O house of Jacob, come ye, and let us walk in the light of the Lord.

Therefore thou hast forsaken thy people the house of Jacob; because they be replenished from the east, and are soothsayers like the Philistines, and they please themselves in the children of strangers. Their land also is full of silver and gold, neither is there any end of their treasures: their land is also full of horses; neither is there any end of their chariots. Their land also is full of idols: they worship the work of their own hands, that which their own fingers have made. And the mean man boweth down, and the great man humbleth himself; therefore forgive them not.

Enter into the rock, and hide thee in the dust, for fear of the
Lord, and for the glory of his majesty. The lofty looks of man
shall be humbled, and the haughtiness of men shall be bowed down:
and the Lord alone shall be exalted in that day. For the day of the
Lord of hosts shall be upon every one that is proud and lofty,
and upon every one that is lifted up, and he shall be brought
low; and upon all the cedars of Lebanon that are high and lifted
up, and upon all the oaks of Bashan, and upon all the high mountains, and upon all the hills that are lifted up, and upon every
high tower, and upon every fenced wall, and upon all the ships of
Tarshish, and upon all pleasant pictures. And the loftiness of man
shall be bowed down, and the haughtiness of men shall be made
low: and the Lord alone shall be exalted in that day. And the idols
he shall utterly abolish. And they shall go into the holes of the
rocks, and into the caves of the earth, for fear of the Lord, and for
the glory of his majesty; when he ariseth to shake terribly the earth.
In that day a man shall cast his idols of silver, and his idols of gold,
which they made each one for himself to worship, to the moles and
to the bats: to go into the clefts of the rocks, and into the tops of
the ragged rocks, for fear of the Lord, and for the glory of his
majesty; when he ariseth to shake terribly the earth. Cease ye from
man, whose breath is in his nostrils: for wherein is he to be
accounted of?

3 For behold, the Lord, the Lord of hosts, doth take away from
Jerusalem, and from Judah, the stay and the staff, the whole
stay of bread, and the whole stay of water, the mighty man, and
the man of war, the judge, and the prophet, and the prudent, and the
ancient, the captain of fifty, and the honourable man, and the counsellor, and the cunning artificer, and the eloquent orator. And I
will give children to be their princes, and babes shall rule over
them. And the people shall be oppressed, every one by another, and
every one by his neighbour: the child shall behave himself proudly
against the ancient, and the base against the honourable. When a
man shall take hold of his brother of the house of his father, saying,
"Thou hast clothing, be thou our ruler, and let this ruin be under
thy hand": in that day shall he swear, saying, "I will not be an
healer: for in my house is neither bread nor clothing: make me not

a ruler of the people." For Jerusalem is ruined, and Judah is fallen: because their tongue and their doings are against the Lord, to provoke the eyes of his glory.

The show of their countenance doth witness against them, and they declare their sin as Sodom, they hide it not: woe unto their soul, for they have rewarded evil unto themselves. Say ye to the righteous, that it shall be well with him: for they shall eat the fruit of their doings. Woe unto the wicked, it shall be ill with him: for the reward of his hands shall be given him.

As for my people, children are their oppressors, and women rule over them: O my people, they which lead thee cause thee to err, and destroy the way of thy paths. The Lord standeth up to plead, and standeth to judge the people. The Lord will enter into judgment with the ancients of his people, and the princes thereof: "For ye have eaten up the vineyard; the spoil of the poor is in your houses. What mean ye that ye beat my people to pieces, and grind the faces of the poor?" saith the Lord God of hosts.

Moreover the Lord saith, "Because the daughters of Zion are haughty, and walk with stretched forth necks, and wanton eyes, walking and mincing as they go, and making a tinkling with their feet: therefore the Lord will smite with a scab the crown of the head of the daughters of Zion, and the Lord will discover their secret parts." In that day the Lord will take away the bravery of their tinkling ornaments about their feet, and their cauls,[1] and their round tires[2] like the moon, the chains, and the bracelets, and the mufflers, the bonnets, and the ornaments of the legs, and the headbands, and the tablets, and the earrings, the rings, and nose jewels, the changeable suits of apparel, and the mantles, and the wimples, and the crisping pins, the glasses, and the fine linen, and the hoods, and the veils. And it shall come to pass, that instead of sweet smell, there shall be stink; and instead of a girdle, a rent; and instead of well set hair, baldness; and instead of a stomacher, a girding of sackcloth; and burning instead of beauty. Thy men shall fall by the sword, and thy mighty in the war. And her gates shall lament and mourn; and she being desolate shall sit upon the ground.

[1] Probably a shawl or hood.
[2] Probably a headdress of some sort.

4 And in that day seven women shall take hold of one man, saying, "We will eat our own bread, and wear our own apparel: only let us be called by thy name, to take away our reproach." In that day shall the branch of the Lord be beautiful and glorious, and the fruit of the earth shall be excellent and comely for them that are escaped of Israel. And it shall come to pass, that he that is left in Zion, and he that remaineth in Jerusalem, shall be called holy, even every one that is written among the living in Jerusalem, when the Lord shall have washed away the filth of the daughters of Zion, and shall have purged the blood of Jerusalem from the midst thereof, by the spirit of judgment, and by the spirit of burning. And the Lord will create upon every dwelling place of mount Zion, and upon her assemblies, a cloud and smoke by day, and the shining of a flaming fire by night; for upon all the glory shall be a defense. And there shall be a tabernacle for a shadow in the daytime from the heat, and for a place of refuge, and for a covert from storm and from rain.

5 Now will I sing to my well-beloved a song of my beloved touching his vineyard: my well-beloved hath a vineyard in a very fruitful hill. And he fenced it, and gathered out the stones thereof, and planted it with the choicest vine, and built a tower in the midst of it, and also made a winepress therein: and he looked that it should bring forth grapes, and it brought forth wild grapes. And now, O inhabitants of Jerusalem, and men of Judah, judge, I pray you, betwixt me and my vineyard. What could have been done more to my vineyard, that I have not done in it? wherefore when I looked that it should bring forth grapes, brought it forth wild grapes? And now go to; I will tell you what I will do to my vineyard: I will take away the hedge thereof, and it shall be eaten up; and break down the wall thereof, and it shall be trodden down. And I will lay it waste; it shall not be pruned, nor digged; but there shall come up briers and thorns: I will also command the clouds, that they rain no rain upon it. For the vineyard of the Lord of hosts is the house of Israel, and the men of Judah his pleasant plant: and he looked for judgment, but behold oppression; for righteousness, but behold a cry.

Woe unto them that join house to house, that lay field to field, till there be no place, that they may be placed alone in the midst of the earth. In mine ears said the Lord of hosts, "Of a truth many houses shall be desolate, even great and fair, without inhabitant. Yea, ten acres of vineyard shall yield one bath,[3] and the seed of an homer[4] shall yield an ephah."

Woe unto them that rise up early in the morning, that they may follow strong drink, that continue until night, till wine inflame them. And the harp and the viol, the tabret and pipe, and wine are in their feasts: but they regard not the work of the Lord, neither consider the operation of his hands.

Therefore my people are gone into captivity, because they have no knowledge: and their honourable men are famished, and their multitude dried up with thirst. Therefore hell[5] hath enlarged herself, and opened her mouth without measure: and their glory, and their multitude, and their pomp, and he that rejoiceth, shall descend into it. And the mean man shall be brought down, and the mighty man shall be humbled, and the eyes of the lofty shall be humbled. But the Lord of hosts shall be exalted in judgment, and God that is holy shall be sanctified in righteousness. Then shall the lambs feed after their manner, and the waste places of the fat ones shall strangers eat. Woe unto them that draw iniquity with cords of vanity, and sin as it were with a cart rope: that say, "Let him make speed, and hasten his work, that we may see it: and let the counsel of the Holy One of Israel draw nigh and come, that we may know it."

Woe unto them that call evil good, and good evil, that put darkness for light, and light for darkness, that put bitter for sweet, and sweet for bitter. Woe unto them that are wise in their own eyes, and prudent in their own sight. Woe unto them that are mighty to drink wine, and men of strength to mingle strong drink: which justify the wicked for the reward, and take away the righteousness of the righteous from him. Therefore as the fire devoureth the stubble, and the flame consumeth the chaff, so their root shall be as rottenness, and their blossom shall go up as dust: because they have cast away the law of the Lord of hosts, and despised the word of the Holy One of Israel. Therefore is the anger of the Lord kindled against his people, and he hath stretched forth his hand against them

[3] Approximately 6 gallons.
[4] Approximately 10 bushels: 10 times as much as an ephah.
[5] The land of the dead, where men are, at most, mere shadows.

and hath smitten them: and the hills did tremble, and their carcasses were torn in the midst of the streets: for all this his anger is not turned away, but his hand is stretched out still.

And he will lift up an ensign to the nations from far, and will hiss unto them from the end of the earth: and behold, they shall come with speed swiftly. None shall be weary nor stumble amongst them: none shall slumber nor sleep, neither shall the girdle of their loins be loosed, nor the latchet of their shoes be broken. Whose arrows are sharp, and all their bows bent, their horses' hoofs shall be counted like flint, and their wheels like a whirlwind. Their roaring shall be like a lion, they shall roar like young lions: yea they shall roar and lay hold of the prey, and shall carry it away safe, and none shall deliver it. And in that day they shall roar against them like the roaring of the sea: and if one look unto the land, behold darkness and sorrow, and the light is darkened in the heavens thereof.

6 In the year that King Uzziah died, I saw also the Lord sitting upon a throne, high and lifted up, and his train filled the temple. Above it stood the seraphim: each one had six wings; with twain he covered his face, and with twain he covered his feet, and with twain he did fly. And one cried unto another, and said, "Holy, holy, holy, is the Lord of hosts, the whole earth is full of his glory." And the posts of the door moved at the voice of him that cried, and the house was filled with smoke.

Then said I, "Woe is me; for I am undone, because I am a man of unclean lips, and I dwell in the midst of a people of unclean lips: for mine eyes have seen the king, the Lord of hosts." Then flew one of the seraphim unto me, having a live coal in his hand, which he had taken with the tongs from off the altar. And he laid it upon my mouth, and said, "Lo, this hath touched thy lips, and thine iniquity is taken away, and thy sin purged." Also I heard the voice of the Lord, saying, "Whom shall I send, and who will go for us?" Then I said, "Here am I, send me."

And he said, "Go and tell this people: 'Hear ye indeed, but understand not: and see ye indeed, but perceive not.' Make the heart of this people fat, and make their ears heavy, and shut their eyes: lest they see with their eyes, and hear with their ears, and understand with their heart, and convert and be healed." Then said I, "Lord, how long?" And he answered, "Until the cities be wasted without inhabitant, and the houses without man, and the land be utterly desolate, and the Lord have removed men far away, and there be a great forsaking in the midst of the land. . . ." [6]

9 Nevertheless the dimness shall not be such as was in her vexation, when at the first he lightly afflicted the land of Zebulun, and the land of Naphtali, and afterward did more grievously afflict her by the way of the sea, beyond Jordan, in Galilee of the nations. The people that walked in darkness have seen a great light: they that dwell in the land of the shadow of death, upon them hath the light shined. Thou hast multiplied the nation, and not increased the joy: they joy before thee according to the joy in harvest, and as men rejoice when they divide the spoil. For thou hast broken the yoke of his burden, and the staff of his shoulder, the rod of his oppressor, as in the day of Midian. For every battle of the warrior is with confused noise, and garments rolled in blood; but this shall be with burning and fuel of fire. For unto us a child is born, unto us a son is given, and the government shall be upon his shoulder: and his name shall be called Wonderful, Counsellor, The mighty God, The everlasting Father, The Prince of Peace. Of the increase of his government and peace there shall be no end, upon the throne of David and upon his kingdom, to order it, and to establish it with judgment and with justice, from henceforth even for ever: the zeal of the Lord of hosts will perform this.

The Lord sent a word into Jacob, and it hath lighted upon Israel. And all the people shall know, even Ephraim and the inhabitant of Samaria, that say in the pride and stoutness of heart, "The bricks are fallen down, but we will build with hewn stones: the sycamores are cut down, but we will change them into cedars." Therefore the Lord shall set up the adversaries of Rezin against him, and join his enemies together; the Syrians before, and the Philistines behind, and they shall devour Israel with open mouth: for all this his anger is not turned away, but his hand is stretched out still.

For the people turneth not unto him that smiteth them, neither do they seek the Lord of hosts. Therefore the Lord will cut off from Israel head and tail, branch and rush, in one day. The ancient and honourable, he is the head: and the prophet that teacheth lies, he is

[6] God's concluding sentence, the final verse of chapter 6, is omitted because without elaborate commentary it is confusing.

the tail. For the leaders of this people cause them to err, and they that are led of them are destroyed. Therefore the Lord shall have no joy in their young men, neither shall have mercy on their fatherless and widows: for every one is an hypocrite and an evildoer, and every mouth speaketh folly: for all this his anger is not turned away, but his hand is stretched out still.

For wickedness burneth as the fire: it shall devour the briers and thorns, and shall kindle in the thickets of the forest, and they shall mount up like the lifting up of smoke. Through the wrath of the Lord of hosts is the land darkened, and the people shall be as the fuel of the fire: no man shall spare his brother. And he shall snatch on the right hand, and be hungry, and he shall eat on the left hand, and they shall not be satisfied: they shall eat every man the flesh of his own arm: Manasseh, Ephraim: and Ephraim, Manasseh: and they together shall be against Judah: for all this his anger is not turned away, but his hand is stretched out still.

11 And there shall come forth a rod out of the stem of Jesse, and a branch shall grow out of his roots. And the spirit of the Lord shall rest upon him, the spirit of wisdom and understanding, the spirit of counsel and might, the spirit of knowledge, and of the fear of the Lord: and shall make him of quick understanding in the fear of the Lord, and he shall not judge after the sight of his eyes, neither reprove after the hearing of his ears. But with righteousness shall he judge the poor, and reprove with equity for the meek of the earth: and he shall smite the earth with the rod of his mouth, and with the breath of his lips shall he slay the wicked. And righteousness shall be the girdle of his loins, and faithfulness the girdle of his reins. The wolf also shall dwell with the lamb, and the leopard shall lie down with the kid: and the calf and the young lion and the fatling together, and a little child shall lead them. And the cow and the bear shall feed, their young ones shall lie down together: and the lion shall eat straw like the ox. And the sucking child shall play on the hole of the asp, and the weaned child shall put his hand on the cockatrice' den. They shall not hurt nor destroy in all my holy mountain: for the earth shall be full of the knowledge of the Lord, as the waters cover the sea.

And in that day there shall be a root of Jesse, which shall stand for an ensign of the people; to it shall the Gentiles seek, and his rest shall be glorious. And it shall come to pass in that day, that the Lord shall set his hand again the second time to recover the remnant of his people, which shall be left, from Assyria, and from Egypt, and from Pathros, and from Cush, and from Elam, and from Shinar, and from Hamath, and from the islands of the sea. And he shall set up an ensign for the nations, and shall assemble the outcasts of Israel, and gather together the dispersed of Judah, from the four corners of the earth. The envy also of Ephraim shall depart, and the adversaries of Judah shall be cut off: Ephraim shall not envy Judah, and Judah shall not vex Ephraim. But they shall fly upon the shoulders of the Philistines toward the west, they shall spoil them of the east together: they shall lay their hand upon Edom and Moab, and the children of Ammon shall obey them. And the Lord shall utterly destroy the tongue of the Egyptian sea, and with his mighty wind shall he shake his hand over the river, and shall smite it in the seven streams, and make men go over dry-shod. And there shall be an highway for the remnant of his people, which shall be left, from Assyria; like as it was to Israel in the day that he came up out of the land of Egypt.

13 The burden of Babylon, which Isaiah the son of Amoz did see. Lift ye up a banner upon the high mountain, exalt the voice unto them, shake the hand, that they may go into the gates of the nobles. I have commanded my sanctified ones: I have also called my mighty ones for mine anger, even them that rejoice in my highness. The noise of a multitude in the mountains, like as of a great people: a tumultuous noise of the kingdoms of nations gathered together: the Lord of hosts mustereth the host of the battle. They come from a far country, from the end of heaven, even the Lord, and the weapons of his indignation, to destroy the whole land.

Howl ye; for the day of the Lord is at hand; it shall come as a destruction from the Almighty. Therefore shall all hands be faint, and every man's heart shall melt. And they shall be afraid: pangs and sorrows shall take hold of them, they shall be in pain as a woman that travaileth: they shall be amazed one at another, their faces shall be as flames. Behold, the day of the Lord cometh, cruel both with wrath and fierce anger, to lay the land desolate; and he shall destroy the sinners thereof out of it. For the stars of heaven and the constellations thereof shall not give their light: the sun shall be darkened in his going forth, and the moon shall not cause her light to shine. And I will punish the world for their evil, and the wicked for their iniquity; and I will cause the arrogancy of the proud to cease, and will lay low the haughtiness of the terrible. I will make a man more precious than fine gold; even a man than the golden wedge of Ophir. Therefore I will shake the heavens, and the earth shall remove out of her place in the wrath of the Lord of hosts, and in the day of his fierce anger. And it shall be as the chased roe, and as a sheep that no man taketh up: they shall every man turn to his own people, and flee every one into his own land. Every one that is found shall be thrust through: and every one that is joined unto them shall fall by the sword. Their children also shall be dashed to pieces before their eyes, their houses shall be spoiled, and their wives ravished. Behold, I will stir up the Medes against them, which shall not regard silver; and as for gold, they shall not delight in it. Their bows also shall dash the young men to pieces, and they shall have no pity on the fruit of the womb; their eye shall not spare children.

And Babylon, the glory of kingdoms, the beauty of the Chaldees' excellency, shall be as when God overthrew Sodom and Gomorrah. It shall never be inhabited, neither shall it be dwelt in from generation to generation: neither shall the Arabian pitch tent there, neither shall the shepherds make their fold there. But wild beasts of the desert shall lie there, and their houses shall be full of doleful creatures, and owls shall dwell there, and satyrs shall dance there. And the wild beasts of the islands shall cry in their desolate houses, and dragons in their pleasant palaces: and her time is near to come, and her days shall not be prolonged.

14 For the Lord will have mercy on Jacob, and will yet choose Israel, and set them in their own land: and the strangers shall be joined with them, and they shall cleave to the house of Jacob. And the people shall take them, and bring them to their place: and the house of Israel shall possess them in the land of the Lord for servants and handmaids: and they shall take them captives, whose captives they were, and they shall rule over their oppressors.

And it shall come to pass in the day that the Lord shall give thee rest from thy sorrow, and from thy fear, and from the hard bondage wherein thou wast made to serve, that thou shalt take up this proverb against the king of Babylon, and say, "How hath the oppressor ceased? the golden city ceased? The Lord hath broken the staff of the wicked, and the sceptre of the rulers. He who smote the people in wrath with a continual stroke, he that ruled the nations in anger, is persecuted, and none hindereth. The whole earth is at rest and is quiet: they break forth into singing. Yea, the fir trees rejoice at thee, and the cedars of Lebanon, saying, 'Since thou art laid down, no feller is come up against us.' Hell from beneath is moved for thee to meet thee at thy coming: it stirreth up the dead for thee, even all the chief ones of the earth; it hath raised up from their thrones all the kings of the nations. All they shall speak and say unto thee, 'Art thou also become weak as we? art thou become like unto us?' Thy pomp is brought down to the grave, and the noise of thy viols: the worm is spread under thee, and the worms cover thee. How art thou fallen from heaven, O Lucifer, son of the morning? how art thou cut down to the ground, which didst weaken the nations? For thou hast said in thine heart, 'I will ascend into heaven, I will exalt my throne above the stars of God: I will sit also upon the mount of the congregation, in the sides of the north. I will ascend above the heights of the clouds, I will be like the most High.' Yet thou shalt be brought down to hell, to the sides of the pit. They that see thee shall narrowly look upon thee, and consider thee, saying, 'Is this the man that made the earth to tremble, that did shake kingdoms? that made the world as a wilderness, and destroyed the cities thereof? that opened not the house of his prisoners?' All the kings of the nations, even all of them, lie in glory, every one in his own house. But thou art cast out of thy grave, like an abominable branch: and as the raiment of those that are slain, thrust through with a sword, that go down to the stones of the pit, as a carcass trodden under feet. Thou shalt not be joined with them in burial, because thou hast destroyed thy land, and slain thy people: the seed of evildoers shall never be renowned. Prepare slaughter for his children for the iniquity of their fathers, that they do not rise nor possess the land, nor fill the face of the world with cities." "For I will rise up against them," saith the Lord of hosts, "and cut off from Babylon the name, and remnant, and son, and nephew," saith the Lord. "I will also make it a possession for the bittern, and pools of water: and I will sweep it with the besom[7] of destruction," saith the Lord of hosts.

The Lord of hosts hath sworn, saying, "Surely as I have thought, so shall it come to pass; and as I have purposed, so shall it stand: that I will break the Assyrian in my land, and upon my mountains tread him under foot: then shall his yoke depart from off them, and his burden depart from off their shoulders." This is the purpose that is purposed upon the whole earth: and this is the hand that is stretched out upon all the nations. For the Lord of hosts hath purposed, and who shall disannul it? and his hand is stretched out, and who shall turn it back? In the year that king Ahaz died was this burden.

Rejoice not thou whole Palestina, because the rod of him that smote thee is broken: for out of the serpent's root shall come forth a cockatrice, and his fruit shall be a fiery flying serpent. And the first-born of the poor shall feed, and the needy shall lie down in safety: and I will kill thy root with famine, and he shall slay thy remnant. Howl, O gate, cry, O city, thou whole Palestina art dissolved, for there shall come from the north a smoke, and none shall be alone in his appointed times. What shall one then answer the messengers of the nation? "That the Lord hath founded Zion, and the poor of his people shall trust in it."

40 Comfort ye, comfort ye my people, saith your God. Speak ye comfortably to Jerusalem, and cry unto her, that her warfare is accomplished, that her iniquity is pardoned: for she hath received of the Lord's hand double for all her sins.

The voice of him that crieth in the wilderness, "Prepare ye the way of the Lord, make straight in the desert a highway for our God. Every valley shall be exalted, and every mountain and hill shall be made low: and the crooked shall be made straight, and the rough places plain. And the glory of the Lord shall be revealed, and all flesh shall see it together: for the mouth of the Lord hath spoken it." The voice said, "Cry." And he said, "What shall I cry?" All flesh is grass, and all the goodliness thereof is as the flower of the field. The grass withereth, the flower fadeth, because the spirit of the Lord bloweth upon it: surely the people is grass. The grass

[7] I.e., broom.

withereth, the flower fadeth: but the word of our God shall stand for ever.

O Zion, that bringest good tidings, get thee up into the high mountain: O Jerusalem, that bringest good tidings, lift up thy voice with strength, lift it up, be not afraid: say unto the cities of Judah, "Behold your God." Behold, the Lord God will come with strong hand, and his arm shall rule for him: behold, his reward is with him, and his work before him. He shall feed his flock like a shepherd: he shall gather the lambs with his arm, and carry them in his bosom, and shall gently lead those that are with young.

Who hath measured the waters in the hollow of his hand? and meted out heaven with the span, and comprehended the dust of the earth in a measure, and weighed the mountains in scales, and the hills in a balance? Who hath directed the spirit of the Lord, or, being his counsellor, hath taught him? With whom took he counsel, and who instructed him, and taught him in the path of judgment? and taught him knowledge, and showed to him the way of understanding? Behold, the nations are as a drop of a bucket, and are counted as the small dust of the balance: behold, he taketh up the isles as a very little thing. And Lebanon is not sufficient to burn, nor the beasts thereof sufficient for a burnt offering. All nations before him are as nothing, and they are counted to him less than nothing, and vanity.

To whom then will ye liken God? or what likeness will ye compare unto him? The workman melteth a graven image, and the goldsmith spreadeth it over with gold, and casteth silver chains. He that is so impoverished that he hath no oblation chooseth a tree that will not rot; he seeketh unto him a cunning workman, to prepare a graven image that shall not be moved. Have ye not known? have ye not heard? hath it not been told you from the beginning? have ye not understood from the foundations of the earth? It is he that sitteth upon the circle of the earth, and the inhabitants thereof are as grasshoppers; that stretcheth out the heavens as a curtain, and spreadeth them out as a tent to dwell in: that bringeth the princes to nothing; he maketh the judges of the earth as vanity. Yea they shall not be planted, yea they shall not be sown, yea their stock shall not take root in the earth: and he shall also blow upon them, and they shall wither, and the whirlwind shall take them away as stubble. "To whom then will ye liken me, or shall I be equal?" saith the Holy One. Lift up your eyes on high, and behold who hath created these things, that bringeth out their host by number: he calleth them all by names, by the greatness of his might, for that he is strong in power; not one faileth. Why sayest thou, O Jacob, and speakest, O Israel, "My way is hid from the Lord, and my judgment is passed over from my God"?

Hast thou not known? hast thou not heard, that the everlasting God, the Lord, the Creator of the ends of the earth, fainteth not, neither is weary? there is no searching of his understanding. He giveth power to the faint, and to them that have no might he increaseth strength. Even the youths shall faint, and be weary, and the young men shall utterly fall. But they that wait upon the Lord shall renew their strength: they shall mount up with wings as eagles, they shall run and not be weary, and they shall walk, and not faint.

52 Awake, awake, put on thy strength, O Zion, put on thy beautiful garments, O Jerusalem the holy city: for henceforth there shall no more come into thee the uncircumcised, and the unclean. Shake thyself from the dust; arise, and sit down, O Jerusalem: loose thyself from the bands of thy neck, O captive daughter of Zion. For thus saith the Lord, "Ye have sold yourselves for nought: and ye shall be redeemed without money." For thus saith the Lord God, "My people went down aforetime into Egypt to sojourn there, and the Assyrian oppressed them without cause. Now therefore, what have I here," saith the Lord, "that my people is taken away for nought? they that rule over them make them to howl," saith the Lord, "and my name continually every day is blasphemed. Therefore my people shall know my name: therefore they shall know in that day that I am he that doth speak. Behold, it is I."

How beautiful upon the mountains are the feet of him that bringeth good tidings, that publisheth peace, that bringeth good tidings of good, that publisheth salvation, that saith unto Zion, "Thy God reigneth"? Thy watchmen shall lift up the voice, with the voice together shall they sing: for they shall see eye to eye when the Lord shall bring again Zion.

Break forth into joy, sing together, ye waste places of Jerusalem: for the Lord hath comforted his people, he hath redeemed Jerusalem. The Lord hath made bare his holy arm in the eyes of all the nations, and all the ends of the earth shall see the salvation of our God.

Depart ye, depart ye, go ye out from thence, touch no unclean thing; go ye out of the midst of her; be ye clean, that bear the vessels of the Lord. For ye shall not go out with haste, nor go by flight: for the Lord will go before you: and the God of Israel will be your rereward.[8]

Behold, my servant shall deal prudently, he shall be exalted and extolled, and be very high. As many were astonished at thee (his visage was so marred more than any man, and his form more than the sons of men): so shall he sprinkle many nations, the kings shall shut their mouths at him: for that which had not been told them shall they see, and that which they had not heard shall they consider.

53 Who hath believed our report? and to whom is the arm of the Lord revealed? For he shall grow up before him as a tender plant, and as a root out of a dry ground: he hath no form nor comeliness: and when we shall see him, there is no beauty that we should desire him. He is despised and rejected of men, a man of sorrows, and acquainted with grief: and we hid as it were our faces from him; he was despised, and we esteemed him not.

Surely he hath borne our griefs, and carried our sorrows: yet we did esteem him stricken, smitten of God, and afflicted. But he was wounded for our transgressions, he was bruised for our iniquities: the chastisement of our peace was upon him, and with his stripes we are healed. All we like sheep have gone astray: we have turned every one to his own way, and the Lord hath laid on him the iniquity of us all. He was oppressed, and he was afflicted, yet he opened not his mouth: he is brought as a lamb to the slaughter, and as a sheep before her shearers is dumb, so he openeth not his mouth. He was taken from prison, and from judgment: and who shall declare his generation? for he was cut off out of the land of the living, for the transgression of my people was he stricken. And he made his grave with the wicked, and with the rich in his death, because he had done no violence, neither was any deceit in his mouth.

Yet it pleased the Lord to bruise him, he hath put him to grief: when thou shalt make his soul an offering for sin, he shall see his seed, he shall prolong his days, and the pleasure of the Lord shall prosper in his hand. He shall see of the travail of his soul, and shall be satisfied: by his knowledge shall my righteous servant justify

[8] *I.e.*, rear guard.

many: for he shall bear their iniquities. Therefore will I divide him a portion with the great, and he shall divide the spoil with the strong: because he hath poured out his soul unto death: and he was numbered with the transgressors, and he bare the sin of many, and made intercession for the transgressors.

55 Ho, every one that thirsteth, come ye to the waters, and he that hath no money: come ye, buy and eat, yea come, buy wine and milk without money, and without price. Wherefore do ye spend money for that which is not bread? and your labour for that which satisfieth not? hearken diligently unto me, and eat ye that which is good, and let your soul delight itself in fatness. Incline your ear, and come unto me: hear, and your soul shall live, and I will make an everlasting covenant with you, even the sure mercies of David. Behold, I have given him for a witness to the people, a leader and commander to the people. Behold, thou shalt call a nation that thou knowest not, and nations that knew not thee shall run unto thee, because of the Lord thy God, and for the Holy One of Israel, for he hath glorified thee.

Seek ye the Lord, while he may be found, call ye upon him while he is near. Let the wicked forsake his way, and the unrighteous man his thoughts: and let him return unto the Lord, and he will have mercy upon him, and to our God, for he will abundantly pardon.

"For my thoughts are not your thoughts, neither are your ways my ways," saith the Lord. "For as the heavens are higher than the earth, so are my ways higher than your ways, and my thoughts than your thoughts. For as the rain cometh down, and the snow from heaven, and returneth not thither, but watereth the earth, and maketh it bring forth and bud, that it may give seed to the sower, and bread to the eater: so shall my word be that goeth forth out of my mouth: it shall not return unto me void, but it shall accomplish that which I please, and it shall prosper in the thing whereto I sent it. For ye shall go out with joy, and be led forth with peace: the mountains and the hills shall break forth before you into singing, and all the trees of the fields shall clap their hands. Instead of the thorn shall come up the fir tree, and instead of the brier shall come up the myrtle tree, and it shall be to the Lord for a name, for an everlasting sign that shall not be cut off."

JOB

INTRODUCTION

Many readers feel that The Book of Job is the literary masterpiece of the Bible. A poem, a drama, a philosophical debate, it fits into no clearly defined category. Yet it is the work of a great artist. Of him, though, we know almost nothing, not even if he was a Hebrew. (Job contains no direct reference to the history or religion of Israel.) Probably he lived in the sixth century B.C. Certainly he was the most deeply and widely learned of all biblical authors. His artistic control is unsurpassed in either Testament, whether in the manipulation of an unusually large vocabulary, the effective use of metaphor and simile, or the depth of psychological penetration. He was thus able to transform the patient sufferer of ancient oriental folklore into a titanic figure who challenges God—and us.

How did the author achieve this work of art? On the level of over-all form, he took a widespread legend and inserted into it a probing dramatic-philosophical poem.[1] (Note that the first two chapters and the conclusion are in prose, and that they are ostensibly simple and naïve, suggestive of the traditional fairy tale: "Once upon a time . . ." and "They lived happily ever after.") On the level of drama, he builds up tension by having the three "comforters" become increasingly vehement in their denunciations of Job, while the protagonist himself becomes more and more isolated and, at the same time, more and more self-aware. On the level of psychology, the author sharply etches Job's profound, sometimes sudden, changes of mood. On the level of philosophy, he has what can be called a strong sense of reality—a sensitive, even anguished, feeling for the contrast between the vast wonders of the natural world and the plight of insignificant man. Finally, on the level of religion, the writer is concerned with the belief of an individual, not with ritual or with the religion of a nation.

[1] For a discussion of the characteristics of Hebrew poetry see the Introduction to the Psalms.

What did this concern with the belief of an individual involve? If we assume, as the author wants us to, that Job was eminently pious and innocent (so much so that he even worried about sinning mentally rather than actively), why should Job be punished? This is the age-old problem of theodicy: how can one equate the existence of evil with an all-powerful deity? Various religions and philosophies have supplied different answers, extending from the concept that God is good but not omnipotent to its reverse, or postulating an indifferent cosmos. The author of Job was aware of how certain non-Hebrew thinkers had dealt with this problem, but he was also specifically questioning what is called the Deuteronomic view of suffering. This view holds that God is interested in individual rather than collective retribution: that He rewards the good man and punishes the evil man, not the whole community. Yet if this explanation is correct, how can one explain the apparent paradox that bad men are often secure and happy, good men degraded and miserable? This is the question Job puts to God, and which God essentially does not answer. Or, if He does, it is with a display of power, not with a reasoned explanation.

But at the poem's end Job is rewarded by an approving God, and his comforters, the representatives of unquestioning orthodoxy, are reprimanded. Thus God appears to respect man for seeking truth and not blindly accepting tradition. Even so, The Book of Job is ultimately pessimistic. God not only fails to answer Job, but the vast and wonderful cosmos—with its behemoths and leviathans—rolls on and on, indifferent to the fate of man. God is a remote metaphysical force, powerful but not benevolent. (That He personally speaks from the whirlwind is a device essential to keeping the poem dramatic. Moreover, the fact that He talks to man but does not help him to understand the universe adds to the irony.)

Two specific elements in the work also require preliminary mention. First, Satan, who appears in the opening chapters, is not the gigantic figure of medieval legend, but is modeled on a type of cynical inspector who traveled around a province and then reported back to the king to whom he owed allegiance—in this case to God. Second, at the end of chapter 19 Job declares that his "redeemer liveth" and that he, Job, after his death will actually see God. In all probability the protagonist is neither foretelling Christ nor stating a doctrine of personal immortality. Instead, out of the depths of his despair he is calling for his future vindication by posterity, and also, because all around him appears so bleak, reaching desperately for the assurance that some day God will side with him. (Then, too, the Hebrew text of these verses is so corrupt that there is little hope of accurately recapturing their original meaning.) But regardless of how one interprets the end of chapter 19, he is likely to be impressed by the psychological anguish portrayed here and throughout the poem, an anguish different from the more detached and less dramatic reaction of Ecclesiastes to the problem of human suffering and divine justice.

The following selection is not complete. The third cycle of speeches by Job's comforters and his replies, along with the so-called Hymn on Wisdom, have been omitted. In these seven chapters (22-28), the text is badly garbled and there is much repetition of earlier speeches. Also left out are chapters 32-37, wherein a fourth and even more orthodox comforter indignantly rebukes Job, in the process adding little to what has gone before. A later interpolation, this section detracts from the cumulative power and momentum of The Book of Job. ♣ ♣ ♣

Suggested Reading

Aeschylus, Sophocles, Euripides: Plays—the classical Greek treatment of guilt, suffering, and punishment.

Christopher Marlowe, *Doctor Faustus*—a Renaissance drama about a man who, defying orthodoxy, sells his soul to the devil for knowledge and power.

William Shakespeare, Tragedies—probably literature's most profound dramatic investigations of the problem of evil.

Goethe, *Faust*—a Romantic retelling of the Faustus story in which aspiration leads to salvation.

Nathaniel Hawthorne, *The Scarlet Letter*—a mid-nineteenth-century American novel that examines the problem of sin and its consequences.

Dostoevski, *Crime and Punishment; The Brothers Karamazov*—nineteenth century Russian novels that probe the psychology of crime and guilt.

Joseph Conrad, *Heart of Darkness*—a modern novella about a trip up the Congo River, but also an exploration into the heart of evil.

Franz Kafka, *The Trial*—an allegorical novel concerned with the theme of unmerited suffering.

Archibald MacLeish, *J.B.*—a recent American play based on The Book of Job.

William Golding, *Lord of the Flies*—an English novel which explores evil in the midst of apparent innocence.

JOB

1 There was a man in the land of Uz, whose name was Job, and that man was perfect and upright, and one that feared God, and eschewed evil. And there were born unto him seven sons and three daughters. His substance also was seven thousand sheep, and three thousand camels, and five hundred yoke of oxen, and five hundred she-asses, and a very great household; so that this man was the greatest of all the men of the east. And his sons went and feasted in their houses, every one his day, and sent and called for their three sisters to eat and to drink with them. And it was so, when the days of their feasting were gone about, that Job sent and sanctified them, and rose up early in the morning, and offered burnt offerings according to the number of them all: for Job said, "It may be that my sons have sinned, and cursed God in their hearts." Thus did Job continually.

Now there was a day when the sons of God came to present themselves before the Lord, and Satan came also among them. And the Lord said unto Satan, "Whence comest thou?" Then Satan answered the Lord, and said, "From going to and fro in the earth, and from walking up and down in it." And the Lord said unto Satan, "Hast thou considered my servant Job, that there is none like him in the earth, a perfect and an upright man, one that feareth God, and escheweth evil?" Then Satan answered the Lord, and said, "Doth Job fear God for nought? Hast not thou made an hedge about him, and about his house, and about all that he hath on every side? thou hast blessed the work of his hands, and his substance is increased in the land. But put forth thine hand now, and touch all that he hath, and he will curse thee to thy face." And the Lord said unto Satan, "Behold, all that he hath is in thy power, only upon himself put not forth thine hand." So Satan went forth from the presence of the Lord.

And there was a day when his sons and his daughters were eating and drinking wine in their eldest brother's house: and there came a messenger unto Job, and said, "The oxen were plowing, and the asses feeding beside them, and the Sabeans fell upon them, and took them away: yea, they have slain the servants with the edge of the sword, and I only am escaped alone to tell thee." While he was yet speaking, there came also another, and said, "The fire of God is fallen from heaven, and hath burnt up the sheep, and the servants, and consumed them, and I only am escaped alone to tell thee." While he was yet speaking, there came also another, and said, "The Chaldeans made out three bands, and fell upon the camels, and have carried them away, yea, and slain the servants with the edge of the sword, and I only am escaped alone to tell thee." While he was yet speaking, there came also another, and said, "Thy sons and thy daughters were eating and drinking wine in their eldest brother's house. And behold, there came a great wind from the wilderness, and smote the four corners of the house, and it fell upon the young men, and they are dead, and I only am escaped alone to tell thee." Then Job arose, and rent his mantle, and shaved his head, and fell down upon the ground, and worshipped, and said, "Naked came I out of my mother's womb, and naked shall I return thither: the Lord gave, and the Lord hath taken away, blessed be the name of the Lord." In all this Job sinned not, nor charged God foolishly.

2   Again there was a day when the sons of God came to present themselves before the Lord, and Satan came also among them to present himself before the Lord. And the Lord said unto Satan, "From whence comest thou?" And Satan answered the Lord, and said, "From going to and fro in the earth, and from walking up and down in it." And the Lord said unto Satan, "Hast thou considered my servant Job, that there is none like him in the earth, a perfect and an upright man, one that feareth God, and escheweth evil? and still he holdeth fast his integrity, although thou movedst me against him, to destroy him without cause." And Satan answered the Lord, and said, "Skin for skin, yea all that a man hath, will he give for his life. But put forth thine hand now, and touch his bone and his flesh, and he will curse thee to thy face." And the Lord said unto Satan, "Behold, he is in thine hand, but save his life."

So went Satan forth from the presence of the Lord, and smote Job with sore boils, from the sole of his foot unto his crown. And he took him a potsherd to scrape himself withal; and he sat down among the ashes.

Then said his wife unto him, "Dost thou still retain thine integrity? curse God, and die." But he said unto her, "Thou speakest as one of the foolish women speaketh; what? shall we receive good at the hand of God, and shall we not receive evil?" In all this did not Job sin with his lips.

Now when Job's three friends heard of all this evil that was come upon him, they came every one from his own place: Eliphaz the Temanite, and Bildad the Shuhite, and Zophar the Naamathite; for they had made an appointment together to come to mourn with him, and to comfort him. And when they lifted up their eyes afar off, and knew him not, they lifted up their voice, and wept; and they rent every one his mantle, and sprinkled dust upon their heads toward heaven. So they sat down with him upon the ground seven days and seven nights, and none spake a word unto him; for they saw that his grief was very great.

3 After this, opened Job his mouth, and cursed his day.

And Job spake, and said,

"Let the day perish wherein I was born, and the night in which it was said, 'There is a man-child conceived.'

Let that day be darkness, let not God regard it from above, neither let the light shine upon it.

Let darkness and the shadow of death stain it, let a cloud dwell upon it, let the blackness of the day terrify it.

As for that night, let darkness seize upon it, let it not be joined unto the days of the year, let it not come into the number of the months.

Lo, let that night be solitary, let no joyful voice come therein.

Let them curse it that curse the day, who are ready to raise up their mourning.

Let the stars of the twilight thereof be dark, let it look for light but have none, neither let it see the dawning of the day:

Because it shut not up the doors of my mother's womb, nor hid sorrow from mine eyes.

Why died I not from the womb? why did I not give up the ghost when I came out of the belly?

Why did the knees prevent me? or why the breasts, that I should suck?

For now should I have lain still and been quiet, I should have slept; then had I been at rest,

With kings and counsellors of the earth, which built desolate places for themselves,

Or with princes that had gold, who filled their houses with silver:

Or as an hidden untimely birth, I had not been; as infants which never saw light.

There the wicked cease from troubling: and there the weary be at rest.

There the prisoners rest together, they hear not the voice of the oppressor.

The small and great are there, and the servant is free from his master.

Wherefore is light given to him that is in misery, and life unto the bitter in soul?

Which long for death, but it cometh not, and dig for it more than for hid treasures:

Which rejoice exceedingly, and are glad when they can find the grave?

Why is light given to a man, whose way is hid, and whom God hath hedged in?

For my sighing cometh before I eat, and my roarings are poured out like the waters.

For the thing which I greatly feared is come upon me, and that which I was afraid of is come unto me.

I was not in safety, neither had I rest, neither was I quiet: yet trouble came."

4 Then Eliphaz the Temanite answered, and said,

"If we assay to commune with thee, wilt thou be grieved? But who can withhold himself from speaking?

Behold, thou hast instructed many, and thou hast strengthened the weak hands.

Thy words have upholden him that was falling, and thou hast strengthened the feeble knees.

But now it is come upon thee, and thou faintest; it toucheth thee, and thou art troubled.

Is not this thy fear, thy confidence, thy hope, and the uprightness of thy ways?

Remember, I pray thee, who ever perished, being innocent? or where were the righteous cut off?

Even as I have seen, they that plow iniquity, and sow wickedness, reap the same.

By the blast of God they perish, and by the breath of his nostrils are they consumed.

The roaring of the lion, and the voice of the fierce lion, and the teeth of the young lions, are broken.

The old lion perisheth for lack of prey, and the stout lion's whelps are scattered abroad.

Now a thing was secretly brought to me, and mine ear received a little thereof.

In thoughts from the visions of the night, when deep sleep falleth on men:

Fear came upon me, and trembling, which made all my bones to shake.

Then a spirit passed before my face: the hair of my flesh stood up.

It stood still, but I could not discern the form thereof: an image was before mine eyes, there was silence, and I heard a voice saying,

'Shall mortal man be more just than God? shall a man be more pure than his maker?

'Behold, he put no trust in his servants; and his angels he charged with folly:

'How much less on them that dwell in houses of clay, whose foundation is in the dust, which are crushed before the moth.

'They are destroyed from morning to evening: they perish for ever, without any regarding it.

'Doth not their excellency which is in them go away? they die, even without wisdom.' "

5 "Call now, if there be any that will answer thee, and to which of the saints wilt thou turn?

For wrath killeth the foolish man, and envy slayeth the silly one.

I have seen the foolish taking root: but suddenly I cursed his habitation.

His children are far from safety, and they are crushed in the gate, neither is there any to deliver them.

Whose harvest the hungry eateth up, and taketh it even out of the thorns, and the robber swalloweth up their substance.

Although affliction cometh not forth of the dust, neither doth trouble spring out of the ground:

Yet man is born unto trouble, as the sparks fly upward.

I would seek unto God, and unto God would I commit my cause:

Which doeth great things and unsearchable: marvelous things without number.

Who giveth rain upon the earth, and sendeth waters upon the fields:

To set up on high those that be low; that those which mourn may be exalted to safety.

He disappointeth the devices of the crafty, so that their hands cannot perform their enterprise.

He taketh the wise in their own craftiness: and the counsel of the froward is carried headlong.

They meet with darkness in the daytime, and grope in the noonday as in the night.

But he saveth the poor from the sword, from their mouth, and from the hand of the mighty.

So the poor hath hope, and iniquity stoppeth her mouth.

Behold, happy is the man whom God correcteth: therefore despise not thou the chastening of the Almighty.

For he maketh sore, and bindeth up: he woundeth, and his hands make whole.

He shall deliver thee in six troubles, yea in seven there shall no evil touch thee.

In famine he shall redeem thee from death: and in war from the power of the sword.

Thou shalt be hid from the scourge of the tongue: neither shalt thou be afraid of destruction when it cometh.

At destruction and famine thou shalt laugh: neither shalt thou be afraid of the beasts of the earth.

For thou shalt be in league with the stones of the field: and the beasts of the field shall be at peace with thee.

And thou shalt know that thy tabernacle shall be in peace; and thou shalt visit thy habitation, and shalt not sin.

Thou shalt know also that thy seed shall be great, and thine offspring as the grass of the earth.

Thou shalt come to thy grave in a full age, like as a shock of corn cometh in, in his season.

Lo this, we have searched it, so it is; hear it, and know thou it for thy good."

6 But Job answered, and said,

"Oh that my grief were thoroughly weighed, and my calamity laid in the balances together.

For now it would be heavier than the sand of the sea, therefore my words are swallowed up.

For the arrows of the Almighty are within me, the poison whereof drinketh up my spirit: the terrors of God do set themselves in array against me.

Doth the wild ass bray when he hath grass? or loweth the ox over his fodder?

Can that which is unsavoury be eaten without salt? or is there any taste in the white of an egg?

The things that my soul refused to touch are as my sorrowful meat.

O that I might have my request! and that God would grant me the thing that I long for!

Even that it would please God to destroy me, that he would let loose his hand, and cut me off.

Then should I yet have comfort, yea I would harden myself in sorrow; let him not spare, for I have not concealed the words of the holy One.

What is my strength, that I should hope? and what is mine end, that I should prolong my life?

Is my strength the strength of stones? or is my flesh of brass?

Is not my help in me? and is wisdom driven quite from me?

To him that is afflicted pity should be showed from his friend; but he forsaketh the fear of the Almighty.

My brethren have dealt deceitfully as a brook, and as the stream of brooks they pass away,

Which are blackish by reason of the ice, and wherein the snow is hid:

What time they wax warm, they vanish: when it is hot, they are consumed out of their place.

The paths of their way are turned aside; they go to nothing, and perish.

The troops of Tema looked, the companies of Sheba waited for them.

They were confounded because they had hoped; they came thither, and were ashamed.

For now ye are nothing; ye see my casting down, and are afraid.

Did I say, 'Bring unto me'? or 'Give a reward for me of your substance'?

Or 'Deliver me from the enemy's hand,' or 'Redeem me from the hand of the mighty'?

Teach me, and I will hold my tongue: and cause me to understand wherein I have erred.

How forcible are right words? but what doth your arguing reprove?

Do ye imagine to reprove words, and the speeches of one that is desperate, which are as wind?

Yea, ye overwhelm the fatherless, and you dig a pit for your friend.

Now therefore be content, look upon me, for it is evident unto you if I lie.

Return, I pray you, let it not be iniquity; yea return again: my righteousness is in it.

Is there iniquity in my tongue? cannot my taste discern perverse things?

7 "Is there not an appointed time to man upon earth? are not his days also like the days of an hireling?

As a servant earnestly desireth the shadow, and as an hireling looketh for the reward of his work:

So am I made to possess months of vanity, and wearisome nights are appointed to me.

When I lie down, I say, 'When shall I arise, and the night be gone?' and I am full of tossings to and fro, unto the dawning of the day.

My flesh is clothed with worms and clods of dust, my skin is broken, and become loathsome.

My days are swifter than a weaver's shuttle, and are spent without hope.

O remember that my life is wind: mine eye shall no more see good.

The eye of him that hath seen me shall see me no more: thine eyes are upon me, and I am not.

As the cloud is consumed and vanisheth away: so he that goeth down to the grave shall come up no more.

He shall return no more to his house: neither shall his place know him any more.

Therefore I will not refrain my mouth, I will speak in the anguish of my spirit, I will complain in the bitterness of my soul.

Am I a sea, or a whale, that thou settest a watch over me?

When I say, 'My bed shall comfort me, my couch shall ease my complaint':

Then thou scarest me with dreams, and terrifiest me through visions:

So that my soul chooseth strangling, and death rather than my life.

I loathe it, I would not live alway: let me alone, for my days are vanity.

What is man, that thou shouldest magnify him? and that thou shouldest set thine heart upon him?

And that thou shouldest visit him every morning, and try him every moment?

How long wilt thou not depart from me? nor let me alone till I swallow down my spittle?

I have sinned: what shall I do unto thee, O thou preserver of men? why hast thou set me as a mark against thee, so that I am a burden to myself?

And why dost thou not pardon my transgression, and take away mine iniquity? for now shall I sleep in the dust, and thou shalt seek me in the morning, but I shall not be."

8 Then answered Bildad the Shuhite, and said,

"How long wilt thou speak these things? and how long shall the words of thy mouth be like a strong wind?

Doth God pervert judgment? or doth the Almighty pervert justice?

If thy children have sinned against him, and he have cast them away for their transgression:

If thou wouldst seek unto God betimes, and make thy supplication to the Almighty:

If thou wert pure and upright, surely now he would awake for thee, and make the habitation of thy righteousness prosperous.

Though thy beginning was small, yet thy latter end should greatly increase.

For inquire, I pray thee, of the former age, and prepare thyself to the search of their fathers.

(For we are but of yesterday, and know nothing, because our days upon earth are a shadow.)

Shall not they teach thee, and tell thee, and utter words out of their heart?

Can the rush grow up without mire? can the flag grow without water?

Whilst it is yet in his greenness, and not cut down, it withereth before any other herb.

So are the paths of all that forget God, and the hypocrite's hope shall perish:

Whose hope shall be cut off, and whose trust shall be a spider's web.

He shall lean upon his house, but it shall not stand: he shall hold it fast, but it shall not endure.

He is green before the sun, and his branch shooteth forth in his garden.

His roots are wrapped about the heap, and seeth the place of stones.

If he destroy him from his place, then it shall deny him, saying, 'I have not seen thee.'

Behold, this is the joy of his way, and out of the earth shall others grow.

Behold, God will not cast away a perfect man, neither will he help the evildoers:

Till he fill thy mouth with laughing, and thy lips with rejoicing.

They that hate thee shall be clothed with shame, and the dwelling place of the wicked shall come to nought."

9 Then Job answered, and said,

"I know it is so of a truth: but how should man be just with God?

If he will contend with him, he cannot answer him one of a thousand.

He is wise in heart, and mighty in strength: who hath hardened himself against him, and hath prospered?

Which removeth the mountains, and they know not: which overturneth them in his anger:

Which shaketh the earth out of her place, and the pillars thereof tremble:

Which commandeth the sun, and it riseth not: and sealeth up the stars:

Which alone spreadeth out the heavens, and treadeth upon the waves of the sea:

Which maketh Arcturus, Orion, and Pleiades, and the chambers of the south:

Which doeth great things past finding out, yea and wonders without number.

Lo, he goeth by me, and I see him not: he passeth on also, but I perceive him not.

Behold, he taketh away, who can hinder him? who will say unto him, 'What doest thou?'

If God will not withdraw his anger, the proud helpers do stoop under him.

How much less shall I answer him, and choose out my words to reason with him?

Whom, though I were righteous, yet would I not answer, but I would make supplication to my judge.

If I had called, and he had answered me, yet would I not believe that he had hearkened unto my voice:

For he breaketh me with a tempest, and multiplieth my wounds without cause.

He will not suffer me to take my breath, but filleth me with bitterness.

If I speak of strength, lo, he is strong: and if of judgment, who shall set me a time to plead?

If I justify myself, mine own mouth shall condemn me: If I say, 'I am perfect,' it shall also prove me perverse.

Though I were perfect, yet would I not know my soul: I would despise my life.

This is one thing, therefore I said it: 'He destroyeth the perfect and the wicked.'

If the scourge slay suddenly, he will laugh at the trial of the innocent.

The earth is given into the hand of the wicked: he covereth the faces of the judges thereof; if not, where, and who is he?

Now my days are swifter than a post: they flee away, they see no good.

They are passed away as the swift ships, as the eagle that hasteth to the prey.

If I say, 'I will forget my complaint, I will leave off my heaviness, and comfort myself';

I am afraid of all my sorrows, I know that thou wilt not hold me innocent.

If I be wicked, why then labour I in vain?

If I wash myself with snow-water, and make my hands never so clean:

Yet shalt thou plunge me in the ditch, and mine own clothes shall abhor me.

For he is not a man as I am, that I should answer him, and we should come together in judgment.

Neither is there any daysman[1] betwixt us, that might lay his hand upon us both.

Let him take his rod away from me, and let not his fear terrify me:

Then would I speak, and not fear him; but it is not so with me."

10 "My soul is weary of my life, I will leave my complaint upon myself; I will speak in the bitterness of my soul.

I will say unto God, 'Do not condemn me; show me wherefore thou contendest with me.

Is it good unto thee that thou shouldest oppress? that thou shouldest despise the work of thine hands? and shine upon the counsel of the wicked?

Hast thou eyes of flesh? or seest thou as man seeth?

Are thy days as the days of man? are thy years as man's days,

That thou inquirest after mine iniquity, and searchest after my sin?

Thou knowest that I am not wicked, and there is none that can deliver out of thine hand.

Thine hands have made me and fashioned me together round about; yet thou dost destroy me.

Remember, I beseech thee, that thou hast made me as the clay, and wilt thou bring me into dust again?

Hast thou not poured me out as milk, and curdled me like cheese?

Thou hast clothed me with skin and flesh, and hast fenced me with bones and sinews.

---

[1] *I.e.*, arbiter.

Thou hast granted me life and favour, and thy visitation hath preserved my spirit.

And these things hast thou hid in thine heart; I know that this is with thee.

If I sin, then thou markest me, and thou wilt not acquit me from mine iniquity.

If I be wicked, woe unto me; and if I be righteous, yet will I not lift up my head: I am full of confusion, therefore see thou mine affliction:

For it increaseth: thou huntest me as a fierce lion: and again thou showest thyself marvelous upon me.

Thou renewest thy witnesses against me, and increasest thine indignation upon me; changes and war are against me.

Wherefore then hast thou brought me forth out of the womb? Oh that I had given up the ghost, and no eye had seen me!

I should have been as though I had not been, I should have been carried from the womb to the grave.

Are not my days few? cease then, and let me alone that I may take comfort a little,

Before I go whence I shall not return, even to the land of darkness and the shadow of death,

A land of darkness, as darkness itself, and of the shadow of death, without any order, and where the light is as darkness.' "

11 Then answered Zophar the Naamathite, and said,
"Should not the multitude of words be answered? and should a man full of talk be justified?

Should thy lies make men hold their peace? and when thou mockest, shall no man make thee ashamed?

For thou hast said, 'My doctrine is pure, and I am clean in thine eyes.'

But O that God would speak, and open his lips against thee,

And that he would show thee the secrets of wisdom, that they are double to that which is: know therefore that God exacteth of thee less than thine iniquity deserveth.

Canst thou by searching find out God? canst thou find out the Almighty unto perfection?

It is as high as heaven, what canst thou do? deeper than hell, what canst thou know?

The measure thereof is longer than the earth, and broader than the sea.

If he cut off, and shut up, or gather together, then who can hinder him?

For he knoweth vain men: he seeth wickedness also, will he not then consider it?

For vain man would be wise, though man be born like a wild ass's colt.

If thou prepare thine heart, and stretch out thine hands toward him:

If iniquity be in thine hand, put it far away, and let not wickedness dwell in thy tabernacles.

For then shalt thou lift up thy face without spot, yea thou shalt be steadfast, and shalt not fear:

Because thou shalt forget thy misery, and remember it as waters that pass away:

And thine age shall be clearer than the noonday; thou shalt shine forth, thou shalt be as the morning.

And thou shalt be secure because there is hope, yea thou shalt dig about thee, and thou shalt take thy rest in safety.

Also thou shalt lie down, and none shall make thee afraid; yea many shall make suit unto thee.

But the eyes of the wicked shall fail, and they shall not escape, and their hope shall be as the giving up of the ghost."

12 And Job answered, and said,

"No doubt but ye are the people, and wisdom shall die with you.

But I have understanding as well as you, I am not inferior to you: yea who knoweth not such things as these?

I am as one mocked of his neighbour, who calleth upon God, and he answereth him: the just upright man is laughed to scorn.

He that is ready to slip with his feet is as a lamp despised in the thought of him that is at ease.

The tabernacles of robbers prosper, and they that provoke God are secure, into whose hand God bringeth abundantly.

But ask now the beasts, and they shall teach thee; and the fowls of the air, and they shall tell thee.

Or speak to the earth, and it shall teach thee; and the fishes of the sea shall declare unto thee.

Who knoweth not in all these that the hand of the Lord hath wrought this?

In whose hand is the soul of every living thing, and the breath of all mankind.

Doth not the ear try words? and the mouth taste his meat?

With the ancient is wisdom, and in length of days understanding.

With him is wisdom and strength, he hath counsel and understanding.

Behold, he breaketh down, and it cannot be built again: he shutteth up a man, and there can be no opening.

Behold, he withholdeth the waters, and they dry up: also he sendeth them out, and they overturn the earth.

With him is strength and wisdom: the deceived and the deceiver are his.

He leadeth counsellors away spoiled, and maketh the judges fools.

He looseth the bond of kings, and girdeth their loins with a girdle.

He leadeth princes away spoiled, and overthroweth the mighty.

He removeth away the speech of the trusty, and taketh away the understanding of the aged.

He poureth contempt upon princes, and weakeneth the strength of the mighty.

He discovereth deep things out of darkness, and bringeth out to light the shadow of death.

He increaseth the nations and destroyeth them: he enlargeth the nations, and straiteneth them again.

He taketh away the heart of the chief of the people of the earth, and causeth them to wander in a wilderness where there is no way.

They grope in the dark without light, and he maketh them to stagger like a drunken man.

13 "Lo, mine eye hath seen all this, mine ear hath heard and understood it.

What ye know, the same do I know also, I am not inferior unto you.

Surely I would speak to the Almighty, and I desire to reason with God.

But ye are forgers of lies, ye are all physicians of no value.

O that you would altogether hold your peace, and it should be your wisdom.

Hear now my reasoning, and hearken to the pleadings of my lips.

Will you speak wickedly for God? and talk deceitfully for him?

Will ye accept his person? will ye contend for God?

Is it good that he should search you out? or as one man mocketh another, do ye so mock him?

He will surely reprove you, if ye do secretly accept persons.

Shall not his excellency make you afraid? and his dread fall upon you?

Your remembrances are like unto ashes, your bodies to bodies of clay.

Hold your peace, let me alone that I may speak, and let come on me what will.

Wherefore do I take my flesh in my teeth, and put my life in mine hand?

Though he slay me, yet will I trust in him: but I will maintain mine own ways before him.

He also shall be my salvation: for an hypocrite shall not come before him.

Hear diligently my speech, and my declaration with your ears.

Behold now, I have ordered my cause, I know that I shall be justified.

Who is he that will plead with me? for now if I hold my tongue, I shall give up the ghost.

Only do not two things unto me: then will I not hide myself from thee.

Withdraw thine hand far from me, and let not thy dread make me afraid.

Then call thou, and I will answer: or let me speak, and answer thou me.

How many are mine iniquities and sins? make me to know my transgression and my sin.

Wherefore hidest thou thy face, and holdest me for thine enemy?

Wilt thou break a leaf driven to and fro? and wilt thou pursue the dry stubble?

For thou writest bitter things against me, and makest me to possess the iniquities of my youth.

Thou puttest my feet also in the stocks, and lookest narrowly unto all my paths; thou settest a print upon the heels of my feet.

And he, as a rotten thing, consumeth, as a garment that is moth-eaten."

14 "Man that is born of a woman is of few days, and full of trouble.

He cometh forth like a flower, and is cut down: he fleeth also as a shadow, and continueth not.

And dost thou open thine eyes upon such an one, and bringest me into judgment with thee?

Who can bring a clean thing out of an unclean? not one.

Seeing his days are determined, the number of his months are with thee, thou hast appointed his bounds that he cannot pass.

Turn from him that he may rest, till he shall accomplish, as an hireling, his day.

For there is hope of a tree, if it be cut down, that it will sprout again, and that the tender branch thereof will not cease.

Though the root thereof wax old in the earth, and the stock thereof die in the ground:

Yet through the scent of water it will bud, and bring forth boughs like a plant.

But man dieth, and wasteth away; yea, man giveth up the ghost, and where is he?

As the waters fail from the sea, and the flood decayeth and dryeth up:

So man lieth down, and riseth not: till the heavens be no more, they shall not awake, nor be raised out of their sleep.

O that thou wouldest hide me in the grave, that thou wouldest keep me secret, until thy wrath be past, that thou wouldest appoint me a set time, and remember me.

If a man die, shall he live again? All the days of my appointed time will I wait, till my change come.

Thou shalt call, and I will answer thee: thou wilt have a desire to the work of thine hands.

For now thou numberest my steps: dost thou not watch over my sin?

My transgression is sealed up in a bag, and thou sewest up mine iniquity.

And surely the mountain falling cometh to nought: and the rock is removed out of his place.

The waters wear the stones, thou washest away the things which grow out of the dust of the earth, and thou destroyest the hope of man.

Thou prevailest for ever against him, and he passeth: thou changest his countenance, and sendest him away.

His sons come to honour, and he knoweth it not; and they are brought low, but he perceiveth it not of them.

But his flesh upon him shall have pain, and his soul within him shall mourn."

15 Then answered Eliphaz the Temanite, and said,
"Should a wise man utter vain knowledge, and fill his belly with the east wind?

Should he reason with unprofitable talk? or with speeches wherewith he can do no good?

Yea thou castest off fear, and restrainest prayer before God.

For thy mouth uttereth thine iniquity, and thou choosest the tongue of the crafty.

Thine own mouth condemneth thee, and not I: yea thine own lips testify against thee.

Art thou the first man that was born? or wast thou made before the hills?

Hast thou heard the secret of God? and dost thou restrain wisdom to thyself?

What knowest thou that we know not? what understandest thou which is not in us?

With us are both the grayheaded and very aged men, much elder than thy father.

Are the consolations of God small with thee? is there any secret thing with thee?

Why doth thine heart carry thee away? and what do thine eyes wink at,

That thou turnest thy spirit against God, and lettest such words go out of thy mouth?

What is man, that he should be clean? and he which is born of a woman, that he should be righteous?

Behold, he putteth no trust in his saints, yea, the heavens are not clean in his sight.

How much more abominable and filthy is man, which drinketh iniquity like water?

I will show thee, hear me, and that which I have seen I will declare,

Which wise men have told from their fathers, and have not hid it:

Unto whom alone the earth was given, and no stranger passed among them.

The wicked man travaileth with pain all his days, and the number of years is hidden to the oppressor.

A dreadful sound is in his ears; in prosperity the destroyer shall come upon him.

He believeth not that he shall return out of darkness, and he is waited for of the sword.

He wandereth abroad for bread, saying, 'Where is it?' he knoweth that the day of darkness is ready at his hand.

Trouble and anguish shall make him afraid; they shall prevail against him, as a king ready to the battle.

For he stretcheth out his hand against God, and strengtheneth himself against the Almighty.

He runneth upon him, even on his neck, upon the thick bosses of his bucklers:

Because he covereth his face with his fatness, and maketh collops of fat on his flanks.

And he dwelleth in desolate cities, and in houses which no man inhabiteth, which are ready to become heaps.

He shall not be rich, neither shall his substance continue, neither shall he prolong the perfection thereof upon the earth.

He shall not depart out of darkness, the flame shall dry up his branches, and by the breath of his mouth shall he go away.

Let not him that is deceived trust in vanity: for vanity shall be his recompense.

It shall be accomplished before his time, and his branch shall not be green.

He shall shake off his unripe grape as the vine, and shall cast off his flower as the olive.

For the congregation of hypocrites shall be desolate, and fire shall consume the tabernacles of bribery.

They conceive mischief, and bring forth vanity, and their belly prepareth deceit."

16 Then Job answered, and said,
"I have heard many such things: miserable comforters are ye all.

Shall vain words have an end? or what emboldeneth thee that thou answerest?

I also could speak as ye do: if your soul were in my soul's stead, I could heap up words against you, and shake mine head at you.

But I would strengthen you with my mouth, and the moving of my lips should assuage your grief.

Though I speak, my grief is not assuaged: and though I forbear, what am I eased?

But now he hath made me weary: thou hast made desolate all my company.

And thou hast filled me with wrinkles, which is a witness against me: and my leanness rising up in me beareth witness to my face.

He teareth me in his wrath, who hateth me: he gnasheth upon me with his teeth; mine enemy sharpeneth his eyes upon me.

They have gaped upon me with their mouth, they have smitten me upon the cheek reproachfully, they have gathered themselves together against me.

God hath delivered me to the ungodly, and turned me over into the hands of the wicked.

I was at ease, but he hath broken me asunder: he hath also taken me by my neck, and shaken me to pieces, and set me up for his mark.

His archers compass me round about, he cleaveth my reins asunder, and doth not spare; he poureth out my gall upon the ground.

He breaketh me with breach upon breach, he runneth upon me like a giant.

I have sewed sackcloth upon my skin, and defiled my horn in the dust.

My face is foul with weeping, and on mine eyelids is the shadow of death;

Not for any injustice in mine hands: also my prayer is pure.

O earth, cover not thou my blood, and let my cry have no place

Also now, behold, my witness is in heaven, and my record is on high.

My friends scorn me: but mine eye poureth out tears unto God.

O that one might plead for a man with God, as a man pleadeth for his neighbor.

When a few years are come, then I shall go the way whence I shall not return."

17 "My breath is corrupt, my days are extinct, the graves are ready for me.

Are there not mockers with me? and doth not mine eye continue in their provocation?

Lay down now, put me in a surety with thee; who is he that will strike hands[2] with me?

For thou hast hid their heart from understanding: therefore shalt thou not exalt them.

He that speaketh flattery to his friends, even the eyes of his children shall fail.

He hath made me also a byword of the people, and aforetime I was as a tabret.

Mine eye also is dim by reason of sorrow, and all my members are as a shadow.

Upright men shall be astonished at this, and the innocent shall stir up himself against the hypocrite.

The righteous also shall hold on his way, and he that hath clean hands shall be stronger and stronger.

But as for you all, do you return, and come now, for I cannot find one wise man among you.

My days are past, my purposes are broken off, even the thoughts of my heart:

They change the night into day: the light is short because of darkness.

If I wait, the grave is mine house: I have made my bed in the darkness.

I have said to corruption, 'Thou art my father': to the worm, 'Thou art my mother, and my sister.'

And where is now my hope? as for my hope, who shall see it?

[2] *I.e.,* shake hands, here implying "who will assure me that he will appear before God on my behalf?"

They shall go down to the bars of the pit, when our rest together is in the dust."

18 Then answered Bildad the Shuhite, and said,
"How long will it be ere you make an end of words? Mark, and afterwards we will speak.

Wherefore are we counted as beasts, and reputed vile in your sight?

He teareth himself in his anger: shall the earth be forsaken for thee? and shall the rock be removed out of his place?

Yea, the light of the wicked shall be put out, and the spark of his fire shall not shine.

The light shall be dark in his tabernacle, and his candle shall be put out with him.

The steps of his strength shall be straitened, and his own counsel shall cast him down.

For he is cast into a net by his own feet, and he walketh upon a snare.

The gin shall take him by the heel, and the robber shall prevail against him.

The snare is laid for him in the ground, and a trap for him in the way.

Terrors shall make him afraid on every side, and shall drive him to his feet.

His strength shall be hunger-bitten, and destruction shall be ready at his side.

It shall devour the strength of his skin: even the firstborn of death shall devour his strength.

His confidence shall be rooted out of his tabernacle, and it shall bring him to the king of terrors.

It shall dwell in his tabernacle, because it is none of his: brimstone shall be scattered upon his habitation.

His roots shall be dried up beneath: and above shall his branch be cut off.

His remembrance shall perish from the earth, and he shall have no name in the street.

He shall be driven from light into darkness, and chased out of the world.

He shall neither have son nor nephew among his people, nor any remaining in his dwellings.

They that come after him shall be astonished at his day, as they that went before were affrighted.

Surely such are the dwellings of the wicked, and this is the place of him that knoweth not God."

19 Then Job answered, and said,
"How long will ye vex my soul, and break me in pieces with words?

These ten times have ye reproached me: you are not ashamed that you make yourselves strange to me.

And be it indeed that I have erred, mine error remaineth with myself.

If indeed ye will magnify yourselves against me, and plead against me my reproach:

Know now that God hath overthrown me, and hath compassed me with his net.

Behold, I cry out of wrong, but I am not heard: I cry aloud, but there is no judgment.

He hath fenced up my way that I cannot pass; and he hath set darkness in my paths.

He hath stripped me of my glory, and taken the crown from my head.

He hath destroyed me on every side, and I am gone: and mine hope hath he removed like a tree.

He hath also kindled his wrath against me, and he counteth me unto him as one of his enemies.

His troops come together, and raise up their way against me, and encamp round about my tabernacle.

He hath put my brethren far from me, and mine acquaintance are verily estranged from me.

My kinsfolk have failed, and my familiar friends have forgotten me.

They that dwell in mine house, and my maids, count me for a stranger: I am an alien in their sight.

I called my servant, and he gave me no answer: I entreated him with my mouth.

My breath is strange to my wife, though I entreated for the children's sake of mine own body.

Yea, young children despised me; I arose, and they spake against me.

All my inward friends abhorred me: and they whom I loved are turned against me.

My bone cleaveth to my skin, and to my flesh, and I am escaped with the skin of my teeth.

Have pity upon me, have pity upon me, O ye my friends; for the hand of God hath touched me.

Why do ye persecute me as God, and are not satisfied with my flesh?

Oh that my words were now written, oh that they were printed in a book!

That they were graven with an iron pen and lead in the rock for ever!

For I know that my redeemer liveth, and that he shall stand at the latter day upon the earth:

And though after my skin worms destroy this body, yet in my flesh shall I see God:

Whom I shall see for myself, and mine eyes shall behold, and not another, though my reins be consumed within me.

But ye should say, 'Why persecute we him?' seeing the root of the matter is found in me.

Be ye afraid of the sword: for wrath bringeth the punishments of the sword, that ye may know there is a judgment."

20 Then answered Zophar the Naamathite, and said,
"Therefore do my thoughts cause me to answer, and for this I make haste.

I have heard the check of my reproach, and the spirit of my understanding causeth me to answer.

Knowest thou not this of old, since man was placed upon earth,

That the triumphing of the wicked is short, and the joy of the hypocrite but for a moment?

Though his excellency mount up to the heavens, and his head reach unto the clouds:

Yet he shall perish for ever, like his own dung: they which have seen him, shall say, 'Where is he?'

He shall fly away as a dream, and shall not be found: yea he shall be chased away as a vision of the night.

The eye also which saw him shall see him no more; neither shall his place any more behold him.

His children shall seek to please the poor, and his hands shall restore their goods.

His bones are full of the sin of his youth, which shall lie down with him in the dust.

Though wickedness be sweet in his mouth, though he hide it under his tongue,

Though he spare it, and forsake it not, but keep it still within his mouth:

Yet his meat in his bowels is turned, it is the gall of asps within him.

He hath swallowed down riches, and he shall vomit them up again: God shall cast them out of his belly.

He shall suck the poison of asps: the viper's tongue shall slay him.

He shall not see the rivers, the floods, the brooks of honey and butter.

That which he laboured for shall he restore, and shall not swallow it down: according to his substance shall the restitution be, and he shall not rejoice therein.

Because he hath oppressed and hath forsaken the poor, because he hath violently taken away an house which he builded not:

Surely he shall not feel quietness in his belly, he shall not save of that which he desired.

There shall none of his meat be left, therefore shall no man look for his goods.

In the fulness of his sufficiency he shall be in straits: every hand of the wicked shall come upon him.

When he is about to fill his belly, God shall cast the fury of his wrath upon him, and shall rain it upon him while he is eating.

He shall flee from the iron weapon, and the bow of steel shall strike him through.

It is drawn, and cometh out of the body; yea the glistering sword cometh out of his gall; terrors are upon him.

All darkness shall be hid in his secret places: a fire not blown shall consume him; it shall go ill with him that is left in his tabernacle.

The heaven shall reveal his iniquity: and the earth shall rise up against him.

The increase of his house shall depart, and his goods shall flow away in the day of his wrath.

This is the portion of a wicked man from God, and the heritage appointed unto him by God."

21 But Job answered, and said,

"Hear diligently my speech, and let this be your consolations. Suffer me that I may speak, and after that I have spoken, mock on.

As for me, is my complaint to man? and if it were so, why should not my spirit be troubled?

Mark me, and be astonished, and lay your hand upon your mouth.

Even when I remember, I am afraid, and trembling taketh hold on my flesh.

Wherefore do the wicked live, become old, yea, are mighty in power?

Their seed is established in their sight with them, and their offspring before their eyes.

Their houses are safe from fear, neither is the rod of God upon them.

Their bull gendereth and faileth not, their cow calveth, and casteth not her calf.

They send forth their little ones like a flock, and their children dance.

They take the timbrel and harp, and rejoice at the sound of the organ.

They spend their days in wealth, and in a moment go down to the grave.

Therefore they say unto God, 'Depart from us: for we desire not the knowledge of thy ways.

What is the Almighty, that we should serve him? and what profit should we have, if we pray unto him?'

Lo, their good is not in their hand: the counsel of the wicked is far from me.

How oft is the candle of the wicked put out? and how oft cometh their destruction upon them? God distributeth sorrows in his anger.

They are as stubble before the wind, and as chaff that the storm carrieth away.

God layeth up his iniquity for his children: he rewardeth him, and he shall know it.

His eyes shall see his destruction, and he shall drink of the wrath of the Almighty.

For what pleasure hath he in his house after him, when the number of his months is cut off in the midst?

Shall any teach God knowledge? seeing he judgeth those that are high.

One dieth in his full strength, being wholly at ease and quiet.

His breasts are full of milk, and his bones are moistened with marrow.

And another dieth in the bitterness of his soul, and never eateth with pleasure.

They shall lie down alike in the dust, and the worms shall cover them.

Behold, I know your thoughts, and the devices which ye wrongfully imagine against me.

For ye say, 'Where is the house of the prince? and where are the dwelling places of the wicked?'

Have ye not asked them that go by the way? and do ye not know their tokens,

That the wicked is reserved to the day of destruction? they shall be brought forth to the day of wrath.

Who shall declare his way to his face? and who shall repay him what he hath done?

Yet shall he be brought to the grave, and shall remain in the tomb.

The clods of the valley shall be sweet unto him, and every man shall draw after him, as there are innumerable before him.

How then comfort ye me in vain, seeing in your answers there remaineth falsehood?"

29 Moreover Job continued his parable, and said,
"O that I were as in months past, as in the days when God preserved me:

When his candle shined upon my head, and when by his light I walked through darkness:

As I was in the days of my youth, when the secret of God was upon my tabernacle:

When the Almighty was yet with me, when my children were about me:

When I washed my steps with butter, and the rock poured me out rivers of oil:

When I went out to the gate through the city, when I prepared my seat in the street.

The young men saw me, and hid themselves: and the aged arose, and stood up.

The princes refrained talking, and laid their hand on their mouth.

The nobles held their peace, and their tongue cleaved to the roof of their mouth.

When the ear heard me, then it blessed me, and when the eye saw me, it gave witness to me:

Because I delivered the poor that cried, and the fatherless, and him that had none to help him.

The blessing of him that was ready to perish came upon me: and I caused the widow's heart to sing for joy.

I put on righteousness, and it clothed me: my judgment was as a robe and a diadem.

I was eyes to the blind, and feet was I to the lame.

I was a father to the poor: and the cause which I knew not, I searched out.

And I brake the jaws of the wicked, and plucked the spoil out of his teeth.

Then I said, 'I shall die in my nest, and I shall multiply my days as the sand.'

My root was spread out by the waters, and the dew lay all night upon my branch.

My glory was fresh in me, and my bow was renewed in my hand.

Unto me men gave ear, and waited, and kept silence at my counsel.

After my words they spake not again, and my speech dropped upon them,

And they waited for me as for the rain, and they opened their mouth wide as for the latter rain.

If I laughed on them, they believed it not, and the light of my countenance they cast not down.

I chose out their way, and sat chief, and dwelt as a king in the army, as one that comforteth the mourners."

30 "But now they that are younger than I have me in derision, whose fathers I would have disdained to have set with the dogs of my flock.

Yea whereto might the strength of their hands profit me, in whom old age was perished?

For want and famine they were solitary: flying into the wilderness in former time desolate and waste:

Who cut up mallows by the bushes, and juniper roots for their meat.

They were driven forth from among men (they cried after them, as after a thief),

To dwell in the cliffs of the valleys, in caves of the earth, and in the rocks.

Among the bushes they brayed: under the nettles they were gathered together.

They were children of fools, yea children of base men: they were viler than the earth.

And now am I their song, yea I am their byword.

They abhor me, they flee far from me, and spare not to spit in my face.

Because he hath loosed my cord and afflicted me, they have also let loose the bridle before me.

Upon my right hand rise the youth, they push away my feet, and they raise up against me the ways of their destruction.

They mar my path, they set forward my calamity, they have no helper.

They came upon me as a wide breaking in of waters: in the desolation they rolled themselves upon me.

Terrors are turned upon me: they pursue my soul as the wind: and my welfare passeth away as a cloud.

And now my soul is poured out upon me: the days of affliction have taken hold upon me:

My bones are pierced in me in the night season: and my sinews take no rest.

By the great force of my disease is my garment changed: it bindeth me about as the collar of my coat.

He hath cast me into the mire, and I am become like dust and ashes.

I cry unto thee, and thou dost not hear me: I stand up, and thou regardest me not.

Thou art become cruel to me: with thy strong hand thou opposest thyself against me.

Thou liftest me up to the wind: thou causest me to ride upon it, and dissolvest my substance.

For I know that thou wilt bring me to death, and to the house appointed for all living.

Howbeit he will not stretch out his hand to the grave, though they cry in his destruction.

Did not I weep for him that was in trouble? was not my soul grieved for the poor?

When I looked for good, then evil came unto me: and when I waited for light, there came darkness.

My bowels boiled and rested not: the days of affliction prevented me.

I went mourning without the sun: I stood up, and I cried in the congregation.

I am a brother to dragons, and a companion to owls.

My skin is black upon me, and my bones are burnt with heat.

My harp also is turned to mourning, and my organ into the voice of them that weep."

31 "I made a covenant with mine eyes; why then should I think upon a maid?

For what portion of God is there from above? and what inheritance of the Almighty from on high?

Is not destruction to the wicked? and a strange punishment to the workers of iniquity?

Doth not he see my ways, and count all my steps?

If I have walked with vanity, or if my foot hath hasted to deceit:

Let me be weighed in an even balance, that God may know mine integrity.

If my step hath turned out of the way, and mine heart walked after mine eyes, and if any blot hath cleaved to my hands:

Then let me sow, and let another eat, yea let my offspring be rooted out.

If mine heart have been deceived by a woman, or if I have laid wait at my neighbour's door:

Then let my wife grind unto another, and let others bow down upon her.

For this is an heinous crime, yea, it is an iniquity to be punished by the judges.

For it is a fire that consumeth to destruction, and would root out all mine increase.

If I did despise the cause of my manservant, or of my maidservant, when they contended with me:

What then shall I do when God riseth up? and when he visiteth, what shall I answer him?

Did not he that made me in the womb, make him? and did not one fashion us in the womb?

If I have withheld the poor from their desire, or have caused the eyes of the widow to fail:

Or have eaten my morsel myself alone, and the fatherless hath not eaten thereof:

(For from my youth he was brought up with me as with a father, and I have guided her from my mother's womb.)

If I have seen any perish for want of clothing, or any poor without covering:

If his loins have not blessed me, and if he were not warmed with the fleece of my sheep:

If I have lifted up my hand against the fatherless, when I saw my help in the gate:

Then let mine arm fall from my shoulder blade, and mine arm be broken from the bone.

For destruction from God was a terror to me: and by reason of his highness I could not endure.

If I have made gold my hope, or have said to the fine gold, 'Thou art my confidence':

If I rejoiced because my wealth was great, and because mine hand had gotten much:

If I beheld the sun when it shined, or the moon walking in brightness:

And my heart hath been secretly enticed, or my mouth hath kissed my hand:

This also were an iniquity to be punished by the judge: for I should have denied the God that is above.

If I rejoiced at the destruction of him that hated me, or lifted up myself when evil found him:

(Neither have I suffered my mouth to sin by wishing a curse to his soul.)

If the men of my tabernacle said not, 'Oh that we had of his flesh! we cannot be satisfied.'

The stranger did not lodge in the street: but I opened my doors to the traveler.

If I covered my transgressions, as Adam, by hiding mine iniquity in my bosom:

Did I fear a great multitude, or did the contempt of families terrify me, that I kept silence, and went not out of the door?

O that one would hear me! Behold, my desire is that the Almighty would answer me, and that mine adversary had written a book.

Surely I would take it upon my shoulder, and bind it as a crown to me.

I would declare unto him the number of my steps, as a prince would I go near unto him.

If my land cry against me, or that the furrows likewise thereof complain:

If I have eaten the fruits thereof without money, or have caused the owners thereof to lose their life:

Let thistles grow instead of wheat, and cockle instead of barley." The words of Job are ended.

38 Then the Lord answered Job out of the whirlwind, and said, "Who is this that darkeneth counsel by words without knowledge?

Gird up now thy loins like a man; for I will demand of thee, and answer thou me.

Where wast thou when I laid the foundations of the earth? declare, if thou hast understanding.

Who hath laid the measures thereof, if thou knowest? or who hath stretched the line upon it?

Whereupon are the foundations thereof fastened? or who laid the cornerstone thereof;

When the morning stars sang together, and all the sons of God shouted for joy?

Or who shut up the sea with doors, when it brake forth as if it had issued out of the womb?

When I made the cloud the garment thereof, and thick darkness a swaddling band for it,

And brake up for it my decreed place, and set bars and doors,

And said, 'Hitherto shalt thou come, but no further: and here shall thy proud waves be stayed'?

Hast thou commanded the morning since thy days? and caused the day-spring to know his place,

That it might take hold of the ends of the earth, that the wicked might be shaken out of it?

It is turned as clay to the seal, and they stand as a garment.

And from the wicked their light is withholden, and the high arm shall be broken.

Hast thou entered into the springs of the sea? or hast thou walked in the search of the depth?

Have the gates of death been opened unto thee? or hast thou seen the doors of the shadow of death?

Hast thou perceived the breadth of the earth? Declare if thou knowest it all.

Where is the way where light dwelleth? and as for darkness, where is the place thereof,

That thou shouldest take it to the bound thereof, and that thou shouldest know the paths to the house thereof?

Knowest thou it, because thou wast then born? or because the number of thy days is great?

Hast thou entered into the treasures of the snow? or hast thou seen the treasures of the hail,

Which I have reserved against the time of trouble, against the day of battle and war?

By what way is the light parted, which scattereth the east wind upon the earth?

Who hath divided a watercourse for the overflowing of waters? or a way for the lightning of thunder,

To cause it to rain on the earth, where no man is: on the wilderness wherein there is no man;

To satisfy the desolate and waste ground, and to cause the bud of the tender herb to spring forth?

Hath the rain a father? or who hath begotten the drops of dew?

Out of whose womb came the ice? and the hoary frost of heaven, who hath gendered it?

The waters are hid as with a stone, and the face of the deep is frozen.

Canst thou bind the sweet influences of Pleiades? or loose the bands of Orion?

Canst thou bring forth Mazzaroth[3] in his season, or canst thou guide Arcturus with his sons?

Knowest thou the ordinances of heaven? canst thou set the dominion thereof in the earth?

Canst thou lift up thy voice to the clouds, that abundance of waters may cover thee?

Canst thou send lightnings, that they may go, and say unto thee, 'Here we are'?

Who hath put wisdom in the inward parts? or who hath given understanding to the heart?

Who can number the clouds in wisdom? or who can stay the bottles of heaven,

When the dust groweth into hardness, and the clods cleave fast together?

Wilt thou hunt the prey for the lion? or fill the appetite of the young lions,

When they couch in their dens, and abide in the covert to lie in wait?

Who provideth for the raven his food? when his young ones cry unto God, they wander for lack of meat."

39 "Knowest thou the time when the wild goats of the rock bring forth? or canst thou mark when the hinds do calve?

Canst thou number the months that they fulfill? or knowest thou the time when they bring forth?

They bow themselves, they bring forth their young ones, they cast out their sorrows.

Their young ones are in good liking, they grow up with corn: they go forth, and return not unto them.

Who hath sent out the wild ass free? or who hath loosed the bands of the wild ass?

---

[3] A constellation.

Whose house I have made the wilderness, and the barren land his dwellings.

He scorneth the multitude of the city, neither regardeth he the crying of the driver.

The range of the mountains is his pasture, and he searcheth after every green thing.

Will the unicorn[4] be willing to serve thee? or abide by thy crib?

Canst thou bind the unicorn with his band in the furrow? or will he harrow the valleys after thee?

Wilt thou trust him because his strength is great? or wilt thou leave thy labour to him?

Wilt thou believe him that he will bring home thy seed? and gather it into thy barn?

Gavest thou the goodly wings unto the peacocks, or wings and feathers unto the ostrich?

Which leaveth her eggs in the earth, and warmeth them in the dust,

And forgetteth that the foot may crush them, or that the wild beast may break them.

She is hardened against her young ones, as though they were not hers: her labour is in vain without fear:

Because God hath deprived her of wisdom, neither hath he imparted to her understanding.

What time she lifteth up herself on high, she scorneth the horse and his rider.

Hast thou given the horse strength? hast thou clothed his neck with thunder?

Canst thou make him afraid as a grasshopper? the glory of his nostrils is terrible.

He paweth in the valley, and rejoiceth in his strength: he goeth on to meet the armed men.

He mocketh at fear, and is not affrighted: neither turneth he back from the sword.

The quiver rattleth against him, the glittering spear and the shield.

He swalloweth the ground with fierceness and rage: neither believeth he that it is the sound of the trumpet.

[4] Probably a type of wild ox.

He saith among the trumpets, 'Ha, ha': and he smelleth the battle afar off, the thunder of the captains, and the shouting.

Doth the hawk fly by thy wisdom, and stretch her wings toward the south?

Doth the eagle mount up at thy command? and make her nest on high?

She dwelleth and abideth on the rock, upon the crag of the rock, and the strong place.

From thence she seeketh the prey, and her eyes behold afar off.

Her young ones also suck up blood: and where the slain are, there is she."

40 Moreover the Lord answered Job, and said,
"Shall he that contendeth with the Almighty instruct him? he that reproveth God, let him answer it."

Then Job answered the Lord, and said,
"Behold, I am vile, what shall I answer thee? I will lay my hand upon my mouth.

Once have I spoken, but I will not answer: yea twice, but I will proceed no further."

Then answered the Lord unto Job out of the whirlwind, and said,
"Gird up thy loins now like a man: I will demand of thee, and declare thou unto me.

Wilt thou also disannul my judgment? wilt thou condemn me, that thou mayest be righteous?

Hast thou an arm like God? or canst thou thunder with a voice like him?

Deck thyself now with majesty and excellency, and array thyself with glory and beauty.

Cast abroad the rage of thy wrath: and behold every one that is proud, and abase him.

Look on every one that is proud, and bring him low: and tread down the wicked in their place.

Hide them in the dust together, and bind their faces in secret.

Then will I also confess unto thee, that thine own right hand can save thee.

Behold now behemoth,[5] which I made with thee, he eateth grass as an ox.

[5] Almost certainly the hippopotamus.

Lo now, his strength is in his loins, and his force is in the navel of his belly.

He moveth his tail like a cedar: the sinews of his stones are wrapped together.

His bones are as strong pieces of brass: his bones are like bars of iron.

He is the chief of the ways of God: he that made him can make his sword to approach unto him.

Surely the mountains bring him forth food, where all the beasts of the field play.

He lieth under the shady trees, in the covert of the reed, and fens.

The shady trees cover him with their shadow: the willows of the brook compass him about.

Behold, he drinketh up a river, and hasteth not: he trusteth that he can draw up Jordan into his mouth.

He taketh it with his eyes: his nose pierceth through snares."

41 "Canst thou draw out leviathan[6] with an hook? or his tongue with a cord which thou lettest down?

Canst thou put an hook into his nose? or bore his jaw through with a thorn?

Will he make many supplications unto thee? will he speak soft words unto thee?

Will he make a covenant with thee? wilt thou take him for a servant for ever?

Wilt thou play with him as with a bird? or wilt thou bind him for thy maidens?

Shall the companions make a banquet of him? shall they part him among the merchants?

Canst thou fill his skin with barbed irons? or his head with fish spears?

Lay thine hand upon him, remember the battle: do no more.

Behold, the hope of him is in vain: shall not one be cast down even at the sight of him?

None is so fierce that dare stir him up: who then is able to stand before me?

Who hath prevented me that I should repay him? whatsoever is under the whole heaven is mine.

[6] A crocodile, but one with many mythical attributes.

I will not conceal his parts, nor his power, nor his comely proportion.

Who can discover the face of his garment? or who can come to him with his double bridle?

Who can open the doors of his face? his teeth are terrible round about.

His scales are his pride, shut up together as with a close seal.

One is so near to another that no air can come between them.

They are joined one to another, they stick together, that they cannot be sundered.

By his neesings[7] a light doth shine, and his eyes are like the eyelids of the morning.

Out of his mouth go burning lamps, and sparks of fire leap out.

Out of his nostrils goeth smoke, as out of a seething pot or caldron.

His breath kindleth coals, and a flame goeth out of his mouth.

In his neck remaineth strength, and sorrow is turned into joy before him.

The flakes of his flesh are joined together: they are firm in themselves, they cannot be moved.

His heart is as firm as a stone, yea as hard as a piece of the nether millstone.

When he raiseth up himself, the mighty are afraid: by reason of breakings they purify themselves.

The sword of him that layeth at him cannot hold: the spear, the dart, nor the habergeon.[8]

He esteemeth iron as straw, and brass as rotten wood.

The arrow cannot make him flee: slingstones are turned with him into stubble.

Darts are counted as stubble: he laugheth at the shaking of a spear.

Sharp stones are under him: he spreadeth sharp pointed things upon the mire.

He maketh the deep to boil like a pot: he maketh the sea like a pot of ointment.

He maketh a path to shine after him; one would think the deep to be hoary.

[7] *I.e.,* sneezings.
[8] A coat of mail.

Upon earth there is not his like, who is made without fear.

He beholdeth all high things: he is a king over all the children of pride."

42 Then Job answered the Lord, and said,

"I know that thou canst do every thing, and that no thought can be withholden from thee.

Who is he that hideth counsel without knowledge? therefore have I uttered that I understood not, things too wonderful for me, which I knew not.

Hear, I beseech thee, and I will speak: I will demand of thee, and declare thou unto me.

I have heard of thee by the hearing of the ear: but now mine eye seeth thee.

Wherefore I abhor myself, and repent in dust and ashes."

And it was so, that after the Lord had spoken these words unto Job, the Lord said to Eliphaz the Temanite, "My wrath is kindled against thee, and against thy two friends: for ye have not spoken of me the thing that is right, as my servant Job hath. Therefore take unto you now seven bullocks, and seven rams, and go to my servant Job, and offer up for yourselves a burnt offering, and my servant Job shall pray for you, for him will I accept: lest I deal with you after your folly, in that ye have not spoken of me the thing which is right, like my servant Job." So Eliphaz the Temanite, and Bildad the Shuhite, and Zophar the Naamathite went, and did according as the Lord commanded them: the Lord also accepted Job. And the Lord turned the captivity of Job, when he prayed for his friends: also the Lord gave Job twice as much as he had before.

Then came there unto him all his brethren, and all his sisters, and all they that had been of his acquaintance before, and did eat bread with him in his house: and they bemoaned him, and comforted him over all the evil that the Lord had brought upon him: every man also gave him a piece of money, and every one an earring of gold. So the Lord blessed the latter end of Job more than his beginning: for he had fourteen thousand sheep, and six thousand camels, and a thousand yoke of oxen, and a thousand she-asses. He had also seven sons, and three daughters. And he called the name of the first Jemima, and the name of the second Kezia, and the name of the third Keren-happuch. And in all the land were no women found so fair as the daughters of Job: and their father gave them inheritance among their brethren. After this lived Job an hundred and forty years, and saw his sons, and his sons' sons, even four generations. So Job died, being old, and full of days.

Jonah

INTRODUCTION

Though the book of Jonah appears among the works of the twelve minor prophets, it is very different from them. First, it is not an oracle but a story about a prophet. Second, it is not even semi-historical but fictional. Third, it was not written in the eighth century B.C., the time of the historical Jonah mentioned in The Second Book of the Kings, but around 350 B.C. Like The Book of Ruth, that of Jonah is both a well told story and a liberal message. Jonah, however, is closer to being a parable, a tale specifically designed to convey a moral. Saturated with the supernatural—miracles, coincidences, large-scale distortions of history—the story nevertheless preaches tolerance. Jonah stands for the many Jews who, the author felt, were retreating into a citadel of pride and nationalism. God, in contrast, is willing to recognize and reward the piety of the regenerated heathen. The ending of the tale may seem abrupt, but the author has skillfully and cumulatively made his point. ♣ ♣ ♣

Suggested Reading

Herman Melville, *Moby Dick*—a nineteenth-century American novel about the pursuit of a whale, but also a story about truth, tolerance, and the ultimate meaning of life. (One chapter, "The Sermon," is a vivid retelling of the Jonah story.)

JONAH

1 Now the word of the Lord came unto Jonah the son of Amittai, saying, "Arise, go to Nineveh that great city, and cry against it: for their wickedness is come up before me." But Jonah rose up to flee unto Tarshish, from the presence of the Lord, and went down to Joppa, and he found a ship going to Tarshish: so he paid the fare thereof, and went down into it, to go with them unto Tarshish from the presence of the Lord.

But the Lord sent out a great wind into the sea, and there was a mighty tempest in the sea, so that the ship was like to be broken. Then the mariners were afraid, and cried every man unto his god, and cast forth the wares that were in the ship, into the sea, to lighten it of them: but Jonah was gone down into the sides of the ship, and he lay, and was fast asleep. So the shipmaster came to him, and said unto him, "What meanest thou, O sleeper? Arise, call upon thy God, if so be that God will think upon us, that we perish not." And they said every one to his fellow, "Come, and let us cast lots, that we may know for whose cause this evil is upon us." So they cast lots, and the lot fell upon Jonah. Then said they unto him, "Tell us, we pray thee, for whose cause this evil is upon us: what is thine occupation? and whence comest thou? What is thy country? and of what people art thou?" And he said unto them, "I am an Hebrew, and I fear the Lord the God of heaven, which hath made the sea and the dry land." Then were the men exceedingly afraid, and said unto him, "Why hast thou done this?" (For the men knew that he fled from the presence of the Lord, because he had told them.)

Then said they unto him, "What shall we do unto thee, that the sea may be calm unto us?" (For the sea wrought and was tempestuous.) And he said unto them, "Take me up, and cast me forth into the sea; so shall the sea be calm unto you: for I know that for my sake this great tempest is upon you." Nevertheless the men rowed hard to bring it to the land, but they could not: for the sea wrought, and was tempestuous against them. Wherefore they cried unto the Lord, and said, "We beseech thee, O Lord, we beseech thee, let us not perish for this man's life, and lay not upon us innocent blood: for thou, O Lord, hast done as it pleased thee." So they took up Jonah, and cast him forth into the sea, and the sea ceased from her raging. Then the men feared the Lord exceedingly, and offered a sacrifice unto the Lord, and made vows.

Now the Lord had prepared a great fish to swallow up Jonah, and Jonah was in the belly of the fish three days, and three nights.

2 Then Jonah prayed unto the Lord his God, out of the fish's belly, and said, "I cried by reason of mine affliction unto the Lord, and he heard me; out of the belly of hell cried I, and thou heardest my voice. For thou hadst cast me into the deep, in the midst of the seas, and the floods compassed me about: all thy billows and thy waves passed over me. Then I said, 'I am cast out of thy sight; yet I will look again toward thy holy temple.' The waters compassed me about even to the soul; the depth closed me round about; the weeds were wrapped about my head. I went down to the bottoms of the mountains: the earth with her bars was about me for ever: yet hast thou brought up my life from corruption, O Lord my God. When my soul fainted within me, I remembered the Lord, and my prayer came in unto thee, into thine holy temple. They that observe lying vanities forsake their own mercy. But I will sacrifice unto thee with the voice of thanksgiving, I will pay that that I have vowed: salvation is of the Lord."

And the Lord spake unto the fish, and it vomited out Jonah upon the dry land.

3 And the word of the Lord came unto Jonah the second time, saying, "Arise, go unto Nineveh that great city, and preach unto it the preaching that I bid thee." So Jonah arose and went unto Nineveh, according to the word of the Lord: now Nineveh was an exceeding great city of three days' journey.[1] And Jonah began to enter into the city a day's journey, and he cried, and said, "Yet forty days, and Nineveh shall be overthrown."

So the people of Nineveh believed God, and proclaimed a fast, and put on sackcloth from the greatest of them even to the least of them. For word came unto the king of Nineveh, and he arose from his throne, and he laid his robe from him, and covered him with sackcloth, and sat in ashes. And he caused it to be proclaimed and published through Nineveh (by the decree of the king and his nobles), saying, "Let neither man nor beast, herd nor flock, taste any thing; let them not feed, nor drink water. But let man and beast be covered with sackcloth, and cry mightily unto God: yea, let them turn every one from his evil way, and from the violence that is in their hands. Who can tell if God will turn and repent, and turn away from his fierce anger, that we perish not?"

And God saw their works, that they turned from their evil way, and God repented of the evil that he had said that he would do unto them, and he did it not.

[1] I.e., it would take three days to walk across it.

4 But it displeased Jonah exceedingly, and he was very angry.
And he prayed unto the Lord, and said, "I pray thee, O Lord, was not this my saying, when I was yet in my country? Therefore I fled before unto Tarshish: for I knew that thou art a gracious God, and merciful, slow to anger, and of great kindness, and repentest thee of the evil. Therefore now, O Lord, take, I beseech thee, my life from me; for it is better for me to die than to live."

Then said the Lord, "Doest thou well to be angry?" So Jonah went out of the city, and sat on the east side of the city, and there made him a booth, and sat under it in the shadow, till he might see what would become of the city. And the Lord God prepared a gourd, and made it to come up over Jonah, that it might be a shadow over his head, to deliver him from his grief. So Jonah was exceeding glad of the gourd. But God prepared a worm when the morning rose the next day, and it smote the gourd that it withered. And it came to pass when the sun did arise, that God prepared a vehement east wind; and the sun beat upon the head of Jonah, that he fainted, and wished in himself to die, and said, "It is better for me to die than to live." And God said to Jonah, "Doest thou well to be angry for the gourd?" And he said, "I do well to be angry, even unto death." Then said the Lord, "Thou hast had pity on the gourd, for the which thou hast not laboured, neither madest it grow, which came up in a night, and perished in a night: and should not I spare Nineveh that great city, wherein are more than sixscore thousand persons that cannot discern between their right hand and their left hand,[2] and also much cattle?"

[2] *I.e.*, children not yet old enough to distinguish right from left.

psalms

INTRODUCTION

In certain respects The Book of Psalms is a miniature Bible. The 150 poems which constitute it range, for instance, from bitter vindictiveness to spiritual exaltation. Like the complete Bible, it shows the influence of other cultures, here especially those of Egypt and Babylonia. But unlike the Bible, most of the psalms represent an individual talking to God, rather than God talking to men or nations. Consequently The Book of Psalms rapidly became an anthology for private or semi-private devotion, associated with the small local synagogue rather than with the large national temple in Jerusalem. Originally, however, most of these poems were designed for use in that temple and, like modern hymns, they were sung by the congregation to some sort of instrumental accompaniment. The vast majority were written between 400 and 100 B.C., after the Babylonian Captivity and the rebuilding of the temple.

Stylistically these poems are closer to the relatively sophisticated technique of Second Isaiah than they are to the more primitive poetry of the Song of Miriam or David's lament for Saul. Yet the psalms are rooted in ancient tradition, and some of them may echo songs coming from an age before the invention of writing. In the main they adhere to the basic characteristics of all Old Testament poetry, from the most ancient verses, through Job, to the Song of Songs. The dominant characteristic is parallelism: the division of each line into two approximately equal parts. (This device was probably inherited from the pre-Hebrew inhabitants of Palestine, the Canaanites.) In terms of sound, each part usually contains the same number of beats, but not necessarily the same number of syllables, with the most common meter employing four beats in each half-line. Here, for instance, is the Song of Miriam:

Sing ye to the **Lord,** for he hath **triumphed glo**riously:
The **horse** and his **ri**der hath he **thrown** into the **sea.** (Exodus 15)

(Note how well here—as in many other psalms—the English translation reproduces the Hebrew sound pattern.) In terms of meaning, the two half-lines are also usually parallel, almost always in one of three ways:

(1) *Synonymous*—where the two parts repeat each other:

   The heavens declare the glory of God: // and the firmament showeth his handiwork. (Psalm XIX)

(2) *Antithetic*—where the second part presents an antithesis to the first:

   For the Lord knoweth the way of the righteous: // but the way of the ungodly shall perish. (Psalm I)

(3) *Synthetic*—where the second half supplements or completes the first:

   Have mercy upon me, O Lord, for I am weak: // O Lord, heal me, for my bones are vexed. (Psalm VI)

The following selection is intended to illustrate these techniques, to convey the potentially intense individualism of Hebrew piety, and to suggest the aesthetic and religious impact the psalms have exerted over the centuries.[1] ♣ ♣ ♣

Suggested Reading

George Herbert, Richard Crashaw, Poems—devout and personal religious lyrics by two seventeenth-century English poets, one a Protestant, the other a Catholic.

PSALMS

1 Blessed is the man that walketh not in the counsel of the ungodly, nor standeth in the way of sinners, nor sitteth in the seat of the scornful.

But his delight is in the law of the Lord, and in his law doth he meditate day and night.

And he shall be like a tree planted by the rivers of water, that bringeth forth his fruit in his season, his leaf also shall not wither, and whatsoever he doeth shall prosper.

[1] Titles and ascription of separate poems to various ancient authors have been omitted: the titles are no longer revealing; and David, despite the fact that 73 psalms are attributed to him, was almost certainly the direct author of none.

The ungodly are not so: but are like the chaff, which the wind driveth away.

Therefore the ungodly shall not stand in the judgment, nor sinners in the congregation of the righteous.

For the Lord knoweth the way of the righteous: but the way of the ungodly shall perish.

6 O Lord, rebuke me not in thine anger, neither chasten me in thy hot displeasure.

Have mercy upon me, O Lord, for I am weak: O Lord, heal me, for my bones are vexed.

My soul is also sore vexed: but thou, O Lord, how long?

Return, O Lord, deliver my soul: oh save me, for thy mercies' sake.

For in death there is no remembrance of thee: in the grave who shall give thee thanks?

I am weary with my groaning, all the night make I my bed to swim: I water my couch with my tears.

Mine eye is consumed because of grief; it waxeth old because of all mine enemies.

Depart from me, all ye workers of iniquity; for the Lord hath heard the voice of my weeping.

The Lord hath heard my supplication; the Lord will receive my prayer.

Let all mine enemies be ashamed and sore vexed: let them return and be ashamed suddenly.

19 The heavens declare the glory of God: and the firmament showeth his handiwork.

Day unto day uttereth speech, and night unto night showeth knowledge.

There is no speech nor language, where their voice is not heard.

Their line is gone out through all the earth, and their words to the end of the world: in them hath he set a tabernacle for the sun,

Which is as a bridegroom coming out of his chamber, and rejoiceth as a strong man to run a race.

His going forth is from the end of the heaven, and his circuit unto the ends of it: and there is nothing hid from the heat thereof.

The law of the Lord is perfect, converting the soul: the testimony of the Lord is sure, making wise the simple.

The statutes of the Lord are right, rejoicing the heart: the commandment of the Lord is pure, enlightening the eyes.

The fear of the Lord is clean, enduring for ever: the judgments of the Lord are true, and righteous altogether.

More to be desired are they than gold, yea, than much fine gold: sweeter also than honey, and the honeycomb.

Moreover by them is thy servant warned: and in keeping of them there is great reward.

Who can understand his errors? cleanse thou me from secret faults.

Keep back thy servant also from presumptuous sins, let them not have dominion over me: then shall I be upright, and I shall be innocent from the great transgression.

Let the words of my mouth, and the meditation of my heart, be acceptable in thy sight, O Lord, my strength, and my redeemer.

23 The Lord is my shepherd, I shall not want.

He maketh me to lie down in green pastures: he leadeth me beside the still waters.

He restoreth my soul: he leadeth me in the paths of righteousness, for his name's sake.

Yea though I walk through the valley of the shadow of death, I will fear no evil: for thou art with me, thy rod and thy staff they comfort me.

Thou preparest a table before me, in the presence of mine enemies: thou anointest my head with oil, my cup runneth over.

Surely goodness and mercy shall follow me all the days of my life: and I will dwell in the house of the Lord for ever.

46 God is our refuge and strength: a very present help in trouble.

Therefore will not we fear, though the earth be removed, and though the mountains be carried into the midst of the sea;

Though the waters thereof roar and be troubled, though the mountains shake with the swelling thereof. Selah.[1]

---

[1] A musical direction, but its precise meaning is now unknown.

There is a river, the streams whereof shall make glad the city of God: the holy place of the tabernacles of the most High.

God is in the midst of her: she shall not be moved; God shall help her, and that right early.

The heathen raged, the kingdoms were moved: he uttered his voice, the earth melted.

The Lord of hosts is with us; the God of Jacob is our refuge. Selah.

Come, behold the works of the Lord, what desolations he hath made in the earth.

He maketh wars to cease unto the end of the earth: he breaketh the bow, and cutteth the spear in sunder, he burneth the chariot in the fire.

Be still, and know that I am God: I will be exalted among the heathen, I will be exalted in the earth.

The Lord of hosts is with us; the God of Jacob is our refuge. Selah.

90 Lord, thou hast been our dwelling place in all generations.

Before the mountains were brought forth, or ever thou hadst formed the earth and the world: even from everlasting to everlasting thou art God.

Thou turnest man to destruction; and sayest: "Return ye children of men."

For a thousand years in thy sight are but as yesterday when it is past: and as a watch in the night.

Thou carriest them away as with a flood, they are as a sleep: in the morning they are like grass which groweth up.

In the morning it flourisheth, and groweth up: in the evening it is cut down, and withereth.

For we are consumed by thine anger: and by thy wrath are we troubled.

Thou hast set our iniquities before thee: our secret sins in the light of thy countenance.

For all our days are passed away in thy wrath: we spend our years as a tale that is told.

The days of our years are threescore years and ten, and if by reason of strength they be fourscore years, yet is their strength labour and sorrow: for it is soon cut off, and we fly away.

Who knoweth the power of thine anger? even according to thy fear, so is thy wrath.

So teach us to number our days: that we may apply our hearts unto wisdom.

Return (O Lord) how long? and let it repent thee concerning thy servants.

O satisfy us early with thy mercy: that we may rejoice, and be glad all our days.

Make us glad according to the days wherein thou hast afflicted us: and the years wherein we have seen evil.

Let thy work appear unto thy servants: and thy glory unto their children.

And let the beauty of the Lord our God be upon us, and establish thou the work of our hands upon us: yea, the work of our hands establish thou it.

96 O sing unto the Lord a new song: sing unto the Lord, all the earth.

Sing unto the Lord, bless his name: show forth his salvation from day to day.

Declare his glory among the heathen: his wonders among all people.

For the Lord is great, and greatly to be praised: he is to be feared above all gods.

For all the gods of the nations are idols: but the Lord made the heavens.

Honour and majesty are before him: strength and beauty are in his sanctuary.

Give unto the Lord (O ye kindreds of the people): give unto the Lord glory and strength.

Give unto the Lord the glory due unto his name: bring an offering, and come into his courts.

O worship the Lord in the beauty of holiness: fear before him all the earth.

Say among the heathen that the Lord reigneth: the world also shall be established that it shall not be moved: he shall judge the people righteously.

Let the heavens rejoice, and let the earth be glad: let the sea roar, and the fulness thereof.

Let the field be joyful, and all that is therein: then shall all the trees of the wood rejoice

Before the Lord, for he cometh, for he cometh to judge the earth: he shall judge the world with righteousness, and the people with his truth.

121 I will lift up mine eyes unto the hills, from whence cometh my help.

My help cometh from the Lord, which made heaven and earth.

He will not suffer thy foot to be moved: he that keepeth thee will not slumber.

Behold, he that keepeth Israel shall neither slumber nor sleep.

The Lord is thy keeper: the Lord is thy shade upon thy right hand.

The sun shall not smite thee by day, nor the moon by night.

The Lord shall preserve thee from all evil: he shall preserve thy soul.

The Lord shall preserve thy going out, and thy coming in, from this time forth and even for evermore.

130 Out of the depths have I cried unto thee, O Lord.

Lord, hear my voice: let thine ears be attentive to the voice of my supplications.

If thou, Lord, shouldest mark iniquities, O Lord, who shall stand?

But there is forgiveness with thee: that thou mayest be feared.

I wait for the Lord, my soul doth wait: and in his word do I hope.

My soul waiteth for the Lord, more than they that watch for the morning: I say, more than they that watch for the morning.

Let Israel hope in the Lord, for with the Lord there is mercy: and with him is plenteous redemption.

And he shall redeem Israel from all his iniquities.

137 By the rivers of Babylon, there we sat down, yea we wept, when we remembered Zion.

We hanged our harps upon the willows, in the midst thereof.

For there they that carried us away captive required of us a song, and they that wasted us required of us mirth: saying, "Sing us one of the songs of Zion."

How shall we sing the Lord's song in a strange land?

If I forget thee, O Jerusulam, let my right hand forget her cunning.

If I do not remember thee, let my tongue cleave to the roof of my mouth; if I prefer not Jerusalem above my chief joy.

Remember, O Lord, the children of Edom, in the day of Jerusalem, who said, "Rase it, rase it: even to the foundation thereof."

O daughter of Babylon, who art to be destroyed: happy shall he be that rewardeth thee, as thou hast served us.

Happy shall he be that taketh and dasheth thy little ones against the stones.

139 O Lord, thou hast searched me, and known me.

Thou knowest my downsitting, and mine uprising: thou understandest my thought afar off.

Thou compassest my path, and my lying down, and art acquainted with all my ways.

For there is not a word in my tongue, but lo, O Lord, thou knowest it altogether.

Thou hast beset me behind, and before: and laid thine hand upon me.

Such knowledge is too wonderful for me: it is high, I cannot attain unto it.

Whither shall I go from thy spirit? or whither shall I fly from thy presence?

If I ascend up into heaven, thou art there: if I make my bed in hell, behold, thou art there.

If I take the wings of the morning, and dwell in the uttermost parts of the sea,

Even there shall thy hand lead me: and thy right hand shall hold me.

If I say, "Surely the darkness shall cover me": even the night shall be light about me.

Yea the darkness hideth not from thee, but the night shineth as the day: the darkness and the light are both alike to thee.

For thou hast possessed my reins: thou hast covered me in my mother's womb.

I will praise thee, for I am fearfully and wonderfully made, marvelous are thy works: and that my soul knoweth right well.

My substance was not hid from thee when I was made in secret, and curiously wrought in the lowest parts of the earth.

Thine eyes did see my substance yet being unperfect, and in thy book all my members were written, which in continuance were fashioned, when as yet there was none of them.[2]

How precious also are thy thoughts unto me, O God: how great is the sum of them?

If I should count them, they are more in number than the sand: when I awake, I am still with thee.

Surely thou wilt slay the wicked, O God: depart from me therefore, ye bloody men.

For they speak against thee wickedly: and thine enemies take thy name in vain.

Do not I hate them, O Lord, that hate thee? and am not I grieved with those that rise up against thee?

I hate them with perfect hatred: I count them mine enemies.

Search me, O God, and know my heart: try me, and know my thoughts:

And see if there be any wicked way in me: and lead me in the way everlasting.

[2] The Revised Standard Version clarifies this verse as follows: "Thy eyes beheld my unformed substance; in thy book were written, every one of them, the days that were formed for me, when as yet there was none of them."

the sonq of solomon

INTRODUCTION

The Song of Solomon is a short anthology of love lyrics, not a consecutive narrative, and some of the lyrics are sung by a man, some by a woman. As in Egyptian love poetry, from which this collection ultimately derives, the tone is erotic, the setting springtime, the atmosphere idyllic. These passionate and glowing poems were accepted as part of the Bible, after some difficulty, because of their popularity and their attribution to Solomon, though almost certainly they did not achieve written form much before 250 B.C. Once accepted, they gained in religious stature by being read allegorically: first as portraying God's love for His chosen people, then as illustrating Christ's love for his church. No matter how they are interpreted, and whether they are the work of one man or the skillful compilation of an editor, these lyrics, individually and collectively, still pulse with life. ♣ ♣ ♣

Suggested Reading

Edmund Spenser, *The Faerie Queene*—a long allegorical and chivalric poem, written during the Renaissance, about the nature of various virtues, including love; *Epithalamion*—a poem in celebration of marriage that is both personal and universal.

William Shakespeare, Sonnets—beautiful, disciplined poems about love, fame, and death.

John Donne, Lyrics—cynical and passionate love poems and intensely personal religious lyrics, written in the late sixteenth and early seventeenth century.

John Keats, Poems—lyrics by the most sensuous of English Romantic poets.

George Meredith, *Modern Love*—a Victorian sonnet sequence which poignantly depicts the break-up of a marriage.

299

THE SONG OF SOLOMON

1 The song of songs, which is Solomon's.

Let him kiss me with the kisses of his mouth: for thy love is better than wine.

Because of the savour of thy good ointments, thy name is an ointment poured forth, therefore do the virgins love thee.

Draw me, we will run after thee: the king hath brought me into his chambers: we will be glad and rejoice in thee, we will remember thy love more than wine: the upright love thee.

I am black, but comely, O ye daughters of Jerusalem, as the tents of Kedar, as the curtains of Solomon.

Look not upon me, because I am black, because the sun hath looked upon me: my mother's children were angry with me, they made me the keeper of the vineyards, but mine own vineyard have I not kept.

Tell me, O thou whom my soul loveth, where thou feedest, where thou makest thy flock to rest at noon: for why should I be as one that turneth aside by the flocks of thy companions?

If thou know not, O thou fairest among women, go thy way forth by the footsteps of the flock, and feed thy kids beside the shepherds' tents.

I have compared thee, O my love, to a company of horses in Pharaoh's chariots.

Thy cheeks are comely with rows of jewels, thy neck with chains of gold.

We will make thee borders of gold with studs of silver.

While the king sitteth at his table, my spikenard sendeth forth the smell thereof.

A bundle of myrrh is my wellbeloved unto me; he shall lie all night betwixt my breasts.

My beloved is unto me as a cluster of camphire in the vineyards of Engedi.

Behold, thou art fair, my love: behold, thou art fair, thou hast doves' eyes.

Behold, thou art fair, my beloved, yea pleasant: also our bed is green.

The beams of our house are cedar, and our rafters of fir.

2 I am the rose of Sharon, and the lily of the valleys.

As the lily among thorns, so is my love among the daughters.

As the apple tree among the trees of the wood, so is my beloved among the sons. I sat under his shadow with great delight, and his fruit was sweet to my taste.

He brought me to the banqueting house, and his banner over me was love.

Stay me with flagons, comfort me with apples, for I am sick of [1] love.

His left hand is under my head, and his right hand doth embrace me.

I charge you, O ye daughters of Jerusalem, by the roes, and by the hinds of the field, that ye stir not up, nor awake my love, till he please.

The voice of my beloved! behold! he cometh leaping upon the mountains, skipping upon the hills.

My beloved is like a roe or a young hart: behold, he standeth behind our wall, he looketh forth at the window, showing himself through the lattice.

My beloved spake, and said unto me, "Rise up, my love, my fair one, and come away.

"For lo, the winter is past, the rain is over, and gone.

"The flowers appear on the earth, the time of the singing of birds is come, and the voice of the turtle [2] is heard in our land.

"The fig tree putteth forth her green figs, and the vines with the tender grape give a good smell. Arise, my love, my fair one, and come away."

O my dove, that art in the clefts of the rock, in the secret places of the stairs: let me see thy countenance, let me hear thy voice, for sweet is thy voice, and thy countenance is comely.

[1] I.e., with.
[2] I.e., turtledove.

Take us the foxes, the little foxes, that spoil the vines: for our vines have tender grapes.

My beloved is mine, and I am his: he feedeth among the lilies.

Until the day break, and the shadows flee away: turn, my beloved, and be thou like a roe, or a young hart, upon the mountains of Bether.

3 By night on my bed I sought him whom my soul loveth. I sought him, but I found him not.

I will rise now, and go about the city in the streets, and in the broad ways I will seek him whom my soul loveth: I sought him, but I found him not.

The watchmen that go about the city found me: to whom I said, "Saw ye him whom my soul loveth?"

It was but a little that I passed from them, but I found him whom my soul loveth: I held him, and would not let him go, until I had brought him into my mother's house, and into the chamber of her that conceived me.

I charge you, O ye daughters of Jerusalem, by the roes and by the hinds of the field, that ye stir not up, nor awake my love, till he please.

Who is this that cometh out of the wilderness like pillars of smoke, perfumed with myrrh and frankincense, with all powders of the merchant?

Behold his bed, which is Solomon's: threescore valiant men are about it, of the valiant of Israel.

They all hold swords, being expert in war: every man hath his sword upon his thigh, because of fear in the night.

King Solomon made himself a chariot of the wood of Lebanon.

He made the pillars thereof of silver, the bottom thereof of gold, the covering of it of purple; the midst thereof being paved with love, for the daughters of Jerusalem.

Go forth, O ye daughters of Zion, and behold king Solomon with the crown wherewith his mother crowned him in the day of his espousals, and in the day of the gladness of his heart.

4 Behold, thou art fair, my love, behold thou art fair, thou hast doves' eyes within thy locks: thy hair is as a flock of goats, that appear from mount Gilead.

Thy teeth are like a flock of sheep that are even shorn, which came up from the washing: whereof every one bear twins, and none is barren among them.

Thy lips are like a thread of scarlet, and thy speech is comely: thy temples are like a piece of a pomegranate within thy locks.

Thy neck is like the tower of David builded for an armoury, whereon there hang a thousand bucklers, all shields of mighty men.

Thy two breasts are like two young roes that are twins, which feed among the lilies.

Until the day break, and the shadows flee away, I will get me to the mountain of myrrh, and to the hill of frankincense.

Thou art all fair, my love, there is no spot in thee.

Come with me from Lebanon, my spouse, with me from Lebanon: look from the top of Amana, from the top of Shenir and Hermon, from the lions' dens, from the mountains of the leopards.

Thou hast ravished my heart, my sister, my spouse; thou hast ravished my heart with one of thine eyes, with one chain of thy neck.

How fair is thy love, my sister, my spouse! how much better is thy love than wine! and the smell of thine ointments than all spices!

Thy lips, O my spouse, drop as the honeycomb: honey and milk are under thy tongue, and the smell of thy garments is like the smell of Lebanon.

A garden inclosed is my sister, my spouse: a spring shut up, a fountain sealed.

Thy plants are an orchard of pomegranates, with pleasant fruits, camphire, with spikenard,

Spikenard and saffron, calamus and cinnamon, with all trees of frankincense, myrrh and aloes, with all the chief spices:

A fountain of gardens, a well of living waters, and streams from Lebanon.

Awake, O north wind, and come thou south; blow upon my garden, that the spices thereof may flow out: let my beloved come into his garden, and eat his pleasant fruits.

5 I am come into my garden, my sister, my spouse, I have gathered my myrrh with my spice, I have eaten my honeycomb with my honey, I have drunk my wine with my milk: eat, O friends; drink, yea drink abundantly, O beloved!

I sleep, but my heart waketh: it is the voice of my beloved that knocketh, saying, "Open to me, my sister, my love, my dove, my undefiled: for my head is filled with dew, and my locks with the drops of the night."

I have put off my coat, how shall I put it on? I have washed my feet, how shall I defile them?

My beloved put in his hand by the hole of the door, and my bowels were moved for him.

I rose up to open to my beloved, and my hands dropped with myrrh, and my fingers with sweet smelling myrrh, upon the handles of the lock.

I opened to my beloved, but my beloved had withdrawn himself, and was gone: my soul failed when he spake: I sought him, but I could not find him: I called him, but he gave me no answer.

The watchmen that went about the city found me, they smote me, they wounded me; the keepers of the walls took away my veil from me.

I charge you, O daughters of Jerusalem, if ye find my beloved, that ye tell him that I am sick of love.

What is thy beloved more than another beloved, O thou fairest among women? what is thy beloved more than another beloved, that thou dost so charge us?

My beloved is white and ruddy, the chiefest among ten thousand.

His head is as the most fine gold, his locks are bushy, and black as a raven.

His eyes are as the eyes of doves by the rivers of waters, washed with milk, and fitly set.

His cheeks are as a bed of spices, as sweet flowers: his lips like lilies, dropping sweet smelling myrrh.

His hands are as gold rings set with the beryl: his belly is as bright ivory, overlaid with sapphires.

His legs are as pillars of marble, set upon sockets of fine gold: his countenance is as Lebanon, excellent as the cedars.

His mouth is most sweet, yea he is altogether lovely. This is my beloved, and this is my friend, O daughters of Jerusalem.

6 Whither is thy beloved gone? O thou fairest among women, whither is thy beloved turned aside? that we may seek him with thee.

My beloved is gone down into his garden, to the beds of spices, to feed in the gardens, and to gather lilies.

I am my beloved's, and my beloved is mine: he feedeth among the lilies.

Thou art beautiful, O my love, as Tirzah, comely as Jerusalem, terrible as an army with banners.

Turn away thine eyes from me, for they have overcome me: thy hair is as a flock of goats that appear from Gilead.

Thy teeth are as a flock of sheep which go up from the washing, whereof every one beareth twins, and there is not one barren among them.

As a piece of a pomegranate are thy temples within thy locks.

There are threescore queens, and fourscore concubines, and virgins without number.

My dove, my undefiled is but one; she is the only one of her mother, she is the choice one of her that bare her. The daughters saw her, and blessed her; yea the queens and the concubines, and they praised her.

Who is she that looketh forth as the morning, fair as the moon, clear as the sun, and terrible as an army with banners?

I went down into the garden of nuts to see the fruits of the valley, and to see whether the vine flourished, and the pomegranates budded.

Or ever I was aware, my soul made me like the chariots of Amminadib.

Return, return, O Shulamite; return, return, that we may look upon thee: what will ye see in the Shulamite? as it were the company of two armies.

7 How beautiful are thy feet with shoes, O prince's daughter! the joints of thy thighs are like jewels, the work of the hands of a cunning workman.

Thy navel is like a round goblet, which wanteth not liquor: thy belly is like an heap of wheat, set about with lilies.

Thy two breasts are like two young roes that are twins.

Thy neck is as a tower of ivory: thine eyes like the fish-pools in Heshbon, by the gate of Bathrabbim: thy nose is as the tower of Lebanon, which looketh toward Damascus.

Thine head upon thee is like Carmel, and the hair of thine head like purple; the king is held in the galleries.

How fair, and how pleasant art thou, O love, for delights!

This thy stature is like to a palm tree, and thy breasts to clusters of grapes.

I said, "I will go up to the palm tree, I will take hold of the boughs thereof": now also thy breasts shall be as clusters of the vine, and the smell of thy nose like apples;

And the roof of thy mouth like the best wine for my beloved, that goeth down sweetly, causing the lips of those that are asleep to speak.

I am my beloved's, and his desire is towards me.

Come, my beloved, let us go forth into the field: let us lodge in the villages.

Let us get up early to the vineyards, let us see if the vine flourish, whether the tender grape appear, and the pomegranates bud forth: there will I give thee my loves.

The mandrakes give a smell, and at our gates are all manner of pleasant fruits, new and old, which I have laid up for thee, O my beloved.

8 O that thou wert as my brother that sucked the breasts of my mother! when I should find thee without, I would kiss thee, yea, I should not be despised.

I would lead thee, and bring thee into my mother's house, who would instruct me: I would cause thee to drink of spiced wine, of the juice of my pomegranate.

His left hand should be under my head, and his right hand should embrace me.

I charge you, O daughters of Jerusalem, that ye stir not up, nor awake my love, until he please.

(Who is this that cometh up from the wilderness, leaning upon her beloved?) I raised thee up under the apple tree: there thy mother brought thee forth, there she brought thee forth that bare thee.

Set me as a seal upon thine heart, as a seal upon thine arm: for love is strong as death, jealousy is cruel as the grave: the coals thereof are coals of fire, which hath a most vehement flame.

Many waters cannot quench love, neither can the floods drown it: if a man would give all the substance of his house for love, it would utterly be contemned.

We have a little sister, and she hath no breasts: what shall we do for our sister, in the day when she shall be spoken for?

If she be a wall, we will build upon her a palace of silver: and if she be a door, we will inclose her with boards of cedar.

I am a wall, and my breasts like towers: then was I in his eyes as one that found favour.

Solomon had a vineyard at Baal-hamon, he let out the vineyard unto keepers: every one for the fruit thereof was to bring a thousand pieces of silver.

My vineyard, which is mine, is before me: thou, O Solomon, must have a thousand, and those that keep the fruit thereof two hundred.

Thou that dwellest in the gardens, the companions hearken to thy voice: cause me to hear it.

Make haste, my beloved, and be thou like to a roe, or to a young hart upon the mountains of spices.

ecclesiastes

INTRODUCTION

Whereas the author of Job wrung his hands at the problem of theodicy, Ecclesiastes seemed to shrug his shoulders. Yet his answer to the problem of evil and suffering is not just skeptical and pessimistic; it is also daring. Traditional religion was to the writer of Ecclesiastes largely a form of wishful thinking. God is remote. Earthly rewards and punishments are haphazard and in no way based on justice. There is no assurance of life after death. Moreover, reality is only "the ceaseless flux of phenomena in a purely arbitrary order"[1]; and this order, even if it is cyclical, is unknowable by man. Hence human beings are powerless to control their fate or to know their future, and hence any messianic hopes are subjective and chimerical.

How did a work that views life in the manner of *The Rubáiyát of Omar Khayyám* get into the Bible? Probably the answer is threefold. First, written late (around 200 B.C.), Ecclesiastes was immediately popular. This popularity, in turn, can be explained by the author's brilliant style, a mixture of prose and poetry that rises to a climax in the allegory of old age in the concluding chapter; and by his attempt, conscious or unconscious, to synthesize Greek philosophy, especially Epicureanism, with Jewish thought. Second, the book of Ecclesiastes was attributed to Solomon, thereby giving its "wisdom" an aura of sanctity.[2] Third, it was promptly and extensively diluted by pious annotations, and the text is full of glosses that uphold the orthodox views of Job's comforters. (For instance, the editor or editors add a note saying that "of making many books there is no end"—so do not worry about this book; and in the final paragraph they diametrically contradict Ecclesiastes' central thesis.) But if such glosses got this book into the Bible, they were more than worth it. Ecclesiastes is more than a cynic, for running through

[1] Pfeiffer, *Introduction to the Old Testament*, p. 727.
[2] Much of the wisdom in Ecclesiastes is proverbial, akin to that section of the Old Testament called The Proverbs.

308

his thought is a stoical belief in moderation. Further, underneath his pessimism is the affirmation that life itself can be good, that a living dog is better than a dead lion. Indeed, the Bible would be a smaller collection, in every sense, if it did not include this provocative work. ♣ ♣ ♣

Suggested Reading

Lucretius, *De rerum natura*—a philosophical poem of the first century B.C. which examines the universe and human behavior from an Epicurean point of view.

Montaigne, *Essays*—urbane, personal, and generally skeptical essays by a Renaissance Frenchman.

Jonathan Swift, *Gulliver's Travels*—a sometimes cynical account by an eighteenth-century English rationalist of travels to four imaginary lands.

Jean-Paul Sartre, Plays—contemporary Existentialist dramas which have much in common with the underlying thought patterns in Ecclesiastes.

ECCLESIASTES

1   The words of the Preacher, the son of David, king in Jerusalem.
      Vanity of vanities, saith the Preacher, vanity of vanities, all is vanity. What profit hath a man of all his labour which he taketh under the sun? One generation passeth away, and another generation cometh: but the earth abideth for ever. The sun also ariseth, and the sun goeth down, and hasteth to the place where he arose. The wind goeth toward the south, and turneth about unto the north; it whirleth about continually, and the wind returneth again according to his circuits. All the rivers run into the sea, yet the sea is not full: unto the place from whence the rivers come, thither they return again. All things are full of labour, man cannot utter it: the eye is not satisfied with seeing, nor the ear filled with hearing. The thing that hath been, it is that which shall be: and that which is done is that which shall be done; and there is no new thing under the sun. Is there any thing whereof it may be said, "See, this is new"? it hath been already of old time, which was before us. There is no remembrance of former things; neither shall there be any remembrance of things that are to come, with those that shall come after.
      I the Preacher was king over Israel in Jerusalem. And I gave my

heart to seek and search out by wisdom, concerning all things that are done under heaven: this sore travail hath God given to the sons of man, to be exercised therewith. I have seen all the works that are done under the sun, and behold, all is vanity and vexation of spirit. That which is crooked cannot be made straight: and that which is wanting cannot be numbered. I communed with mine own heart, saying, "Lo, I am come to great estate, and have gotten more wisdom than all they that have been before me in Jerusalem: yea, my heart had great experience of wisdom and knowledge." And I gave my heart to know wisdom, and to know madness and folly: I perceived that this also is vexation of spirit. For in much wisdom is much grief: and he that increaseth knowledge increaseth sorrow.

2 I said in mine heart, "Go to now, I will prove thee with mirth, therefore enjoy pleasure": and behold, this also is vanity. I said of laughter, "It is mad": and of mirth, "What doeth it?" I sought in mine heart to give myself unto wine (yet acquainting mine heart with wisdom), and to lay hold on folly, till I might see what was that good for the sons of men, which they should do under the heaven all the days of their life. I made me great works, I builded me houses, I planted me vineyards. I made me gardens and orchards, and I planted trees in them of all kind of fruits. I made me pools of water, to water therewith the wood that bringeth forth trees: I got me servants and maidens, and had servants born in my house; also I had great possessions of great and small cattle, above all that were in Jerusalem before me. I gathered me also silver and gold, and the peculiar treasure of kings and of the provinces: I gat me men singers and women singers, and the delights of the sons of men, as musical instruments, and that of all sorts. So I was great, and increased more than all that were before me in Jerusalem; also my wisdom remained with me. And whatsoever mine eyes desired, I kept not from them; I withheld not my heart from any joy: for my heart rejoiced in all my labour; and this was my portion of all my labour. Then I looked on all the works that my hands had wrought, and on the labour that I had laboured to do: and behold, all was vanity, and vexation of spirit, and there was no profit under the sun.

And I turned myself to behold wisdom, and madness and folly: for what can the man do that cometh after the king? even that which hath been already done. Then I saw that wisdom excelleth folly, as far as light excelleth darkness. The wise man's eyes are in his head, but the fool walketh in darkness: and I myself perceived also that one event happeneth to them all. Then said I in my heart, "As it happeneth to the fool, so it happeneth even to me; and why was I then more wise?" Then I said in my heart, that this also is vanity. For there is no remembrance of the wise more than of the fool for ever; seeing that which now is, in the days to come shall all be forgotten; and how dieth the wise man? as the fool. Therefore I hated life, because the work that is wrought under the sun is grievous unto me: for all is vanity, and vexation of spirit.

Yea, I hated all my labour which I had taken under the sun: because I should leave it unto the man that shall be after me. And who knoweth whether he shall be a wise man or a fool? yet shall he have rule over all my labour, wherein I have laboured, and wherein I have showed myself wise under the sun. This is also vanity. Therefore I went about to cause my heart to despair of all the labour which I took under the sun. For there is a man whose labour is in wisdom and in knowledge, and in equity: yet to a man that hath not laboured therein shall he leave it for his portion; this also is vanity, and a great evil. For what hath man of all his labour, and of the vexation of his heart, wherein he hath laboured under the sun? For all his days are sorrows, and his travail grief; yea, his heart taketh not rest in the night. This is also vanity.

There is nothing better for a man, than that he should eat and drink, and that he should make his soul enjoy good in his labour. This also I saw, that it was from the hand of God. For who can eat? or who else can hasten hereunto more than I? For God giveth to a man that is good in his sight, wisdom, and knowledge, and joy: but to the sinner he giveth travail, to gather and to heap up, that he may give to him that is good before God. This also is vanity and vexation of spirit.

3 To every thing there is a season, and a time to every purpose under the heaven: a time to be born, and a time to die; a time to plant, and a time to pluck up that which is planted; a time to kill, and a time to heal; a time to break down, and a time to build up; a time to weep, and a time to laugh; a time to mourn, and a time to dance; a time to cast away stones, and a time to gather stones together; a time to embrace, and a time to refrain from embracing;

a time to get, and a time to lose; a time to keep, and a time to cast away; a time to rend, and a time to sew; a time to keep silence, and a time to speak; a time to love, and a time to hate; a time of war, and a time of peace.

What profit hath he that worketh in that wherein he laboureth? I have seen the travail which God hath given to the sons of men, to be exercised in it. He hath made every thing beautiful in his time: also he hath set the world in their heart, so that no man can find out the work that God maketh from the beginning to the end. I know that there is no good in them, but for a man to rejoice, and to do good in his life. And also that every man should eat and drink, and enjoy the good of all his labour: it is the gift of God. I know that, whatsoever God doeth, it shall be for ever: nothing can be put to it, nor any thing taken from it: and God doeth it, that men should fear before him. That which hath been, is now: and that which is to be, hath already been, and God requireth that which is past.

And moreover, I saw under the sun the place of judgment, that wickedness was there; and the place of righteousness, that iniquity was there. I said in mine heart, "God shall judge the righteous and the wicked: for there is a time there for every purpose and for every work." I said in mine heart concerning the estate of the sons of men, that God might manifest them, and that they might see that they themselves are beasts. For that which befalleth the sons of men befalleth beasts, even one thing befalleth them: as the one dieth, so dieth the other; yea, they have all one breath, so that a man hath no preeminence above a beast: for all is vanity. All go unto one place, all are of the dust, and all turn to dust again. Who knoweth the spirit of man that goeth upward, and the spirit of the beast that goeth downward to the earth? Wherefore I perceive that there is nothing better, than that a man should rejoice in his own works: for that is his portion; for who shall bring him to see what shall be after him?

4 So I returned, and considered all the oppressions that are done under the sun; and behold the tears of such as were oppressed, and they had no comforter: and on the side of their oppressors there was power, but they had no comforter. Wherefore I praised the dead which are already dead, more than the living which are yet alive. Yea, better is he than both they, which hath not yet been, who hath not seen the evil work that is done under the sun.

Again I considered all travail, and every right work, that for this a man is envied of his neighbour: this is also vanity, and vexation of spirit. The fool foldeth his hands together, and eateth his own flesh. Better is an handful with quietness, than both the hands full with travail and vexation of spirit.

Then I returned, and I saw vanity under the sun. There is one alone, and there is not a second; yea, he hath neither child nor brother: yet is there no end of all his labour, neither is his eye satisfied with riches, neither saith he, "For whom do I labour, and bereave my soul of good?" This is also vanity, yea it is a sore travail.

Two are better than one; because they have a good reward for their labour. For if they fall, the one will lift up his fellow; but woe to him that is alone when he falleth: for he hath not another to help him up. Again, if two lie together, then they have heat; but how can one be warm alone? And if one prevail against him, two shall withstand him; and a threefold cord is not quickly broken.

Better is a poor and a wise child than an old and foolish king who will no more be admonished. For out of prison he cometh to reign, whereas also he that is born in his kingdom becometh poor. I considered all the living which walk under the sun, with the second child that shall stand up in his stead. There is no end of all the people, even of all that have been before them: they also that come after shall not rejoice in him: surely this also is vanity, and vexation of spirit.

5 Keep thy foot when thou goest to the house of God, and be more ready to hear, than to give the sacrifice of fools: for they consider not that they do evil. Be not rash with thy mouth, and let not thine heart be hasty to utter any thing before God: for God is in heaven, and thou upon earth: therefore let thy words be few. For a dream cometh through the multitude of business, and a fool's voice is known by multitude of words. When thou vowest a vow unto God, defer not to pay it: for he hath no pleasure in fools; pay that which thou hast vowed. Better is it that thou shouldest not vow, than that thou shouldest vow and not pay. Suffer not thy mouth to cause thy flesh to sin, neither say thou before the angel, that it was an error: wherefore should God be angry at thy voice, and destroy the work of thine hands? For in the multitude of dreams and many words there are also divers vanities: but fear thou God.

If thou seest the oppression of the poor, and violent perverting of judgment and justice in a province, marvel not at the matter: for he that is higher than the highest regardeth, and there be higher than they.

Moreover the profit of the earth is for all: the king himself is served by the field. He that loveth silver shall not be satisfied with silver; nor he that loveth abundance, with increase: this is also vanity. When goods increase, they are increased that eat them: and what good is there to the owners thereof, saving the beholding of them with their eyes? The sleep of a labouring man is sweet, whether he eat little or much: but the abundance of the rich will not suffer him to sleep. There is a sore evil which I have seen under the sun, namely, riches kept for the owners thereof to their hurt. But those riches perish by evil travail; and he begetteth a son, and there is nothing in his hand. As he came forth of his mother's womb, naked shall be return to go as he came, and shall take nothing of his labour, which he may carry away in his hand. And this also is a sore evil, that in all points as he came, so shall he go: and what profit hath he that hath laboured for the wind? All his days also he eateth in darkness, and he hath much sorrow and wrath with his sickness.

Behold that which I have seen: it is good and comely for one to eat and to drink, and to enjoy the good of all his labour that he taketh under the sun, all the days of his life, which God giveth him: for it is his portion. Every man also to whom God hath given riches and wealth, and hath given him power to eat thereof, and to take his portion, and to rejoice in his labour; this is the gift of God. For he shall not much remember the days of his life: because God answereth him in the joy of his heart.

6 There is an evil which I have seen under the sun, and it is common among men: a man to whom God hath given riches, wealth, and honour, so that he wanteth nothing for his soul of all that he desireth, yet God giveth him not power to eat thereof, but a stranger eateth it: this is vanity, and it is an evil disease.

If a man beget an hundred children, and live many years, so that the days of his years be many: and his soul be not filled with good, and also that he have no burial; I say, that an untimely birth is better than he. For he cometh in with vanity, and departeth in darkness, and his name shall be covered with darkness. Moreover he hath not seen the sun, nor known any thing: this hath more rest than the other.

Yea though he live a thousand years twice told, yet hath he seen no good: do not all go to one place? All the labour of man is for his mouth, and yet the appetite is not filled. For what hath the wise more than the fool? what hath the poor, that knoweth to walk before the living?

Better is the sight of the eyes than the wandering of the desire: this is also vanity and vexation of spirit. That which hath been, is named already, and it is known that it is man: neither may he contend with him that is mightier than he.

Seeing there be many things that increase vanity, what is man the better? For who knoweth what is good for man in this life, all the days of his vain life, which he spendeth as a shadow? for who can tell a man what shall be after him under the sun?

7 A good name is better than precious ointment: and the day of death than the day of one's birth.

It is better to go to the house of mourning, than to go to the house of feasting: for that is the end of all men, and the living will lay it to his heart. Sorrow is better than laughter: for by the sadness of the countenance the heart is made better. The heart of the wise is in the house of mourning: but the heart of fools is in the house of mirth. It is better to hear the rebuke of the wise, than for a man to hear the song of fools. For as the crackling of thorns under a pot, so is the laughter of the fool: this also is vanity.

Surely oppression maketh a wise man mad: and a gift destroyeth the heart. Better is the end of a thing than the beginning thereof: and the patient in spirit is better than the proud in spirit. Be not hasty in thy spirit to be angry: for anger resteth in the bosom of fools. Say not thou, "What is the cause that the former days were better than these?" for thou dost not inquire wisely concerning this.

Wisdom is good with an inheritance: and by it there is profit to them that see the sun. For wisdom is a defense, and money is a defense: but the excellency of knowledge is, that wisdom giveth life to them that have it. Consider the work of God: for who can make that straight, which he hath made crooked? In the day of prosperity be joyful, but in the day of adversity consider: God also hath set the one over against the other, to the end that man should find nothing after him. All things have I seen in the days of my vanity: there is a just man that perisheth in his righteousness, and there is a wicked man that prolongeth his life in his wickedness. Be not righteous overmuch, neither make thyself overwise: why shouldest thou destroy thyself? Be not overmuch wicked, neither be thou foolish: why shouldest thou die before thy time? It is good that thou should-est take hold of this; yea, also from this withdraw not thine hand: for he that feareth God shall come forth of them all. Wisdom strength-eneth the wise more than ten mighty men which are in the city. For there is not a just man upon earth, that doeth good, and sinneth not. Also take no heed unto all words that are spoken; lest thou hear thy servant curse thee. For oftentimes also thine own heart knoweth that thou thyself likewise hast cursed others.

All this have I proved by wisdom: I said, "I will be wise," but it was far from me. That which is far off, and exceeding deep, who can find it out? I applied mine heart to know, and to search, and to seek out wisdom, and the reason of things, and to know the wicked-ness of folly, even of foolishness and madness. And I find more bitter than death the woman whose heart is snares and nets, and her hands as bands: whoso pleaseth God shall escape from her, but the sinner shall be taken by her. Behold, this have I found (saith the preacher), counting one by one to find out the account: which yet my soul seeketh, but I find not: one man among a thousand have I found, but a woman among all those have I not found. Lo, this only have I found, that God hath made man upright: but they have sought out many inventions.

8 Who is as the wise man? and who knoweth the interpretation of a thing? a man's wisdom maketh his face to shine, and the boldness of his face shall be changed. I counsel thee to keep the king's commandment, and that in regard of the oath of God. Be not hasty to go out of his sight: stand not in an evil thing, for he doeth whatsoever pleaseth him. Where the word of a king is, there is power: and who may say unto him, "What doest thou?" Whoso keepeth the commandment shall feel no evil thing: and a wise man's heart discerneth both time and judgment.

Because to every purpose there is time, and judgment; therefore the misery of man is great upon him. For he knoweth not that which shall be: for who can tell him when it shall be? There is no man that hath power over the spirit to retain the spirit; neither hath he power in the day of death: and there is no discharge in that war, neither shall wickedness deliver those that are given to it. All this have I seen, and applied my heart unto every work that is done under the sun: there is a time wherein one man ruleth over another to his own hurt. And so I saw the wicked buried, who had come and gone from the place of the holy, and they were forgotten in the city where they had so done: this is also vanity. Because sentence against an evil work is not executed speedily, therefore the heart of the sons of men is fully set in them to do evil.

Though a sinner do evil an hundred times, and his days be prolonged, yet surely I know that it shall be well with them that fear God, which fear before him. But it shall not be well with the wicked, neither shall he prolong his days, which are as a shadow; because he feareth not before God. There is a vanity which is done upon the earth, that there be just men, unto whom it happeneth according to the work of the wicked: again, there be wicked men, to whom it happeneth according to the work of the righteous: I said that this also is vanity. Then I commended mirth, because a man hath no better thing under the sun, than to eat, and to drink, and to be merry: for that shall abide with him of his labour, the days of his life, which God giveth him under the sun.

When I applied mine heart to know wisdom, and to see the business that is done upon the earth (for also there is that neither day nor night seeth sleep with his eyes): then I beheld all the work of God, that a man cannot find out the work that is done under the sun: because though a man labour to seek it out, yet he shall not find it; yea further, though a wise man think to know it, yet shall he not be able to find it.

9 For all this I considered in my heart, even to declare all this, that the righteous, and the wise, and their works, are in the hand of God: no man knoweth either love, or hatred, by all that is before them. All things come alike to all: there is one event to the righteous, and to the wicked, to the good and to the clean, and to the unclean; to him that sacrificeth, and to him that sacrificeth not: as is the good, so is the sinner, and he that sweareth, as he that feareth an oath. This is an evil among all things that are done under the sun, that there is one event unto all: yea also the heart of the sons of men is

full of evil, and madness is in their heart while they live, and after
that they go to the dead.

For to him that is joined to all the living there is hope: for a living
dog is better than a dead lion. For the living know that they shall
die: but the dead know not any thing, neither have they any more a
reward, for the memory of them is forgotten. Also their love, and
their hatred, and their envy, is now perished; neither have they any
more a portion for ever in any thing that is done under the sun.

Go thy way, eat thy bread with joy, and drink thy wine with a
merry heart; for God now accepteth thy works. Let thy garments be
always white; and let thy head lack no ointment. Live joyfully with
the wife, whom thou lovest, all the days of the life of thy vanity,
which he hath given thee under the sun, all the days of thy vanity:
for that is thy portion in this life, and in thy labour which thou
takest under the sun. Whatsoever thy hand findeth to do, do it with
thy might: for there is no work, nor device, nor knowledge, nor
wisdom, in the grave, whither thou goest.

I returned, and saw under the sun, that the race is not to the swift,
nor the battle to the strong, neither yet bread to the wise, nor yet
riches to men of understanding, nor yet favour to men of skill; but
time and chance happeneth to them all. For man also knoweth not
his time: as the fishes that are taken in an evil net, and as the birds
that are caught in the snare, so are the sons of men snared in an
evil time, when it falleth suddenly upon them.

This wisdom have I seen also under the sun, and it seemed great
unto me: there was a little city, and few men within it; and there
came a great king against it, and besieged it, and built great bulwarks
against it: now there was found in it a poor wise man, and he by
his wisdom delivered the city; yet no man remembered that same
poor man. Then said I, "Wisdom is better than strength": nevertheless, the poor man's wisdom is despised, and his words are not heard.
The words of wise men are heard in quiet, more than the cry of him
that ruleth among fools. Wisdom is better than weapons of war: but
one sinner destroyeth much good.

10 Dead flies cause the ointment of the apothecary to send forth
a stinking savour: so doth a little folly him that is in reputation
for wisdom and honour. A wise man's heart is at his right hand: but
a fool's heart at his left. Yea also when he that is a fool walketh by

the way, his wisdom faileth him, and he saith to every one that he is a fool. If the spirit of the ruler rise up against thee, leave not thy place; for yielding pacifieth great offenses. There is an evil which I have seen under the sun, as an error which proceedeth from the ruler: folly is set in great dignity, and the rich sit in low place. I have seen servants upon horses, and princes walking as servants upon the earth. He that diggeth a pit shall fall into it; and whoso breaketh an hedge, a serpent shall bite him. Whoso removeth stones shall be hurt therewith: and he that cleaveth wood shall be endangered thereby. If the iron be blunt, and he do not whet the edge, then must he put to more strength: but wisdom is profitable to direct. Surely the serpent will bite without enchantment, and a babbler is no better. The words of a wise man's mouth are gracious: but the lips of a fool will swallow up himself. The beginning of the words of his mouth is foolishness: and the end of his talk is mischievous madness. A fool also is full of words; a man cannot tell what shall be; and what shall be after him, who can tell him? The labour of the foolish wearieth every one of them, because he knoweth not how to go to the city.

Woe to thee, O land, when thy king is a child, and thy princes eat in the morning. Blessed art thou, O land, when thy king is the son of nobles, and thy princes eat in due season, for strength, and not for drunkenness.

By much slothfulness the building decayeth; and through idleness of the hands the house droppeth through.

A feast is made for laughter, and wine maketh merry: but money answereth all things.

Curse not the king, no not in thy thought, and curse not the rich in thy bedchamber: for a bird of the air shall carry the voice, and that which hath wings shall tell the matter.

11 Cast thy bread upon the waters: for thou shalt find it after many days. Give a portion to seven, and also to eight; for thou knowest not what evil shall be upon the earth. If the clouds be full of rain, they empty themselves upon the earth: and if the tree fall toward the south, or toward the north, in the place where the tree falleth, there it shall be. He that observeth the wind shall not sow: and he that regardeth the clouds shall not reap. As thou knowest not what is the way of the spirit, nor how the bones do grow in the womb of her that is with child: even so thou knowest not the works of God who maketh all. In the morning sow thy seed, and in the evening withhold not thine hand: for thou knowest not whether shall prosper, either this or that, or whether they both shall be alike good.

Truly the light is sweet, and a pleasant thing it is for the eyes to behold the sun. But if a man live many years, and rejoice in them all; yet let him remember the days of darkness, for they shall be many. All that cometh is vanity.

Rejoice, O young man, in thy youth, and let thy heart cheer thee in the days of thy youth, and walk in the ways of thine heart, and in the sight of thine eyes: but know thou, that for all these things, God will bring thee into judgment. Therefore remove sorrow from thy heart, and put away evil from thy flesh; for childhood and youth are vanity.

12 Remember now thy Creator in the days of thy youth, while the evil days come not, nor the years draw nigh, when thou shalt say, "I have no pleasure in them": while the sun, or the light, or the moon, or the stars, be not darkened, nor the clouds return after the rain: in the day when the keepers of the house shall tremble, and the strong men shall bow themselves, and the grinders cease because they are few, and those that look out of the windows be darkened: and the doors shall be shut in the streets, when the sound of the grinding is low, and he shall rise up at the voice of the bird, and all the daughters of music shall be brought low. Also when they shall be afraid of that which is high, and fears shall be in the way, and the almond tree shall flourish, and the grasshopper shall be a burden, and desire shall fail: because man goeth to his long home, and the mourners go about the streets: or ever the silver cord be loosed, or the golden bowl be broken, or the pitcher be broken at the fountain, or the wheel broken at the cistern. Then shall the dust return to the earth as it was: and the spirit shall return unto God who gave it.

Vanity of vanities (saith the preacher), all is vanity. And moreover because the preacher was wise, he still taught the people knowledge, yea, he gave good heed, and sought out, and set in order many proverbs. The preacher sought to find out acceptable words, and that which was written was upright, even words of truth. The words of the wise are as goads, and as nails fastened by the masters of assemblies, which are given from one shepherd. And further, by these, my son, be admonished: of making many books there is no end, and much study is a weariness of the flesh.

Let us hear the conclusion of the whole matter: fear God, and keep his commandments, for this is the whole duty of man. For God shall bring every work into judgment, with every secret thing, whether it be good, or whether it be evil.

the
new
testament

the Gospels

INTRODUCTION

The New Testament has been more important than the Old in shaping our ideas and institutions because for almost two thousand years the dominant religion of the Western world has been Christianity. In purely literary terms, however, the New Testament is inferior. It is less than one-third as long as the Old, and the twenty-seven books which make it up are far more homogeneous. These books were composed within a period of one hundred years, not over many centuries: Paul's earliest Epistle dates from about 50 A.D., The Second Epistle of Peter from a century later. Also, the New Testament is mainly concerned with one subject: the life, death, and resurrection of Jesus—and their impact on his immediate followers. This concern generally excluded an interest in world figures and events; and since most New Testament writers felt that the end of the world was imminent, they further minimized the importance of secular history. Then, too, these authors were evangelists of a new faith. As such they had both to defend that faith from internal and external attack and to deal with practical ecclesiastical problems. Finally, the New Testament was written in colloquial, not classic, Greek, with the result that its language was not well endowed with the resources of a fully developed literary tradition. None the less, the literary superiority of the Old Testament is neither overwhelming nor consistent. Moreover, the New Testament in many of its ideas and techniques is a continuation of its predecessor: together they make up one Bible.

Approximately half of the New Testament consists of the four Gospels, four different interpretations of the meaning of Jesus. The first three (the Synoptic Gospels) are more narrative than interpretative; while in the fourth, that of John, the function of the interpreter seems to have taken over completely. The word "gospel" means good news, and all four are characterized by the zeal and excitement of an apparently new belief. To choose the one to be included in this selection was a difficult problem. The Gospel According to St. Luke is the most extended treatment of Christ's life and teachings, and a majority of critics consider it the best written of the four. In addition, its author was almost certainly the man who continued his story in The Acts of the Apostles. (Two fragments from other Gospels, however, seem indispensable: the Beatitudes from Matthew's version of the Sermon on the Mount, which are inserted in their proper place in Luke's narrative; and the opening of John, which is given at the end of Luke.)

Of the author of Luke we know little, and much of that is conjectural. He may have been a companion of Paul on some of the latter's missionary journeys, the man to whom Paul refers as the "beloved physician." Unlike most other writers of the New Testament, Luke may not have been Jewish by birth, though he was obviously familiar with the Old Testament. His Gospel is primarily addressed to a Greek audience; and where Matthew, for instance, is mainly speaking to Jewish readers, Luke has the broader Gentile community in mind.

The Gospel According to St. Luke was written, most modern scholars believe, around 90 A.D., concurrently with that of Matthew and some years before John's. Because it was set down long after the events it describes, Luke must have drawn on sources other than his own memory and imagination. Three of them are evident: an early collection of Christ's sayings also used by Matthew; his own special source of material; and The Gospel According to St. Mark, composed in all probability shortly after the destruction of Jerusalem in 70 A.D. (That Luke used several sources is corroborated by the opening sentence of his Gospel.) Out of these earlier records he wove a coherent and affecting narrative, the motive force of which is the conviction that Jesus, crucified and risen, is now Lord of the world. ♣ ♣ ♣

Suggested Reading

"The Second Shepherds' Play"—a medieval drama about the nativity. John Milton, *Paradise Regained*—a short epic about Christ's temptation in the wilderness.

LUKE

1   Forasmuch as many have taken in hand to set forth in order a declaration of those things which are most surely believed among us, even as they delivered them unto us, which from the beginning were eyewitnesses, and ministers of the word: it seemed good to me also, having had perfect understanding of all things from

the very first, to write unto thee in order, most excellent Theophilus,[1] that thou mightest know the certainty of those things, wherein thou hast been instructed.

There was in the days of Herod, the king of Judea, a certain priest named Zacharias, of the course[2] of Abia, and his wife was of the daughters of Aaron, and her name was Elizabeth. And they were both righteous before God, walking in all the commandments and ordinances of the Lord, blameless. And they had no child, because that Elizabeth was barren, and they both were now well stricken in years. And it came to pass, that while he executed the priest's office before God in the order of his course, according to the custom of the priest's office, his lot was to burn incense when he went into the temple of the Lord. And the whole multitude of the people were praying without, at the time of incense. And there appeared unto him an angel of the Lord, standing on the right side of the altar of incense. And when Zacharias saw him, he was troubled, and fear fell upon him. But the angel said unto him, "Fear not, Zacharias, for thy prayer is heard, and thy wife Elizabeth shall bear thee a son, and thou shalt call his name John. And thou shalt have joy and gladness, and many shall rejoice at his birth: for he shall be great in the sight of the Lord, and shall drink neither wine, nor strong drink, and he shall be filled with the Holy Ghost, even from his mother's womb. And many of the children of Israel shall he turn to the Lord their God. And he shall go before him in the spirit and power of Elias,[3] to turn the hearts of the fathers to the children, and the disobedient to the wisdom of the just, to make ready a people prepared for the Lord."

And Zacharias said unto the angel, "Whereby shall I know this? For I am an old man, and my wife well stricken in years." And the angel answering, said unto him, "I am Gabriel, that stand in the presence of God, and am sent to speak unto thee, and to show thee these glad tidings. And behold, thou shalt be dumb, and not able to speak, until the day that these things shall be performed, because thou believest not my words, which shall be fulfilled in their season."

[1] This name means "one who loves God," and apparently it was then fairly common. The preceding phrase, "most excellent," indicates that Theophilus was a high government official—just as today we use the title "your excellency."
[2] I.e., division.
[3] I.e., Elijah.

And the people waited for Zacharias, and marvelled that he tarried so long in the temple. And when he came out, he could not speak unto them: and they perceived that he had seen a vision in the temple: for he beckoned unto them, and remained speechless. And it came to pass, that as soon as the days of his ministration were accomplished, he departed to his own house. And after those days his wife Elizabeth conceived, and hid herself five months, saying, "Thus hath the Lord dealt with me in the days wherein he looked on me, to take away my reproach among men."

And in the sixth month the angel Gabriel was sent from God unto a city of Galilee, named Nazareth, to a virgin espoused to a man whose name was Joseph, of the house of David, and the virgin's name was Mary. And the angel came in unto her, and said, "Hail, thou that art highly favoured, the Lord is with thee: blessed art thou among women." And when she saw him, she was troubled at his saying, and cast in her mind what manner of salutation this should be. And the angel said unto her, "Fear not, Mary, for thou hast found favour with God. And behold, thou shalt conceive in thy womb, and bring forth a son, and shalt call his name Jesus.[4] He shall be great, and shall be called the Son of the Highest, and the Lord God shall give unto him the throne of his father David. And he shall reign over the house of Jacob for ever, and of his kingdom there shall be no end." Then said Mary unto the angel, "How shall this be, seeing I know not a man?" And the angel answered and said unto her, "The Holy Ghost shall come upon thee, and the power of the Highest shall overshadow thee. Therefore also that holy thing which shall be born of thee shall be called the Son of God. And behold, thy cousin Elizabeth, she hath also conceived a son in her old age, and this is the sixth month with her, who was called barren. For with God nothing shall be unpossible." And Mary said, "Behold the handmaid of the Lord, be it unto me according to thy word." And the angel departed from her.

And Mary arose in those days, and went into the hill country with haste, into a city of Judah, and entered into the house of Zacharias, and saluted Elizabeth. And it came to pass that when Elizabeth heard the salutation of Mary, the babe leaped in her womb, and Elizabeth was filled with the Holy Ghost. And she spake out with a loud voice, and said, "Blessed art thou among women, and blessed

[4] The Greek equivalent of Joshua, which means "the Lord is salvation."

is the fruit of thy womb. And whence is this to me, that the mother of my Lord should come to me? For lo, as soon as the voice of thy salutation sounded in mine ears, the babe leaped in my womb for joy. And blessed is she that believed, for there shall be a performance of those things which were told her from the Lord."

And Mary said, "My soul doth magnify the Lord.

And my spirit hath rejoiced in God my Saviour.

For he hath regarded the low estate of his handmaiden: for behold, from henceforth all generations shall call me blessed.

For he that is mighty hath done to me great things, and holy is his name.

And his mercy is on them that fear him, from generation to generation.

He hath showed strength with his arm, he hath scattered the proud in the imagination of their hearts.

He hath put down the mighty from their seats, and exalted them of low degree.

He hath filled the hungry with good things, and the rich he hath sent empty away.

He hath holpen his servant Israel, in remembrance of his mercy,

As he spake to our fathers, to Abraham, and to his seed for ever."

And Mary abode with her about three months, and returned to her own house. Now Elizabeth's full time came, that she should be delivered, and she brought forth a son. And her neighbours and her cousins heard how the Lord had showed great mercy upon her, and they rejoiced with her. And it came to pass that on the eighth day they came to circumcise the child, and they called him Zacharias, after the name of his father. And his mother answered and said, "Not so, but he shall be called John." And they said unto her, "There is none of thy kindred that is called by this name." And they made signs to his father, how he would have him called. And he asked for a writing table,[5] and wrote, saying, "His name is John": and they marvelled all. And his mouth was opened immediately, and his tongue loosed, and he spake, and praised God. And fear came on all that dwelt round about them, and all these sayings were noised abroad throughout all the hill country of Judea. And all they that heard them laid them up in their hearts, saying, "What manner of child shall this be?" And the hand of the Lord was with him.

[5] *I.e.*, tablet.

And his father Zacharias was filled with the Holy Ghost, and prophesied, saying,

"Blessed be the Lord God of Israel, for he hath visited and redeemed his people,

And hath raised up an horn of salvation for us, in the house of his servant David,

As he spake by the mouth of his holy prophets, which have been since the world began:

That we should be saved from our enemies, and from the hand of all that hate us,

To perform the mercy promised to our fathers, and to remember his holy covenant,

The oath which he sware to our father Abraham,

That he would grant unto us, that we being delivered out of the hand of our enemies, might serve him without fear,

In holiness and righteousness before him, all the days of our life.

And thou child shalt be called the prophet of the Highest: for thou shalt go before the face of the Lord to prepare his ways,

To give knowledge of salvation unto his people, by the remission of their sins,

Through the tender mercy of our God, whereby the dayspring from on high hath visited us,

To give light to them that sit in darkness and in the shadow of death, to guide our feet into the way of peace."

And the child grew, and waxed strong in spirit, and was in the deserts till the day of his showing unto Israel.

2 And it came to pass in those days, that there went out a decree from Caesar Augustus, that all the world should be taxed. (And this taxing was first made when Cyrenius was governor of Syria.) And all went to be taxed, every one into his own city. And Joseph also went up from Galilee, out of the city of Nazareth, into Judea, unto the city of David, which is called Bethlehem (because he was of the house and lineage of David), to be taxed with Mary his espoused wife, being great with child. And so it was, that while they were there, the days were accomplished that she should be delivered. And she brought forth her firstborn son, and wrapped him in swaddling clothes, and laid him in a manger, because there was no room for them in the inn.

And there were in the same country shepherds abiding in the field, keeping watch over their flock by night. And lo, the angel of the Lord came upon them, and the glory of the Lord shone round about them, and they were sore afraid. And the angel said unto them, "Fear not: for behold, I bring you good tidings of great joy, which shall be to all people. For unto you is born this day, in the city of David, a Saviour, which is Christ[6] the Lord. And this shall be a sign unto you; ye shall find the babe wrapped in swaddling clothes lying in a manger." And suddenly there was with the angel a multitude of the heavenly host praising God, and saying, "Glory to God in the highest, and on earth peace, good will toward men."

And it came to pass, as the angels were gone away from them into heaven, the shepherds said one to another, "Let us now go even unto Bethlehem, and see this thing which is come to pass, which the Lord hath made known unto us." And they came with haste, and found Mary and Joseph, and the babe lying in a manger. And when they had seen it, they made known abroad the saying which was told them concerning this child. And all they that heard it wondered at those things which were told them by the shepherds. But Mary kept all these things, and pondered them in her heart. And the shepherds returned, glorifying and praising God for all the things that they had heard and seen, as it was told unto them.

And when eight days were accomplished for the circumcising of the child, his name was called Jesus, which was so named of[7] the angel before he was conceived in the womb. And when the days of her purification according to the law of Moses were accomplished, they brought him to Jerusalem, to present him to the Lord (as it is written in the law of the Lord, "Every male that openeth the womb shall be called holy to the Lord"), and to offer a sacrifice according to that which is said in the law of the Lord, a pair of turtledoves, or two young pigeons. And behold, there was a man in Jerusalem, whose name was Simeon, and the same man was just and devout, waiting for the consolation of Israel: and the Holy Ghost was upon him. And it was revealed unto him by the Holy Ghost, that he should not see death before he had seen the Lord's Christ. And he came by the Spirit into the temple: and when the parents brought in the child Jesus, to do for him after the custom of the law, then

[6] "Christ" means "anointed one," and therefore "Messiah."
[7] I.e., by.

took he him up in his arms, and blessed God, and said, "Lord, now lettest thou thy servant depart in peace, according to thy word. For mine eyes have seen thy salvation, which thou hast prepared before the face of all people: a light to lighten the Gentiles, and the glory of thy people Israel." And Joseph and his mother marvelled at those things which were spoken of him. And Simeon blessed them, and said unto Mary his mother, "Behold, this child is set for the fall and rising again of many in Israel: and for a sign which shall be spoken against (yea, a sword shall pierce through thy own soul also), that the thoughts of many hearts may be revealed."

And there was one Anna a prophetess, the daughter of Phanuel, of the tribe of Aser: she was of a great age, and had lived with an husband seven years from her virginity. And she was a widow of about fourscore and four years, which departed not from the temple, but served God with fastings and prayers night and day. And she coming in that instant gave thanks likewise unto the Lord, and spake of him to all them that looked for redemption in Jerusalem. And when they had performed all things according to the law of the Lord, they returned into Galilee, to their own city Nazareth.

And the child grew, and waxed strong in spirit, filled with wisdom, and the grace of God was upon him. Now his parents went to Jerusalem every year, at the feast of the Passover. And when he was twelve years old, they went up to Jerusalem, after the custom of the feast. And when they had fulfilled the days, as they returned, the child Jesus tarried behind in Jerusalem, and Joseph and his mother knew not of it. But they, supposing him to have been in the company, went a day's journey, and they sought him among their kinsfold and acquaintance. And when they found him not, they turned back again to Jerusalem, seeking him. And it came to pass, that after three days they found him in the temple, sitting in the midst of the doctors, both hearing them, and asking them questions. And all that heard him were astonished at his understanding and answers. And when they saw him, they were amazed: and his mother said unto him, "Son, why hast thou thus dealt with us? Behold, thy father and I have sought thee sorrowing." And he said unto them, "How is it that ye sought me? Wist ye not that I must be about my Father's business?" And they understood not the saying which he spake unto them. And he went down with them, and came to Nazareth, and was subject unto them: but his mother kept all these sayings in her heart. And Jesus increased in wisdom and stature, and in favour with God and man.

3 Now in the fifteenth year of the reign of Tiberius Caesar,[8] Pontius Pilate being governor of Judea, and Herod being tetrarch[9] of Galilee, and his brother Philip tetrarch of Iturea and of the region of Trachonitis, and Lysanias the tetrarch of Abilene, Annas and Caiaphas being the high priests, the word of God came unto John the son of Zacharias, in the wilderness. And he came into all the country about Jordan, preaching the baptism of repentance for the remission of sins, as it is written in the book of the words of Esaias[10] the prophet, saying, "The voice of one crying in the wilderness, prepare ye the way of the Lord, make his paths straight. Every valley shall be filled, and every mountain and hill shall be brought low, and the crooked shall be made straight, and the rough ways shall be made smooth. And all flesh shall see the salvation of God." Then said he to the multitude that came forth to be baptized of him, "O generation of vipers, who hath warned you to flee from the wrath to come? Bring forth therefore fruits worthy of repentance, and begin not to say within yourselves, 'We have Abraham to our father': for I say unto you, that God is able of these stones to raise up children unto Abraham. And now also the axe is laid unto the root of the tree: every tree therefore which bringeth not forth good fruit is hewn down, and cast into the fire." And the people asked him, saying, "What shall we do then?" He answereth, and saith unto them, "He that hath two coats, let him impart to him that hath none, and he that hath meat, let him do likewise." Then came also publicans[11] to be baptized, and said unto him, "Master, what shall we do?" And he said unto them, "Exact no more than that which is appointed you." And the soldiers likewise demanded of him, saying, "And what shall we do?" And he said unto them, "Do violence to no man, neither accuse any falsely, and be content with your wages."

And as the people were in expectation, and all men mused in their hearts of John, whether he were the Christ or not: John

[8] 28-29 A.D.
[9] *I.e.*, a ruler over part of a province.
[10] *I.e.*, Isaiah.
[11] *I.e.*, tax collectors—hence their unpopularity, especially since most Palestinians considered Roman taxes an unwarranted and alien burden.

answered, saying unto them all, "I indeed baptize you with water, but one mightier than I cometh, the latchet of whose shoes I am not worthy to unloose: he shall baptize you with the Holy Ghost, and with fire: whose fan[12] is in his hand, and he will thoroughly purge his floor, and will gather the wheat into his garner, but the chaff he will burn with fire unquenchable." And many other things in his exhortation preached he unto the people. But Herod the tetrarch being reproved by him for Herodias his brother Philip's wife, and for all the evils which Herod had done, added yet this above all, that he shut up John in prison. Now when all the people were baptized, it came to pass that Jesus also being baptized, and praying, the heaven was opened: and the Holy Ghost descended in a bodily shape like a dove upon him, and a voice came from heaven, which said, "Thou art my beloved Son, in thee I am well pleased." . . .[13]

4 And Jesus being full of the Holy Ghost returned from Jordan, and was led by the Spirit into the wilderness, being forty days tempted of the devil, and in those days he did eat nothing: and when they were ended, he afterward hungered. And the devil said unto him, "If thou be the Son of God, command this stone that it be made bread." And Jesus answered him, saying, "It is written, 'That man shall not live by bread alone, but by every word of God.' " And the devil, taking him up into an high mountain, showed unto him all the kingdoms of the world in a moment of time. And the devil said unto him, "All this power will I give thee, and the glory of them; for that is delivered unto me, and to whomsoever I will, I give it. If thou therefore wilt worship me, all shall be thine." And Jesus answered and said unto him, "Get thee behind me, Satan: for it is written, 'Thou shalt worship the Lord thy God, and him only shalt thou serve.' " And he brought him to Jerusalem, and set him on a pinnacle of the temple, and said unto him, "If thou be the Son of God, cast thyself down from hence. For it is written, 'He shall give his angels charge over thee, to keep thee. And in their hands they shall bear thee up, lest at any time thou dash thy foot against a stone.' " And Jesus answering, said unto him, "It is said,

[12] I.e., an implement for separating the wheat from the chaff.
[13] Here follows a genealogy of Jesus, from Joseph, through David, back to Adam.

'Thou shalt not tempt the Lord thy God.' " And when the devil had ended all the temptation, he departed from him for a season.

And Jesus returned in the power of the Spirit into Galilee, and there went out a fame of him through all the region round about. And he taught in their synagogues, being glorified of all.

And he came to Nazareth, where he had been brought up, and as his custom was, he went into the synagogue on the sabbath day, and stood up for to read. And there was delivered unto him the book of the prophet Esaias, and when he had opened the book, he found the place where it was written, "The Spirit of the Lord is upon me, because he hath anointed me to preach the gospel to the poor, he hath sent me to heal the broken-hearted, to preach deliverance to the captives, and recovering of sight to the blind, to set at liberty them that are bruised, to preach the acceptable year of the Lord." And he closed the book, and he gave it again to the minister, and sat down. And the eyes of all them that were in the synagogue were fastened on him. And he began to say unto them, "This day is this scripture fulfilled in your ears." And all bare him witness, and wondered at the gracious words which proceeded out of his mouth. And they said, "Is not this Joseph's son?" And he said unto them, "Ye will surely say unto me this proverb, 'Physician, heal thyself: whatsoever we have heard done in Capernaum, do also here in thy country.' " And he said, "Verily I say unto you, no prophet is accepted in his own country. But I tell you of a truth, many widows were in Israel in the days of Elias, when the heaven was shut up three years and six months: when great famine was throughout all the land: but unto none of them was Elias sent, save unto Sarepta, a city of Sidon, unto a woman that was a widow. And many lepers were in Israel in the time of Eliseus[14] the prophet: and none of them was cleansed, saving Naaman the Syrian." And all they in the synagogue, when they heard these things, were filled with wrath, and rose up, and thrust him out of the city, and led him unto the brow of the hill (whereon their city was built), that they might cast him down headlong. But he passing through the midst of them went his way, and came down to Capernaum, a city of Galilee, and taught them on the sabbath days. And they were astonished at his doctrine: for his word was with power.

And in the synagogue there was a man which had a spirit of an

[14] *I.e.*, Elisha.

unclean devil, and cried out with a loud voice, saying, "Let us alone, what have we to do with thee, thou Jesus of Nazareth? art thou come to destroy us? I know thee who thou art, the Holy One of God." And Jesus rebuked him, saying, "Hold thy peace, and come out of him." And when the devil had thrown him in the midst, he came out of him, and hurt him not. And they were all amazed, and spake among themselves, saying, "What a word is this? for with authority and power he commandeth the unclean spirits, and they come out." And the fame of him went out into every place of the country round about.

And he arose out of the synagogue, and entered into Simon's house: and Simon's wife's mother was taken with a great fever, and they besought him for her. And he stood over her, and rebuked the fever, and it left her. And immediately she arose, and ministered unto them.

Now when the sun was setting, all they that had any sick with diverse diseases brought them unto him: and he laid his hands on every one of them, and healed them. And devils also came out of many, crying out, and saying, "Thou art Christ the Son of God." And he rebuking them, suffered them not to speak: for they knew that he was Christ. And when it was day, he departed, and went into a desert place: and the people sought him, and came unto him, and stayed him, that he should not depart from them. And he said unto them, "I must preach the kingdom of God to other cities also: for therefore am I sent." And he preached in the synagogues of Galilee.

5 And it came to pass, that as the people pressed upon him to hear the word of God, he stood by the lake of Gennesaret, and saw two ships standing by the lake: but the fishermen were gone out of them, and were washing their nets. And he entered into one of the ships, which was Simon's, and prayed him that he would thrust out a little from the land: and he sat down, and taught the people out of the ship. Now when he had left speaking, he said unto Simon, "Launch out into the deep, and let down your nets for a draught." [15] And Simon answering, said unto him, "Master, we have toiled all the night, and have taken nothing: nevertheless at thy word I will let down the net." And when they had this done, they inclosed a

[15] I.e., catch.

great multitude of fishes, and their net brake: and they beckoned unto their partners, which were in the other ship, that they should come and help them. And they came, and filled both the ships, so that they began to sink. When Simon Peter saw it, he fell down at Jesus' knees, saying, "Depart from me, for I am a sinful man, O Lord." For he was astonished, and all that were with him, at the draught of the fishes which they had taken. And so was also James, and John, the sons of Zebedee, which were partners with Simon. And Jesus said unto Simon, "Fear not, from henceforth thou shalt catch men." And when they had brought their ships to land, they forsook all, and followed him.

And it came to pass, when he was in a certain city, behold a man full of leprosy: who seeing Jesus fell on his face, and besought him, saying, "Lord, if thou wilt, thou canst make me clean." And he put forth his hand, and touched him, saying, "I will: be thou clean." And immediately the leprosy departed from him. And he charged him to tell no man: "But go, and show thyself to the priest, and offer for thy cleansing, according as Moses commanded, for a testimony unto them." But so much the more went there a fame abroad of him, and great multitudes came together to hear, and to be healed by him of their infirmities.

And he withdrew himself into the wilderness, and prayed. And it came to pass on a certain day, as he was teaching, that there were Pharisees[16] and doctors of the law sitting by, which were come out of every town of Galilee, and Judea, and Jerusalem: and the power of the Lord was present to heal them.

And behold, men brought in a bed a man which was taken with a palsy: and they sought means to bring him in, and to lay him before him. And when they could not find by what way they might bring him in, because of the multitude, they went upon the housetop, and let him down through the tiling with his couch, into the midst before Jesus. And when he saw their faith, he said unto him, "Man, thy sins are forgiven thee." And the scribes[17] and the Pharisees began to reason, saying, "Who is this which speaketh blasphemies? Who can forgive sins, but God alone?" But when

[16] A Jewish sect that adhered strictly to the Law and to its supplementary interpretations.
[17] One of the professional guilds of Judaism: its members were especially learned in the Law.

Jesus perceived their thoughts, he answering, said unto them. "What reason ye in your hearts? Whether is easier, to say, 'Thy sins be forgiven thee'; or to say, 'Rise up and walk'? But that ye may know that the Son of man hath power upon earth to forgive sins (he said unto the sick of the palsy), I say unto thee, 'Arise, and take up thy couch, and go into thine house.'" And immediately he rose up before them, and took up that whereon he lay, and departed to his own house, glorifying God. And they were all amazed, and they glorified God, and were filled with fear, saying, "We have seen strange things today."

And after these things he went forth, and saw a publican, named Levi, sitting at the receipt of custom: and he said unto him, "Follow me." And he left all, rose up, and followed him. And Levi made him a great feast in his own house: and there was a great company of publicans and of others that sat down with them. But their scribes and Pharisees murmured against his disciples, saying, "Why do ye eat and drink with publicans and sinners?" And Jesus answering, said unto them, "They that are whole need not a physician: but they that are sick. I came not to call the righteous, but sinners to repentance."

And they said unto him, "Why do the disciples of John fast often, and make prayers, and likewise the disciples of the Pharisees: but thine eat and drink?" And he said unto them, "Can ye make the children of the bridechamber fast, while the bridegroom is with them? But the days will come, when the bridegroom shall be taken away from them, and then shall they fast in those days."

And he spake also a parable unto them, "No man putteth a piece of a new garment upon an old: if otherwise, then both the new maketh a rent, and the piece that was taken out of the new agreeth not with the old. And no man putteth new wine into old bottles: else the new wine will burst the bottles, and be spilled, and the bottles shall perish. But new wine must be put into new bottles, and both are preserved. No man also having drunk old wine, straightway desireth new: for he saith, 'The old is better.'"

6 And it came to pass on the second sabbath after the first, that he went through the corn fields: and his disciples plucked the ears of corn, and did eat, rubbing them in their hands. And certain of the Pharisees said unto them, "Why do ye that which is not

lawful to do on the sabbath days?" And Jesus answering them, said, "Have ye not read so much as this, what David did, when himself was an hungered, and they which were with him: how he went into the house of God, and did take and eat the showbread, and gave also to them that were with him, which it is not lawful to eat but for the priests alone?" And he said unto them, "That the Son of man is Lord also of the sabbath." And it came to pass also on another sabbath, that he entered into the synagogue, and taught: and there was a man whose right hand was withered. And the scribes and Pharisees watched him, whether he would heal on the sabbath day: that they might find an accusation against him. But he knew their thoughts, and said to the man which had the withered hand, "Rise up, and stand forth in the midst." And he arose, and stood forth. Then said Jesus unto them, "I will ask you one thing, Is it lawful on the sabbath days to do good, or to do evil? to save life, or to destroy it?" And looking round about upon them all, he said unto the man, "Stretch forth thy hand." And he did so: and his hand was restored whole as the other. And they were filled with madness, and communed one with another what they might do to Jesus. And it came to pass in those days, that he went out into a mountain to pray, and continued all night in prayer to God.

And when it was day, he called unto him his disciples: and of them he chose twelve, whom also he named apostles: Simon (whom he also named Peter), and Andrew his brother, James and John, Philip and Bartholomew, Matthew and Thomas, James the son of Alpheus, and Simon called Zelotes, and Judas the brother of James, and Judas Iscariot, which also was the traitor.

And he came down with them, and stood in the plain, and the company of his disciples, and a great multitude of people, out of all Judea and Jerusalem, and from the sea coast of Tyre and Sidon, which came to hear him, and to be healed of their diseases, and they that were vexed with unclean spirits: and they were healed. And the whole multitude sought to touch him: for there went virtue out of him, and healed them all.

And he lifted up his eyes on his disciples, and said, "Blessed be ye poor: for yours is the kingdom of God. Blessed are ye that hunger now: for ye shall be filled. Blessed are ye that weep now, for ye shall laugh. Blessed are ye when men shall hate you, and when they shall separate you from their company, and shall reproach you, and cast out your name as evil, for the Son of man's sake. Rejoice ye in that day, and leap for joy: for behold, your reward is great in heaven: for in the like manner did their fathers unto the prophets. But woe unto you that are rich: for ye have received your consolation. Woe unto you that are full: for ye shall hunger. Woe unto you that laugh now: for ye shall mourn and weep. Woe unto you, when all men shall speak well of you: for so did their fathers to the false prophets.[18]

"But I say unto you which hear, Love your enemies, do good to them which hate you, bless them that curse you, and pray for them which despitefully use you. And unto him that smiteth thee on the one cheek, offer also the other: and him that taketh away thy cloak, forbid not to take thy coat also. Give to every man that asketh of thee, and of him that taketh away thy goods ask them not again. And as ye would that men should do to you, do ye also to them likewise. For if ye love them which love you, what thank have ye? for sinners also love those that love them. And if ye do good to them which do good to you, what thank have ye? for sinners also do even the same. And if ye lend to them of whom ye hope to receive, what thank have ye? for sinners also lend to sinners, to receive as much again. But love ye your enemies, and do good, and lend, hoping for nothing again: and your reward shall be great, and ye shall be the children of the Highest: for he is kind unto the unthankful and to

[18] The Beatitudes at the beginning of the Sermon on the Mount, as given in the fifth chapter of The Gospel According to St. Matthew, are too familiar and too beautiful to omit:

And seeing the multiudes, he went up into a mountain: and when he was set, his disciples came unto him. And he opened his mouth, and taught them saying,

"Blessed are the poor in spirit: for theirs is the kingdom of heaven.

Blessed are they that mourn: for they shall be comforted.

Blessed are the meek: for they shall inherit the earth.

Blessed are they which do hunger and thirst after righteousness: for they shall be filled.

Blessed are the merciful: for they shall obtain mercy.

Blessed are the pure in heart: for they shall see God.

Blessed are the peacemakers: for they shall be called the children of God.

Blessed are they which are persecuted for righteousness' sake: for theirs is the kingdom of heaven.

Blessed are ye, when men shall revile you, and persecute you, and shall say all manner of evil against you falsely for my sake.

Rejoice, and be exceeding glad: for great is your reward in heaven: for so persecuted they the prophets which were before you."

the evil. Be ye therefore merciful, as your Father also is merciful. Judge not, and ye shall not be judged: condemn not, and ye shall not be condemned: forgive, and ye shall be forgiven. Give, and it shall be given unto you: good measure, pressed down, and shaken together, and running over, shall men give into your bosom: for with the same measure that ye mete withal, it shall be measured to you again."

And he spake a parable unto them, "Can the blind lead the blind? shall they not both fall into the ditch? The disciple is not above his master: but every one that is perfect shall be as his master. And why beholdest thou the mote that is in thy brother's eye, but perceivest not the beam that is in thine own eye? Either how canst thou say to thy brother, 'Brother, let me pull out the mote that is in thine eye,' when thou thyself beholdest not the beam that is in thine own eye? Thou hypocrite, cast out first the beam out of thine own eye, and then shalt thou see clearly to pull out the mote that is in thy brother's eye. For a good tree bringeth not forth corrupt fruit: neither doth a corrupt tree bring forth good fruit. For every tree is known by his own fruit: for of thorns men do not gather figs, nor of a bramble bush gather they grapes. A good man out of the good treasure of his heart bringeth forth that which is good: and an evil man out of the evil treasure of his heart bringeth forth that which is evil: for of the abundance of the heart his mouth speaketh.

"And why call ye me, 'Lord, Lord,' and do not the things which I say? Whosoever cometh to me, and heareth my sayings, and doeth them, I will show you to whom he is like. He is like a man which built an house, and digged deep, and laid the foundation on a rock. And when the flood arose, the stream beat vehemently upon that house, and could not shake it: for it was founded upon a rock. But he that heareth, and doeth not, is like a man that without a foundation built an house upon the earth: against which the stream did beat vehemently, and immediately it fell, and the ruin of that house was great."

7 Now when he had ended all his sayings in the audience of the people, he entered into Capernaum. And a certain centurion's[19] servant, who was dear unto him, was sick and ready to die. And when he heard of Jesus, he sent unto him the elders of the Jews, beseech-

[19] *I.e.*, the commander of 100 soldiers.

ing him that he would come and heal his servant. And when they came to Jesus, they besought him instantly, saying, "That he was worthy for whom he should do this: for he loveth our nation, and he hath built us a synagogue." Then Jesus went with them. And when he was now not far from the house, the centurion sent friends to him, saying unto him, "Lord, trouble not thyself: for I am not worthy that thou shouldest enter under my roof. Wherefore neither thought I myself worthy to come unto thee: but say in a word, and my servant shall be healed. For I also am a man set under authority, having under me soldiers: and I say unto one, 'Go,' and he goeth: and to another, 'Come,' and he cometh: and to my servant, 'Do this,' and he doeth it." When Jesus heard these things, he marvelled at him, and turned him about, and said unto the people that followed him, "I say unto you, I have not found so great faith, no, not in Israel." And they that were sent, returning to the house, found the servant whole that had been sick.

And it came to pass the day after, that he went into a city called Naim: and many of his disciples went with him, and much people. Now when he came nigh to the gate of the city, behold, there was a dead man carried out, the only son of his mother, and she was a widow: and much people of the city was with her. And when the Lord saw her, he had compassion on her, and said unto her, "Weep not." And he came and touched the bier (and they that bare him stood still). And he said, "Young man, I say unto thee, Arise." And he that was dead sat up, and began to speak: and he delivered him to his mother. And there came a fear on all, and they glorified God, saying that a great prophet is risen up among us, and that God hath visited his people. And this rumour of him went forth throughout all Judea, and throughout all the region round about. And the disciples of John showed him of all these things.

And John calling unto him two of his disciples, sent them to Jesus, saying, "Art thou he that should come, or look we for another?" When the men were come unto him, they said, "John Baptist hath sent us unto thee, saying, 'Art thou he that should come, or look we for another?'" And in that same hour he cured many of their infirmities and plagues, and of evil spirits, and unto many that were blind he gave sight. Then Jesus answering, said unto them, "Go your way, and tell John what things ye have seen and heard, how that the blind see, the lame walk, the lepers are cleansed, the deaf hear, the dead are raised, to the poor the gospel is preached. And blessed is he, whosoever shall not be offended in me."

And when the messengers of John were departed, he began to speak unto the people concerning John: "What went ye out into the wilderness for to see? A reed shaken with the wind? But what went ye out for to see? A man clothed in soft raiment? Behold, they, which are gorgeously apparelled, and live delicately, are in kings' courts. But what went ye out for to see? A prophet? Yea, I say unto you, and much more than a prophet. This is he of whom it is written, 'Behold, I send my messenger before thy face, which shall prepare thy way before thee.' For I say unto you, among those that are born of women there is not a greater prophet than John the Baptist: but he that is least in the kingdom of God is greater than he." And all the people that heard him, and the publicans, justified God, being baptized with the baptism of John. But the Pharisees and lawyers rejected the counsel of God against themselves, being not baptized of him.

And the Lord said, "Whereunto then shall I liken the men of this generation? and to what are they like? They are like unto children sitting in the market place, and calling one to another, and saying, 'We have piped unto you, and ye have not danced: we have mourned to you, and ye have not wept.' For John the Baptist came, neither eating bread nor drinking wine, and ye say, 'He hath a devil.' The Son of man is come, eating and drinking, and ye say, 'Behold a gluttonous man, and a winebibber, a friend of publicans and sinners.' But wisdom is justified of all her children."

And one of the Pharisees desired him that he would eat with him. And he went into the Pharisee's house, and sat down to meat. And behold, a woman in the city, which was a sinner, when she knew that Jesus sat at meat in the Pharisee's house, brought an alabaster box of ointment, and stood at his feet behind him, weeping, and began to wash his feet with tears, and did wipe them with the hairs of her head, and kissed his feet, and anointed them with the ointment. Now when the Pharisee which had bidden him saw it, he spake within himself, saying, "This man, if he were a prophet, would have known who and what manner of woman this is that toucheth him: for she is a sinner." And Jesus answering unto him, "Simon, I have somewhat to say unto thee." And he saith, "Master, say on." "There was a certain creditor, which had two debtors: the one owed five hundred pence, and the other fifty. And when they had nothing to pay, he frankly forgave them both. Tell me therefore, which of them will love him most?" Simon answered, and said, "I suppose that he to whom he forgave most." And he said unto him, "Thou hast rightly judged." And he turned to the woman, and said unto Simon, "Seest thou this woman? I entered into thine house, thou gavest me no water for my feet: but she hath washed my feet with tears, and wiped them with the hairs of her head. Thou gavest me no kiss: but this woman, since the time I came in, hath not ceased to kiss my feet. Mine head with oil thou didst not anoint: but this woman hath anointed my feet with ointment. Wherefore I say unto thee, her sins, which are many, are forgiven, for she loved much: but to whom little is forgiven, the same loveth little." And he said unto her, "Thy sins are forgiven." And they that sat at meat with him began to say within themselves, "Who is this that forgiveth sins also?" And he said to the woman, "Thy faith hath saved thee, go in peace."

8 And it came to pass afterward, that he went throughout every city and village, preaching, and showing the glad tidings of the kingdom of God: and the twelve were with him, and certain women which had been healed of evil spirits and infirmities. Mary called Magdalene, out of whom went seven devils, and Joanna the wife of Chuza, Herod's steward, and Susanna, and many others which ministered unto him of their substance.

And when much people were gathered together, and were come to him out of every city, he spake by a parable: "A sower went out to sow his seed: and as he sowed, some fell by the wayside, and it was trodden down, and the fowls of the air devoured it. And some fell upon a rock, and as soon as it was sprung up, it withered away, because it lacked moisture. And some fell among thorns, and the thorns sprang up with it, and choked it. And other fell on good ground, and sprang up, and bare fruit an hundredfold." And when he had said these things, he cried, "He that hath ears to hear, let him hear." And his disciples asked him, saying, "What might this parable be?" And he said, "Unto you it is given to know the mysteries of the kingdom of God: but to others in parables, that seeing, they might not see, and hearing, they might not understand. Now the parable is this: The seed is the word of God. Those by the wayside are they that hear: then cometh the devil, and taketh away the word out of their hearts, lest they should believe, and be saved. They on the rock are they which when they hear, receive the word with joy; and these have no root, which for a while believe, and in time of temptation fall away. And that which fell among thorns are they, which when they have heard, go forth, and are choked with cares and riches, and pleasures of this life, and bring no fruit to perfection. But that on the good ground are they, which in an honest and good heart having heard the word, keep it, and bring forth fruit with patience.

"No man when he hath lighted a candle, covereth it with a vessel, or putteth it under a bed: but setteth it on a candlestick, that they which enter in may see the light. For nothing is secret, that shall not be made manifest; neither any thing hid, that shall not be known and come abroad. Take heed therefore how ye hear: for whosoever hath, to him shall be given; and whosoever hath not, from him shall be taken, even that which he seemeth to have."

Then came to him his mother and his brethren, and could not come at him for the press. And it was told him by certain which said, "Thy mother and thy brethren stand without, desiring to see thee." And he answered and said unto them, "My mother and my brethren are these which hear the word of God, and do it."

Now it came to pass on a certain day, that he went into a ship, with his disciples: and he said unto them, "Let us go over unto the other side of the lake," and they launched forth. But as they sailed, he fell asleep, and there came down a storm of wind on the lake, and they were filled with water, and were in jeopardy. And they came to him, and awoke him, saying, "Master, master, we perish." Then he arose, and rebuked the wind, and the raging of the water: and they ceased, and there was a calm. And he said unto them, "Where is your faith?" And they being afraid wondered, saying one to another, "What manner of man is this? For he commandeth even the winds and water, and they obey him."

And they arrived at the country of the Gadarenes, which is over against Galilee. And when he went forth to land, there met him out of the city a certain man which had devils long time, and ware no clothes, neither abode in any house, but in the tombs. When he saw Jesus, he cried out, and fell down before him, and with a loud voice said, "What have I to do with thee, Jesus, thou Son of God most high? I beseech thee torment me not." (For he had commanded the unclean spirit to come out of the man. For oftentimes it had caught him, and he was kept bound with chains and in fetters: and he brake the bands, and was driven of the devil into the wilderness.) And Jesus asked him, saying, "What is thy name?" And he said, "Legion": because many devils were entered into him. And they besought him that he would not command them to go out into the deep. And there was there an herd of many swine feeding on the mountain: and they besought him that he would suffer them to enter into them: and he suffered them. Then went the devils out of the man, and entered into the swine: and the herd ran violently down a steep place into the lake, and were choked. When they that fed them saw what was done, they fled, and went, and told it in the city and in the country. Then they went out to see what was done, and came to Jesus, and found the man, out of whom the devils were departed, sitting at the feet of Jesus, clothed, and in his right mind: and they were afraid. They also which saw it told them by what means he that was possessed of the devils was healed.

Then the whole multitude of the country of the Gadarenes round about besought him to depart from them, for they were taken with great fear: and he went up into the ship, and returned back again. Now the man, out of whom the devils were departed, besought him that he might be with him: but Jesus sent him away, saying, "Return to thine own house, and show how great things God hath done unto thee." And he went his way, and published throughout the whole city how great things Jesus had done unto him. And it came to pass, that when Jesus was returned, the people gladly received him: for they were all waiting for him.

And behold, there came a man named Jairus, and he was a ruler of the synagogue, and he fell down at Jesus' feet, and besought him that he would come into his house: for he had one only daughter, about twelve years of age, and she lay dying.

(But as he went the people thronged him. And a woman having an issue of blood twelve years, which had spent all her living upon physicians, neither could be healed of any, came behind him, and touched the border of his garment: and immediately her issue of blood stanched. And Jesus said, "Who touched me?" When all denied, Peter and they that were with him said, "Master, the multitude throng thee, and press thee, and sayest thou, 'Who touched me?'" And Jesus said, "Somebody hath touched me: for I perceive that virtue is gone out of me." And when the woman saw that she was not hid, she came trembling, and falling down before him, she declared unto him before all the people for what cause she had touched him, and how she was healed immediately. And he said unto her, "Daughter, be of good comfort, thy faith hath made thee whole, go in peace.")

While he yet spake, there cometh one from the ruler of the synagogue's house, saying to him, "Thy daughter is dead, trouble not the Master." But when Jesus heard it, he answered him, saying, "Fear not, believe only, and she shall be made whole." And when he came into the house, he suffered no man to go in, save Peter, and James, and John, and the father and the mother of the maiden. And all wept, and bewailed her: but he said, "Weep not, she is not dead, but sleepeth." And they laughed him to scorn, knowing that she was dead. And he put them all out, and took her by the hand, and called, saying, "Maid, arise." And her spirit came again, and she arose straightway: and he commanded to give her meat. And her parents were astonished: but he charged them that they should tell no man what was done.

9 Then he called his twelve disciples together, and gave them power and authority over all devils, and to cure diseases. And he sent them to preach the kingdom of God, and to heal the sick. And he said unto them, "Take nothing for your journey, neither staves, nor scrip,[20] neither bread, neither money, neither have two coats apiece. And whatsoever house ye enter into, there abide, and thence depart. And whosoever will not receive you, when ye go out of that city, shake off the very dust from your feet, for a testimony against them." And they departed, and went through the towns, preaching the gospel, and healing everywhere.

Now Herod the tetrarch heard of all that was done by him: and he was perplexed, because that it was said of some, that John was risen from the dead: and of some, that Elias had appeared: and of others, that one of the old prophets was risen again. And Herod said, "John have I beheaded: but who is this of whom I hear such things?" And he desired to see him.

And the apostles, when they were returned, told him all that they had done. And he took them, and went aside privately into a desert

20 *I.e.*, a bag or knapsack.

place, belonging to the city called Bethsaida. And the people, when they knew it, followed him, and he received them, and spake unto them of the kingdom of God, and healed them that had need of healing. And when the day began to wear away, then came the twelve, and said unto him, "Send the multitude away, that they may go into the towns and country round about, and lodge, and get victuals: for we are here in a desert place." But he said unto them, "Give ye them to eat." And they said, "We have no more but five loaves and two fishes, except we should go and buy meat for all this people." For they were about five thousand men. And he said to his disciples, "Make them set down by fifties in a company." And they did so, and made them all sit down. Then he took the five loaves and the two fishes, and looking up to heaven, he blessed them, and brake, and gave to the disciples to set before the multitude. And they did eat, and were all filled. And there was taken up of fragments that remained to them, twelve baskets.

And it came to pass, as he was alone praying, his disciples were with him: and he asked them, saying, "Whom say the people that I am?" They answering, said, "John the Baptist: but some say, Elias: and others say, that one of the old prophets is risen again." He said unto them, "But whom say ye that I am?" Peter answering, said, "The Christ of God." And he straitly charged them, and commanded them to tell no man that thing, saying, "The Son of man must suffer many things, and be rejected of the elders, and chief priests, and scribes, and be slain, and be raised the third day."

And he said to them all, "If any man will come after me, let him deny himself, and take up his cross daily, and follow me. For whosoever will save his life, shall lose it: but whosoever will lose his life for my sake, the same shall save it. For what is a man advantaged, if he gain the whole world, and lose himself, or be cast away? For whosoever shall be ashamed of me, and of my words, of him shall the Son of man be ashamed, when he shall come in his own glory, and in his Father's, and of the holy angels. But I tell you of a truth, there be some standing here, which shall not taste of death, till they see the kingdom of God."

And it came to pass, about an eight days after these sayings, he took Peter, and John, and James, and went up into a mountain to pray: and as he prayed, the fashion of his countenance was altered, and his raiment was white and glistering. And behold, there talked with him two men, which were Moses and Elias, who appeared in glory, and spake of his decease, which he should accomplish at Jerusalem. But Peter, and they that were with him, were heavy with sleep: and when they were awake, they saw his glory, and the two men that stood with him. And it came to pass, as they departed from him, Peter said unto Jesus, "Master, it is good for us to be here, and let us make three tabernacles, one for thee, and one for Moses, and one for Elias": not knowing what he said. While he thus spake, there came a cloud, and overshadowed them, and they feared, as they entered into the cloud. And there came a voice out of the cloud, saying, "This is my beloved Son, hear him." And when the voice was past, Jesus was found alone, and they kept it close, and told no man in those days any of these things which they had seen.

And it came to pass, that on the next day, when they were come down from the hill, much people met him. And behold, a man of the company cried out, saying, "Master, I beseech thee look upon my son, for he is mine only child. And lo, a spirit taketh him, and he suddenly crieth out, and it teareth him that he foameth again, and bruising him, hardly departeth from him. And I besought thy disciples to cast him out, and they could not." And Jesus answering, said, "O faithless and perverse generation, how long shall I be with you, and suffer you? Bring thy son hither." And as he was yet a coming, the devil threw him down, and tare him: and Jesus rebuked the unclean spirit, and healed the child, and delivered him again to his father.

And they were all amazed at the mighty power of God: but while they wondered every one at all things which Jesus did, he said unto his disciples, "Let these sayings sink down into your ears: for the Son of man shall be delivered into the hands of men." But they understood not this saying, and it was hid from them, that they perceived it not: and they feared to ask him of that saying.

Then there arose a reasoning among them, which of them should be greatest. And Jesus, perceiving the thought of their heart, took a child, and set him by him, and said unto them, "Whosoever shall receive this child in my name, receiveth me: and whosoever shall receive me, receiveth him that sent me: for he that is least among you all, the same shall be great."

And John answered, and said, "Master, we saw one casting out devils in thy name, and we forbade him, because he followeth not with us." And Jesus said unto him, "Forbid him not: for he that is not against us is for us."

And it came to pass, when the time was come that he should be received up, he steadfastly set his face to go to Jerusalem, and sent messengers before his face, and they went and entered into a village of the Samaritans[21] to make ready for him. And they did not receive him, because his face was as though he would go to Jerusalem. And when his disciples James and John saw this, they said, "Lord, wilt thou that we command fire to come down from heaven, and consume them, even as Elias did?" But he turned, and rebuked them, and said, "Ye know not what manner of spirit ye are of. For the Son of man is not come to destroy men's lives, but to save them." And they went to another village.

And it came to pass that as they went in the way, a certain man said unto him, "Lord, I will follow thee whithersoever thou goest." And Jesus said unto him, "Foxes have holes, and birds of the air have nests, but the Son of man hath not where to lay his head." And he said unto another, "Follow me." But he said, "Lord, suffer me first to go and bury my father." Jesus said unto him, "Let the dead bury their dead: but go thou and preach the kingdom of God." And another also said, "Lord, I will follow thee: but let me first go bid them farewell, which are at home at my house." And Jesus said unto him, "No man having put his hand to the plough, and looking back, is fit for the kingdom of God."

10 After these things, the Lord appointed other seventy also, and sent them two and two before his face, into every city and place, whither he himself would come. Therefore said he unto them, "The harvest truly is great, but the labourers are few; pray ye therefore the Lord of the harvest, that he would send forth labourers into his harvest. Go your ways: behold, I send you forth as lambs among wolves. Carry neither purse nor scrip, nor shoes, and salute no man by the way. And into whatsoever house ye enter, first say, 'Peace be to this house.' And if the son of peace be there, your peace shall rest upon it: if not, it shall turn to you again. And in the same house remain, eating and drinking such things as they give: for the labourer is worthy of his hire. Go not from house to house. And into

[21] At this time there was much ill feeling between the Samaritans and the orthodox Jews.

whatsoever city ye enter, and they receive you, eat such things as are set before you: and heal the sick that are therein, and say unto them, 'The kingdom of God is come nigh unto you.' But into whatsoever city ye enter, and they receive you not, go your ways out into the streets of the same, and say, 'Even the very dust of your city which cleaveth on us, we do wipe off against you: notwithstanding, be ye sure of this, that the kingdom of God is come nigh unto you.' But I say unto you, that it shall be more tolerable in that day for Sodom, than for that city. Woe unto thee Chorazin, woe unto thee Bethsaida: for if the mighty works had been done in Tyre and Sidon, which have been done in you, they had a great while ago repented, sitting in sackcloth and ashes. But it shall be more tolerable for Tyre and Sidon at the judgment, than for you. And thou Capernaum, which art exalted to heaven, shalt be thrust down to hell. He that heareth you, heareth me: and he that despiseth you, despiseth me: and he that despiseth me, despiseth him that sent me."

And the seventy returned again with joy, saying, "Lord, even the devils are subject unto us through thy name." And he said unto them, "I beheld Satan as lightning fall from heaven. Behold, I give unto you power to tread on serpents and scorpions, and over all the power of the enemy: and nothing shall by any means hurt you. Notwithstanding, in this rejoice not, that the spirits are subject unto you: but rather rejoice, because your names are written in heaven."

In that hour Jesus rejoiced in spirit, and said, "I thank thee, O Father, Lord of heaven and earth, that thou hast hid these things from the wise and prudent, and hast revealed them unto babes: even so, Father, for so it seemed good in thy sight. All things are delivered to me of my Father: and no man knoweth who the Son is, but the Father: and who the Father is, but the Son, and he to whom the Son will reveal him."

And he turned him unto his disciples, and said privately, "Blessed are the eyes which see the things that ye see. For I tell you, that many prophets and kings have desired to see those things which ye see, and have not seen them: and to hear those things which ye hear, and have not heard them."

And behold, a certain lawyer stood up, and tempted him, saying, "Master, what shall I do to inherit eternal life?" He said unto him, "What is written in the law? how readest thou?" And he answering, said, "Thou shalt love the Lord thy God with all thy heart, and with all thy soul, and with all thy strength, and with all thy mind, and thy neighbour as thyself." And he said unto him, "Thou hast answered right: this do, and thou shalt live." But he willing to justify himself, said unto Jesus, "And who is my neighbour?" And Jesus answering, said, "A certain man went down from Jerusalem to Jericho, and fell among thieves, which stripped him of his raiment, and wounded him, and departed, leaving him half dead. And by chance there came down a certain priest that way, and when he saw him, he passed by on the other side. And likewise a Levite,[22] when he was at the place, came and looked on him, and passed by on the other side. But a certain Samaritan, as he journeyed, came where he was; and when he saw him, he had compassion on him, and went to him, and bound up his wounds, pouring in oil and wine, and set him on his own beast, and brought him to an inn, and took care of him. And on the morrow when he departed, he took out two pence, and gave them to the host, and said unto him, 'Take care of him, and whatsoever thou spendest more, when I come again I will repay thee.' Which now of these three, thinkest thou, was neighbour unto him that fell among the thieves?" And he said, "He that showed mercy on him." Then said Jesus unto him, "Go, and do thou likewise."

Now it came to pass, as they went, that he entered into a certain village: and a certain woman named Martha received him into her house. And she had a sister called Mary, which also sat at Jesus' feet, and heard his word: but Martha was cumbered about[23] much serving, and came to him, and said, "Lord, dost thou not care that my sister hath left me to serve alone? Bid her therefore that she help me." And Jesus answered, and said unto her, "Martha, Martha, thou art careful,[24] and troubled about many things: but one thing is needful, and Mary hath chosen that good part, which shall not be taken away from her."

11   And it came to pass, that as he was praying in a certain place, when he ceased, one of his disciples said unto him, "Lord, teach us to pray, as John also taught his disciples." And he said unto them, "When ye pray, say, 'Our Father which art in heaven, hal-

[22] *I.e.,* a priest.
[23] *I.e.,* distracted by.
[24] *I.e.,* anxious.

lowed be thy name, thy kingdom come, thy will be done, as in heaven, so in earth. Give us day by day our daily bread. And forgive us our sins: for we also forgive every one that is indebted to us. And lead us not into temptation, but deliver us from evil.' " And he said unto them, "Which of you shall have a friend, and shall go unto him at midnight, and say unto him, 'Friend, lend me three loaves. For a friend of mine in his journey is come to me, and I have nothing to set before him'? And he from within shall answer and say, 'Trouble me not, the door is now shut, and my children are with me in bed: I cannot rise and give thee.' I say unto you, though he will not rise, and give him, because he is his friend: yet because of his importunity, he will rise and give him as many as he needeth. And I say unto you, ask, and it shall be given you: seek, and ye shall find: knock, and it shall be opened unto you. For every one that asketh, receiveth: and he that seeketh, findeth: and to him that knocketh, it shall be opened. If a son shall ask bread of any of you that is a father, will he give him a stone? Or if he ask a fish, will he for a fish give him a serpent? Or if he shall ask an egg, will he offer him a scorpion? If ye then being evil, know how to give good gifts unto your children: how much more shall your heavenly Father give the holy Spirit to them that ask him?"

And he was casting out a devil, and it was dumb. And it came to pass, when the devil was gone out, the dumb spake: and the people wondered. But some of them said, "He casteth out devils through Beelzebub the chief of the devils." And others, tempting him, sought of him a sign from heaven. But he knowing their thoughts, said unto them, "Every kingdom divided against itself is brought to desolation: and a house divided against a house falleth. If Satan also be divided against himself, how shall his kingdom stand? Because ye say that I cast out devils through Beelzebub. And if I by Beelzebub cast out devils, by whom do your sons cast them out? therefore shall they be your judges. But if I with the finger of God cast out devils, no doubt the kingdom of God is come upon you. When a strong man armed keepeth his palace, his goods are in peace: but when a stronger than he shall come upon him, and overcome him, he taketh from him all his armour wherein he trusted, and divideth his spoils. He that is not with me, is against me: and he that gathereth not with me, scattereth. When the unclean spirit is gone out of a man, he walketh through dry places, seeking rest: and finding none, he saith, 'I will return unto my house whence I came out.' And when he cometh, he findeth it swept and garnished. Then goeth he, and taketh to him seven other spirits more wicked than himself, and they enter in, and dwell there, and the last state of that man is worse than the first."

And it came to pass as he spake these things, a certain woman of the company lifted up her voice, and said unto him, "Blessed is the womb that bare thee, and the paps which thou hast sucked." But he said, "Yea, rather blessed are they that hear the word of God, and keep it."

And when the people were gathered thick together, he began to say, "This is an evil generation, they seek a sign, and there shall no sign be given it, but the sign of Jonas[25] the prophet: for as Jonas was a sign unto the Ninevites, so shall also the Son of man be to this generation. The queen of the south shall rise up in the judgment with the men of this generation, and condemn them: for she came from the utmost parts of the earth to hear the wisdom of Solomon: and behold, a greater than Solomon is here. The men of Nineveh shall rise up in the judgment with this generation, and shall condemn it: for they repented at the preaching of Jonas, and behold, a greater than Jonas is here. No man when he hath lighted a candle, putteth it in a secret place, neither under a bushel, but on a candlestick, that they which come in may see the light. The light of the body is the eye: therefore when thine eye is single, thy whole body also is full of light: but when thine eye is evil, thy body also is full of darkness. Take heed therefore that the light which is in thee be not darkness. If thy whole body therefore be full of light, having no part dark, the whole shall be full of light, as when the bright shining of a candle doth give thee light."

And as he spake, a certain Pharisee besought him to dine with him: and he went in, and sat down to meat. And when the Pharisee saw it, he marvelled that he had not first washed before dinner. And the Lord said unto him, "Now do ye Pharisees make clean the outside of the cup and the platter: but your inward part is full of ravening and wickedness. Ye fools, did not he that made that which is without, make that which is within also? But rather give alms of such things as you have: and behold, all things are clean unto you. But woe unto you Pharisees: for ye tithe mint and rue, and all

[25] I.e., Jonah.

manner of herbs, and pass over judgment, and the love of God: these ought ye to have done, and not to leave the other undone. Woe unto you Pharisees: for ye love the uppermost seats in the synagogues, and greetings in the markets. Woe unto you scribes and Pharisees, hypocrites: for ye are as graves which appear not, and the men that walk over them are not aware of them."

Then answered one of the lawyers, and said unto him, "Master, thus saying, thou reproachest us also." And he said, "Woe unto you also, ye lawyers: for ye lade men with burdens grievous to be borne, and ye yourselves touch not the burdens with one of your fingers. Woe unto you: for ye build the sepulchres of the prophets, and your fathers killed them. Truly ye bear witness that ye allow the deeds of your fathers: for they indeed killed them, and ye build their sepulchres. Therefore also said the wisdom of God, 'I will send them prophets and apostles, and some of them they shall slay and persecute': that the blood of all the prophets, which was shed from the foundation of the world, may be required of this generation, from the blood of Abel unto the blood of Zacharias,[26] which perished between the altar and the temple: verily I say unto you, it shall be required of this generation. Woe unto you lawyers: for ye have taken away the key of knowledge: ye entered not in yourselves, and them that were entering in, ye hindered." And as he said these things unto them, the scribes and the Pharisees began to urge him vehemently, and to provoke him to speak of many things: laying wait for him, and seeking to catch something out of his mouth, that they might accuse him.

12 In the meantime, when there were gathered together an innumerable multitude of people, insomuch that they trod one upon another, he began to say unto his disciples first of all, "Beware ye of the leaven of the Pharisees, which is hypocrisy. For there is nothing covered, that shall not be revealed, neither hid, that shall not be known. Therefore, whatsoever ye have spoken in darkness shall be heard in the light: and that which ye have spoken in the ear, in closets, shall be proclaimed upon the housetops. And I say unto you my friends, be not afraid of them that kill the body, and after that have no more that they can do. But I will forewarn you

[26] Not the father of John the Baptist, but possibly a Jew murdered during the siege of Jerusalem in 68 A.D.

whom you shall fear: fear him, which after he hath killed, hath power to cast into hell: yea, I say unto you, fear him. Are not five sparrows sold for two farthings, and not one of them is forgotten before God? But even the very hairs of your head are all numbered: fear not therefore, ye are of more value than many sparrows. Also I say unto you, whosoever shall confess me before men, him shall the Son of man also confess before the angels of God. But he that denieth me before men shall be denied before the angels of God. And whosoever shall speak a word against the Son of man, it shall be forgiven him: but unto him that blasphemeth against the Holy Ghost, it shall not be forgiven. And when they bring you unto the synagogues, and unto magistrates, and powers, take ye no thought how or what thing ye shall answer, or what ye shall say: for the Holy Ghost shall teach you in the same hour what ye ought to say."

And one of the company said unto him, "Master, speak to my brother, that he divide the inheritance with me." And he said unto him, "Man, who made me a judge, or a divider over you?" And he said unto them, "Take heed and beware of covetousness: for a man's life consisteth not in the abundance of the things which he possesseth." And he spake a parable unto them, saying, "The ground of a certain rich man brought forth plentifully. And he thought within himself, saying, 'What shall I do, because I have no room where to bestow my fruits?' And he said, 'This will I do, I will pull down my barns, and build greater, and there will I bestow all my fruits, and my goods. And I will say to my soul, "Soul, thou hast much goods laid up for many years, take thine ease, eat, drink, and be merry."' But God said unto him, 'Thou fool, this night thy soul shall be required of thee: then whose shall those things be, which thou hast provided?' So is he that layeth up treasure for himself, and is not rich toward God."

And he said unto his disciples, "Therefore I say unto you, take no thought for your life, what ye shall eat, neither for the body what ye shall put on. The life is more than meat, and the body is more than raiment. Consider the ravens, for they neither sow nor reap, which neither have storehouse nor barn, and God feedeth them: how much more are ye better than the fowls? And which of you with taking thought can add to his stature one cubit? If ye then be not able to do that thing which is least, why take ye thought for the rest? Consider the lilies how they grow, they toil not; they spin not: and yet I say unto you, that Solomon in all his glory was not arrayed like one of these. If then God so clothe the grass, which is today in the field, and tomorrow is cast into the oven: how much more will he clothe you, O ye of little faith? And seek not ye what ye shall eat, or what ye shall drink, neither be ye of doubtful mind. For all these things do the nations of the world seek after: and your Father knoweth that ye have need of these things.

"But rather seek ye the kingdom of God, and all these things shall be added unto you. Fear not, little flock, for it is your Father's good pleasure to give you the kingdom. Sell that ye have, and give alms: provide yourselves bags which wax not old, a treasure in the heavens that faileth not, where no thief approacheth, neither moth corrupteth. For where your treasure is, there will your heart be also. Let your loins be girded about, and your lights burning, and ye yourselves like unto men that wait for their lord, when he will return from the wedding, that when he cometh and knocketh, they may open unto him immediately. Blessed are those servants, whom the lord when he cometh shall find watching: verily, I say unto you, that he shall gird himself, and make them to sit down to meat, and will come forth and serve them. And if he shall come in the second watch, or come in the third watch, and find them so, blessed are those servants. And this know, that if the good man of the house had known what hour the thief would come, he would have watched, and not have suffered his house to be broken through. Be ye therefore ready also: for the Son of man cometh at an hour when ye think not."

Then Peter said unto him, "Lord, speakest thou this parable unto us, or even to all?" And the Lord said, "Who then is that faithful and wise steward, whom his lord shall make ruler over his household, to give them their portion of meat in due season? Blessed is that servant, whom his lord when he cometh shall find so doing. Of a truth, I say unto you, that he will make him ruler over all that he hath. But and if that servant say in his heart, 'My lord delayeth his coming': and shall begin to beat the menservants, and maidens, and to eat and drink, and to be drunken: the lord of that servant will come in a day when he looketh not for him, and at an hour when he is not aware, and will cut him in sunder, and will appoint him his portion with the unbelievers. And that servant, which knew his lord's will, and prepared not himself, neither did according to his will, shall be beaten with many stripes. But he that knew not, and did commit things worthy of stripes, shall be beaten with few stripes. For unto whomsoever much is given, of him shall be much required: and to whom men have committed much, of him they will ask the more.

"I am come to send fire on the earth, and what will I, if it be already kindled? But I have a baptism to be baptized with, and how am I straitened till it be accomplished? Suppose ye that I am come to give peace on earth? I tell you, Nay, but rather division. For from henceforth there shall be five in one house divided, three against two, and two against three. The father shall be divided against the son, and the son against the father: the mother against the daughter, and the daughter against the mother: the mother in law against her daughter in law, and the daughter in law against her mother in law."

And he said also to the people, "When ye see a cloud rise out of the west, straightway ye say, 'There cometh a shower,' and so it is. And when ye see the south wind blow, ye say, 'There will be heat,' and it cometh to pass. Ye hypocrites, ye can discern the face of the sky, and of the earth: but how is it that ye do not discern this time? Yea, and why even of yourselves judge ye not what is right?

"When thou goest with thine adversary to the magistrate, as thou art in the way, give diligence that thou mayest be delivered from him, lest he hale thee to the judge, and the judge deliver thee to the officer, and the officer cast thee into prison. I tell thee, thou shalt not depart thence, till thou hast paid the very last mite."

13 There were present at that season some that told him of the Galileans, whose blood Pilate had mingled with their sacrifices. And Jesus answering, said unto them, "Suppose ye that these Galileans were sinners above all the Galileans, because they suffered such things? I tell you, Nay: but, except ye repent, ye shall all likewise perish. Or those eighteen, upon whom the tower in Siloam fell, and slew them, think ye that they were sinners above all men that dwelt in Jerusalem? I tell you, Nay: but, except ye repent, ye shall all likewise perish."

He spake also this parable, "A certain man had a fig tree planted in his vineyard, and he came and sought fruit thereon, and found none. Then said he unto the dresser of his vineyard, 'Behold, these three years I come seeking fruit on this fig tree, and find none: cut it down, why cumbereth it the ground?' And he answering, said unto him, 'Lord, let it alone this year also, till I shall dig about it, and dung it: and if it bear fruit, well: and if not, then after that thou shalt cut it down.' " And he was teaching in one of the synagogues on the sabbath.

And behold, there was a woman which had a spirit of infirmity eighteen years, and was bowed together, and could in no wise lift up herself. And when Jesus saw her, he called her to him, and said unto her, "Woman, thou art loosed from thine infirmity." And he laid his hands on her, and immediately she was made straight, and glorified God. And the ruler of the synagogue answered with indignation, because that Jesus had healed on the sabbath day, and said unto the people, "There are six days in which men ought to work: in them therefore come and be healed, and not on the sabbath day." The Lord then answered him, and said, "Thou hypocrite, doth not each one of you on the sabbath loose his ox or his ass from the stall, and lead him away to watering? And ought not this woman, being a daughter of Abraham, whom Satan hath bound, lo these eighteen years, be loosed from this bond on the sabbath day?" And when he had said these things, all his adversaries were ashamed: and all the people rejoiced for all the glorious things that were done by him.

Then said he, "Unto what is the kingdom of God like? and whereunto shall I resemble it? It is like a grain of mustard seed, which a man took, and cast into his garden, and it grew, and waxed a great tree: and the fowls of the air lodged in the branches of it." And again he said, "Whereunto shall I liken the kingdom of God? It is like leaven, which a woman took and hid in three measures of meal, till the whole was leavened." And he went through the cities and villages, teaching and journeying toward Jerusalem. Then said one unto him, "Lord, are there few that be saved?" And he said unto them, "Strive to enter in at the strait gate: for many, I say unto you, will seek to enter in, and shall not be able. When once the master of the house is risen up, and hath shut to the door, and ye begin to stand without, and to knock at the door, saying, 'Lord, Lord, open unto us,' and he shall answer, and say unto you, 'I know you not whence you are': then shall ye begin to say, 'We have eaten and drunk in thy presence, and thou hast taught in our streets.' But he shall say, 'I tell you, I know you not whence you are; depart from me all ye workers of iniquity.' There shall be weeping and gnashing of teeth, when ye shall see Abraham, and Isaac, and Jacob, and all the prophets in the kingdom of God, and you yourselves thrust out. And they shall come from the east, and from the west, and from the north, and from the south, and shall sit down in the kingdom of God. And behold, there are last, which shall be first; and there are first, which shall be last."

The same day there came certain of the Pharisees, saying unto him, "Get thee out, and depart hence; for Herod will kill thee." And he said unto them, "Go ye and tell that fox, 'Behold, I cast out devils, and I do cures today and tomorrow, and the third day I shall be perfected. Nevertheless, I must walk today and tomorrow, and the day following: for it cannot be that a prophet perish out of Jerusalem.' O Jerusalem, Jerusalem, which killest the prophets, and stonest them that are sent unto thee; how often would I have gathered thy children together, as a hen doth gather her brood under her wings, and ye would not? Behold, your house is left unto you desolate. And verily I say unto you, ye shall not see me, until the time come when ye shall say, 'Blessed is he that cometh in the name of the Lord.' "

14 And it came to pass, as he went into the house of one of the chief Pharisees to eat bread on the sabbath day, that they watched him. And behold, there was a certain man before him, which had the dropsy. And Jesus answering, spake unto the lawyers and Pharisees, saying, "Is it lawful to heal on the sabbath day?" And they held their peace. And he took him, and healed him, and let him go, and answered them, saying, "Which of you shall have an ass or an ox fallen into a pit, and will not straightway pull him out on the sabbath day?" And they could not answer him again to these things.

And he put forth a parable to those which were bidden, when he marked how they chose out the chief rooms, saying unto them, "When thou art bidden of any man to a wedding, sit not down in the highest room: lest a more honourable man than thou be bidden of him, and he that bade thee and him come and say to thee, 'Give this man place': and thou begin with shame to take the lowest room. But when thou art bidden, go and sit down in the lowest room, that when he that bade thee cometh, he may say unto thee, 'Friend, go up higher': then shalt thou have worship in the presence of them that sit at meat with thee. For whosoever exalteth himself shall be abased: and he that humbleth himself shall be exalted."

Then said he also to him that bade him, "When thou makest a dinner or a supper, call not thy friends, nor thy brethren, neither thy kinsmen, nor thy rich neighbours, lest they also bid thee again, and a recompense be made thee. But when thou makest a feast, call the poor, the maimed, the lame, the blind, and thou shalt be blessed, for they cannot recompense thee: for thou shalt be recompensed at the resurrection of the just."

And when one of them that sat at meat with him heard these things, he said unto him, "Blessed is he that shall eat bread in the kingdom of God." Then said he unto him, "A certain man made a great supper, and bade many: and sent his servant at supper time to say to them that were bidden, 'Come, for all things are now ready.' And they all with one consent began to make excuse: the first said unto him, 'I have bought a piece of ground, and I must needs go and see it: I pray thee have me excused.' And another said, 'I have bought five yoke of oxen, and I go to prove them: I pray thee have me excused.' And another said, 'I have married a wife: and therefore I cannot come.' So that servant came, and showed his lord these things. Then the master of the house being angry said to his servant, 'Go out quickly into the streets and lanes of the city, and bring in hither the poor, and the maimed, and the halt, and the blind.' And the servant said, 'Lord, it is done as thou hast commanded, and yet there is room.' And the lord said unto the servant, 'Go out into the highways and hedges, and compel them to come in, that my house may be filled. For I say unto you, that none of those men which were bidden shall taste of my supper.' "

And there went great multitudes with him: and he turned, and said unto them, "If any man come to me, and hate not his father, and mother, and wife, and children, and brethren, and sisters, yea and his own life also, he cannot be my disciple. And whosoever doth not bear his cross, and come after me, cannot be my disciple. For which of you intending to build a tower, sitteth not down first, and counteth the cost, whether he have sufficient to finish it? Lest haply after he hath laid the foundation, and is not able to finish it, all that behold it begin to mock him, saying, 'This man began to build, and was not able to finish.' Or what king going to make war against another king, sitteth not down first, and consulteth whether he be able with ten thousand to meet him that cometh against him with twenty thousand? Or else, while the other is yet a great way off, he sendeth an ambassage, and desireth conditions of peace. So likewise, whosoever he be of you that forsaketh not all that he hath, he cannot be my disciple.

"Salt is good: but if the salt have lost his savour, wherewith shall it be seasoned? It is neither fit for the land, nor yet for the dunghill: but men cast it out. He that hath ears to hear, let him hear."

15 Then drew near unto him all the publicans and sinners, for to hear him. And the Pharisees and scribes murmured, saying, "This man receiveth sinners, and eateth with them."

And he spake this parable unto them, saying, "What man of you having an hundred sheep, if he lose one of them, doth not leave the ninety and nine in the wilderness, and go after that which is lost, until he find it? And when he hath found it, he layeth it on his shoulders, rejoicing. And when he cometh home, he calleth together his friends and neighbours, saying unto them, 'Rejoice with me, for I have found my sheep which was lost.' I say unto you, that likewise joy shall be in heaven over one sinner that repenteth, more than over ninety and nine just persons, which need no repentance.

"Either what woman having ten pieces of silver, if she lose one piece, doth not light a candle, and sweep the house, and seek diligently till she find it? And when she hath found it, she calleth her friends and her neighbours together, saying, 'Rejoice with me, for I have found the piece which I had lost.' Likewise, I say unto you, there is joy in the presence of the angels of God over one sinner that repenteth."

And he said, "A certain man had two sons: and the younger of them said to his father, 'Father, give me the portion of goods that falleth to me.' And he divided unto them his living. And not many days after, the younger son gathered all together, and took his journey into a far country, and there wasted his substance with riotous living. And when he had spent all, there arose a mighty famine in that land, and he began to be in want. And he went and joined himself to a citizen of that country, and he sent him into his fields to feed swine. And he would fain have filled his belly with the husks that the swine did eat: and no man gave unto him. And when he came to himself, he said, 'How many hired servants of my father's have bread enough and to spare, and I perish with hunger? I will arise and go to my father, and will say unto him, "Father, I have sinned against heaven, and before thee. And am no more worthy to be called thy son: make me as one of thy hired servants."' And he arose, and came to his father. But when he was yet a great way off, his father saw him, and had compassion, and ran, and fell on his neck, and kissed him. And the son said unto him, 'Father, I have sinned against heaven, and in thy sight, and am no more worthy to be called thy son.' But the father said to his servants, 'Bring forth the best robe, and put it on him, and put a ring on his hand, and shoes on his feet. And bring hither the fatted calf, and kill it, and let us eat, and be merry. For this my son was dead, and is alive again; he was lost, and is found.' And they began to be merry. Now his elder son was in the field, and as he came and drew nigh to the house, he heard music and dancing. And he called one of the servants, and asked what these things meant. And he said unto him, 'Thy brother is come, and thy father hath killed the fatted calf, because he hath received him safe and sound.' And he was angry, and would not go in: therefore came his father out, and entreated him. And he answering said to his father, 'Lo, these many years do I serve thee, neither transgressed I at any time thy commandment, and yet thou never gavest me a kid, that I might make merry with my friends: but as soon as this thy son was come, which hath devoured thy living with harlots, thou hast killed for him the fatted calf.' And he said unto him, 'Son, thou art ever with me, and all that I have is thine. It was meet that we should make merry, and be glad: for this thy brother was dead, and is alive again: and was lost, and is found.' "

16 And he said also unto his disciples, "There was a certain rich man which had a steward, and the same was accused unto him that he had wasted his goods. And he called him, and said unto him, 'How is it that I hear this of thee? Give an account of thy stewardship: for thou mayest be no longer steward.' Then the steward said within himself, 'What shall I do, for my lord taketh away from me the stewardship? I cannot dig; to beg I am ashamed. I am resolved what to do, that when I am put out of the stewardship, they may receive me into their houses.' So he called every one of his lord's debtors unto him, and said unto the first, 'How much owest thou unto my lord?' And he said, 'An hundred measures of oil.' And he said unto him, 'Take thy bill, and sit down quickly, and write fifty.' Then said he to another, 'And how much owest thou?' And he said, 'An hundred measures of wheat.' And he said unto him, 'Take thy bill and write fourscore.' And the lord commended the unjust steward, because he had done wisely: for the children of this world are in their generation wiser than the children of light. And I say unto you, make to yourselves friends of the mammon of unrighteousness, that when ye fail, they may receive you into everlasting habitations. He that is faithful in that which is least, is faithful also in much: and he that is unjust in the least, is unjust also in much. If therefore ye have not been faithful in the unrighteous mammon, who will commit to your trust the true riches? And if ye have not been faithful in that which is another man's, who shall give you that which is your own?

"No servant can serve two masters, for either he will hate the one, and love the other: or else he will hold to the one, and despise the other: ye cannot serve God and mammon." And the Pharisees also, who were covetous, heard all these things: and they derided him. And he said unto them, "Ye are they which justify yourselves before men, but God knoweth your hearts: for that which is highly esteemed among men is abomination in the sight of God. The law and the prophets were until John: since that time the kingdom of God is preached, and every man presseth into it. And it is easier for heaven and earth to pass, than one tittle[27] of the law to fail. Whosoever putteth away his wife, and marrieth another, committeth adultery: and whosoever marrieth her that is put away from her husband committeth adultery.

"There was a certain rich man, which was clothed in purple and fine linen, and fared sumptuously every day. And there was a certain beggar named Lazarus, which was laid at his gate full of sores, and desiring to be fed with the crumbs which fell from the rich man's table: moreover the dogs came and licked his sores. And it came to pass that the beggar died, and was carried by the angels into Abraham's bosom: the rich man also died, and was buried. And in hell he lifted up his eyes, being in torments, and seeth Abraham afar off, and Lazarus in his bosom: and he cried, and said, 'Father

[27] I.e., a dot over, or part of, a letter in the Hebrew alphabet.

Abraham, have mercy on me, and send Lazarus, that he may dip the tip of his finger in water, and cool my tongue, for I am tormented in this flame.' But Abraham said, 'Son, remember that thou in thy lifetime receivedst thy good things, and likewise Lazarus evil things, but now he is comforted, and thou art tormented. And besides all this, between us and you there is a great gulf fixed, so that they which would pass from hence to you cannot, neither can they pass to us, that would come from thence.' Then he said, 'I pray thee therefore, father, that thou wouldest send him to my father's house: for I have five brethren, that he may testify unto them, lest they also come into this place of torment.' Abraham saith unto him, 'They have Moses and the prophets, let them hear them.' And he said, 'Nay, father Abraham: but if one went unto them from the dead, they will repent.' And he said unto him, 'If they hear not Moses and the prophets, neither will they be persuaded, though one rose from the dead.' "

17 Then said he unto the disciples, "It is impossible but that offenses will come, but woe unto him through whom they come. It were better for him that a millstone were hanged about his neck, and he cast into the sea, than that he should offend one of these little ones.

"Take heed to yourselves: if thy brother trespass against thee, rebuke him, and if he repent, forgive him. And if he trespass against thee seven times in a day, and seven times in a day turn again to thee, saying, 'I repent,' thou shalt forgive him." And the apostles said unto the Lord, "Increase our faith." And the Lord said, "If ye had faith as a grain of mustard seed, ye might say unto this sycamine[28] tree, 'Be thou plucked up by the root, and be thou planted in the sea,' and it should obey you. But which of you having a servant plowing, or feeding cattle, will say unto him by and by when he is come from the field, 'Go and sit down to meat'? And will not rather say unto him, 'Make ready wherewith I may sup, and gird thyself, and serve me, till I have eaten and drunken: and afterward thou shalt eat and drink'? Doth he thank that servant, because he did the things that were commanded him? I trow not. So likewise ye, when ye shall have done all those things which are commanded

28 *I.e.,* mulberry.

you, say, 'We are unprofitable servants: we have done that which was our duty to do.' "

And it came to pass, as he went to Jerusalem, that he passed through the midst of Samaria and Galilee. And as he entered into a certain village, there met him ten men that were lepers, which stood afar off. And they lifted up their voices, and said, "Jesus, master, have mercy on us." And when he saw them, he said unto them, "Go show yourselves unto the priests." And it came to pass, that as they went, they were cleansed. And one of them when he saw that he was healed, turned back, and with a loud voice glorified God, and fell down on his face at his feet, giving him thanks: and he was a Samaritan. And Jesus answering, said, "Were there not ten cleansed? but where are the nine? There are not found that returned to give glory to God, save this stranger." And he said unto him, "Arise, go thy way, thy faith hath made thee whole."

And when he was demanded of the Pharisees, when the kingdom of God should come, he answered them, and said, "The kingdom of God cometh not with observation. Neither shall they say, 'Lo here,' or, 'Lo there': for behold, the kingdom of God is within you." And he said unto the disciples, "The days will come, when ye shall desire to see one of the days of the Son of man, and ye shall not see it. And they shall say to you, 'See here'; or, 'See there': go not after them, nor follow them. For as the lightning, that lighteneth out of the one part under heaven, shineth unto the other part under heaven: so shall also the Son of man be in his day. But first must he suffer many things and be rejected of this generation. And as it was in the days of Noe:[29] so shall it be also in the days of the Son of man. They did eat, they drank, they married wives, they were given in marriage, until the day that Noe entered into the ark: and the flood came, and destroyed them all. Likewise also as it was in the days of Lot, they did eat, they drank, they bought, they sold, they planted, they builded: but the same day that Lot went out of Sodom, it rained fire and brimstone from heaven, and destroyed them all: even thus shall it be in the day when the Son of man is revealed. In that day he which shall be upon the housetop, and his stuff in the house, let him not come down to take it away: and he that is in the field, let him likewise not return back. Remember Lot's wife. Whosoever shall seek to save his life shall lose it, and

[29] *I.e.,* Noah.

whosoever shall lose his life shall preserve it. I tell you, in that night there shall be two men in one bed; the one shall be taken, and the other shall be left. Two women shall be grinding together; the one shall be taken, and the other left. Two men shall be in the field; the one shall be taken, and the other left." And they answered, and said unto him, "Where, Lord?" And he said unto them, "Wheresoever the body is, thither will the eagles be gathered together."

18 And he spake a parable unto them, to this end, that men ought always to pray, and not to faint, saying, "There was in a city a judge, which feared not God, neither regarded man. And there was a widow in that city, and she came unto him, saying, 'Avenge me of mine adversary': and he would not for a while. But afterward he said within himself, 'Though I fear not God, nor regard man, yet because this widow troubleth me, I will avenge her, lest by her continual coming she weary me.'" And the Lord said, "Hear what the unjust judge saith. And shall not God avenge his own elect, which cry day and night unto him, though he bear long with them? I tell you that he will avenge them speedily. Nevertheless, when the Son of man cometh, shall he find faith on the earth?" And he spake this parable unto certain which trusted in themselves that they were righteous, and despised others: "Two men went up into the temple to pray, the one a Pharisee, and the other a publican. The Pharisee stood and prayed thus with himself, 'God, I thank thee, that I am not as other men are, extortioners, unjust, adulterers, or even as this publican. I fast twice in the week, I give tithes of all that I possess.' And the publican standing afar off, would not lift up so much as his eyes unto heaven: but smote upon his breast, saying, 'God be merciful to me a sinner.' I tell you, this man went down to his house justified rather than the other: for every one that exalteth himself shall be abased: and he that humbleth himself shall be exalted."

And they brought unto him also infants, that he would touch them: but when his disciples saw it, they rebuked them. But Jesus called them unto him, and said, "Suffer little children to come unto me, and forbid them not: for of such is the kingdom of God. Verily I say unto you, whosoever shall not receive the kingdom of God as a little child, shall in no wise enter therein." And a certain ruler asked him, saying, "Good master, what shall I do to inherit eternal life?"

And Jesus said unto him, "Why callest thou me good? None is good, save one, that is God. Thou knowest the commandments, Do not commit adultery, Do not kill, Do not steal, Do not bear false witness, Honour thy father and thy mother." And he said, "All these have I kept from my youth up." Now when Jesus heard these things, he said unto him, "Yet lackest thou one thing: sell all that thou hast, and distribute unto the poor, and thou shalt have treasure in heaven, and come, follow me." And when he heard this, he was very sorrowful, for he was very rich. And when Jesus saw that he was very sorrowful, he said, "How hardly shall they that have riches enter into the kingdom of God? For it is easier for a camel to go through a needle's eye, than for a rich man to enter into the kingdom of God." And they that heard it said, "Who then can be saved?" And he said, "The things which are unpossible with men, are possible with God." Then Peter said, "Lo, we have left all, and followed thee." And he said unto them, "Verily I say unto you, there is no man that hath left house, or parents, or brethren, or wife, or children, for the kingdom of God's sake, who shall not receive manifold more in this present time, and in the world to come life everlasting."

Then he took unto him the twelve, and said unto them, "Behold, we go up to Jerusalem, and all things that are written by the prophets concerning the Son of man shall be accomplished. For he shall be delivered unto the Gentiles, and shall be mocked, and spitefully entreated, and spitted on: and they shall scourge him, and put him to death, and the third day he shall rise again." And they understood none of these things: and this saying was hid from them, neither knew they the things which were spoken.

And it came to pass, that as he was come nigh unto Jericho, a certain blind man sat by the wayside, begging: and hearing the multitude pass by, he asked what it meant. And they told him that Jesus of Nazareth passeth by. And he cried, saying, "Jesus thou son of David, have mercy on me." And they which went before rebuked him, that he should hold his peace: but he cried so much the more, "Thou son of David, have mercy on me." And Jesus stood and commanded him to be brought unto him: and when he was come near, he asked him, saying, "What wilt thou that I shall do unto thee?" And he said, "Lord, that I may receive my sight." And Jesus said unto him, "Receive thy sight, thy faith hath saved thee." And immediately he received his sight, and followed him, glorifying God: and all the people, when they saw it gave praise unto God.

19 And Jesus entered, and passed through Jericho. And behold, there was a man named Zaccheus, which was the chief among the publicans, and he was rich. And he sought to see Jesus who he was, and could not for the press, because he was little of stature. And he ran before, and climbed up into a sycamore tree to see him, for he was to pass that way. And when Jesus came to the place, he looked up, and saw him, and said unto him, "Zaccheus, make haste, and come down, for today I must abide at thy house." And he made haste, and came down, and received him joyfully. And when they saw it, they all murmured, saying, "That he was gone to be guest with a man that is a sinner." And Zaccheus stood, and said unto the Lord, "Behold, Lord, the half of my goods I give to the poor, and if I have taken any thing from any man by false accusation, I restore him fourfold." And Jesus said unto him, "This day is salvation come to this house, forsomuch as he also is a son of Abraham. For the Son of man is come to seek, and to save that which was lost." And as they heard these things, he added and spake a parable, because he was nigh to Jerusalem, and because they thought that the kingdom of God should immediately appear. He said therefore, "A certain nobleman went into a far country, to receive for himself a kingdom, and to return. And he called his ten servants, and delivered them ten pounds, and said unto them, 'Occupy till I come.' But his citizens hated him, and sent a message after him, saying, 'We will not have this man to reign over us.' And it came to pass, that when he was returned, having received the kingdom, then he commanded these servants to be called unto him, to whom he had given the money, that he might know how much every man had gained by trading. Then came the first, saying, 'Lord, thy pound hath gained ten pounds.' And he said unto him, 'Well, thou good servant: because thou hast been faithful in a very little, have thou authority over ten cities.' And the second came, saying, 'Lord, thy pound hath gained five pounds.' And he said likewise to him, 'Be thou also over five cities.' And another came, saying, 'Lord, behold here is thy pound, which I have kept laid up in a napkin: for I feared thee, because thou art an austere man: thou takest up that thou layedst not down, and reapest that thou didst not sow.' And he saith unto

him, 'Out of thine own mouth will I judge thee, thou wicked servant: thou knewest that I was an austere man, taking up that I laid
not down, and reaping that I did not sow. Wherefore then gavest
not thou my money into the bank, that at my coming I might have
required mine own with usury?' And he said unto them that stood
by, 'Take from him the pound, and give it to him that hath ten
pounds.' And they said unto him, 'Lord, he hath ten pounds.' For I
say unto you, that unto every one which hath shall be given, and
from him that hath not, even that he hath shall be taken away from
him. But those mine enemies which would not that I should reign
over them, bring hither, and slay them before me."

And when he had thus spoken, he went before, ascending up to
Jerusalem. And it came to pass, when he was come nigh to Beth-
phage and Bethany, at the mount called the Mount of Olives, he
sent two of his disciples, saying, "Go ye into the village over against
you, in the which at your entering ye shall find a colt tied, whereon
yet never man sat: loose him, and bring him hither. And if any
man ask you, 'Why do ye loose him?' thus shall ye say unto him,
'Because the Lord hath need of him.'" And they that were sent went
their way, and found even as he had said unto them. And as they
were loosing the colt, the owners thereof said unto them, "Why loose
ye the colt?" and they said, "The Lord hath need of him." And they
brought him to Jesus: and they cast their garments upon the colt,
and they set Jesus thereon. And as he went, they spread their clothes
in the way. And when he was come nigh, even now at the descent of
the Mount of Olives, the whole multitude of the disciples began to
rejoice and praise God with a loud voice, for all the mighty works
that they had seen, saying, "Blessed be the king that cometh in the
name of the Lord, peace in heaven, and glory in the highest." And
some of the Pharisees from among the multitude said unto him,
"Master, rebuke thy disciples." And he answered, and said unto
them, "I tell you that, if these should hold their peace, the stones
would immediately cry out."

And when he was come near, he beheld the city, and wept over it,
saying, "If thou hadst known, even thou, at least in this thy day, the
things which belong unto thy peace! but now they are hid from
thine eyes. For the days shall come upon thee, that thine enemies
shall cast a trench about thee, and compass thee round, and keep
thee in on every side, and shall lay thee even with the ground, and

thy children within thee: and they shall not leave in thee one stone upon another, because thou knewest not the time of thy visitation." And he went into the temple, and began to cast out them that sold therein, and them that bought, saying unto them, "It is written, 'My house is the house of prayer': but ye have made it a den of thieves." And he taught daily in the temple. But the chief priests and the scribes and the chief of the people sought to destroy him, and could not find what they might do: for all the people were very attentive to hear him.

20 And it came to pass, that on one of those days, as he taught the people in the temple, and preached the gospel, the chief priests and the scribes came upon him, with the elders, and spake unto him, saying, "Tell us, by what authority doest thou these things? or who is he that gave thee this authority?" And he answered, and said unto them, "I will also ask you one thing: and answer me. The baptism of John, was it from heaven, or of men?" And they reasoned with themselves, saying, "If we shall say, 'From heaven,' he will say, 'Why then believed ye him not?' But and if we say, 'Of men,' all the people will stone us: for they be persuaded that John was a prophet." And they answered, that they could not tell whence it was. And Jesus said unto them, "Neither tell I you by what authority I do these things." Then began he to speak to the people this parable: "A certain man planted a vineyard, and let it forth to husbandmen, and went into a far country for a long time. And at the season he sent a servant to the husbandman, that they should give him of the fruit of the vineyard, but the husbandmen beat him, and sent him away empty. And again he sent another servant, and they beat him also, and entreated [30] him shamefully, and sent him away empty. And again he sent a third, and they wounded him also, and cast him out. Then said the lord of the vineyard, 'What shall I do? I will send my beloved son: it may be they will reverence him when they see him.' But when the husbandmen saw him, they reasoned among themselves, saying, 'This is the heir, come, let us kill him, that the inheritance may be ours.' So they cast him out of the vineyard, and killed him. What therefore shall the lord of the vineyard do unto them? He shall come and destroy these husbandmen, and shall give the vineyard to others."

[30] I.e., treated.

And when they heard it, they said, "God forbid." And he beheld them, and said, "What is this then that is written, 'The stone which the builders rejected, the same is become the head of the corner'? Whosoever shall fall upon that stone shall be broken: but on whomsoever it shall fall, it will grind him to powder."

And the chief priests and the scribes the same hour sought to lay hands on him, and they feared the people: for they perceived that he had spoken this parable against them. And they watched him, and sent forth spies, which should feign themselves just men, that they might take hold of his words, that so they might deliver him unto the power and authority of the governor. And they asked him, saying, "Master, we know that thou sayest and teachest rightly, neither acceptest thou the person of any, but teachest the way of God truly. Is it lawful for us to give tribute unto Caesar, or no?" But he perceived their craftiness, and said unto them, "Why tempt ye me? Show me a penny: whose image and superscription hath it?" They answered, and said, "Caesar's." And he said unto them, "Render therefore unto Caesar the things which be Caesar's, and unto God the things which be God's." And they could not take hold of his words before the people, and they marvelled at his answer, and held their peace.

Then came to him certain of the Sadducees (which deny that there is any resurrection) [31] and they asked him, saying, "Master, Moses wrote unto us, 'If any man's brother die, having a wife, and he die without children, that his brother should take his wife, and raise up seed unto his brother.' There were therefore seven brethren, and the first took a wife, and died without children. And the second took her to wife, and he died childless. And the third took her, and in like manner the seven also. And they left no children, and died. Last of all the woman died also. Therefore in the resurrection whose wife of them is she? for seven had her to wife." And Jesus answering, said unto them, "The children of this world marry, and are given in marriage: but they which shall be accounted worthy to obtain that world, and the resurrection from the dead, neither marry, nor are given in marriage. Neither can they die any more; for they are equal unto the angels, and are the children of God, being the

[31] The Sadducees recognized only the Pentateuch, the written Law. In general, the Pharisees belonged to the middle class, the Sadducees to the priestly aristocracy.

children of the resurrection. Now that the dead are raised, even Moses showed at the bush, when he calleth the Lord, the God of Abraham, and the God of Isaac, and the God of Jacob. For he is not a God of the dead, but of the living; for all live unto him."

Then certain of the scribes answering, said, "Master, thou hast well said." And after that they durst not ask him any question at all. And he said unto them, "How say they that Christ is David's son? And David himself saith in the book of Psalms, 'The lord said unto my Lord, "Sit thou on my right hand, till I make thine enemies thy footstool." ' David therefore calleth him Lord, how is he then his son?"

Then in the audience of all the people he said unto his disciples, "Beware of the scribes, which desire to walk in long robes, and love greetings in the markets, and the highest seats in the synagogues, and the chief rooms at feasts: which devour widows' houses, and for a show make long prayers: the same shall receive greater damnation."

21 And he looked up, and saw the rich men casting their gifts into the treasury. And he saw also a certain poor widow, casting in thither two mites. And he said, "Of a truth, I say unto you, that this poor widow hath cast in more than they all. For all these have of their abundance cast in unto the offerings of God, but she of her penury hath cast in all the living that she had."

And as some spake of the temple, how it was adorned with goodly stones, and gifts, he said, "As for these things which ye behold, the days will come, in the which there shall not be left one stone upon another, that shall not be thrown down." And they asked him, saying, "Master, but when shall these things be? and what sign will there be, when these things shall come to pass?" And he said, "Take heed that ye be not deceived: for many shall come in my name, saying, 'I am Christ, and the time draweth near': go ye not therefore after them. But when ye shall hear of wars, and commotions, be not terrified: for these things must first come to pass, but the end is not by and by." Then said he unto them, "Nation shall rise against nation, and kingdom against kingdom: and great earthquakes shall be in divers places, and famines, and pestilences: and fearful sights and great signs shall there be from heaven. But before all these, they shall lay their hands on you, and persecute you, delivering you up to the synagogues, and into prisons, being brought before kings and rulers for my name's sake. And it shall turn to you for a testimony. Settle it therefore in your hearts, not to meditate before what ye shall answer. For I will give you a mouth and wisdom, which all your adversaries shall not be able to gainsay, nor resist. And ye shall be betrayed both by parents, and brethren, and kinsfolks, and friends, and some of you shall they cause to be put to death. And ye shall be hated of all men for my name's sake. But there shall not a hair of your head perish. In your patience possess ye your souls. And when ye shall see Jerusalem compassed with armies, then know that the desolation thereof is nigh. Then let them which are in Judea flee to the mountains, and let them which are in the midst of it depart out, and let not them that are in the countries enter thereinto. For these be the days of vengeance, that all things which are written may be fulfilled. But woe unto them that are with child, and to them that give suck in those days, for there shall be great distress in the land, and wrath upon this people. And they shall fall by the edge of the sword, and shall be led away captive into all nations, and Jerusalem shall be trodden down of the Gentiles, until the times of the Gentiles be fulfilled.

"And there shall be signs in the sun, and in the moon, and in the stars, and upon the earth distress of nations, with perplexity, the sea and the waves roaring, men's hearts failing them for fear, and for looking after those things which are coming on the earth; for the powers of heaven shall be shaken. And then shall they see the Son of man coming in a cloud with power and great glory. And when these things begin to come to pass, then look up, and lift up your heads, for your redemption draweth nigh." And he spake to them a parable, "Behold the fig tree, and all the trees, when they now shoot forth, ye see and know of your own selves that summer is now nigh at hand. So likewise ye, when ye see these things come to pass, know ye that the kingdom of God is nigh at hand. Verily I say unto you, this generation shall not pass away, till all be fulfilled. Heaven and earth shall pass away, but my words shall not pass away.

"And take heed to yourselves, lest at any time your hearts be overcharged with surfeiting, and drunkenness, and cares of this life, and so that day come upon you unawares. For as a snare shall it come on all them that dwell on the face of the whole earth. Watch ye therefore, and pray always, that ye may be accounted worthy to escape all these things that shall come to pass, and to stand before the Son of man." And in the daytime he was teaching in the temple, and at night he went out, and abode in the mount that is called the Mount of Olives. And all the people came early in the morning to him in the temple, for to hear him.

22 Now the feast of unleavened bread drew nigh, which is called the Passover. And the chief priests and scribes sought how they might kill him; for they feared the people.

Then entered Satan into Judas surnamed Iscariot, being of the number of the twelve. And he went his way, and communed with the chief priests and captains, how he might betray him unto them. And they were glad, and covenanted to give him money. And he promised, and sought opportunity to betray him unto them in the absence of the multitude.

Then came the day of unleavened bread, when the passover must be killed. And he sent Peter and John, saying, "Go and prepare us the passover, that we may eat." And they said unto him, "Where wilt thou that we prepare?" And he said unto them, "Behold, when ye are entered into the city, there shall a man meet you, bearing a pitcher of water; follow him into the house where he entereth in. And ye shall say unto the goodman of the house, 'The Master saith unto thee, "Where is the guest-chamber where I shall eat the passover with my disciples."' And he shall show you a large upper room furnished: there make ready." And they went, and found as he had said unto them, and they made ready the passover. And when the hour was come, he sat down, and the twelve apostles with him. And he said unto them, "With desire I have desired to eat this passover with you before I suffer. For I say unto you, I will not any more eat thereof, until it be fulfilled in the kingdom of God." And he took the cup, and gave thanks, and said, "Take this, and divide it among yourselves. For I say unto you, I will not drink of the fruit of the vine, until the kingdom of God shall come."

And he took bread, and gave thanks, and brake it, and gave unto them, saying, "This is my body which is given for you, this do in remembrance of me." Likewise also the cup after supper, saying, "This cup is the new testament in my blood, which is shed for you.

"But behold, the hand of him that betrayeth me is with me on the table. And truly the Son of man goeth as it was determined, but woe unto that man by whom he is betrayed." And they began to inquire among themselves, which of them it was that should do this thing.

And there was also a strife among them, which of them should be accounted the greatest. And he said unto them, "The kings of the Gentiles exercise lordship over them, and they that exercise authority upon them are called benefactors. But ye shall not be so; but he that is greatest among you, let him be as the younger; and he that is chief, as he that doth serve. For whether is greater, he that sitteth at meat, or he that serveth? Is not he that sitteth at meat? But I am among you as he that serveth. Ye are they which have continued with me in my temptations. And I appoint unto you a kingdom, as my Father hath appointed unto me, that ye may eat and drink at my table in my kingdom, and sit on thrones judging the twelve tribes of Israel."

And the Lord said, "Simon, Simon, behold, Satan hath desired to have you, that he may sift you as wheat: but I have prayed for thee, that thy faith fail not; and when thou art converted, strengthen thy brethren." And he said unto him, "Lord, I am ready to go with thee, both into prison, and to death." And he said, "I tell thee Peter, the cock shall not crow this day, before that thou shalt thrice deny that thou knowest me." And he said unto them, "When I sent you without purse, and scrip, and shoes, lacked ye any thing?" And they said, "Nothing." Then said he unto them, "But now he that hath a purse, let him take it, and likewise his scrip: and he that hath no sword, let him sell his garment, and buy one. For I say unto you, that this that is written must yet be accomplished in me, 'And he was reckoned among the transgressors': for the things concerning me have an end." And they said, "Lord, behold, here are two swords." And he said unto them, "It is enough."

And he came out, and went, as he was wont, to the Mount of Olives, and his disciples also followed him. And when he was at the place, he said unto them, "Pray, that ye enter not into temptation." And he was withdrawn from them about a stone's cast, and kneeled down, and prayed, saying, "Father, if thou be willing, remove this cup from me: nevertheless, not my will, but thine be done." And there appeared an angel unto him from heaven, strengthening him. And being in an agony, he prayed more earnestly, and his sweat was as it were great drops of blood falling down to the ground. And when he rose up from prayer, and was come to his disciples, he found them sleeping for sorrow, and said unto them, "Why sleep ye? Rise, and pray, lest ye enter into temptation."

And while he yet spake, behold, a multitude, and he that was called Judas, one of the twelve, went before them, and drew near unto Jesus, to kiss him. But Jesus said unto him, "Judas, betrayest thou the Son of man with a kiss?" When they which were about him saw what would follow, they said unto him, "Lord, shall we smite with the sword?"

And one of them smote the servant of the high priest, and cut off his right ear. And Jesus answered, and said, "Suffer ye thus far." And he touched his ear, and healed him. Then Jesus said unto the chief priests, and captains of the temple, and the elders which were come to him, "Be ye come out as against a thief, with swords and staves? When I was daily with you in the temple, ye stretched forth no hands against me: but this is your hour, and the power of darkness."

Then took they him, and led him, and brought him into the high priest's house, and Peter followed afar off. And when they had kindled a fire in the midst of the hall, and were set down together, Peter sat down among them. But a certain maid beheld him as he sat by the fire, and earnestly looked upon him, and said, "This man was also with him." And he denied him, saying, "Woman, I know him not." And after a little while another saw him, and said, "Thou art also of them." And Peter said, "Man, I am not." And about the space of one hour after, another confidently affirmed, saying, "Of a truth this fellow also was with him; for he is a Galilean." And Peter said, "Man, I know not what thou sayest." And immediately while he yet spake, the cock crew. And the Lord turned, and looked upon Peter; and Peter remembered the word of the Lord, how he had said unto him, "Before the cock crow, thou shalt deny me thrice." And Peter went out, and wept bitterly.

And the men that held Jesus mocked him, and smote him. And when they had blindfolded him, they struck him on the face, and asked him, saying, "Prophesy, who is it that smote thee?" And many other things blasphemously spake they against him.

And as soon as it was day, the elders of the people and the chief priests and the scribes came together, and led him into their council, saying, "Art thou the Christ? Tell us." And he said unto them, "If

I tell you, you will not believe. And if I also ask you, you will not answer me, nor let me go. Hereafter shall the Son of man sit on the right hand of the power of God." Then said they all, "Art thou then the Son of God?" And he said unto them, "Ye say that I am." And they said, "What need we any further witness? For we ourselves have heard of his own mouth."

23 And the whole multitude of them arose, and led him unto Pilate. And they began to accuse him, saying, "We found this fellow perverting the nation, and forbidding to give tribute to Caesar, saying that he himself is Christ a king." And Pilate asked him, saying, "Art thou the king of the Jews?" And he answered him, and said, "Thou sayest it." Then said Pilate to the chief priests, and to the people, "I find no fault in this man." And they were the more fierce, saying, "He stirreth up the people, teaching throughout all Jewry, beginning from Galilee to this place." When Pilate heard of Galilee, he asked whether the man were a Galilean. And as soon as he knew that he belonged unto Herod's jurisdiction, he sent him to Herod, who himself also was at Jerusalem at that time.

And when Herod saw Jesus, he was exceeding glad, for he was desirous to see him of a long season, because he had heard many things of him, and he hoped to have seen some miracle done by him. Then he questioned with him in many words, but he answered him nothing. And the chief priests and scribes stood, and vehemently accused him. And Herod with his men of war set him at nought, and mocked him, and arrayed him in a gorgeous robe, and sent him again to Pilate.

And the same day Pilate and Herod were made friends together; for before they were at enmity between themselves.

And Pilate, when he had called together the chief priests, and the rulers, and the people, said unto them, "Ye have brought this man unto me, as one that perverteth the people, and behold, I having examined him before you, have found no fault in this man, touching those things whereof ye accuse him. No, nor yet Herod: for I sent you to him, and lo, nothing worthy of death is done unto him. I will therefore chastise him, and release him." For of necessity he must release one unto them at the feast. And they cried out all at once, saying, "Away with this man, and release unto us Barabbas," who for a certain sedition made in the city, and for murder, was cast into prison. Pilate therefore willing to release Jesus, spake again to them: but they cried, saying, "Crucify him, crucify him." And he said unto them the third time, "Why, what evil hath he done? I have found no cause of death in him, I will therefore chastise him, and let him go." And they were instant[32] with loud voices, requiring that he might be crucified: and the voices of them and of the chief priests prevailed. And Pilate gave sentence that it should be as they required. And he released unto them him that for sedition and murder was cast into prison, whom they had desired, but he delivered Jesus to their will. And as they led him away, they laid hold upon one Simon, a Cyrenian, coming out of the country, and on him they laid the cross, that he might bear it after Jesus.

And there followed him a great company of people, and of women, which also bewailed and lamented him. But Jesus turning unto them, said, "Daughters of Jerusalem, weep not for me, but weep for yourselves, and for your children. For behold, the days are coming, in the which they shall say, 'Blessed are the barren, and the wombs that never bare, and the paps which never gave suck.' Then shall they begin to say to the mountains, 'Fall on us,' and to the hills, 'Cover us.' For if they do these things in a green tree, what shall be done in the dry?" And there were also two other malefactors led with him, to be put to death. And when they were come to the place which is called Calvary, there they crucified him, and the malefactors, one on the right hand, and the other on the left.

Then said Jesus, "Father, forgive them, for they know not what they do": and they parted[33] his raiment, and cast lots. And the people stood beholding, and the rulers also with them derided him, saying, "He saved others, let him save himself, if he be Christ, the chosen of God." And the soldiers also mocked him, coming to him, and offering him vinegar, and saying, "If thou be the king of the Jews, save thyself." And a superscription also was written over him in letters of Greek, and Latin, and Hebrew, THIS IS THE KING OF THE JEWS.

And one of the malefactors, which were hanged, railed on him, saying, "If thou be Christ, save thyself and us." But the other answer-

[32] *I.e.,* insistent.
[33] *I.e.,* divided.

ing, rebuked him, saying, "Dost not thou fear God, seeing thou art in the same condemnation? And we indeed justly; for we receive the due reward of our deeds, but this man hath done nothing amiss." And he said unto Jesus, "Lord, remember me when thou comest into thy kingdom." And Jesus said unto him, "Verily I say unto thee, today shalt thou be with me in paradise." And it was about the sixth hour, and there was darkness over all the earth, until the ninth hour. And the sun was darkened, and the veil [34] of the temple was rent in the midst.

And when Jesus had cried with a loud voice, he said, "Father, into thy hands I commend my spirit": and having said thus, he gave up the ghost. Now when the centurion saw what was done, he glorified God, saying, "Certainly this was a righteous man." And all the people that came together to that sight, beholding the things which were done, smote their breasts, and returned. And all his acquaintance, and the women that followed him from Galilee, stood afar off, beholding these things.

And behold, there was a man named Joseph, a counsellor, and he was a good man, and a just. (The same had not consented to the counsel and deed of them.) He was of Arimathea, a city of the Jews (who also himself waited for the kingdom of God). This man went unto Pilate, and begged the body of Jesus. And he took it down, and wrapped it in linen, and laid it in a sepulchre that was hewn in stone, wherein never man before was laid. And that day was the preparation, and the sabbath drew on. And the women also, which came with him from Galilee, followed after, and beheld the sepulchre, and how his body was laid. And they returned, and prepared spices and ointments, and rested the sabbath day, according to the commandment.

24 Now upon the first day of the week, very early in the morning, they came unto the sepulchre, bringing the spices which they had prepared, and certain others with them. And they found the stone rolled away from the sepulchre. And they entered in, and found not the body of the Lord Jesus. And it came to pass, as they were much perplexed thereabout, behold, two men stood by them in shining garments. And as they were afraid, and bowed down their

[34] *I.e.*, curtain.

faces to the earth, they said unto them, "Why seek ye the living among the dead? He is not here, but is risen: remember how he spake unto you when he was in Galilee, saying, 'The Son of man must be delivered into the hands of sinful men, and be crucified, and the third day rise again'?" And they remembered his words, and returned from the sepulchre, and told all these things unto the eleven, and to all the rest. It was Mary Magdalene, and Joanna, and Mary the mother of James, and other women that were with them, which told these things unto the apostles. And their words seemed to them as idle tales, and they believed them not. Then arose Peter, and ran unto the sepulchre, and stooping down, he beheld the linen clothes laid by themselves, and departed, wondering in himself at that which was come to pass.

And behold, two of them went that same day to a village called Emmaus, which was from Jerusalem about threescore furlongs. And they talked together of all these things which had happened. And it came to pass, that while they communed together and reasoned, Jesus himself drew near, and went with them. But their eyes were holden,[35] that they should not know him. And he said unto them, "What manner of communications are these that ye have one to another as ye walk, and are sad?" And the one of them, whose name was Cleopas, answering, said unto him, "Art thou only a stranger in Jerusalem, and hast not known the things which are come to pass there in these days?" And he said unto them, "What things?" And they said unto him, "Concerning Jesus of Nazareth, which was a prophet, mighty in deed and word before God, and all the people. And how the chief priests and our rulers delivered him to be condemned to death, and have crucified him. But we trusted that it had been he which should have redeemed Israel: and beside all this, today is the third day since these things were done. Yea, and certain women also of our company made us astonished, which were early at the sepulchre: and when they found not his body, they came, saying, that they had also seen a vision of angels, which said that he was alive. And certain of them which were with us went to the sepulchre, and found it even so as the women had said, but him they saw not." Then he said unto them, "O fools, and slow of heart to believe all that the prophets have spoken: ought not Christ to have

[35] *I.e.*, held.

suffered these things, and to enter into his glory?" And beginning at Moses and all the prophets, he expounded unto them in all the scriptures the things concerning himself. And they drew nigh unto the village, whither they went, and he made as though he would have gone further. But they constrained him, saying, "Abide with us, for it is toward evening, and the day is far spent": and he went in, to tarry with them. And it came to pass, as he sat at meat with them, he took bread, and blessed it, and brake, and gave to them. And their eyes were opened, and they knew him, and he vanished out of their sight. And they said one to another, "Did not our heart burn within us, while he talked with us by the way, and while he opened to us the scriptures?" And they rose up the same hour, and returned to Jerusalem, and found the eleven gathered together, and them that were with them, saying, "The Lord is risen indeed, and hath appeared to Simon." And they told what things were done in the way, and how he was known of them in breaking of bread.

And as they thus spake, Jesus himself stood in the midst of them, and saith unto them, "Peace be unto you." But they were terrified, and affrighted, and supposed that they had seen a spirit. And he said unto them, "Why are ye troubled, and why do thoughts arise in your hearts? Behold my hands and my feet, that it is I myself: handle me, and see, for a spirit hath not flesh and bones, as ye see me have." And when he had thus spoken, he showed them his hands and his feet. And while they yet believed not for joy, and wondered, he said unto them, "Have ye here any meat?" And they gave him a piece of a broiled fish, and of an honeycomb. And he took it, and did eat before them. And he said unto them, "These are the words which I spake unto you, while I was yet with you, that all things must be fulfilled, which were written in the law of Moses, and in the prophets, and in the psalms concerning me." Then opened he their understanding, that they might understand the scriptures, and said unto them, "Thus it is written, and thus it behooved Christ to suffer, and to rise from the dead the third day: and that repentance and remission of sins should be preached in his name among all nations, beginning at Jerusalem. And ye are witnesses of these things.

"And behold, I send the promise of my Father upon you: but tarry ye in the city of Jerusalem, until ye be endued with power from on high."

And he led them out as far as to Bethany, and he lifted up his hands, and blessed them. And it came to pass, while he blessed them, he was parted from them, and carried up into heaven. And they worshipped him, and returned to Jerusalem with great joy: and were continually in the temple, praising and blessing God. Amen.

JOHN

1 In the beginning was the Word, and the Word was with God, and the Word was God. The same was in the beginning with God. All things were made by him, and without him was not any thing made that was made. In him was life, and the life was the light of men. And the light shineth in darkness, and the darkness comprehended it not.

There was a man sent from God, whose name was John. The same came for a witness, to bear witness of the light, that all men through him might believe. He was not that light, but was sent to bear witness of that light. That was the true light, which lighteth every man that cometh into the world. He was in the world, and the world was made by him, and the world knew him not. He came unto his own, and his own received him not. But as many as received him, to them gave he power to become the sons of God, even to them that believe on his name: which were born, not of blood, nor of the will of the flesh, nor of the will of man, but of God. And the Word was made flesh, and dwelt among us (and we beheld his glory, the glory as of the only begotten of the Father) full of grace and truth.

John bare witness of him, and cried, saying, "This was he of whom I spake, 'He that cometh after me is preferred before me, for he was before me.'" And of his fulness have all we received, and grace for grace. For the law was given by Moses, but grace and truth came by Jesus Christ. No man hath seen God at any time: the only begotten Son, which is in the bosom of the Father, he hath declared him. . . .

the acts
of the apostles

INTRODUCTION

The Acts of the Apostles is a continuation of The Gospel According to St. Luke, though what title the author originally gave his two-part work is unknown. Almost certainly Luke wrote this second part shortly after the first: around 90 A.D. His purpose was to tell about the widening influence of Christianity, how this potentially new religion had spread from a small Jewish sect in Palestine to a congregation that was rapidly gaining converts throughout the Roman Empire. Not only was this new religion, according to Luke, essentially harmonious within its own ranks, but it was politically inoffensive to Rome. Acts ends before Paul's conviction by a Roman court in 64 A.D.,[1] probably because the author did not want to conclude with an incident that emphasized controversy between the new church and the established state. Luke was not trying to write a complete history or to expound theology (Paul's Epistles had not yet been collected and made public); rather, he was attempting to celebrate, in a highly selective manner, the early growth of the Christian movement.

To narrate this saga that ranges from Jerusalem to Rome, Luke seems to have relied on three sources: the presumed diary which he kept when he traveled with Paul some thirty or forty years earlier, one or two written accounts of the earliest days of Christianity, and oral tradition. As before, he was able to weave his diverse materials into a graphic story. Luke's artistry shows itself especially in the speeches which he, like the Greek historians, inserts in the mouths of his chief personages, and in his ability to transmit the excitement of the marvelous and the miraculous.

Acts is mostly concerned with the activities of Paul and Peter. The following brief selection, however, concentrates on the personality of

[1] For further details see the Introduction to the Epistles of Paul.

Paul, in many ways the architect of Christianity. But it is also intended to suggest Luke's purpose, scope, and skill in completing the narrative he had begun in his Gospel. ♣ ♣ ♣

Suggested Reading

Cervantes, *Don Quixote*—a seventeenth-century Spanish novel about a crusading idealist in a hostile world.

THE ACTS OF THE APOSTLES

9 And Saul yet breathing out threatenings and slaughter against the disciples of the Lord, went unto the high priest, and desired of him letters to Damascus, to the synagogues, that if he found any of this way, whether they were men or women, he might bring them bound unto Jerusalem. And as he journeyed he came near Damascus, and suddenly there shined round about him a light from heaven. And he fell to the earth, and heard a voice saying unto him, "Saul, Saul, why persecutest thou me?" And he said, "Who art thou Lord?" And the Lord said, "I am Jesus whom thou persecutest: it is hard for thee to kick against the pricks." [1] And he trembling and astonished, said, "Lord, what wilt thou have me to do?" And the Lord said unto him, "Arise, and go into the city, and it shall be told thee what thou must do." And the men which journeyed with him stood speechless, hearing a voice, but seeing no man. And Saul arose from the earth, and when his eyes were opened, he saw no man: but they led him by the hand, and brought him into Damascus. And he was three days without sight, and neither did eat nor drink.

And there was a certain disciple at Damascus, named Ananias, and to him said the Lord in a vision, "Ananias." And he said, "Behold, I am here, Lord." And the Lord said unto him, "Arise, and go into the street, which is called Straight, and inquire in the house of Judas for one called Saul, of Tarsus: for behold, he prayeth, and hath seen in a vision a man named Ananias coming in, and putting his hand on him, that he might receive his sight." Then Ananias answered, "Lord, I have heard by many of this man, how much evil he hath done to thy saints at Jerusalem: and here he hath authority from the chief priests, to bind all that call on thy name." But the Lord said unto him, "Go thy way: for he is a chosen vessel unto me,

[1] *I.e.*, it is painful for you to dispute the will of the gods.

to bear my name before the Gentiles, and kings, and the children of Israel. For I will show him how great things he must suffer for my name's sake." And Ananias went his way, and entered into the house, and putting his hands on him, said, "Brother Saul, the Lord (even Jesus that appeared unto thee in the way as thou camest) hath sent me, that thou mightest receive thy sight, and be filled with the Holy Ghost." And immediately there fell from his eyes as it had been scales, and he received sight forthwith, and arose, and was baptized. And when he had received meat, he was strengthened. Then was Saul certain days with the disciples which were at Damascus. And straightway he preached Christ in the synagogues, that he is the Son of God. But all that heard him were amazed, and said, "Is not this he that destroyed them which called on this name in Jerusalem, and came hither for that intent that he might bring them bound unto the chief priests?" But Saul increased the more in strength, and confounded the Jews which dwelt at Damascus, proving that this is very Christ.

And after that many days were fulfilled, the Jews took counsel to kill him. But their laying await was known of Saul: and they watched the gates day and night to kill him. Then the disciples took him by night, and let him down by the wall in a basket. And when Saul was come to Jerusalem, he assayed to join himself to the disciples, but they were all afraid of him, and believed not that he was a disciple. But Barnabas took him, and brought him to the apostles, and declared unto them how he had seen the Lord in the way, and that he had spoken to him, and how he had preached boldly at Damascus in the name of Jesus. And he was with them coming in and going out at Jerusalem. And he spake boldly in the name of the Lord Jesus, and disputed against the Grecians: but they went about to slay him. Which when the brethren knew, they brought him down to Caesarea, and sent him forth to Tarsus. Then had the churches rest throughout all Judea, and Galilee, and Samaria, and were edified; and walking in the fear of the Lord, and in the comfort of the Holy Ghost, were multiplied.

And it came to pass, as Peter passed throughout all quarters, he came down also to the saints which dwelt at Lydda. And there he found a certain man named Aeneas, which had kept his bed eight years, and was sick of the palsy. And Peter said unto him, "Aeneas,

Jesus Christ maketh thee whole: arise, and make thy bed." [2] And he arose immediately. And all that dwelt at Lydda, and Saron, saw him, and turned to the Lord.

Now there was at Joppa a certain disciple named Tabitha, which by interpretation is called Dorcas.[3] This woman was full of good works, and almsdeeds, which she did. And it came to pass in those days that she was sick, and died: whom when they had washed, they laid her in an upper chamber. And forasmuch as Lydda was nigh to Joppa, and the disciples had heard that Peter was there, they sent unto him two men, desiring him that he would not delay to come to them. Then Peter arose and went with them: when he was come, they brought him into the upper chamber: and all the widows stood by him weeping, and showing the coats and garments which Dorcas made, while she was with them. But Peter put them all forth, and kneeled down, and prayed, and turning him to the body said, "Tabitha, arise." And she opened her eyes, and when she saw Peter, she sat up. And he gave her his hand, and lifted her up: and when he had called the saints and widows, presented her alive. And it was known throughout all Joppa, and many believed in the Lord. And it came to pass, that he tarried many days in Joppa, with one Simon a tanner.

17 . . . Now while Paul waited for them at Athens, his spirit was stirred in him, when he saw the city wholly given to idolatry. Therefore disputed he in the synagogue with the Jews, and with the devout persons, and in the market daily with them that met with him. Then certain philosophers of the Epicureans, and of the Stoics, encountered him: and some said, "What will this babbler say?" other some, "He seemeth to be a setter forth of strange gods": because he preached unto them Jesus, and the resurrection. And they took him, and brought him unto Areopagus,[4] saying, "May we know what this new doctrine, whereof thou speakest, is? For thou bringest certain strange things to our ears: we would know therefore what these things mean." (For all the Athenians, and strangers which were there, spent their time in nothing else, but either to tell or to hear some new thing.)

[2] I.e., take up your bed.
[3] Tabitha is the Aramaic word for gazelle, Dorcas the Greek word.
[4] A hill near the Acropolis; it also signified the Athenian council which had general supervision over religious and educational matters.

Then Paul stood in the midst of Mars' Hill,[5] and said, "Ye men of Athens, I perceive that in all things ye are too superstitious. For as I passed by, and beheld your devotions, I found an altar with this inscription, TO THE UNKNOWN GOD. Whom therefore ye ignorantly worship, him declare I unto you. God that made the world, and all things therein, seeing that he is Lord of heaven and earth, dwelleth not in temples made with hands: neither is worshipped with men's hands as though he needed any thing, seeing he giveth to all, life and breath, and all things, and hath made of one blood all nations of men, for to dwell on all the face of the earth, and hath determined the times before appointed, and the bounds of their habitation: that they should seek the Lord, if haply they might feel after him and find him, though he be not far from every one of us. For in him we live, and move, and have our being, as certain also of your own poets have said, 'For we are also his offspring.' Forasmuch then as we are the offspring of God, we ought not to think that the Godhead is like unto gold, or silver, or stone, graven by art and man's device. And the times of this ignorance God winked at, but now commandeth all men everywhere to repent: because he hath appointed a day in the which he will judge the world in righteousness, by that man whom he hath ordained, whereof he hath given assurance unto all men, in that he hath raised him from the dead."

And when they heard of the resurrection of the dead, some mocked: and others said, "We will hear thee again of this matter." So Paul departed from among them. Howbeit, certain men clave unto him, and believed: among the which was Dionysius the Areopagite, and a woman named Damaris, and others with them.

26 Then Agrippa[6] said unto Paul, "Thou art permitted to speak for thyself." Then Paul stretched forth the hand, and answered for himself, "I think myself happy, king Agrippa, because I shall answer for myself this day before thee touching all the things whereof I am accused of the Jews: especially because I know thee to be expert in all customs and questions which are among the Jews: wherefore I beseech thee to hear me patiently. My manner of life from my youth, which was at the first among mine own nation

[5] I.e., the Areopagus.
[6] Agrippa was Jewish in religion and was governor, for Rome, of a district that included Galilee.

at Jerusalem, know all the Jews, which knew me from the beginning (if they would testify), that after the most straitest sect of our religion I lived a Pharisee. And now I stand and am judged for the hope of the promise made of God unto our fathers: unto which promise our twelve tribes, instantly[7] serving God day and night, hope to come: for which hope's sakes, king Agrippa, I am accused of the Jews. Why should it be thought a thing incredible with you, that God should raise the dead? I verily thought with myself, that I ought to do many things contrary to the name of Jesus of Nazareth: which thing I also did in Jerusalem, and many of the saints did I shut up in prison, having received authority from the chief priests; and when they were put to death, I gave my voice against them. And I punished them oft in every synagogue, and compelled them to blaspheme, and being exceedingly mad against them, I persecuted them even unto strange cities. Whereupon, as I went to Damascus, with authority and commission from the chief priests: at midday, O king, I saw in the way a light from heaven, above the brightness of the sun, shining round about me and them which journeyed with me. And when we were all fallen to the earth, I heard a voice speaking unto me, and saying in the Hebrew tongue, 'Saul, Saul, why persecutest thou me? It is hard for thee to kick against the pricks.' And I said, 'Who art thou, Lord?' And he said, 'I am Jesus whom thou persecutest. But rise, and stand upon thy feet, for I have appeared unto thee for this purpose, to make thee a minister and a witness, both of these things which thou hast seen, and of those things in the which I will appear unto thee, delivering thee from the people, and from the Gentiles, unto whom now I send thee, to open their eyes, and to turn them from darkness to light, and from the power of Satan unto God, that they may receive forgiveness of sins, and inheritance among them which are sanctified by faith that is in me.'

"Whereupon, O king Agrippa, I was not disobedient unto the heavenly vision: but showed first unto them of Damascus, and at Jerusalem, and throughout all the coasts of Judea, and then to the Gentiles, that they should repent and turn to God, and do works meet for repentance. For these causes the Jews caught me in the temple, and went about to kill me. Having therefore obtained help of God, I continue unto this day, witnessing both to small and great, saying none other things than those which the prophets and Moses

[7] I.e., earnestly.

did say should come: that Christ should suffer, and that he should be the first that should rise from the dead, and should show light unto the people, and to the Gentiles."

And as he thus spake for himself, Festus[8] said with a loud voice, "Paul, thou art beside thyself, much learning doth make thee mad." But he said, "I am not mad, most noble Festus, but speak forth the words of truth and soberness. For the king knoweth of these things, before whom also I speak freely: for I am persuaded that none of these things are hidden from him, for this thing was not done in a corner. King Agrippa, believest thou the prophets? I know that thou believest." Then Agrippa said unto Paul, "Almost thou persuadest me to be a Christian." And Paul said, "I would to God, that not only thou, but also all that hear me this day, were both almost, and altogether such as I am, except these bonds." And when he had thus spoken, the king rose up, and the governor, and Bernice,[9] and they that sat with them. And when they were gone aside, they talked between themselves, saying, "This man doeth nothing worthy of death, or of bonds." Then said Agrippa unto Festus, "This man might have been set at liberty, if he had not appealed unto Caesar."

[8] Festus was the Roman governor of Judea.
[9] Bernice was Agrippa's sister.

the epistles of paul

INTRODUCTION

Many of the probable facts of Paul's life are told in Acts and in his own letters, the latter being the more reliable source of information. Born not long after the birth of Christ, in Tarsus, a rich and cosmopolitan city on the eastern Mediterranean, Paul was brought up as an orthodox Jew. For a time in his early manhood he actively persecuted members of a new sect, the Christians. But with his conversion to Christianity in 48 or 49 A.D. he began his lengthy travels in Palestine, Asia Minor, and Greece as a preacher of this new religion. Because he had long claimed Roman citizenship, and after he had been charged with some form of sedition, he was brought to Rome as a prisoner. There, during the persecutions under Nero, he was executed—probably in 64 A.D. Admittedly a poor speaker and apparently of frail health, he was nevertheless a man of vitality, courage, and effectiveness. Indeed it was Paul who, in two major respects, was the founder of Christianity.

First, he was in a sense its theological founder. Peter, the other dominant apostle in Acts, directed his appeal primarily to Jews. He stressed that Christianity was a continuation of Judaism and that Christ was the Messiah long foretold in the Old Testament. Paul, in contrast, addressed himself mainly to a Gentile audience. Appealing largely to the dispossessed, he preached that salvation did not require circumcision or strict observance of the Jewish Law, but that it was a free gift of God's grace. His message of hope and faith—of a potentially joyous immortality—was contagious, and within three centuries Christianity, not Judaism or an Eastern mystery cult, was the leading religion of the Mediterranean world.

Second, Paul was Christianity's practical founder. By his energetic trips, religious zeal, and common sense he established and nurtured a broad network of Christian churches. One of his chief instruments in accomplishing this—and a technique made necessary by the fact that he was constantly traveling—was his letters. Of the fourteen attributed to Paul, ten are certainly by him; and many others may have been lost.

391

Written between 50 and 60 A.D. these letters are both the earliest documents of Christianity and its decisive theological expression. We are quite sure that they were carefully dictated to a scribe and that they were designed to be read in public, not only in the church to which they were addressed but in neighboring churches. Their range is extensive: from light irony, for instance, to involved argumentation, or from the problem of whether women should be veiled in public meetings to the mystery of predestination. But regardless of his mood or topic Paul was a skilled literary craftsman.

In his letters to the church at Corinth we can see Paul in all his strength. Here, as in his other Epistles, he was concerned both with the problems of a specific church and with larger theological questions. Corinth itself was a flourishing variegated city, and here as elsewhere the new church tended to be divided between what can be called Jewish orthodoxy and Greek speculativeness. Thus Paul's doctrine of immortality was in part a compromise. To the Jews life without a body was a meaningless concept, while to many Greeks the body seemed an impediment, a barrier to the immortality which only a disembodied spirit could achieve. But to Paul the true believer will be rewarded by an afterlife in which he will be clothed with a spiritual body.

The short selection which follows illustrates the richness and vitality of Paul's letters. It begins with a passage from The Second Epistle to the Corinthians recapitulating his own adventurous career, and it ends with three chapters from First Corinthians which epitomize his evangelical ardor. ♣ ♣ ♣

Suggested Reading

Plato, *Dialogues*—Platonic Idealism, to which much New Testament theology is closely related.

II CORINTHIANS

11 Would to God ye could bear with me a little in my folly, and indeed bear with me. For I am jealous over you with godly jealousy, for I have espoused you to one husband, that I may present you as a chaste virgin to Christ. But I fear lest by any means, as the serpent beguiled Eve through his subtilty, so your minds should be corrupted from the simplicity that is in Christ. For if he that cometh preacheth another Jesus, whom we have not preached, or if ye receive another spirit, which ye have not received, or another gospel, which ye have not accepted, ye might well bear with him. For I suppose I was not a whit behind the very chiefest apostles. But though I be rude in speech, yet not in knowledge; but we have been thoroughly made manifest among you in all things. Have I committed an offense in abasing myself, that ye might be exalted, because I have preached to you the gospel of God freely? I robbed other churches, taking wages of them to do you service. And when I was present with you, and wanted, I was chargeable to no man: for that which was lacking to me the brethren which came from Macedonia supplied, and in all things I have kept myself from being burdensome unto you, and so will I keep myself.

As the truth of Christ is in me, no man shall stop me of this boasting in the regions of Achaia. Wherefore? because I love you not? God knoweth. But what I do, that I will do, that I may cut off occasion from them which desire occasion; that wherein they glory, they may be found even as we. For such are false apostles, deceitful workers, transforming themselves into the apostles of Christ. And no marvel, for Satan himself is transformed into an angel of light. Therefore it is no great thing if his ministers also be transformed as the ministers of righteousness, whose end shall be according to their works.

I say again, let no man think me a fool; if otherwise, yet as a fool receive me, that I may boast myself a little. That which I speak, I speak it not after the Lord, but as it were foolishly in this confidence of boasting. Seeing that many glory after the flesh, I will glory also. For ye suffer fools gladly, seeing ye yourselves are wise. For ye suffer if a man bring you into bondage, if a man devour you, if a man take of you, if a man exalt himself, if a man smite you on the face. I speak as concerning reproach, as though we had been weak: howbeit, whereinsoever any is bold, I speak foolishly, I am bold also. Are they Hebrews? so am I: are they Israelites? so am I: are they the seed of Abraham? so am I: are they ministers of Christ? I speak as a fool, I am more: in labours more abundant: in stripes above measure: in prisons more frequent: in deaths oft. Of the Jews five times received I forty stripes save one. Thrice was I beaten with rods, once was I stoned: thrice I suffered shipwreck: a night and a day I have been in the deep. In journeyings often, in perils of waters, in perils of robbers, in perils by mine own countrymen, in perils by the heathen, in perils in the city, in perils in the wilderness, in perils in the sea, in perils among false brethren, in weariness and painfulness, in watchings often, in hunger and thirst, in fastings often, in cold and nakedness. Besides those things that are without, that which cometh upon me daily, the care of all the churches. Who is weak, and I am not weak? who is offended, and I burn not? If I must needs glory, I will glory of the things which concern mine infirmities. The God and Father of our Lord Jesus Christ, which is blessed for evermore, knoweth that I lie not. In Damascus the governor under Aretas the king kept the city of the Damascenes with a garrison, desirous to apprehend me. And through a window in a basket was I let down by the wall, and escaped his hands.

I CORINTHIANS

1 . . . For Christ sent me not to baptize, but to preach the gospel: not with wisdom of words, lest the cross of Christ should be made of none effect. For the preaching of the cross is to them that perish, foolishness: but unto us which are saved, it is the power of God. For it is written, "I will destroy the wisdom of the wise, and will bring to nothing the understanding of the prudent." Where is the wise? where is the scribe? where is the disputer of this world? Hath not God made foolish the wisdom of this world? For after that, in the wisdom of God, the world by wisdom knew not God, it pleased God by the foolishness of preaching to save them that believe. For the Jews require a sign, and the Greeks seek after wisdom. But we preach Christ crucified, unto the Jews a stumbling block, and unto the Greeks foolishness: but unto them which are called, both Jews and Greeks, Christ, the power of God, and the wisdom of God. Because the foolishness of God is wiser than men: and the weakness of God is stronger than men. For ye see your calling, brethren, how that not many wise men after the flesh, not many mighty, not many noble, are called. But God hath chosen the foolish things of the world, to confound the wise: and God hath chosen the weak things of the world, to confound the things which are mighty: and base things of the world, and things which are despised, hath God chosen, yea and things which are not, to bring to nought things that are: that no flesh should glory in his presence. But of him are ye in Christ Jesus, who of God is made unto us wisdom, and righteousness, and sanctification, and redemption: that, according as it is written, "He that glorieth, let him glory in the Lord."

13 Though I speak with the tongues of men and of angels, and have not charity, I am become as sounding brass or a tinkling cymbal. And though I have the gift of prophecy, and understand all mysteries and all knowledge: and though I have all faith, so that I could remove mountains, and have not charity, I am nothing. And though I bestow all my goods to feed the poor, and though I give my body to be burned, and have not charity, it profiteth me nothing. Charity suffereth long, and is kind: charity envieth not: charity vaunteth not itself, is not puffed up, doth not behave itself unseemly, seeketh not her own, is not easily provoked, thinketh no evil, rejoiceth not in iniquity, but rejoiceth in the truth: beareth all things, believeth all things, hopeth all things, endureth all things. Charity never faileth: but whether there be prophecies, they shall fail; whether there be tongues, they shall cease; whether there be knowledge, it shall vanish away. For we know in part, and we prophesy in part. But when that which is perfect is come, then that which is in part shall be done away. When I was a child, I spake as a child, I understood as a child, I thought as a child: but when I became a man, I put away childish things. For now we see through a glass, darkly: but then face to face: now I know in part, but then shall I know even as also I am known. And now abideth faith, hope, charity, these three, but the greatest of these is charity.

15 Moreover brethren, I declare unto you the gospel which I preached unto you, which also you have received, and wherein ye stand. By which also ye are saved, if ye keep in memory what I preached unto you, unless ye have believed in vain. For I delivered unto you first of all that which I also received, how that Christ died for our sins according to the scriptures: and that he was buried, and that he rose again the third day according to the scriptures. And that he was seen of Cephas, then of the twelve. After that, he was seen of above five hundred brethren at once: of whom the greater part remain unto this present, but some are fallen asleep. After that, he was seen of James, then of all the apostles. And last of all he was seen of me also, as of one born out of due time. For I am the least of the apostles, that am not meet to be called an apostle because I persecuted the church of God. But by the grace of God I am what I am: and his grace which was bestowed upon me was not in vain:

but I laboured more abundantly than they all, yet not I, but the grace of God which was with me. Therefore, whether it were I or they, so we preach, and so ye believed. Now if Christ be preached that he rose from the dead, how say among you that there is no resurrection of the dead? But if there be no resurrection of the dead, then is Christ not risen. And if Christ be not risen, then is our preaching vain, and your faith is also vain: yea, and we are found false witnesses of God, because we have testified of God, that he raised up Christ: whom he raised not up, if so be that the dead rise not. For if the dead rise not, then is not Christ raised. And if Christ be not raised, your faith is vain, ye are yet in your sins. Then they also which are fallen asleep in Christ are perished. If in this life only we have hope in Christ, we are of all men most miserable.

But now is Christ risen from the dead, and become the first fruits of them that slept. For since by man came death, by man came also the resurrection of the dead. For as in Adam all die, even so in Christ shall all be made alive. But every man in his own order: Christ the first fruits, afterward they that are Christ's, at his coming. Then cometh the end, when he shall have delivered up the kingdom to God, even the Father, when he shall have put down all rule, and all authority and power. For he must reign, till he hath put all enemies under his feet. The last enemy that shall be destroyed is death. For he hath put all things under his feet; but when he saith all things are put under him, it is manifest that he is excepted which did put all things under him. And when all things shall be subdued unto him, then shall the Son also himself be subject unto him that put all things under him, that God may be all in all. Else what shall they do, which are baptized for the dead, if the dead rise not at all? why are they then baptized for the dead? And why stand we in jeopardy every hour? I protest by your rejoicing which I have in Christ Jesus our Lord, I die daily. If after the manner of men I have fought with beasts at Ephesus, what advantageth it me, if the dead rise not? let us eat and drink, for tomorrow we die. Be not deceived: evil communications corrupt good manners. Awake to righteousness, and sin not: for some have not the knowledge of God, I speak this to your shame. But some man will say, "How are the dead raised up? and with what body do they come?" Thou fool, that which thou sowest is not quickened except it die. And that which thou sowest, thou sowest not that body that shall be, but bare grain, it may chance of wheat, or of some other grain. But God giveth it a body as it hath pleased him, and to every seed his own body. All flesh is not the same flesh, but there is one kind of flesh of men, another flesh of beasts, another of fishes, and another of birds. There are also celestial bodies, and bodies terrestrial: but the glory of the celestial is one, and the glory of the terrestrial is another. There is one glory of the sun, and another glory of the moon, and another glory of the stars: for one star differeth from another star in glory. So also is the resurrection of the dead: it is sown in corruption, it is raised in incorruption. It is sown in dishonour, it is raised in glory: it is sown in weakness, it is raised in power: it is sown a natural body, it is raised a spiritual body. There is a natural body, and there is a spiritual body. And so it is written: "The first man Adam was made a living soul, the last Adam was made a quickening spirit." Howbeit that was not first which is spiritual: but that which is natural, and afterward that which is spiritual. The first man is of the earth, earthy: the second man is the Lord from heaven. As is the earthy, such are they also that are earthy: and as is the heavenly, such are they also that are heavenly. And as we have borne the image of the earthy, we shall also bear the image of the heavenly.

Now this I say, brethren, that flesh and blood cannot inherit the kingdom of God: neither doth corruption inherit incorruption. Behold, I show you a mystery: we shall not all sleep, but we shall all be changed, in a moment, in the twinkling of an eye, at the last trump (for the trumpet shall sound, and the dead shall be raised incorruptible, and we shall be changed). For this corruptible must put on incorruption, and this mortal must put on immortality. So when this corruptible shall have put on incorruption, and this mortal shall have put on immortality, then shall be brought to pass the saying that is written, "Death is swallowed up in victory. O death, where is thy sting? O grave, where is thy victory?" The sting of death is sin, and the strength of sin is the law. But thanks be to God, which giveth us the victory, through our Lord Jesus Christ. Therefore my beloved brethren, be ye steadfast, unmoveable, always abounding in the work of the Lord, forasmuch as you know that your labour is not in vain in the Lord.

Revelation

INTRODUCTION

The New Testament ends appropriately with a book that is steeped in the Old; and the John who wrote Revelation is, almost certainly, not the author of the Fourth Gospel. Probably a Palestinian, he seems to have defied the order that the Roman emperor Domitian be worshipped as a god, and around 95 A.D. he was exiled to Patmos. On that small and rugged island he helped to quarry stone for imperial building projects, and there he had his vision. As in the past, a time of massive persecution produced a literature of intense hope. John was deeply familiar with the Old Testament (well over half the verses in Revelation contain echoes from or allusions to the Old Testament), and he especially treasured the apocalyptic writings of First Isaiah, Ezekiel, and Daniel.

By definition an apocalypse is concerned with the ultimate series of events: the final battles between good and evil, the end of an age, the dawn of a new age—either in heaven or on earth. The apocalyptic tradition is found not only in the Old Testament (most explicitly in Daniel), but in other ancient Middle Eastern works. It was, in fact, sufficiently widespread for both John's message and his complex symbolism to be familiar to the common reader of the late first century A.D. Moreover, when the forces of evil seemed to be at their crest, it was easy to imagine that the war between good and evil, between God and Satan, was approaching its climax, that the old evil age was ending, and that the new heavenly age was about to begin. In such an atmosphere, too, apocalypses tend to be deterministic: no matter how bad things are, no matter what an individual does, God will be victorious. The good man must only endure and hope, for his fidelity will soon be vindicated. In such an eschatology God appears as an all-powerful sultan, surrounded by His splendid court. He is not concerned with atonement or forgiveness but with ultimate victory, not with the salvation by faith preached by Paul but with the good works signified by endurance and expectation. (The Lamb in Revelation stands for Christ, but he is a lamb only in the sense that he has been temporarily sacrificed, not in the sense that he is meek.)

Surrounded by what seemed to him the darkness before the dawn, John revitalized this apocalyptic tradition. In a carefully orchestrated crescendo of dire prophecy and vibrant hope he exhorted his coreligionists not to despair: their salvation was at hand. For almost two thousand years his message has been probed and twisted as people have tried to apply it to their own historical situations; yet it may have an especially frightening or exhilarating relevance to today's harried world. ❧ ❧ ❧

Suggested Reading

Dante, *The Divine Comedy*—the great medieval Italian poem about Hell, Purgatory, and Heaven.

Everyman—a late medieval morality play about Christian death.

T. S. Eliot, *The Waste Land*—a poem about the desolation of the modern world, but one which also implies a new apocalypse.

Aldous Huxley, *Brave New World*—the revelation of a nightmarish future utopia.

THE REVELATION OF ST. JOHN THE DIVINE

4 After this I looked, and behold, a door was opened in heaven: and the first voice which I heard was as it were of a trumpet talking with me, which said, "Come up hither, and I will show thee things which must be hereafter." And immediately I was in the spirit: and behold, a throne was set in heaven, and one sat on the throne. And he that sat was to look upon like a jasper, and a sardine stone: and there was a rainbow round about the throne, in sight like unto an emerald. And round about the throne were four and twenty seats, and upon the seats I saw four and twenty elders sitting, clothed in white raiment, and they had on their heads crowns of gold. And out of the throne proceeded lightnings, and thunderings, and voices: and there were seven lamps of fire burning before the throne, which are the seven spirits of God. And before the throne there was a sea of glass like unto crystal: and in the midst of the throne, and round about the throne, were four beasts full of eyes before and behind. And the first beast was like a lion, and the second beast like a calf, and the third beast had a face as a man, and the fourth beast was like a flying eagle. And the four beasts had each of them six wings

about him, and they were full of eyes within, and they rest not day and night, saying, "Holy, holy, holy, Lord God Almighty, which was, and is, and is to come." And when those beasts give glory, and honour, and thanks to him that sat on the throne, who liveth for ever and ever, the four and twenty elders fall down before him that sat on the throne, and worship him that liveth for ever and ever, and cast their crowns before the throne, saying, "Thou art worthy, O Lord, to receive glory, and honour, and power: for thou hast created all things, and for thy pleasure they are, and were created."

5 And I saw in the right hand of him that sat on the throne a book written within, and on the backside, sealed with seven seals. And I saw a strong angel proclaiming with a loud voice, "Who is worthy to open the book, and to loose the seals thereof?" And no man in heaven, nor in earth, neither under the earth, was able to open the book, neither to look thereon. And I wept much, because no man was found worthy to open and to read the book, neither to look thereon. And one of the elders saith unto me, "Weep not: behold, the Lion of the tribe of Judah, the Root of David, hath prevailed to open the book, and to loose the seven seals thereof."

And I beheld, and lo, in the midst of the throne, and of the four beasts, and in the midst of the elders, stood a Lamb as it had been slain, having seven horns and seven eyes, which are the seven spirits of God, sent forth into all the earth. And he came, and took the book out of the right hand of him that sat upon the throne. And when he had taken the book, the four beasts and four and twenty elders fell down before the Lamb, having every one of them harps, and golden vials full of odours, which are the prayers of saints. And they sung a new song, saying, "Thou art worthy to take the book, and to open the seals thereof: for thou wast slain, and hast redeemed us to God by thy blood, out of every kindred, and tongue, and people, and nation: and hast made us unto our God kings and priests, and we shall reign on the earth." And I beheld, and I heard the voice of many angels, round about the throne, and the beasts and the elders: and the number of them was ten thousand times ten thousand, and thousands of thousands, saying with a loud voice, "Worthy is the Lamb that was slain, to receive power, and riches, and wisdom, and strength, and honour, and glory, and blessing." And every creature which is in heaven, and on the earth, and under the earth, and such as are in the sea, and all that are in them, heard I saying, "Blessing, and honour, and glory, and power be unto him that sitteth upon the throne, and unto the Lamb for ever and ever." And the four beasts said, "Amen." And the four and twenty elders fell down and worshipped him that liveth for ever and ever.

6 And I saw when the Lamb opened one of the seals, and I heard as it were the noise of thunder, one of the four beasts saying, "Come and see." And I saw, and behold, a white horse, and he that sat on him had a bow, and a crown was given unto him, and he went forth conquering, and to conquer. And when he had opened the second seal, I heard the second beast say, "Come and see." And there went out another horse that was red: and power was given to him that sat thereon to take peace from the earth, and that they should kill one another: and there was given unto him a great sword. And when he had opened the third seal, I heard the third beast say, "Come and see." And I beheld, and lo, a black horse: and he that sat on him had a pair of balances in his hand. And I heard a voice in the midst of the four beasts say, "A measure of wheat for a penny, and three measures of barley for a penny, and see thou hurt not the oil and the wine." And when he had opened the fourth seal, I heard the voice of the fourth beast say, "Come and see." And I looked, and behold, a pale horse, and his name that sat on him was Death, and Hell followed with him: and power was given unto them over the fourth part of the earth, to kill with sword, and with hunger, and with death, and with the beasts of the earth. And when he had opened the fifth seal, I saw under the altar the souls of them that were slain for the word of God, and for the testimony which they held. And they cried with a loud voice, saying, "How long, O Lord, holy and true, dost thou not judge and avenge our blood on them that dwell on the earth?" And white robes were given unto every one of them, and it was said unto them, that they should rest yet for a little season, until their fellow servants also, and their brethren that should be killed as they were, should be fulfilled.

And I beheld when he had opened the sixth seal, and lo, there was a great earthquake, and the sun became black as sackcloth of hair, and the moon became as blood. And the stars of heaven fell unto the earth, even as a fig tree casteth her untimely figs when she is shaken of a mighty wind. And the heaven departed as a scroll when it is rolled together, and every mountain and island were moved out of their places. And the kings of the earth, and the great men, and the rich men, and the chief captains, and the mighty men, and every bondman, and every free man, hid themselves in the dens, and in the rocks of the mountains, and said to the mountains and rocks, "Fall on us, and hide us from the face of him that sitteth on the throne, and from the wrath of the Lamb: for the great day of his wrath is come, and who shall be able to stand?"

16 And I heard a great voice out of the temple, saying to the seven angels, "Go your ways, and pour out the vials of the wrath of God upon the earth." And the first went, and poured out his vial upon the earth, and there fell a noisome and grievous sore upon the men which had the mark of the beast, and upon them which worshipped his image. And the second angel poured out his vial upon the sea, and it became as the blood of a dead man: and every living soul died in the sea. And the third angel poured out his vial upon the rivers and fountains of waters, and they became blood. And I heard the angel of the waters say, "Thou art righteous, O Lord, which art, and wast, and shalt be, because thou hast judged thus. For they have shed the blood of saints and prophets, and thou hast given them blood to drink: for they are worthy." And I heard another out of the altar say, "Even so, Lord God Almighty, true and righteous are thy judgments."

And the fourth angel poured out his vial upon the sun, and power was given unto him to scorch men with fire. And men were scorched with great heat, and blasphemed the name of God, which hath power over these plagues: and they repented not, to give him glory. And the fifth angel poured out his vial upon the seat of the beast, and his kingdom was full of darkness, and they gnawed their tongues for pain, and blasphemed the God of heaven, because of their pains and their sores, and repented not of their deeds. And the sixth angel poured out his vial upon the great river Euphrates, and the water thereof was dried up, that the way of the kings of the east might be prepared. And I saw three unclean spirits like frogs come out of the mouth of the dragon, and out of the mouth of the beast, and out of the mouth of the false prophet. For they are the spirits of devils working miracles, which go forth unto the kings of the earth, and of the whole world, to gather them to the battle of that great day of God Almighty. "Behold, I come as a thief. Blessed is he that watcheth, and keepeth his garments, lest he walk naked, and they see his shame." And he gathered them together into a place called in the Hebrew tongue Armageddon.

And the seventh angel poured out his vial into the air, and there came a great voice out of the temple of heaven, from the throne, saying, "It is done." And there were voices, and thunders, and lightnings: and there was a great earthquake, such as was not since men were upon the earth, so mighty an earthquake, and so great. And the great city was divided into three parts, and the cities of the nations fell: and great Babylon came in remembrance before God, to give unto her the cup of the wine of the fierceness of his wrath. And every island fled away, and the mountains were not found. And there fell upon men a great hail out of heaven, every stone about the weight of a talent,[1] and men blasphemed God, because of the plague of the hail: for the plague thereof was exceeding great.

20 And I saw an angel come down from heaven, having the key of the bottomless pit and a great chain in his hand. And he laid hold on the dragon, that old serpent, which is the Devil, and Satan, and bound him a thousand years, and cast him into the bottomless pit, and shut him up, and set a seal upon him, that he should deceive the nations no more, till the thousand years should be fulfilled: and after that he must be loosed a little season. And I saw thrones, and they sat upon them, and judgment was given unto them: and I saw the souls of them that were beheaded for the witness of Jesus, and for the word of God, and which had not worshipped the beast, neither his image, neither had received his mark upon their foreheads, or in their hands; and they lived and reigned with Christ a thousand years. But the rest of the dead lived not again until the thousand years were finished. This is the first resurrection. Blessed and holy is he that hath part in the first resurrection: on such the second death hath no power, but they shall be priests of God, and of Christ, and shall reign with him a thousand years. And when the thousand years are expired, Satan shall be loosed out of his prison, and shall go out to deceive the nations which are in the four

[1] Probably about 100 pounds.

quarters of the earth, Gog and Magog,[2] to gather them together to battle: the number of whom is as the sand of the sea. And they went up on the breadth of the earth, and compassed the camp of the saints about, and the beloved city: and fire came down from God out of heaven, and devoured them. And the devil that deceived them was cast into the lake of fire and brimstone, where the beast and the false prophet are, and shall be tormented day and night, for ever and ever. And I saw a great white throne, and him that sat on it, from whose face the earth and the heaven fled away, and there was found no place for them.

And I saw the dead, small and great, stand before God: and the books were opened: and another book was opened, which is the book of life: and the dead were judged out of those things which were written in the books, according to their works. And the sea gave up the dead which were in it: and death and hell delivered up the dead which were in them: and they were judged every man according to their works. And death and hell were cast into the lake of fire: this is the second death. And whosoever was not found written in the book of life was cast into the lake of fire.

21   And I saw a new heaven, and a new earth: for the first heaven and the first earth were passed away, and there was no more sea. And I John saw the holy city, new Jerusalem, coming down from God out of heaven, prepared as a bride adorned for her husband. And I heard a great voice out of heaven, saying, "Behold, the tabernacle of God is with men, and he will dwell with them, and they shall be his people, and God himself shall be with them, and be their God. And God shall wipe away all tears from their eyes: and there shall be no more death, neither sorrow, nor crying, neither shall there be any more pain: for the former things are passed away." . . .

[2] Originally Gog of Magog: the king of a heathen people who, according to Ezekiel, will be destroyed by a revengeful God. (See Ezekiel, chapters 38 and 39.)